LAW'S ALLURE

How Law Shapes, Constrains, Saves, and Kills Politics

Judicial and political power are inextricably linked in America, but, by the time John Roberts and Samuel Alito joined the Supreme Court, that link seemed more important, more significant, and more pervasive than ever before. From war powers to abortion, from tobacco to integration, from the environment to campaign finance, Americans increasingly turn away from the political tools of negotiating, bargaining, and persuading to embrace what they have come to believe is a more effective, more efficient, and even more just world of formal rules, automated procedures, litigation, and judicial decision making.

Using more than ten controversial policy case studies, *Law's Allure: How Law Shapes, Constrains, Saves, and Kills Politics* draws a road map to help politicians, litigators, judges, policy advocates, and those who study them understand the motives and incentives that encourage efforts to legalize, formalize, and judicialize the political process and American public policy, as well as the risks and rewards these choices can generate.

Gordon Silverstein is assistant professor of political science at the University of California, Berkeley. A former journalist with a PhD from Harvard University, Professor Silverstein also has taught at Rice University, Dartmouth College, Lewis & Clark College, and the University of Minnesota. Professor Silverstein has written a number of articles and book chapters on American politics, the separation of powers, and judicial power in comparative perspective and is the author of *Imbalance of Powers: Constitutional Interpretation and the Making of American Foreign Policy* (1996).

Law's Allure

How Law Shapes, Constrains, Saves, and Kills Politics

Gordon Silverstein

University of California, Berkeley

CAMBRIDGE
UNIVERSITY PRESS

CAMBRIDGE UNIVERSITY PRESS
Cambridge, New York, Melbourne, Madrid, Cape Town, Singapore,
São Paulo, Delhi, Dubai, Tokyo

Cambridge University Press
32 Avenue of the Americas, New York, NY 10013-2473, USA

www.cambridge.org
Information on this title: www.cambridge.org/9780521896474

First published 2009

A catalog record for this publication is available from the British Library

Library of Congress Cataloging in Publication data

Silverstein, Gordon.
Law's allure: how law shapes, constrains, saves, and kills politics / Gordon Silverstein.
  p. cm.
Includes bibliographical references and index.
ISBN 978-0-521-89647-4 (hardback) – ISBN 978-0-521-72108-0 (pbk.)
1. Political questions and judicial power – United States. 2. Judicial power – United
States. 3. Justice, Administration of – Political aspects – United States. 4. Law –
Political aspects – United States. I. Title.
KF5130.S55 2009
347.73'12 – dc22   2008035825

ISBN 978-0-521-89647-4 Hardback
ISBN 978-0-521-72108-0 Paperback

Transferred to digital printing 2010

For

Nelson W. Polsby
and our students,
past, present, and future

CONTENTS

ACKNOWLEDGMENTS

This book started as a paper about precedent – what it is, why it matters, and how it has come to play such a central role in American politics, turning judicial nominations into one of the central arenas for political debate in the United States. That paper was meant to be a chapter or two in a book about how and why judicial review emerges and is tolerated, invited, and even embraced in various political systems around the world. That book is next. It turns out that the American case is far more interesting and requires a good deal more thought than I originally imagined. In fact, it required a book of its own.

I owe a great number of people my deepest thanks – those who have helped me with this project both directly and indirectly. Although the book began before I arrived at Berkeley, it would likely never have been completed without the support and inspiration of Nelson W. Polsby and our students, past, present, and future, to whom this book is dedicated.

I had the great good fortune to arrive at Berkeley in time to be one of Nelson W. Polsby's colleagues – which means, of course, one of his students as well. Nelson was a resource, a model, a friend, and an inspiration. Nelson offered a living demonstration of what it means to search for truth and how that search actually can be a lot of fun. The search for knowledge, for answers, and for understanding was the object, the predicate, the purpose, and the motivation for his work and his approach: asking questions, studying those who actually engage in the political process, testing propositions, and debunking conventional wisdom – and then, just as importantly, communicating these findings and his method in clear, concise, and compelling ways in print, in the lecture hall, and in his famously (and literally) open-door office. In a 1968 article defending the work of his own mentor, Robert Dahl, Nelson wrote that Dahl's work was "ambitious, artful, intelligent, persuasive, and on the whole, impressively successful." Those words could just as accurately be written today by any one of Nelson's own legion of devoted students about their mentor, my colleague, and our teacher, Nelson Polsby.

This book is also dedicated to our students – past, present, and future. Although Nelson died in 2007, his intellectual influence lives on in his students, many of whom are now, and will for a long time, be teaching generations of teachers, scholars, politicians, journalists, lawyers, judges, and those who observe, study, and comment on them. As I am sure Nelson would agree, most of us who teach do so for selfish reasons – we learn from our students. They provide the opportunity to explore new ideas and rediscover older ones. They challenge us, inspire us, amaze us, impress us, and make it possible for us to do the impossible – stay in school forever. The insights gained in the undergraduate classroom and in working directly with graduate students on their own original research projects are among the greatest rewards this profession has to offer.

Many students helped make this book possible – and worth the effort. I have been unusually fortunate to have had a chance to teach (and learn from) some of the finest students in the United States, and I thank them all for giving me this opportunity – for listening, for challenging, for questioning, for pushing, and forcing me to hone my arguments, open my mind, and learn how to express my ideas in ways that just might challenge, inspire, and inform them. Although I thank every one of them, a few have made particularly important contributions to this project, and I want to acknowledge that effort. At the University of Minnesota, Dion Farganis quickly shifted from graduate student and teaching assistant to collaborator and colleague. He worked closely with me on a conference paper that grew into the foundation for this work, as well as working with me in my courses on American constitutional law, which also were instrumental in shaping the questions and arguments in this book. At Berkeley, Bruce Huber and John Hanley helped out as the manuscript moved into its final stages. I also want to offer my sincere thanks to the extraordinary group of graduate students who have helped me teach courses on the Supreme Court and American constitutional law at Minnesota and Berkeley – the courses that built the foundation for this work: Melissa Cully Anderson, Sara Chatfield, Andra Crull, Brendan Doherty, Dion Farganis, Alison Gash, Rebecca Hamlin, Peter Hanson, Jill Hargis, James Harney, Amanda Hollis-Brusky, Bruce Huber, Ben Krupicka, Manoj Mate, and Mike Salamone. I want also to thank the more than 2,000 undergraduates who have taken these courses over the years, but particularly I want to acknowledge Kinsey Kiriakos, Kyle Maurer, Fabian Ronisky, and David Wasserman, whose research assistance directly contributed in important ways to this project.

I am also deeply indebted to W.W. Norton's Roby Harrington, who encouraged this work and made important contributions to the manuscript along the way. Ed Parsons, my editor at Cambridge University Press, has done everything right, and I thank him for his support, his encouragement, and his help on this project.

As are so many who study the separation of powers and the interaction of law and politics, I owe a real debt to Mark Graber, a prolific, original, and provocative scholar, teacher, and friend. For years, he has sponsored one of the most intellectually stimulating annual gatherings of a wide range of people who share these interests – gatherings at which I have tested a number of the arguments in this book. Mark Graber also has earned my deep appreciation for having been an encouraging reader of many parts of this manuscript in its early phases and a tremendously helpful reader of the full manuscript as it came into the home stretch.

I am indebted as well to my colleagues at a number of extraordinary institutions with which I have had the good fortune to be affiliated over the years, including Harvard University, Rice University, Dartmouth College, the University of Minnesota, Lewis & Clark College, and, above all, the University of California, Berkeley. Some I have known and have counted on for a long time, and I particularly thank Jeb Barnes, Tom Burke, Tom Buerkle, Jonathan Cohn, Jamie Druckman, Andrew and Lois Cortell, Matthew Dickinson, Robert Eisinger, Linda Fowler, Paul Glastris, Virginia Gray, Mike Grunwald, Eric Heineman, Brian and Adrienne Hoblit, Dan and Lisa Hurwitz, Christine Harrington, Charlie Johnson, Sally Kenney, Sam Krislov, Sandy Levinson, Lynn Mather, Eric Paley, Barbara Rosen, Andrew Schader, W. Phillips Shively, Debora Spar, and Paul Starr for their help and friendship throughout the years.

Some of the ideas for this book began to take shape in Washington, D.C., at the New America Foundation, an innovative new think tank that brings together young writers, policy experts, and journalists from a wide ideological spectrum to think, write, argue, and advance original ideas and invigorate a policy community in Washington that seemed increasingly moribund, divided, and anything but productive. I benefited greatly from my time there as the director of the Fellows Program, and I thank New America's founder and president, Ted Halstead, as well as Steve Clemons, Debra Dickerson, James Forman, Michael Lind, Maya MacGuineas, Jedediah Purdy, Sherle Schwenninger, Margaret Talbot, and especially Gregory Rodriguez for their thoughts, ideas, arguments, and inspiration.

Berkeley has long been a special place for me. Before starting graduate school at Harvard, I was a professional journalist, working for the *Wall Street Journal* in New York and Hong Kong and for the *San Francisco Chronicle*. When I was trying to decide whether to head off to graduate school, it was the *Chronicle's* assistant managing editor, Jack Breibart, who encouraged me to go, and it was Breibart who offered to hire me back for four summers during which I worked as an editor at night but researched and wrote much of my doctoral dissertation in the Berkeley libraries during the day. I never imagined that I might someday have a chance to return to the Bay Area as a member of the Berkeley faculty, but I was in the right place at the right time to be able to be a part of one of the very best institutions of higher education in the world. Berkeley is an extraordinary place, a public institution that draws the very finest students and faculty from across the nation and around the world, one that encourages interdisciplinary work and has the resources to make it happen. I have had the rare privilege of being a part of this institution and have benefited enormously from working with and learning from an incredible group of genuine colleagues. I am particularly indebted to my colleagues in the Department of Political Science, who are (incredibly) too many to list here. I do want to mention Wendy Brown, Beppe Di Palma, Paul Pierson, Eric Schickler, and Shannon Stimson, however, all of whom provided valuable comments on this manuscript at various points. I am also very much indebted to Jack Citrin, director of the Institute of Governmental Studies at Berkeley who has supported me – and my work – when it was most needed and most welcome. I also want to thank Judy Gruber, the department chair when I was hired, who died shortly after I arrived. It was Judy who told me that Berkeley was a place that encouraged, that embraced big ideas. One would think this is true of all universities, but sadly it is not. It is, however, true of Berkeley, and it is part of what makes this such a special place. Outside of the department, I have been very fortunate to have colleagues and friends such as Dan Farber, Malcolm Feeley, Kathy Frydl, Anya Grant, Rosann Greenspan, David Kirp, Linda Polsby, Emily Polsby, and Martin Shapiro, all of whom have greatly enriched my experience here.

I turn now to Robert A. Kagan, a scholar, teacher, and friend who has redefined the meaning of colleague and who, by his example, sets standards that – although I might hope to emulate – I can never possibly meet or exceed. Bob Kagan has been a source of support and encouragement; he has challenged me to be better, to reach higher; he has pressed me, urged me, and goaded me to fortify, deepen, and broaden my vision, arguments, and evidence. He has taught me new ways to teach and, in teaching with him, new ways to learn from teaching. His own work has been inspirational and of central utility in this project. Look in the dictionary for the proper definition of what a colleague is or should be, and I have no doubt you will find a picture of Bob Kagan. Here is an extraordinarily accomplished scholar with unbelievable demands on his time who nevertheless found the time and energy to comment on draft after draft after draft after draft of this manuscript; who eagerly replies to any question; and who unquestioningly responds to any request for his time or expertise. Bob redefines above and beyond. He saw things in my work that I did not know were there. Bob helped me see and understand that this was, in fact, a far more ambitious project than I had initially imagined, and he helped me, pushed me, pulled me, and pressed me to make it better, stronger, and more rigorous. Although Bob and I inhabit different corners of the world of people who study public law, he never pressed me to adopt his methods, or his questions, or his approach. Instead, he welcomed and encouraged me to pursue my thoughts, my arguments, and my research agenda. It was always clear that his objective was to help me achieve my own objectives and more effectively express my own ideas. This is a vastly better book than it would have been had I not had a chance to work with him, and I cannot begin to adequately express my appreciation and admiration. The best I can do is to try, in a small way, to follow his example.

In an interview with Berkeley's Harry Kreisler some years ago, Nelson Polsby said that there is "a very large array of possible ways of going about social science," and Nelson believed that each of his students had to find his or her own path. "The most important thing in the world," Nelson insisted, "is to have a mind of your own." It is a conviction that Bob Kagan obviously shares. I am a better teacher, a better student, a better writer, and a better person for having had a chance to work with Bob Kagan and Nelson Polsby, and I thank them profoundly for that opportunity.

Finally, there is my family. It has been wonderful to get to know my West Coast relatives, particularly my cousins, Jim and Marie Silverstein, and their daughters Mikayla and Alyssa, who keep me grounded, regularly reminding me that I have one of the best jobs in the world. They're right. My deepest debt is, as always, to my brother Frank and his family, Esther and Maya, and above all to my parents – my inspiration, my support, my models, and my teachers. Marilyn Cooper Silverstein and Josef Silverstein taught me to ask questions and pursue knowledge always and everywhere. Everything I am, everything I have done, and everything I will do, I owe to them.

LAW'S ALLURE

How Law Shapes, Constrains, Saves, and Kills Politics

INTRODUCTION

Law's Allure: The Juridification of American Politics and Public Policy

THE MEMBERS OF THE U.S. SENATE assembled what they like to call the "world's greatest deliberative body" on a crisp November evening a few years ago for a debate that would last more than forty hours. This great gathering was not about public health or civil rights; it was not about individual liberty, or property, or prosperity. It did not focus on war or peace. Instead, these orators had assembled to filibuster against the filibusters that were blocking the confirmation of presidential nominees to serve as federal judges.

This effort was seen by many as a practice run for the struggle that would ensue when Supreme Court Justice Sandra Day O'Connor announced her retirement, an event triggering carefully rehearsed plans that "would rival a presidential campaign, complete with extensive television advertising, mass e-mails, special Internet sites, opposition research, public rallies and news conferences."[1] President George W. Bush's supporters pledged more than $18 million for the effort, and Democrats tapped into their own war chests, using veterans of the Clinton and Gore campaigns to mount an all-out battle.

Judicial and political power are inextricably linked in America, but by the time John Roberts and Samuel Alito joined the Supreme Court, that link seemed more significant and more pervasive than ever before. Efforts to regulate and even eliminate tobacco, to reform the criminal justice system, to protect privacy, and save the environment; efforts to define and defend a woman's right to choose an abortion; efforts to integrate

---

1 Peter Baker, "Parties Gear Up for High Court Battle," *Washington Post*, June 27, 2005, p A2. Mark Miller notes that what is most notable is not Senate concern with Supreme Court nominations, but rather with fights over lower federal judicial nominations. Mark C. Miller, "The View of the Courts from the Hill," in Mark C. Miller and Jeb Barnes (eds), *Making Policy, Making Law*. Washington, DC: Georgetown University Press, 2004, p 61, citing Colton Campbell and John Stack, *Congress Confronts the Court: The Struggle for Legitimacy and Authority in Lawmaking*, Lanham: Rowman & Littlefield, 2001, p 11. See also Keith Perine, "Both Parties Find Political Benefit from Battle over Judicial Nominees," *Congressional Quarterly Weekly Report*, Oct. 4, 2003, p 2431.

schools and reform prison systems; efforts to control and automate the federal budget, to define and limit the exercise of war powers, and contain and prosecute federal corruption – in each of these and more, the answer increasingly was a legalistic one: politicians and policy entrepreneurs turning to the courts and the adjudicative process as a substitute for the persuasion, negotiation, bargaining, and tradeoffs of political decision making. Even in their legislative efforts, there has been a growing reliance on judicial language, formal structures, and automated procedures. In some instances, the courts were seen as a substitute for the ordinary political process; in others, the courts were asked merely to ratify or ignore the reallocation of powers within the political system itself.

Sometimes the U.S. Supreme Court allows these innovations, and sometimes the Justices say no. And in some cases, judicial rulings are only the start of a complex iterated game, a game of leap-frog in which one decision serves as the jumping-off point for the next. These are games in which a judicial decision responds to legislative choices, and the next round of legislative choices is built on that legal ruling, leading to yet another round of legal rulings and legislative actions. Finally, there are instances in which legal language, legal forms, and legal frames shape and constrain political behavior, even when the courts play little or no direct role.[2] This process does not determine results, but shapes, frames, and constrains the choices that legislators and those they represent tend to most readily consider. The narrowing, formalizing, and hardening of the terms of debate add up to what might be called juridification – efforts to legalize, formalize, and proceduralize; efforts to strip out the ambiguity of politics and the U.S. Constitution and replace it with unambiguous rules and automated default procedures. Although these efforts have been part of the American system from the start, juridification is more frequent, more important, and more deeply embedded now than ever before. But why? And what sorts of risks or costs might these choices entail? Are there times when these risks are more or less tolerable for those making these choices? This book is an effort to draw a road map to help politicians, policy entrepreneurs, lawyers, judges, and those who study them understand how law shapes and frames, constrains, sometimes saves, and sometimes kills politics.

Law and politics cannot be disentangled in the United States. This has something to do with American political culture itself. Americans have never quite embraced politics. It is necessary. It is useful. It is unavoidable. It is to be tolerated and tamed. It can be great sport, but it can also be an

---

2 Frederick Schauer argues persuasively that a great deal of important political issues do not end up in Court. This does not mean that many of these issues are not still subject to juridification – merely that they are not determined by an explicit judicial ruling. See Frederick Schauer, "The Supreme Court 2005 Term, Foreword: The Court's Agenda – and the Nation's," 120 *Harvard Law Review* 4, 2006.

embarrassment and even (and often) a genuine danger. For Americans, law is different. Law suggests predictability, propriety, and fairness. We celebrate truth, *justice*, and the American way – not truth, *politics*, and the American way. Law, Judith Shklar writes, "aims at justice, while politics looks only to expediency. The former is neutral and objective, the latter the uncontrolled child of competing interests and ideologies. Justice is thus not only the policy of legalism, it is treated as a policy superior to and unlike any other."[3] Fear of the abuse of political power and concerns about corruption have long been met by demands for more law and less politics, for increasingly legalistic solutions to our problems, including what Lawrence Friedman calls a demand for "total justice."[4] These are among the driving forces behind the expansion and acceleration of juridification: efforts that include attempts to solve policy problems by judicial means, as well as efforts to formalize, proceduralize, and automate the political process itself.

North Carolina's Senator Sam Ervin once noted that we "have a national tendency when something happens that we think ought not to happen to demand that new laws be passed, regardless of the laws we already have on the books."[5] This inclination, this insistence, plays out not only in legalistic approaches to social policy, but also in demands for the formalization and depoliticization of the political process itself. Ours is a political culture in which "social problems increasingly are approached as problems to be solved through comprehensive legal strategies." When these comprehensive approaches fail to work, rather than questioning these legalistic efforts, the failure often "is attributed to poor drafting and not enough law; typically the solution is 'smarter' legal interventions."[6] As Karl Llewellyn reminds novice law students, in America there is "no cure for law but more law."[7]

The Juridification of American Politics

Terminology is tricky here. In a system in which law and politics are intimately related, it is difficult to craft a term that distinguishes what

---

3 Judith Shklar, *Legalism: Law, Morals, and Political Trials*, Cambridge: Harvard University Press, 1964, p 111.
4 Lawrence Friedman, *Total Justice*, New York: Russell Sage Foundation, 1995.
5 Senator Sam Ervin (D-NC), testifying in "Removing Politics from the Administration of Justice," hearings on S. 2803 and S. 2978 before the Subcommittee on Separation of Power of the Committee on the Judiciary of the United States Senate, 93rd Congress, 2nd session, March 28, 1974, p 155.
6 Frank Anechiarico and James Jacob, *The Pursuit of Absolute Integrity: How Corruption Control Makes Government Ineffective*, Chicago: University of Chicago Press, 1996, p 12 (Cited in Katy Harriger, *The Special Prosecutor in American Politics* (2nd ed.), Lawrence: University Press of Kansas, 2000, p 230.
7 Karl Llewellyn, *The Bramble Bush: On Our Law and its Study*, Dobbs Ferry: Oceana, 1960, pp 102–8.

might be called a traditional role of law, courts, and judicial reasoning in policy and politics from a world in which legalistic approaches to institutional and political and policy problems substitute for, displace, and even undermine or kill the ordinary political process. Judicialization captures just one part of the change – instances in which policymakers come to rely directly on the courts and on judicial decisions to advance their goals. Legalization captures another part of the story, but again only one part of the efforts to formalize, proceduralize, and regularize the political process itself. Because politicians mostly engage in writing laws and regulations, it is confusing to talk about the legalization of politics and the political process.

Therefore, the best term may be the least elegant – *juridification*. It is a term that is rarely used in the United States and only somewhat more commonly in Europe, where Jurgen Habermas and other social theorists use the word to describe the degree to which areas of social life once free of rules, laws, and statutes, are increasingly controlled by a profusion, an overgrowth of such things. This is close, but not precisely the American experience.[8] In the United States, it is not so much a question of a once unregulated and unrestrained arena of life now bound and tied and structured and ordered by law, but rather a question of the degree to which what had been *part* of a process – an essential tool or instrument or weapon – came to dominate, structure, frame, and constrain the debate and the product of that debate.

Juridification is not the product of an imperial judiciary imposing its will or of an abdicating legislature or weak executive. In some policy areas, the Supreme Court led, and in others, the Court followed; in some, the Court merely acquiesced or largely stood to one side. Juridification is, instead, the product of the *interaction* of these institutions, along with interest groups, parties, lobbyists, and policy entrepreneurs alike. To understand how law's allure shapes and constrains politics and the political process we have to go beyond the zero-sum, gladiatorial struggle for dominance that is the focus of much of the academic study of law and politics in America. Although there certainly are instances of direct struggles between the branches, an exclusive focus on these obscures another dimension of the juridification process – the *interaction* between and among these institutions. To understand law's

8 See Jurgen Habermas, "Law as Medium and Law as Institution," in Gunther Teubner (ed), *Dilemmas of Law in the Welfare State*, New York: Walter de Gruyter, 1986, pp 203–20. See also Lars Tragardh and Michael X. Delli Carpini, "The Juridification of Politics in the United States and Europe: Historical Roots, Contemporary Debates and Future Prospects," in Lars Tragardh (ed), *After National Democracy: Rights, Law and Power in America and the New Europe*, Portland: Hart Publishing, 2004; and Lars Chr. Blichner and Anders Molander, "What is Juridification?" University of Oslo, Centre for European Studies, Working Paper, no. 14, March 2005.

allure, its risks and its rewards, we need to think of the interaction of courts and legislators, of law and politics, not as a series of individual, one-off contests – something like individual hands of poker – and instead think about juridification as the end product of a long chain of interactions, more like a poker tournament. Juridification is the product of a dialogue of courts, legislators, policy entrepreneurs, opinion leaders, the general public, and individual litigants. Sometimes, this is a cooperative process; sometimes, it is antagonistic; and, at other times, parallel and coincidental.

Juridification – relying on legal process and legal arguments, using legal language, substituting or replacing ordinary politics with judicial decisions and legal formality – can shape and constrain the political and policy horizon. But when is that risk worth taking? When is it essential and when should it be tempered or avoided? These are questions that those who study politics and political institutions in isolation from the third branch of government sometimes miss, just as they are also missed by those who study law and judicial doctrine in isolation from the political process in which courts and judicial decisions play a prominent role. What is needed is a cross-institutional approach, one that actually incorporates and evaluates the role of ideas and the ways in which ideas and arguments shape and constrain policy and politics across, between, and among the branches of government.[9] This project is a first step in that direction. There are no comprehensive, cross-institutional theories about juridification. Before we can hope to build and test those theories, we have to understand and map out the problem itself.

A Road Map to the Road Map

Chapter 1 sets out a road map to help answer these questions, laid out along two primary dimensions: the motives and incentives that drive the choice to opt for legalistic solutions (or abandon traditional political means to achieve these solutions) and the various patterns (and therefore various risks) these choices tend to generate. Why one and not another? For those facing profound political and institutional barriers to their goals, a judicial or legalistic path might well be the only viable option, and their risk tolerance would and should be quite high. Others embrace and even choose juridification not because they must, but because they believe it to be more efficient, more effective, or even morally superior. Juridification poses risks for everyone involved, but before accepting,

---

9 Jeb Barnes, "Bringing the Courts Back In: Interbranch Perspectives on the Role of Courts in American Politics and Policy Making," 10 *Annual Review of Political Science*, pp 25–43 (2007); Mark C. Miller and Jeb Barnes, *Making Policy, Making Law: An Interbranch Perspective*, Washington, D.C.: Georgetown University Press, 2004.

embracing, or even choosing juridification, policy entrepreneurs and politicians alike ought to better understand the nature of this risk and better calculate the level they might be willing to tolerate.

Law's allure for Americans is not new – but something changed in America's recent past that allowed a significant expansion and acceleration of juridification. Chapter 2 strives to explain why these changes occurred. In a constitutional system of limited government, some one or some institution must define and interpret those limits. That an independent federal judiciary arose to fill this demand is hardly surprising. Before the 1960s, the Court's role largely was that of a traffic cop, saying what government could and could not do.[10] Because America's fragmented political system guarantees a struggle for power between the states and the national government – and among the branches of the national government itself – this blocking function became a source of great power. The Supreme Court effectively built on this power to say yes and no, playing a critical role in the nationalization of power and the expansion of the American economy and in policing everything from trade and commerce to labor law, territorial expansion, taxes, and the constitutionality of paper money. The Court's role was dramatic and powerful – but it was a particular sort of role. The blocking function meant the Court was the place to go to stop government action or to certify its legitimacy. The Court could be an important ally or an enemy. But for those seeking government action, those advocating new policy, those who wanted to get the government to act, it was necessary to rely on the ordinary political process of legislation and administrative rules arrived at through bargaining, negotiation, persuasion, and electoral and popular pressure. This continues to be the dominant avenue to policy goals, but within ten years of becoming Chief Justice in 1953, Earl Warren and the U.S. Supreme Court signaled that the Court might offer an additional, alternative path to political and policy goals by being willing to say not only what government could and could not do – but what it must do as well.

Brown v. Board of Education and its progeny eventually led the Court to tell local, state, and national governments that they *must* desegregate their schools. In 1962, the Court intervened in the allocation of political

---

10 Martin Shapiro identifies this role as something present in all societies in which two individuals or institutions have a dispute: They will turn to a third party to settle the fight. Shapiro refers to this as "triadic dispute resolution," articulated first in *Courts: A Comparative and Political Analysis*, Chicago: University of Chicago Press, 1981. That the federal courts would develop this role, though it is not explicitly spelled out in the U.S. Constitution, fits rather well with the assumptions made by Alexander Hamilton in the *Federalist* #78, in which he suggested that judicial review was a logical necessity in a federal system of limited government. That this has played out so powerfully in the American system is well explained by Robert A. Kagan, who develops the argument about the central importance of a fragmented system of government and power in the development of the American legal-political system in *Adversarial Legalism: The American Way of Law*, Cambridge: Harvard University Press, 2001.

power within the individual states in *Baker v. Carr*, telling the state of Tennessee that it was required to more closely assure that each voter was equally represented in the political process.[11] The Court also intervened and demanded that government do what few politicians could possibly advocate – expand and extend the rights of criminal defendants and even convicted felons.[12] This new command function would open a new path, an alternative path, for policy entrepreneurs. Policy goals that once had been achievable only through the legislative and political process, it was thought, might now be advanced in large part – and perhaps even exclusively – through judicial decisions and judicial orders.

The Supreme Court opened its doors in the early years of what some refer to as the "long-1960s" – a period when government shifted from being the solution to being seen as the problem; it was an era in which public trust in government was tested, eroded, and finally shattered.[13] From Cold War loyalty inquisitions to the assassination of key political figures, from the escalation of the war in Vietnam to the political melt-down of the Democrats' 1968 convention in Chicago, to the increasingly violent racial conflicts in America's inner cities, the long 1960s was an era in which the political system seemed to fail and one in which the formality, apparent transparency, predictability, and moral superiority of legal alternatives became increasingly attractive.[14] The judicial path

11 *Brown v. Board of Education*, 347 U.S. 483 (1954); *Baker v. Carr*, 369 U.S. 186 (1962).
12 *Mapp v. Ohio* 367 U.S. 643 (1961), *Miranda v. Arizona*, 378 U.S. 478 (1964). For a thorough examination of the court's role in reforming prisons, see the definitive book by Malcolm M. Feeley and Edward L. Rubin, *Judicial Policy Making and the Modern State: How the Courts Reformed America's Prisons*, New York: Cambridge University Press, 1998.
13 Historian M. J. Heale suggests that Fredric Jameson was among the first to consider the problems of identifying the scope and boundaries of the 1960s. In "Periodizing the Sixties," (a chapter in Sohnia Sayres (ed), *The 60s without Apology*, Minneapolis: University of Minnesota Press, 1984), Jameson "began his analysis with the late 1950s and located an end in the general area of 1972–1974.'" It was Arthur Marwick, according to Heale, who was among the first to employ the term the "long 1960s" as encompassing "a cultural transformation between about 1958 and 1974" in four western countries, including the United States (see Arthur Marwick, *The Sixties*, New York: Oxford University Press, 1998). Theda Skocpol argues for a "long 1960s" that stretches "from the mid-1950s through the mid-1970s;" see Skocpol, "Advocates without Members: The Recent Transformation of Civic Life" in Skocpol and Morris Fiorina (eds), *Civic Engagement in American Democracy*, Washington, DC: Brookings Institution Press, 1999; and Skocpol, *Diminished Democracy*, Norman: University of Oklahoma Press, 2003. Heale notes that "there is also a case for a short 1960s. Jon Margolis in a recent book insists that the Sixties began in 1964. If we are to believe Bruce Schulman, the Sixties ended rather abruptly in 1968. That leaves us with a truncated era sometimes characterized as the 'high Sixties.'" Heale's article does an admirable job of laying out this debate; see M. J. Heale, "The Sixties as History: A Review of the Political Historiography," 2005 *Reviews in American History* 33, 133–52.
14 John F. Kennedy was assassinated in 1963, Martin Luther King in April 1968, and Robert F. Kennedy in June of that same year. Urban riots ripped through the West (the Watts neighborhood in Los Angeles in 1965), the Midwest (Detroit in 1967), and the East Coast (Newark, New Jersey in 1967); Washington, D.C., was one of many cities that burned in the wake of King's assassination in 1968.

seemed to offer a clean, efficient and alluring alternative to a discredited political system.

And then came Watergate, a parade of horribles that only served to reinforce the growing conviction that politicians (and politics) were venal and corrupt – whereas judges, lawyers, and journalists emerged as heroic saviors.[15] "Watergate made me a lawyer," one professor wrote. He wanted to be like his heroes: "Archibald Cox, Sam Ervin, Peter Rodino, Barbara Jordan." He wanted "to be like these people, wanted a part, however small, in the high drama of American public life."[16] Public opinion reflected this trend – and drove it.[17] Polls taken in the 1970s "reflected a steady decline in confidence in government that became marked during and following the Watergate crisis." Eighty-eight percent of those surveyed in a 1976 Harris poll said that "cleaning up corruption in government" was a very important goal for Congress, and making sure that "no more Watergates take place" was identified as "very important" by 78 percent of the respondents."[18] Framed as a struggle between "the rule of law" and "the abuse of power," the public clearly "aligned itself with the former."[19]

In the wake of the Watergate crisis, Congress passed a number of dramatic pieces of legislation designed to shift policy disputes out of the murky and discredited realm of politics and into what appeared to be the far more legitimate arena of law.[20] Each of these innovations – ranging from campaign finance reform to the formal allocation and proceduralization of the war powers to the creation of an independent office of special prosecutor to deal with political corruption – would raise serious constitutional and legal challenges, and each would end up in Court. Unlike the legalistic solutions to more traditional policy problems – such

---

15 It should be noted that many disgraced politicians – including Richard Nixon, Attorney General John Mitchell, John Ehrlichman, Charles Colson, and John Dean, to name just a few – were all trained lawyers.

16 Frank Bowman, "Falling Out of Love with America: The Clinton Impeachment and the Madisonian Constitution," 60 *Maryland Law Review* 5, 5–6 (2001). It is true, as Bowman points out, that nearly all the key players in Watergate – heroes and villains alike – were lawyers. But that only reinforced the shift, demonstrating that the real battlefield was on legal, not political, turf.

17 And it has been a dominant feature of public opinion ever since. See John R. Hibbing and Elizabeth Theiss-Morse, *Congress as Public Enemy: Public Attitudes toward American Political Institutions*, New York: Cambridge University Press, 1995; Arthur Miller, "Political Issues and Trust in Government, 1964–1970," 68 *American Political Science Review* 3, 951–72 (1974); Jack Citrin, "Comment: The Political Relevance of Trust in Government," 68 *American Political Science Review* 3, 973–988 (1974); Jack Citrin, Herbert McClosky, John Shanks, and Paul Sniderman, "Personal and Political Sources of Political Alienation," 5 *British Journal of Political Science* 1, 1–31 (1975).

18 Katy Harriger, *The Special Prosecutor in American Politics* (2nd ed.), Lawrence: University Press of Kansas, 2000, p 44, 46.

19 Harriger, *The Special Prosecutor*, p 209.

20 In one important example, Congress overrode President Nixon's veto and passed the War Powers Resolution in November 1973, attempting to codify and control by law what it had failed to control through the political process.

as environmental regulation – in these cases, Congress was explicitly attempting to adopt and emulate the approach, the precision, and what some thought and hoped was the clarity of law and achieve the equitable results that they came to believe could be accomplished by substituting procedural efficiency for the frustrating and prone-to-corruption gray of politics.[21]

The appeal of formal rules, formal procedures, and automated political decision making took on a life of its own. Even when law and formal procedure were inappropriate, the answer to one failed effort at a legalistic solution was another. But when these laws are passed and corruption continues, Frank Anechiarico and James Jacob note, the "failure is attributed to poor drafting and not enough law; typically the solution is 'smarter' legal interventions."[22]

As the 1960s gave way to the 1970s and 1980s, talented and public-spirited young people flocked into law schools and from there to a host of public interest litigation positions. Organizations such as Ralph Nader and Alan Morrison's Public Citizen Litigation Group (which opened its doors in February 1972) increasingly focused on law as an alternative – and preferred – route to social change in areas ranging from struggles to end poverty to battles for consumers' rights, from fights for environmental protection to demands for gender equity. The traditional tools of political change – bargaining, negotiation, and elections – increasingly were seen as "defeats for justice," leading many to embrace what Judith Shklar refers to as "the politics of legalism" in which the adjudicative process came to be seen as a more efficient, more effective, and more just model for government – and as a "substitute for politics."[23]

What difference does this shift toward juridification make? Does it really matter whether policy goals are pressed in courts or through legislation and administrative choices? And if it does, how and why? Chapter 3 sets out to answer these questions. Legal decisions may be political, but law nevertheless is different from politics. Judicial decision making follows different rules and is driven by different incentives, limited by different constraints, and addressed to different audiences in a different language than the political process. The way judges articulate, explain, and rationalize their choices and the way earlier decisions influence, shape, and constrain later judicial decisions are distinctly different from the patterns, practices, rhetoric, internal rules, and driving incentives that operate in the elected branches and among bureaucrats. Policy that is driven in large measure by litigation and judicial rulings may produce similar

---

21 Hibbing and Theiss-Morse, *Congress as Public Enemy*, pp 14–15.
22 Harriger, *The Special Prosecutor*, quoting Frank Anechiarico and James Jacob, *The Pursuit of Absolute Integrity: How Corruption Control Makes Government Ineffective*, Chicago: University of Chicago Press, 1996, p 12.
23 Shklar, *Legalism*, p 17.

results as that produced by the political process in the short term, but it can and often does limit, direct, shape, and constrain those policies in the longer run in ways quite different from what might have been expected by those who chose a judicial route in the first place.

Having provided a road map in Chapter 1, an explanation for how and when and why law's allure – always present in the American political system – expanded and accelerated so rapidly in the middle of the twentieth century in Chapter 2, and an argument about why law, legal decision making, and, therefore, the juridification of policy and politics can generate risks as well as rewards in Chapter 3, the book moves to a series of paradigmatic case studies to illustrate the patterns and process of juridification.

In Chapter 4, abortion and the move to use courts and the judicial process to fight poverty in America offer two very different patterns of juridification: one that asked the courts to say what government may not do (impose limits on abortion) and one that asked courts to tell the government what it must do (to end poverty). Chapter 5 explores a constructive pattern of juridification – the work of the courts together with the elected branches to advance and shape a dramatic change in America's environmental policy. A deconstructive pattern of juridification, illustrated by the struggles over campaign finance reform, is the subject of Chapter 6. Turning to the separation of powers, Chapter 7 explores two different patterns – (1) where the Court says yes and allows the elected branches to experiment with creating an independent prosecutor's office to pursue charges of political corruption and illegal activity and (2) where the Court says no, blocking efforts to automate the budget-cutting process and to delegate to the president the power to impose line-item vetoes. Chapter 8 looks at war and emergency powers to consider the risks of juridification when the Court is relatively silent or reluctant to intervene.

In Chapter 9, the final case study looks at tobacco. Here is a textbook example of how law can save politics – and yet, ultimately, a textbook example of how law kills politics. Here we see in one case both the promise and peril of law's allure. Facing profound political and institutional barriers – effective and committed political support for tobacco from key Senators and members of Congress, a public unwilling to punish tobacco companies for the health consequences of those who generally were expected to have known and understood the risks their habit entailed, and the deep pockets of a very profitable industry – lawsuits, and the threat of more lawsuits, actually brought these companies to the table, willing to accept a political settlement that had previously been unimaginable. This success added luster to law's allure. If law and legal process could bring the large tobacco makers to their knees, those who had battled tobacco for decades reasoned, then why not rely on this same force to vanquish and destroy them? Justice could be done, and no political compromise would be needed. They were wrong. The deal collapsed. The tobacco companies settled separately with forty-six states. The novel legal theories upon which opponents confidently relied were denied or reversed. Far from eliminating tobacco, these settlements actually allowed tobacco not only to survive, but also to thrive as a beacon of profitability in a sea of losses on Wall Street.

In some large part, the expansion and acceleration of juridification in our recent past can be understood as a reaction to the adaptations needed to govern a twenty-first-century, continent-spanning, global economic and military nation of nearly 300 million people under the rules and institutional arrangements of an eighteenth-century Constitution. Turning to the courts and formalizing, legalizing, and automating a political system that was built to make change and innovation extraordinarily difficult to accomplish may have great appeal as an end run around these institutional barriers and costly political impediments – but there are real risks involved as well.

When and why should we embrace juridification? What are the risks involved in our ever-greater reliance on judicial decisions, judicial forms, and judicial language? How and when and why do legalistic solutions, approaches, language, and frames of analysis influence, direct, constrain, sometimes save and sometimes threaten, sometimes undermine, and sometimes even kill our public policy and the political process itself? To help answer these questions, this book maps out the incentives, motives, patterns, and pathways of American juridification in an effort to help politicians, policy entrepreneurs, litigators, judges, and those who study them evaluate the risks and rewards of law's allure.[24]

---

24 Note that law is alluring not only to liberals, but to conservatives as well. Where once conservatives employed legal terms, legal approaches, formal codification, and judicial rulings to assure property rights, to enforce contracts, and to check the expansion of national power, now growing numbers of conservative groups are doing so to fight affirmative action, to press for school vouchers, assure government support for religious organizations and causes, and, once again, to protect private property. See, for example, Brian Z. Tamanaha, *Law as a Means to an End: Threat to the Rule of Law*, New York: Cambridge University Press, 2006, pp 162–3; Karen O'Conner and Lee Epstein, "The Rise of Conservative Interest Group Litigation," 45 *Journal of Politics* 479 (1983); Karen O'Conner and Lee Epstein, "Rebalancing the Scales of Justice," 7 *Harvard Journal of Law and Public Policy* 483 (1984).

Part I
Law's Allure: Why, Why Now,
and Why it Matters

1   MOTIVES, INCENTIVES, PATTERNS, AND PROCESS

TURNING TO THE COURTS, relying on judicial decision making, and formalizing, proceduralizing, and automating the political process as substitutes or replacements for the traditional methods of politics – organizing, electioneering, negotiating, and bargaining – can shape, frame, and constrain policy choices and politics itself. But when are these risks higher or lower? When are they more or less tolerable?

Juridification is not an all-or-nothing proposition.[1] It is a continuum. At one extreme, policy entrepreneurs and elected officials might come to rely on the courts and judicial decisions to define and impose, block, or redirect policy preferences – although, even at this extreme, administrative procedures and statutory provisions will still be needed to apply and enforce these rulings. At the other end of the spectrum, policy is debated, negotiated, approved, and implemented through the ordinary legislative and administrative channels – although, even at this extreme, individual cases will arise in which courts will be asked to interpret and apply these laws and administrative rulings.[2]

The relative risks (and rewards) of juridification need to be evaluated along two primary dimensions: (1) the motives and incentives that might lead politicians, policy entrepreneurs, litigators, and legislators alike to embrace juridification and (2) the patterns and the process of juridification that develop, which are a product of the interaction of law and politics. The motives and incentives tell us a great deal about risk tolerance. When court rulings and juridification offer what appears to be the only viable way around profound institutional barriers (such as super-majority requirements, federalism, and minority-veto instruments, including the filibuster), risk tolerance would likely be quite high. Juridification might

---

1 A full discussion of this term and of its use in this book can be found in the Introduction.
2 Somewhere in the middle, various individuals or some interested groups might litigate and others might pursue a primarily political path to their goals in overlapping, conflicting, or cooperative strategies.

be costly and might skew and undercut long-term policy goals, but given the lack of alternatives, such risks likely would be relatively tolerable. By contrast, when there are viable (even if very costly) ways to achieve these ends through the ordinary political process, risk tolerance ought to be considerably lower, and a more careful risk-benefit analysis might be well advised.

Risk tolerance, of course, is only half the story. Different strategies and different patterns of juridification will generate different levels and kinds of risk. These patterns and processes are the product of the interaction of political and judicial actors, institutions, and practices in a way that "progressively shapes" their strategic behavior.[3] Juridification is the product of a long series of interactive and interdependent choices, rather than the sum of a series of individual contests in which there is a winner and a loser and then everyone starts all over. It is an iterated process, one in which the results of earlier rounds of play shape and constrain current choices, as do expectations about future behavior that also are calculated into each choice in the present. Juridification – legalistic solutions, the judicialization of policy, the formalization and automation of the political process – can be "blocked or reversed," and sometimes it is. But in many cases, "unwilling to forgo the benefits" the legal process seems to offer, or "unable to agree on alternative arrangements," the choice to juridify is taken without much attention paid to the ways in which this choice can skew and shape future choices and options, framing and constraining the terms of public debate and discourse.[4]

This chapter explores and charts these two critical dimensions – the motives and incentives for legalistic solutions and the different patterns and processes those solutions might trigger or follow – that, when combined, generate a road map of the risks and rewards of law's allure.

Juridification: Motives and Incentives

There are all sorts of reasons why politicians and policy entrepreneurs alike might opt for a legalistic solution (see Figure 1.1). Grouping and sorting these motives and incentives can start with a fairly simple question: Is the turn to judicial forms, legal language, and judicial decision making a matter of preference, or is it realistically understood as the only viable alternative? In other words, is it seen as a *preferred choice*, perhaps

---

3 Alec Stone Sweet, "Judicialization and the Construction of Governance," in Martin Shapiro and Alec Stone Sweet, *On Law, Politics and Judicialization*, New York: Oxford University Press, 2002, p 71. This chapter appeared originally in 32 *Comparative Political Studies* 2, 147–84 (1999).
4 Stone Sweet, "Judicialization," p 87. Although the definitions of judicialization are a bit different, these words seem to have solid application to the version of judicialization addressed in this book.

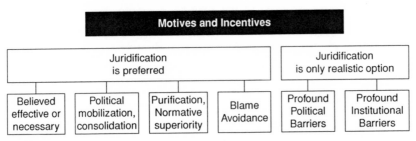

Figure 1.1.

believed to be the best, or easiest, or cheapest path to follow? Or is there good reason to believe that the courts and litigation offer the *only realistic option*?

Institutional Barriers

The only realistic option? Consider segregation – for those fighting to end this practice in the United States, and particularly in the South in the 1950s and 1960s, it would not be enough to secure a national majority in favor of desegregation. That was because two fundamental, institutional barriers in the American system – federalism and the procedural rules of the U.S. Senate – blocked any chance that even a strong national majority could end segregation. Because most of our daily lives are (and certainly were in the 1950s) governed by state, not national, law, issues such as education and access to public accommodations (parks, restaurants, hotels, swimming pools) were governed by state and local law and enforced by state and local police. Short of a constitutional amendment, a national majority – even a strong national majority – would have faced a nearly impossible task in trying to reverse these state laws by simple statute.[5] And a constitutional amendment requires the support of three-quarters of the states (thirty-six of forty-eight in 1954); negative votes from the eleven states that had seceded from the Union in the Civil War, plus from just two additional states, would doom any such amendment.[6]

---

5 One could have made a constitutional case for a statute under Section 5 of the Fourteenth Amendment, which gives Congress the power to pass laws to enforce the provisions of that amendment, including protections for the privileges and immunities of national citizenship, guarantees for the equal protection of the laws, and provisions for due process. But each of these faced profound barriers erected by the Supreme Court itself – the privileges and immunities clause having been circumscribed by a narrow interpretation in the *Slaughterhouse Cases*, 83 U.S. 36 (1873); and the application of Section 5, as well as the Fourteenth Amendment in general, and the equal protection clause in particular, and particularly in reference to civil rights and racial discrimination having been largely precluded by the Court's ruling in the *Civil Rights Cases*, 109 U.S. 3 (1883).

6 The eleven states are Alabama, Arkansas, Florida, Georgia, Louisiana, Mississippi, North Carolina, South Carolina, Tennessee, Texas, and Virginia.

Given that Delaware, Maryland, Missouri, Kentucky, and Oklahoma all had strict segregation laws (and others, such as Kansas, allowed local governments to impose segregation), we can fairly well assume that passing a constitutional amendment was impossible.

Even if segregation somehow could, constitutionally, have been brought under national control through an ordinary statute, and even if there was a national majority that might have supported such an effort (both rather doubtful propositions in 1954), that effort unquestionably would have been defeated by the minority-veto provision of the U.S. Senate's Rule XXII – the innocuous-sounding provision that governs "the precedence of motions," more commonly known as the Senate filibuster rule.[7] Until 1975, Senate Rule XXII required the formal support of two-thirds of those present and voting in the Senate to end debate and allow a vote on challenged legislation. The problem with the filibuster rule is that even if one side (those favoring an end to segregation or other civil rights legislation) has a solid majority that favors passage, a determined minority of senators can block action.[8] Under these circumstances, a turn to the courts by those opposed to segregation – even if risky – might well have been the only viable route, the most promising of a very unpromising set of alternatives.[9]

Political Barriers

Another motive to turn to the courts arises when there are profound political barriers. Here, as with the institutional barriers, we might expect politicians and policy entrepreneurs to make very different calculations about the risks involved in juridification because the alternative to a

---

7 http://rules.senate.gov/senaterules/rule22.php.

8 Here again, if we assume that the senators from the eleven states of the Confederacy (twenty-two senators) were joined by the senators of the other states with mandatory segregation laws (Maryland, Delaware, West Virginia, Kentucky, Missouri, and Oklahoma) that would be thirty-four votes – and the filibuster would be unbeatable.

9 And indeed, the reliance on the courts has been a mixed blessing. *Brown v. Board of Education* was met by massive southern resistance, and there are profound disagreements to this day about the unintended consequences of this approach; urban schools are in many places as segregated today as they ever were, and, in some instances, particularly in northern cities, they are even more segregated today after decades of court orders. See, among many others: Leo Graglia, *Disaster by Decree: The Supreme Court Decisions on Race and the Schools*, Ithaca: Cornell University Press, 1976; Gary Orfield, *Dismantling Desegregation: The Quiet Reversal of* Brown v. Board of Education, New York: New Press, 1996; Gary Orfield and Chungmei Lee, "Brown at 50: King's Dream or 'Plessy's' Nightmare?" Civil Rights Project at Harvard University, Harvard Education Publishing Group, 2004; Charles Ogletree, *All Deliberate Speed: Reflections on the First Half-Century of* Brown v. Board of Education, New York: W.W. Norton, 2004; Derrick Bell, *Silent Covenants:* Brown v. Board of Education *and the Unfulfilled Hopes for Racial Reform*, New York: Oxford University Press, 2004; Michael Klarman, *From Jim Crow to Civil Rights: The Supreme Court and the Struggle for Racial Equality*, New York: Oxford University Press, 2006.

risky legalistic solution might be no hope for any policy gain at all. One example of a profound political barrier serving as an incentive is found in the struggle over abortion rights in the United States (see Chapter 4).

Those looking to change abortion laws divided into two groups – one pressing for the reform and liberalization of existing abortion restrictions (which would leave significant restrictions and limits in place) and another insisting that the choice about abortion must be entirely left to each individual woman. For those urging reform and liberalization, a judicial strategy was one, but not the only, plausible route to their goal. Turning to the courts, for them, might be seen as a preference or as an alternative to the normal state-by-state political process of organizing, electioneering, negotiating, and bargaining. By contrast, for those seeking the total and unequivocal repeal of all restrictions on a woman's choice about abortion, a judicial path seemed the only way to achieve their goal. Public opinion had shifted hardly at all in their direction in the period during which the liberalization of abortion restrictions was winning greater and greater support.[10] For those urging total repeal, there may not have been a profound institutional barrier blocking them – but politically, it seems clear that securing total repeal was a virtually impossible task. The only viable hope for advocates of a woman's unrestricted choice, then, was through the courts. If the Supreme Court ruled that the choice about abortion was a fundamental right, then it would not be necessary to change minds or secure majority support.[11]

Prison reform provides another example of a case in which there were no institutional barriers to reform, but there were considerable, perhaps insurmountable, political barriers. Though law enforcement officials, elected politicians, and administrators, along with advocates and policy entrepreneurs in the 1960s, all largely agreed that many American prisons were desperately in need of expansion and modernization, it was almost impossible for anyone to imagine that voters would support these expensive reforms.[12] Although a political leader might emerge who could accomplish these goals through the ordinary political and policy process, prison reform would only be possible at some staggering political cost, if

---

10 As Rosemary Nossiff notes, there were low levels of public support for abortion liberalization in cases where "the woman was unmarried (18 percent) or where she was married but did not want any more children (16 percent) and the family income was low (22 percent)." Rosemary Nossiff, "Abortion Policy before *Roe*: Grassroots and Interest Group Mobilization," 13 *Journal of Policy History* 4 (2001), p 465.

11 For a comprehensive survey of public opinion on the courts and abortion, see Samantha Luks and Michael Salamone, "Abortion," in Nathaniel Persily, Jack Citrin, and Patrick J. Egan (eds.), *Public Opinion and Constitutional Controversy*, New York: Oxford University Press, 2008.

12 Malcolm M. Feeley and Edward Rubin, *Judicial Policy Making and the Modern State: How the Courts Reformed America's Prisons*, New York: Cambridge University Press, 1998.

at all. The courts seemed to be a plausible and perhaps the *only* plausible path around severe political barriers.

INSTITUTIONAL AND POLITICAL BARRIERS AND THE POLITICAL PROCESS. That an eighteenth-century Constitution might produce significant barriers to the governance needs of a twentieth- and now twenty-first-century superpower should come as no surprise. The seemingly intractable problem of budget deficits is one example of a policy area that some felt only a legalistic, formal, automated process could resolve. With inflation running at staggering levels in the 1970s, with the control of government divided between increasingly antagonistic political parties, and amid soaring levels of cynicism and mistrust in government and politics, Congress tried to formalize, legalize, narrow, and tame the political nightmare of the budget.[13] In 1985, for example, Congress tried to control runaway deficits and inflation by mandating automatic budget-cutting provisions into law. In 1998, members of Congress attempted to hand the president a line-item veto in an effort to do what, politically, they felt they could not. The decision to create an office of special prosecutor is another example of a legalistic effort to correct the political process itself, motivated by what were believed to be fundamental and profound institutional and political barriers.

The post-Watergate 1974 midterm elections swept into Congress candidates for whom reform of the government's ability to investigate and prosecute government corruption and criminal behavior was a top priority. Lawbreaking by executive branch officials and corruption were both very real and far from easy to solve, thanks, in part, to an institutional arrangement that leaves choices about criminal prosecution to the attorney general, a political appointee and member of the president's cabinet. Although this system provides political accountability for law enforcement choices and priorities, it creates a very difficult problem when the alleged lawbreaking, as was the case with the Watergate break-in and cover-up, is being done not only by members of the attorney general's own administration, but by the attorney general him- or herself, as well as by White House officials and even by the person to whom the attorney general reports and at whose pleasure the attorney general serves. The answer embraced by a congressional majority was to create an independent special prosecutor, stripping politics (and, as it turns out, political accountability) from decisions about the prosecution of government corruption (see Chapter 7).

---

13 Some of these efforts were sincere; some were cynically designed to produce political advantage. House Speaker Tip O'Neill (D-MA) called the Gramm-Rudman-Hollings balanced budget proposal "the Senate Incumbents Protection Act of 1986," because it would promise to deliver in the future what the Senate was unwilling to support in the face of an election cycle. Michael Barone, "The Deficit Panic: If We Won't Pay Now, Why Will We Later?," *Washington Post*, October 27, 1985, p B-1.

Juridification by Preference

Profound political and institutional barriers – real and imagined – are not the only motives and incentives for juridification. In some cases politicians and policy entrepreneurs *prefer* legalistic approaches; they prefer to rely on the courts, and they prefer formalized legal procedures and an automated political process. Some may believe these approaches to be more effective or efficient; others see a legalistic strategy as a means of indirectly advancing their objectives, using legal rulings (both positive and negative) to mobilize and consolidate their political organizations, followers, or the public at large. For some, the legal route seems morally superior; for others, particularly those aiming to reform the political process itself, legalistic solutions offer a way to claim credit or, more important, avoid blame for politically costly choices.

EFFECTIVENESS AND EFFICIENCY. The promise of policy success is the most obvious – but by no means the only – motive for juridification.[14] These approaches also may appeal because they appear to be faster and cheaper, allowing policy advocates to focus their limited resources. Rather than requiring mass mobilization, voter drives in 50 states and 435 congressional districts, legislative lobbying, and public campaigns, a legalistic approach, one that relies on judicial rulings, can be staffed and supported by a fairly small coterie of young, well-trained lawyers marching out of the nation's top law schools and into lightly staffed offices in key judicial centers like New York City and Washington, D.C.[15]

Are the courts effective and efficient? Although some follow Gerald Rosenberg and insist that the courts are no more than a "hollow hope," unable to effect real change, legions of policy entrepreneurs continue to litigate in the hope and expectation that the courts will provide a pathway to their policy ends. Should they? That is an important, but slightly different debate. Rosenberg himself agrees that, even if there is no empirical evidence to support any strong claims of efficacy, practitioners – policy entrepreneurs, politicians, and lawyers alike – assume there is and act on that assumption. An early example was provided by those trying to end poverty in America in the early 1960s (see Chapter 4). Two Yale Law School graduates, the husband-and-wife team of Edgar and Jean

---

14 Whether or not a court-centered strategy actually is efficient and effective is the source of one of the great debates in political science. But while that debate rages, many policy entrepreneurs, politicians, litigators, and politicians alike act on their perception, assumption, and belief that the courts can be an efficient and effective means to accomplish their ends. Whether that assumption is valid or not, it is the assumption that drives many – but not all – turns to the courts.

15 Theda Skocpol makes a similar point about the shift from mass-membership civic organizations to small, professionally managed advocacy groups in Washington, D.C. Theda Skocpol, *Diminished Democracy: From Membership to Management in Civic Life*, Norman: University of Oklahoma Press, 2003.

Cahn, insisted in a seminal article in the *Yale Law Journal*, in 1964, that the "case and controversy focus of legal activity can provide one possible alternative to middle class forms of organization and protest." Perhaps more importantly, they argued that a legal approach to the problems of trying to end poverty that relied on the courts rather than the political process might be far quicker and more effective. It may, they wrote, "take less time and effort" for a lawyer "to articulate a concern than to press the same demand by organizing citizens groups."[16]

Struggles over poverty were not the first time that policy entrepreneurs saw the courts as a potentially effective or efficient means to their ends. Howard Gillman demonstrates that political parties have long seen judicial rulings as a way to secure their policy agendas, insulating them from electoral politics.[17] In civil rights, Paul Frymer argues, federal courts played a critical role in the development and enforcement of civil rights for African Americans in the U.S. labor movement, not only because the courts offered a way around significant political and institutional barriers, but also because advocates believed that the courts were more effective and efficient than was the ordinary political process. But, as Frymer notes, this turn to the courts ultimately shaped and constrained the development of future policy choices, in part because the adversarial legal process focused narrowly on the particular issues being litigated (in this case efforts to integrate labor union membership) without considering the consequences this focus might have for the development and power of the union movement more generally.[18] The "choice by civil rights activists to pursue goals through litigation enabled" and encouraged further and later turns away from politics and toward the courts and law.[19] Others – ranging from environmentalists to those concerned with welfare policy,[20] from those struggling to regulate the use and sale of

---

16 Edgar Cahn and Jean Cahn, "The War on Poverty: A Civilian Perspective," 73 *Yale Law Journal* 1335 (1964).

17 Howard Gillman, "How Political Parties Can Use the Courts to Advance Their Agendas: Federal Courts in the United States, 1875–1891," 96 *American Political Science Review* 3, 511 (2002).

18 "The single-mindedness with which many judges and lawyers focused on integrating unions led them to ignore less adversarial ways in which the process might have been resolved. As a result, when racial minorities were provided access to unions, they often found them gravely weakened by financial problems and social discord, leaving unions less power to negotiate collective bargaining agreements. One of the ironies of this story... is that courts were arguably *too* powerful in promoting civil rights in labor unions." Paul Frymer, "Acting When Elected Officials Won't: Federal Courts and Civil Rights Enforcement in U.S. Labor Unions, 1935–85," 97 *American Political Science Review* 3, 496 (2003).

19 Paul Frymer, "Acting When Elected Officials Won't: Federal Courts and Civil Rights Enforcement in U.S. Labor Unions, 1935–85," 97 *American Political Science Review* 3, 484 (2003)

20 Robert Kagan, *Adversarial Legalism: The American Way of Law*, Cambridge: Harvard University Press, 2001; Richard Lazarus, *The Making of Environmental Law*, Chicago:

tobacco, to those demanding that states perform and recognize same-sex marriages, to those fighting to end the death penalty[21] – were clearly convinced that judicial rulings might prove an effective and efficient means to their goals. Their assumptions may or may not have been correct, but correct or not, these assumptions were among the *motives and incentives* driving these advocates into court.

POLITICAL MOBILIZATION. Effectiveness and efficiency are not the only motives for going to court out of preference rather than necessity. A second motive for turning to the courts is provided by what Marc Galanter insists are the important, though perhaps indirect, "radiating effects" that legal advocacy has on political mobilization[22] – effects that serve what Michael McCann calls a "constitutive function," indirectly advancing policy objectives by facilitating political organizing efforts, unifying political movements, or energizing individuals and policy entrepreneurs.[23]

University of Chicago Press, 2004; R. Shep Melnick, *Regulation and the Courts: The Case of the Clean Air Act*, Washington, DC: Brookings Institution Press, 1983; R. Shep Melnick, *The Politics of the New Property: Welfare Rights in Congress and the Courts*, Washington, DC: Brookings Institution Press, 1991; Douglas S. Reed, *On Equal Terms: The Constitutional Politics of Equal Opportunity*, Princeton: Princeton University Press, 2001; Thomas Burke, *Lawyers, Lawsuits and Legal Rights: The Battle over Litigation in American Society*, Berkeley: University of California Press, 2002; Elizabeth Bussiere, "The Failure of Constitutional Welfare Rights in the Warren Court," 109 *Political Science Quarterly* 1, 105–31 (1994); Elizabeth Bussiere, *(Dis)Entitling the Poor: The Warren Court, Welfare Rights, and the American Political Tradition*, University Park: Pennsylvania State University Press, 1997; Philip B. Kurland, "The Judicial Road to Social Welfare," *Social Service Review* 48, 481–93 (December 1974).

21 Peter D. Jacobson and Kenneth E. Warner, "Litigation and Public Health Policy Making: The Case of Tobacco Control," 24 *Journal of Health Politics, Policy and Law* 4, 769–804 (1999); Martha Derthick, *Up in Smoke: From Legislation to Litigation in Tobacco Control* (2nd ed.), Washington, DC: CQ Press, 2005; Evan Gerstmann, "Litigating Same-Sex Marriage: Might the Courts Actually Be Bastions of Rationality?", 38 *PS: Political Science and Politics* 2, 217–20 (2005); Evan Gerstmann, *Same-Sex Marriage and the Constitution*, New York: Cambridge University Press, 2003; Lee Epstein and Joseph Kobylka, *The Supreme Court and Legal Change: Abortion and the Death Penalty*, Chapel Hill: University of North Carolina Press, 1992.

22 Marc Galanter, "The Radiating Effects of Courts," in Keith Boyum and Lynn Mather (eds), *Empirical Theories of Courts*, New York: Longman Press, 1983.

23 In recent years, this struggle has been framed around Gerald Rosenberg's controversial and influential work, *The Hollow Hope: Can Courts Bring about Social Change?* (Chicago: University of Chicago Press, 1991). For contrary, positivist views, see Feeley and Rubin, *Judicial Policy Making and the Modern State*. For a constitutive perspective, consider Michael W. McCann (ed), *Law and Social Movements*, Burlington: Ashgate, 2006; Michael W. McCann, *Rights at Work: Pay Equity Reform and the Politics of Legal Mobilization*, Chicago: University of Chicago Press, 1994; Michael W. McCann, "Causal versus Constitutive Explanations (or, On the Difficulty of Being So Positive ...)," 21 *Law & Social Inquiry* 2, 457–82 (1996); and a series of books written and edited by Austin Sarat and Stuart Scheingold, including *Cause Lawyers and Social Movements*, Stanford: Stanford University Press, 2006; Stuart Scheingold and Austin Sarat, *Something to Believe in: Politics, Professionalism and Cause Lawyering*, Stanford: Stanford University Press, 2004; and Kagan, *Adversarial Legalism*.

These effects are appealing not only to those who use rulings in their own policy arena to motivate and mobilize, but also to those who see the success of other litigation strategies and are, in turn, encouraged to pursue their own.[24] "Such indirect effects," McCann notes, "may include catalyzng movement-building efforts, generating public support for new rights claims, or providing pressure to supplement other political tactics."[25] Although there might be policy advocates who see the courts as a clean, instrumental means to their objectives, we need to consider the power of court rulings (both favorable and adverse rulings) as powerful organizing tools and rallying points. Entrepreneurs might well turn to the courts in an indirect effort, recognizing, as McCann suggests, that "legal rights advocacy can in some circumstances provide a useful resource for social movement building and strategic political action."[26] McCann, Galanter, Joel Handler, and others have well documented the links between social movements and the constitutive effects of law and litigation.

And, of course, these effects can work in two directions: Court rulings can goad social movements affirmatively (by providing an inspiring, organizing, or rallying set of arguments) or negatively, as groups organize in resistance to, or rejection of, a court ruling, as so clearly happened with the anti-abortion movement, which did not exist before the Supreme Court's ruling in *Roe v. Wade*. That Court decision, still law, has helped generate and embed a powerful political movement that profoundly shaped the modern Republican party, not to mention having radiating effects in state and national politics more generally.[27]

Brown v. Board of Education is perhaps the most vivid example of a ruling with widespread radiating effects. Did *Brown* really change American policy? Some say yes; some say no. But did *Brown* fundamentally shift the debate, frame the issue, and come to dominate our political culture, galvanizing and helping motivate and organize generations of lawyers, litigants, politicians, and citizens alike? Michael Klarman notes that *Brown* had a powerful effect, even if it failed to accomplish the objectives set out in the decision itself. *Brown* put racial segregation, and segregation in public schools in particular, on the national agenda, front and center. "*Brown* forced many people to take a position on school segregation.... Before *Brown*, desegregation of the military and major league baseball had been salient issues; school segregation was not. In 1947, Truman's civil rights committee took a position on nearly all salient race

24 David S. Meyer and Steven A. Boutcher, "Signals and Spillover: *Brown v. Board of Education* and Other Social Movements," 5 *Perspectives on Politics* 1, 81–93 (2007).
25 Michael W. McCann, "Legal Mobilization and Social Reform Movements: Notes on Theory and its Application," in McCann (ed), *Law and Social Movements*, p 8.
26 McCann, "Legal Mobilization," p 4.
27 William Saletan, *Bearing Right: How Conservatives Won the Abortion War*, Berkeley: University of California Press, 2003; David J. Garrow, *Liberty and Sexuality: The Right to Privacy and the Making of* Roe v. Wade, Berkeley: University of California Press, 1998; Linda Greenhouse, *Becoming Justice Blackmun*, New York: Times Books, 2005.

issues; school segregation was not among them. *Brown* changed this."[28] *Brown*, Klarman argues, had a motivational effect for African Americans, prompting southern blacks to challenge Jim Crow more aggressively than they might otherwise have done in the mid-1950s.[29]

Turning to the courts because advocates believe that judicial rulings might actually offer an efficient path to their goals (as opposed to the *only* viable route) or because court rulings might serve to galvanize and consolidate a political movement are two motivations for the juridification of policy. But there is at least one more to consider, one that very clearly motivates and inspires not only efforts to pursue public policy through judicial rulings, but also to seek legalistic solutions for the inefficiencies and failures of the political process itself.

NORMATIVE, MORAL SUPERIORITY. Politics is about compromise, deals, and tradeoffs – deals that often require each party to abide and tolerate what it sincerely believes to be fundamentally evil institutions and policies.[30] In contrast, law is about justice, and courts and judicial decisions seem to offer a morally superior path. Ours is and has been a legalistic culture from the start, a fact that was grudgingly accepted by Thomas Paine in 1776,[31] explored by Alexis de Tocqueville after a visit in the 1830s,[32] noted by English observer James Bryce in the 1880s,[33] analyzed by Max Weber in the early years of the twentieth century, and examined by historians and social analysts like Michael Kammen and Seymour Martin Lipset in the last half of that same century.[34] It is a theme that continues to resonate in modern writing on political science.[35] Law has a luster, a power, an appeal, an allure. The presumed clarity and neutrality of law,

---

28 Klarman, *From Jim Crow to Civil Rights*, p 364.

29 Klarman, *From Jim Crow to Civil Rights*, pp 368–9. Also, see Christopher Coleman, Lawrence Nee, & Leonard Rubinowitz, "Social Movements and Social-Change Litigation: Synergy in the Montgomery Bus Protest," 30 *Law & Social Inquiry* 4, 663–701 (2005), arguing that it was the synergy of judicial rulings and political mobilization, each *together with* the other, that led to a successful result. For a full discussion of public opinion and desegregation, see Michael Murakami, "Desegregation," in Persily, Citrin, and Egan (eds), *Public Opinion and Constitutional Controversy*.

30 Mark A. Graber, *Dred Scott and the Problem of Constitutional Evil*, New York: Cambridge University Press, 2006.

31 Thomas Paine, *Common Sense*, 1776.

32 Alexis de Tocqueville, *Democracy in America*, 1835.

33 James Bryce, *The American Commonwealth*, 1893.

34 Michael Kammen, *A Machine That Would Go of Itself: The Constitution in American Culture*, New York: Knopf, 1986. In *American Exceptionalism: A Two-Edged Sword* (New York: W.W. Norton, 1996), Seymour Martin Lipset notes, "In the United States, 'only law is sovereign.' The weakness of the state, the emphasis on individual rights, and a constitutionally mandated division of powers give lawyers a uniquely powerful role in America and makes its people exceptionally litigious" (p 40).

35 See, for example, Sanford Levinson, *Constitutional Faith*, Princeton: Princeton University Press, 1990; John Brigham, *The Cult of the Court*, Philadelphia: Temple University Press, 1987; Barbara Perry, *The Priestly Tribe: The Supreme Court's Image in the American Mind*, Westport: Praeger, 1999.

and of the judges who declare and interpret that law, elevate the courts in the minds of many Americans, suggesting the moral superiority of a legal route to policy goals, even if it is not the most effective or efficient approach. This is particularly true for those who may define morality itself in legalistic terms, as "a matter of rule following" in which moral relationships "consist of duties and rights determined by rules."[36]

Following this approach, juridification may promise more than a faster way to a goal; it may be an essential part of the goal itself. In *Federalist 51*, James Madison insisted that "justice is the end of government. It is the end of civil society. It ever has been and ever will be pursued until it be obtained, or until liberty be lost in the pursuit."[37] This motivation emerges far more explicitly in legalistic efforts to formalize, proceduralize, automate, cleanse, and purify politics and the political process itself. But it is an incentive, a motivation that is shared by many who choose a judicial path to their policy goals as well, as is clearly evident in everything from the struggles over abortion and poverty to the fights over environmental policy, segregation, capital punishment, and even the tobacco conflict detailed in the cases examined in this book.

Policy movements are not always unified, single minded, and hierarchical, but may include individuals with very different agendas and objectives, as well as coalitions of people moved to different degrees by different incentives. Recall the movement around abortion. Even for those seeking liberalization and reform and not necessarily the total repeal of all abortion restrictions, this effort was still a question about rights and about human autonomy, liberty, and dignity – questions many felt should not be subject to the marketplace of politics. For them, as for many whose turn to the courts is motivated by normative preferences, the risks of skewed policy choices in the future have to be weighed against the profoundly more normatively superior path that juridification seems to offer.

How we do what we do is at the very core of the American constitutional system and is among the most strongly held constitutional values. Is the U.S. Constitution essentially the means to a set of clear normative ends – or are the means themselves the ends? In an extraordinary exchange with Lieutenant Colonel Oliver North during the hearings into the Iran-Contra affair in 1987, Indiana's Democratic Congressman Lee Hamilton suggested that the means matter at least as much, if not more, than the ends: "A democratic government, as I understand it," Hamilton said, "is not a solution, but it's a way of seeking solutions. It's not a government devoted to a particular objective, but a form of government which specifies means and methods of achieving objectives. Methods and means are

---

36 Shklar, *Legalism*, p 1.
37 James Madison, *Federalist 51*.

what this country is all about."[38] Although one-person-one-vote may not, in fact, be the best way to ensure fair and equal representation in America's odd federal system, it has a moral clarity that was and continues to be nearly impossible to oppose.[39] And although political control of prosecutorial decisions may, in fact, be the best way to protect against the abuse of power, it is, as Justice Scalia noted, "difficult to vote not to enact, and even more difficult to vote to repeal, a statute called, appropriately enough, the Ethics in Government Act."[40]

The normative, moral impulse runs deep in the American political tradition, stretching back to the Puritans. Whether in the abolitionist movement; the Jacksonian, Progressive, or Populist eras; or the long-1960s, it flourishes and then recedes – but never disappears. Historically, Samuel Huntington argues, "American society seems to evolve through periods of creedal passion and creedal passivity." There is, he argues, an "ever-present gap" between American political ideals and the American political institutions and practices that simply cannot deliver the policies those ideals seem to demand.[41] That gap has ripped wide a few times in American history – and when it has, it often has been followed by a demand for more law and less politics.

Americans long have had great ambivalence about politics and the political process, craving the purity, clarity, and efficiency of judicial rulings and rejecting or barely tolerating the gray ambiguity and frustrating inefficiency of the political process. This trend, this tendency, was fed by the political resistance to the end of racial segregation during the Cold War and then fanned by frustration with the inability to force an end to the war in Vietnam. Richard Nixon's assertion of prerogative budgetary, war, and emergency powers, as well as the use and misuse of executive power in struggles over intelligence gathering – the misuse of the Internal Revenue Service, the Department of Justice, and the Federal Bureau of Investigation – added fuel to the fire. And then came Watergate.

The Watergate-era reforms took the form of statutory, procedural attempts to solve political problems – legalizing, constitutionalizing, and even criminalizing the political process. Politics was to be cleansed, formalized, and contained. The budget process would be automated; war powers allocated, assigned, formalized, and proceduralized; campaign finance regularized and regulated; and political corruption controlled by

38 Lee Hamilton (D-IN), Select Committee on Secret Military Assistance to Iran and the Nicaraguan Opposition, July 14, 1987, published in *Taking the Stand: The Testimony of Lieutenant Colonel Oliver L. North*, New York: Pocket Books, 1987, p 744.
39 See *Baker v. Carr*, 369 U.S. 186 (1962) and its progeny, discussed in Chapter 2.
40 *Morrison v. Olson*, 487 U.S. 654, 733 (1988) (Scalia, J., dissenting).
41 Samuel P. Huntington, *American Politics: The Promise of Disharmony*, Cambridge: Harvard University Press, 1981, p 4.

prosecutors independent of all political influence. These were efforts by Congress to adopt the approach, the precision, and what some thought and hoped was the black-and-white of law. And they were efforts driven by another important element in law's allure – blame shifting or blame avoidance.[42]

BLAME AVOIDANCE. Although a reform-minded Congress swept into office following the Watergate crisis, its members were still elected officials, and they were not immune to the primary goal shared by most elected officials, which, as David Mayhew teaches, is to pursue their interests as "single-minded reelection seekers."[43] Juridification offers a great deal to politicians who want to cut deficits, or terminate a war, or prosecute corruption, but fear the heavy political price these choices might pose – it allows them to avoid blame.[44]

It was a temptation the 99th Congress could not resist. Facing what was (for the time) a historically unprecedented debt, with projected deficits in fiscal 1986 of more than $180 billion, there were no good choices. To support draconian spending cuts seemed political suicide. Instead, a proposal by Republican Senators Phil Gramm of Texas and Warren Rudman of New Hampshire offered a way to shed blame, rather than a real solution to the problem. "If Congress [failed to] achieve its budget targets, responsibility for the painful choices would shift to the president to implement cuts specified" by the law.[45] It was, Connecticut's Republican Senator Lowell Weicker said, a "legislative substitute for the guts we don't have to do what needs to be done."[46] Maryland's Republican Senator Charles Mathias insisted that the law "searches for a way to evade the hard choices that deficit reduction demands. It strives for a way to reach that goal without taking responsibility."[47]

If the goal is to galvanize, or organize, or define a political movement, legalistic solutions may have a very different sort of appeal than they might if the goal were to actually force specific change; if the political process itself is seen as corrupt, then legalistic solutions in general and solutions that automate or even surrender power to the courts might be seen as superior, even if the courts ultimately may not support the goals

---

42 R. Kent Weaver, *The Politics of Blame Avoidance*, Washington, DC: Brookings Institution Press, 1987.

43 David Mayhew, *Congress: The Electoral Connection*, New Haven: Yale University Press, 1974, p 17.

44 Weaver, *The Politics of Blame Avoidance*.

45 Carl E. Van Horn, "Fear and Loathing on Capitol Hill: The 99th Congress and Economic Policy," 19 *PS* 1 (Winter 1986), p 25.

46 Elizabeth Wehr, "Support Grows for Balancing Federal Budget," *Congressional Quarterly Weekly Report*, October 5, 1985, pp 1975–8.

47 David Broder, "The Rudman-Gramm Balanced Budget Sham," *Washington Post*, December 11, 1985, p A-23.

initially sought by policy advocates. Better to lose in court than to corrupt the cause with the taint of politics.

Juridification seems to be most defensible and least costly in those cases where the courts offer the only viable path to get around fundamental institutional barriers posed by federalism, the separation of powers, or institutional rules like the filibuster. By contrast, juridification seems most problematic when it dilutes or deflects the ordinary political process that might have been quite capable, not only of accomplishing the desired goals, but also of doing so through means and methods of political persuasion and bargaining – means and methods that might actually build public and political support for controversial policies by changing minds, an often necessary condition for changing votes.[48]

Juridification Patterns and Process

Although the motives and incentives tell us something about whether a policy entrepreneur *ought* to be more or less risk adverse, they do not tell us which patterns generate which types of risks nor do they suggest which patterns are more and less likely to be followed. This is the second dimension that needs to be considered here: the different patterns and processes that juridification tends to follow (see Figure 1.2).

Before the 1960s, the courts were a place to go to stop the government, to block and obstruct policy initiatives. This blocking function is with us still, but when the Warren Court first signaled the possibility that, in addition to its traditional function of saying what government *could* and what it could *not* do, the courts might now also be available to say what government *must* do as well, the Justices opened a new path to policy goals. Was this simply an alternative route to the same goal – or would the path chosen, the pattern and process that would follow,

---

48 Justice Ruth Bader Ginsburg, for example, argues that becoming overly dependent on courts and overemphasizing the rights argument about abortion may have been a significant strategic error. The error, she insists, was not the use of the courts as *part* of the strategy, but the near total dependence on the courts. Had the courts struck down individual abortion regulations as violations of the equal protection clause or as violations of procedural requirements, Ginsburg argues, and these decisions were paired with a full-scale political effort to pass reform legislation state by state, the net result of this sort of courts *together with* strategy might have been far more powerful and lasting than the more exclusively legalistic solution of asking the Court to articulate, defend, and expand a fundamental right. See Ruth Bader Ginsburg, "Speaking in a Judicial Voice," 57 *NYU Law Review* 1185 (1992); "A Moderate View on Roe," *Constitution*, Spring-Summer 1992, p 17; "Some Thoughts on Autonomy and Equality in Relation to *Roe v. Wade*," 63 *North Carolina Law Review* 375 (1985). Similar arguments have been made in a number of controversial areas, including desegregation. One study suggests that the success of the struggle against racial discrimination in buses in Montgomery, Alabama, was precisely because it was a combined, *together with* strategy of judicial rulings and political tactics that actually made a difference. See, for example, Coleman, Nee, and Rubinowitz, "Social Movements and Social-Change Litigation."

Figure 1.2.

make a difference? To begin to sort out these questions, we can divide these patterns into four categories: cases in which the Court (1) remains relatively silent; (2) authorizes or defers; (3) blocks or rejects, in whole or in part; or (4) commands. Sometimes, these patterns appear to end right at this point – if the Court says no and Congress accepts that choice, the pattern ends. Conversely, if the Court commands and the elected branches comply, the pattern ends. But more often, these are but the first step in a long, iterated chain, in which policies and decisions spiral from Court to elected branches, to administrative agencies, and back into Court – each decision at each step shaped by those that came before and, in turn, shaping and constraining those that will follow (see Figure 1.3).

The Court Authorizes or Blocks – May and May Not

Like any traffic cop, the courts' primary power is to say what is and what is not allowed. What is the national government allowed to do? What are the states allowed to do? And what is each forbidden to do? Long ago, the Supreme Court became a place to go to stop the government or to certify the government's authority to act. Unlike agencies or administrators and elected officials, Martin Shapiro notes, judges "often exercise negative power by striking down laws through juridical review,

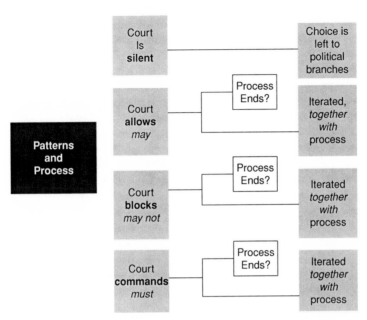

Figure 1.3.

as opposed to positively shaping policy through the promulgation of specific regulations."[49] Impressively, this simple blocking function became an enormous source of power for the courts (though compliance with these orders was far from universal): The Supreme Court blocked efforts by the state governments to tax a nationally chartered bank; courts blocked the reach and narrowed the scope of antitrust legislation; the courts blocked efforts to strike a deal in the days before the Civil War, overturning the Missouri Compromise[50]; the Court's narrow reading of the Fourteenth Amendment blocked the efforts of the Reconstruction Congress to ban segregation in transportation and public accommodations; the Court blocked the government from imposing a graduated income tax (requiring a constitutional amendment to remove the impediment); and the Court

49 Martin Shapiro, *The Supreme Court and Administrative Agencies*, New York: Free Press, 1968, p 60 (quoted in Barnes, "Bringing the Courts Back In," p 38).
50 The Supreme Court certainly did not foreclose the possibility of a legislative compromise in the *Dred Scott* decision, simply ruling that the particular compromise that had been reached over Missouri was not constitutionally valid. As Mark Graber notes, the "legislative decision to foist responsibility onto the courts" was one the Court may have invited, but was also one that legislators from across the political spectrum welcomed. The Court did not preclude compromise, but in fact, the decision to hand the problem over to the courts was itself the "last great territorial compromise" of the antebellum era. See Mark A. Graber, *Dred Scott and the Problem of Constitutional Evil*, New York: Cambridge University Press, 2006, p 35, quoting Keith Whittington, "The Road Not Taken: Dred Scott, Judicial Authority and Political Questions," 63 *Journal of Politics* 2, 365 (2001) p 378.

blocked a great deal of labor legislation at the turn of the century and on into the era of the New Deal. The Court continued to exercise its blocking function in the modern era, blocking President Truman's efforts to take over steel mills during the Korean War, banning government efforts to impose mandatory prayers in schools, rejecting government restrictions on abortions in the first trimester, and banning the imposition of race-based quotas in school integration, to name just a few rulings.

President Theodore Roosevelt devoted almost one-quarter of his final State of the Union address in 1908 to an attack on the courts and their blocking function.[51] After urging Congress to raise judicial salaries and condemning class conflict, Roosevelt called on the courts to abandon the judges' insistence on classical, hidebound readings of the Constitution. "The rapid changes in our social and industrial life," he said, "make it necessary that, in applying to concrete cases the great rule of right laid down in our Constitution, there should be a full understanding and appreciation of the new conditions to which the rules are to be applied. What would have been an infringement upon liberty half a century ago may be the necessary safeguard of liberty today." He returned to this theme in 1912, when again campaigning for the White House, he insisted that when a judge "decides what the people as a whole can or cannot do, the people should have a right to recall that decision if they think it is wrong. If the courts have the first say as to all legislative acts, and if no appeal can lie from them to the people, then they are irresponsible masters of the people."[52]

Teddy Roosevelt's cousin, Franklin, saw the Supreme Court as a major barrier to his agenda – and his political mandate. After winning a landslide reelection in 1936, Franklin Roosevelt proposed a dramatic reorganization of the Supreme Court. Since the rise of "the modern movement for social and economic progress through legislation," Franklin Roosevelt noted in his Fireside Chat of March 9, 1937, "the Court has more and more often and more and more boldly asserted a power to veto laws passed by the Congress and State Legislatures." In blocking legislative efforts to "stabilize national agriculture, to improve the conditions of labor, to safeguard business against unfair competition, to protect our national resources, and in many other ways, to serve our clearly national needs, the majority of the Court has been assuming the power to pass on the wisdom of these acts of the Congress – and to approve or disapprove the public policy written into these laws."[53] Such views were not – and are not – limited to liberals and Democrats, but continue to be widely shared

---

51 More than 4400 words of his nearly 19,400 word speech were focused on the courts. See: http://www.presidency.ucsb.edu/ws/index.php?pid=29549.
52 Frances Leupp, "Roosevelt the Politician," *The Atlantic*, June 1912.
53 Franklin D. Roosevelt, *Fireside Chat*, March 9, 1937. See http://www.millercenter. virginia.edu/scripps/digitalarchive/speeches/spe_1937_0309_roosevelt.

and expressed by conservative presidents in the modern era, including Ronald Reagan and both the younger and elder George Bush.

These complaints tend to suggest that the problem is one of judicial overreach or judicial imperialism The judges are not, however, alone responsible for the growth of judicial power. As Keith Whittington, Mark Graber, Howard Gillman, George Lovell, and Paul Frymer, among others, clearly demonstrate, elected officials often facilitate, request, and plead for judicial intervention, happy to surrender responsibility (and blame) for tough choices.[54] And so the courts, *together with* Congress and the administration, turned the power to say what the government *can* and what it can *not* do into the foundation for the nationalization of American government, the expansion of the American economy, and, with it, supervision of everything from slavery to contracts, from property to war.[55]

Though the focus of conventional interest in the blocking model tends to be on cases where the Court says no, there are important instances in which the Court's decision to say yes are equally if not more momentous; one might argue this was the case with the Court's decision to allow the creation of the Office of Special Prosecutor. When the Court says yes or no, juridification ostensibly is left largely in the hands of the other branches – but even then, the Court's decision shapes, frames, and constrains the strategic choices made by politicians, policy entrepreneurs, private litigants, and their attorneys as they evaluate court decisions retrospectively and prospectively before making their next move.

The Court's Command Function – Thou Must

The Court never surrendered its blocking function, but, in 1954, the Justices signaled that they might be willing to add a new function. Starting with the Supreme Court's dramatic school desegregation ruling in

---

54 Keith Whittington, *Political Foundations of Judicial Supremacy: The Presidency, the Supreme Court and Constitutional Leadership in U.S. History*, Princeton: Princeton University Press, 2007; George Lovell, *Legislative Deferrals: Statutory Ambiguity, Judicial Power and American Democracy*, Cambridge: Cambridge University Press, 2003; Frymer, "Acting When Elected Officials Won't"; Howard Gillman, "How Political Parties Can Use the Courts to Advance Their Agendas: Federal Courts in the United States, 1875–1891," 96 *American Political Science Review* 3, 511–24 (2002); Mark Graber, "The Non-Majoritarian Difficulty: Legislative Deference to the Judiciary," 7 *Studies in American Political Development* (Spring 1993), pp 35–73.

55 A taste of these can be found in *McCulloch v. Maryland*, 17 U.S. 316 (1819); *Gibbons v. Ogden*, 22 U.S. 1 (1824); *U.S. v. E.C. Knight*, 156 U.S. 1 (1895) (economic expansion); *The Antelope*, 10 Wheaton 66 (1825); *U.S. v. the Schooner Amistad*, 40 U.S. 518 (1841); *Prigg v. Pennsylvania*, 41 U.S. 539 (1842); and *Dred Scott v. Sanford*, 60 U.S. 393 (1857) (slavery); *Pollock v. Farmers' Loan & Trust Co.*, 157 U.S. 429 (1895) (taxation); *Dartmouth College v. Woodward*, 17 U.S. 518 (1819), and *Charles River Bridge v. Warren Bridge*, 36 U.S. 420 (1837) (contracts); *Little v. Barreme*, 6 U.S. 170 (1804) (war).

Brown vs. Board of Education in 1954 and confirmed by a series of decisions ordering state governments to redraw their political districting lines, starting in *Baker v. Carr* in 1962, the Court began to clear a new path. This path led not only to orders telling government what it could and could not do – but also to orders telling the government what it *must* do as well. It was an invitation that was eagerly accepted: In some cases because it provided a means around profound political and institutional barriers; in some because it seemed to offer a more effective or efficient path to policy goals; in some because of law's normative allure; and in still others as a way to galvanize, motivate, and consolidate political movements.[56] Here, we can find litigation efforts aimed at social policy objectives, ranging from struggles over welfare and prison reform, to education, disability law, environmental protection, and poverty abatement.[57] In addition. we can find efforts to command the states to reallocate legislative districts, with profound effects on the political process itself.

Both of these patterns – those triggered by the Court's blocking function and those triggered by the Court's command function – raise real risks (and offer real attractions) for policy advocates. In some instances, these rulings may be one-off single shots, in which the Court says do this – and the government complies – or the Court says do not do this, and the government stops.[58] These are relatively lower risk patterns – lower, but not without risk. In such cases, the elected branches have some viable political tools to reverse the Court's decision or work around it. Congress can strip the court of jurisdiction, and, in statutory rulings, Congress can pass override legislation.[59] Presidents can (over time) shift the courts through appointments,[60] and there is even the ultimate recourse of constitutional amendment. However, when the Court remains relatively silent or when the courts actively engage in the policymaking process, the process becomes more complicated and far more difficult to unwind, terminate, or reverse.

---

56 Meyer and Boutcher, "Signals and Spillover," p 81.
57 Kagan, *Adversarial Legalism*; Lazarus, *The Making of Environmental Law*; Melnick, *Regulation and the Courts*; Reed, *On Equal Terms*; Melnick, *The Politics of the New Property*; Burke, *Lawyers, Lawsuits and Legal Rights*; Bussiere, "The Failure of Constitutional Welfare Rights"; Bussiere, *(Dis)Entitling the Poor*; Kurland, "The Judicial Road to Social Welfare."
58 There are, of course, instances in which the Court says "do this" and the government fails to comply, as well as instances in which the Supreme Court's orders are misinterpreted or willfully ignored by lower courts.
59 See Jeb Barnes, *Overruled? Legislative Overrides, Pluralism and Contemporary Court-Congress Relations*, Stanford: Stanford University Press, 2004.
60 Judges from the federal courts serve an average of 18.3 years in office. See Albert Yoon, "Love's Labor Lost: Judicial Tenure among Federal Court Judges: 1945–2000," 91 *California Law Review* 1029 (2003). Even the Supreme Court, with rare exception, experiences at least one vacancy every four years; that the Rehnquist Court was unchanged for eleven years (1994–2005) was an exception, and far from the rule.

The Court Is Reluctant to Intervene and Remains Relatively Silent

This category is largely limited to efforts to juridify the political process and the allocation or reallocation of power within the government. These cases might involve internal, institutional procedures or separation of powers disputes in which the two branches have worked out a legalistic, formalized, or proceduralized set of rules. Legalistic solutions such as the effort to structure the allocation and exercise of war powers, or the more recent technique of statutory authorizations for the use of military force short of a declaration of war (employed in both Gulf Wars and in Afghanistan) rarely involve the Court directly or extensively. Such cases may well be examples of an interbranch issue that has yet to become ripe, or, as Justice Powell said in a case concerning the abrogation of a defense treaty in 1979, "If the Congress chooses not to confront the President, it is not our task to do so."[61]

Silence by the courts, however, does not mean a lack of juridification. At a minimum, the Court's reticence leaves it as something of a "brooding omnipresence" in the background, able to interpose and engage should the question become ripe in the eyes of the Justices.[62] Judicial silence does not prevent juridification; it merely leaves the process largely in the hands of the other branches – where efforts to eliminate ambiguity, to formalize, and to automate may continue.

Courts Together with the Elected Branches

Each of these processes – in which the Court blocks (may or may not), commands, or remains relatively silent – can trigger a variety of patterns of juridification. What happens next and the relative degree of risk involved have a great deal to do with the way in which the elected branches, administrative agencies, and interest groups respond to these initial court rulings. When Congress and the president build on court rulings, trying to work within the boundaries and frames established by court rulings past, present, and those they anticipate are likely to come, a very different set of patterns may emerge – patterns that will be far harder to undo and will be far more likely to shape and constrain policy and politics in important ways.

---

61 *Goldwater v. Carter*, 444 U.S. 996, 998 (1979) (Powell, J., concurring in the order to deny certiorari).

62 This is, of course, the much-abused phrase Justice Oliver Wendell Holmes used to describe what the common law was *not*: "The common law is not a brooding omnipresence in the sky," Holmes wrote, "but the articulate voice of some sovereign or quasi sovereign that can be identified; although some decisions with which I have disagreed seem to me to have forgotten the fact." *Southern Pacific Co. v. Jensen* 244 U.S. 205, 222 (1917) (Holmes, J., dissenting).

There is a tendency for most observers – academic and nonacademic alike – to see and evaluate the interaction of courts and politics as something of a gladiatorial struggle, in which judicial power and the judicial role are seen as "instrumental, linear, and unidirectional."[63] More often, however, court rulings are anything but single-shot games. If we look at a Court ruling as a snapshot, there is of course a winner and loser. But if we think about Court rulings and how they shape and constrain policy goals over time, we get a very different picture. Consider the death penalty.[64] Capital punishment is a fine example of an area in which opponents of the policy must overcome significant, even profound, political barriers. Frustrated by the endless stream of challenges to the death penalty that filled the Court's docket, in 1971, Hugo Black convinced his brethren on the Supreme Court to hear arguments in a set of death penalty cases during the Court's next term, in 1972. Black's hope was that the Court might settle the issue, one way or the other, "once and for all."[65] Black prevailed, but suffered a massive stroke shortly after, dying just eight days after he retired from the Court. His seat would be filled by Lewis Powell.

One of the cases the Supreme Court elected to hear was *Furman v. Georgia*, in which the Court handed down a stunning 5–4 decision striking down every death penalty law in the United States, state and national alike, thereby commuting the sentences of 600 inmates on death rows across the country.[66] A June 1972 snapshot would certainly give the appearance of an active, aggressive Court delivering the prize that death penalty opponents had long sought in court.[67] Realistically, Chief Justice Warren Burger confided to two reporters, it was the end of the line for capital punishment. He told them that, after the 5–4 *Furman* decision, there would "never be another execution in this country."[68]

This was not, however, the end of the story. *Furman* may have terminated death sentences in 1972, but the Court's opinion also provided the outline of a judicially drawn road map for the entrenchment of a

---

63 Michael McCann, "Causal versus Constitutive Explanations," p 459.
64 My thanks to Robert Kagan for goading me to think about how the blocking pattern can trip a precedent spiral.
65 William J. Brennan, "Constitutional Adjudication and the Death Penalty: A View from the Court," 100 *Harvard Law Review* 313, 322 (1986).
66 *Furman v. Georgia*, 408 U.S. 238 (1972); Fred Graham, "Court Spares 600," *New York Times*, June 30, 1972, p 1.
67 Fred Graham, "'68 Ending With No Executions, First Such Year in U.S. Records." *New York Times*, December 31, 1968, p 17.
68 Bob Woodward and Scott Armstrong, *The Brethren: Inside the Supreme Court*, New York: Simon & Schuster, 1979, p 259 (cited in Lee Epstein and Joseph Kobylka, *The Supreme Court and Legal Change: Abortion and the Death Penalty*, Chapel Hill: University of North Carolina Press, 1992, p 80).

far more resilient future for capital punishment, signaling the sorts of laws and procedures that would be needed to withstand constitutional challenge.[69] And, just four years after *Furman*, the Supreme Court sanctioned the return of a rebuilt, reinforced death penalty – one that had been designed to fit precisely the specifications the Court itself had outlined.[70] The post-*Furman* death penalty was a very different thing from the pre-*Furman* death penalty. The post-*Furman* death penalty was one that was directed, shaped, constrained, and defined by the courts and by legal precedent. This certainly was not a case of an imperial court imposing its will nor did this happen because elected officials overrode the courts. It was very much a case of one layer atop another, a case of the courts *together with* the elected branches. Although those opposed to the death penalty had a plausible incentive to turn to the courts, in hindsight it may have been a Faustian bargain. They gambled that the Court and the Court alone could eliminate the death penalty – and it did. But they failed to consider that this is not a single-round game, they failed to understand that the Court's rulings were part of a colloquy, and ultimately they failed to imagine that the very ruling that would end the

---

69 "Today the Court has not ruled that capital punishment is per se violative of the Eighth Amendment; nor has it ruled that the punishment is barred for any particular class or classes of crimes. The substantially similar concurring opinions of Mr. Justice Stewart and Mr. Justice White, which are necessary to support the judgment setting aside petitioners' sentences, stop short of reaching the ultimate question. The actual scope of the Court's ruling, which I take to be embodied in these concurring opinions, is not entirely clear. This much, however, seems apparent: If the legislatures are to continue to authorize capital punishment for some crimes, juries and judges can no longer be permitted to make the sentencing determination in the same manner they have in the past. . . . While I would not undertake to make a definitive statement as to the parameters of the Court's ruling, it is clear that if state legislatures and the Congress wish to maintain the availability of capital punishment, significant statutory changes will have to be made. Since the two pivotal concurring opinions turn on the assumption that the punishment of death is now meted out in a random and unpredictable manner, legislative bodies may seek to bring their laws into compliance with the Court's ruling by providing standards for juries and judges to follow in determining the sentence in capital cases or by more narrowly defining the crimes for which the penalty is to be imposed. . . . Since there is no majority of the Court on the ultimate issue presented in these cases, the future of capital punishment in this country has been left in an uncertain limbo. Rather than providing a final and unambiguous answer on the basic constitutional question, the collective impact of the majority's ruling is to demand an undetermined measure of change from the various state legislatures and the Congress. While I cannot endorse the process of decision-making that has yielded today's result and the restraints that that result imposes on legislative action, I am not altogether displeased that legislative bodies have been given the opportunity, and indeed unavoidable responsibility, to make a thorough re-evaluation of the entire subject of capital punishment. If today's opinions demonstrate nothing else, they starkly show that this is an area where legislatures can act far more effectively than courts." *Furman v. Georgia*, 408 U.S. 238, 396–403 (1972), Chief Justice Burger (dissenting).

70 This came in *Gregg v. Georgia*, 428 U.S. 153 (1976), and two companion cases, *Proffitt v. Florida*, 428 U.S. 242 (1976), and *Jurek v. Texas*, 428 U.S. 262 (1976).

death penalty would, ultimately provide a far more stable platform for its revival and entrenchment.[71]

This is a good reminder that the juridification process is not an all-or-nothing proposition, but rather spreads across a continuum. At one extreme, courts play an important but fairly simple role of saying what is and what is not allowed. Congress accepts it or (where it can) reverses it. But, far more often, court rulings are part of an iterated sequence, in which a court ruling triggers new legislation, which triggers further litigation, which triggers more legislation. At the other end of the spectrum, the branches are interlaced, each dependent on the other, each reacting to the other, each trying to anticipate the other. Sometimes, these iterated patterns find Court and Congress largely on the same page, at least headed in roughly the same direction. Like a team of skilled craftsmen, each is adding bricks to a wall that together they build high and strong in what might be called a *constructive pattern*. Sometimes, though, they are very much on different pages. They misread each others' signals, they respond to different incentives, and they are constrained by different institutional barriers. As one group lays bricks in place, the other removes them, rearranges them, or substitutes different bricks that may not fit as well – or at all. Far from building a strong wall, together they engage in something more like a *deconstructive pattern*, building something neither would recognize or likely choose had it been left to them alone. The risks for policy entrepreneurs are higher here, not only because a deconstructive pattern more deeply embeds the problem but also because these decisions and choices may not be limited to the particular policy question in play. Because of the way judicial decision making works (Chapter 3), decisions in one substantive area (religious liberty, for example) can influence, shape, and constrain – and be influenced, shaped, and constrained by – decisions in other substantive areas (such as free speech), making it even harder to unwind these tangles.

Far from being limited to the policy sphere, some of the most complex and risky cases of interbranch constructive and deconstructive patterns are those that actually involve both policy and the political process itself. The effort to improve the environment that took hold in the 1970s is one of the better examples of the constructive model of juridification (Chapter 5). The continuing struggle over campaign finance reform (Chapter 6) is a powerful example of a deconstructive pattern of juridification, one that shapes and constrains policy as well as the political process itself.

---

71 In fact, it was those pressing to carry out death sentences who turned to politics, persuading Congress, in 1996, to pass a new statute that would severely limit access to the courts, shorten litigation delays, and make sure death penalties would be less likely to clog the Supreme Court's docket. (The Antiterrorism and Effective Death Penalty Act of 1996 – see http://thomas.loc.gov/cgi-bin/query/z?c104:S.735.ENR:)

Constructive and Deconstructive Patterns

There can be no question that America's air and water are vastly cleaner and healthier today than they were in 1969 when a massive oil spill in Santa Barbara was followed just two months later by the sight of the Cuyahoga River, in Cleveland, Ohio, catching fire and burning. These crises helped jumpstart a leap-frog process of legislation and litigation, leading to more legislation, which in turn was expanded and developed by more litigation that – produced yet more legislation. Each round added ever greater reliance on litigation and built in more provisions to encourage yet more litigation to help define, expand, and enforce the legislation. The process began with the vague and platitudinous National Environmental Policy Act that Richard Nixon signed into law on January 1, 1970, after it flew through the House without a roll-call vote. And no wonder – on its face, the legislation provided a good opportunity for members of Congress to claim credit with environmentalists at little if any cost: There was scant reason to believe that the law would actually require very much from recalcitrant agencies save another stack of reports to add to their blizzard of paperwork. And it might never have amounted to much, had it not been for a couple of key federal judges who interpreted the statute broadly and whose broad interpretation, in turn, was welcomed by a congressional majority, which built new legislation on the foundations laid by these interpretations – a process that would play out with the Clean Air Act of 1970, the Endangered Species Act of 1973, the Clean Water Act of 1977, and a host of other provisions, administrative rulings, extensions, and revisions. Legislation built on court interpretations that were then expanded and deepened by yet more court rulings that then fed back into new statutes, creating new legislative history that would then enable further judicial interpretation.

It is a very open question whether this game of interbranch leap-frog produced anything like what any of the key players expected or wanted. But it is hard to doubt that Court and Congress were at least heading in something of a similar direction and that the courts *together with* Congress and many administrators were working furiously in what certainly appeared to be a *constructive* pattern – meaning simply that, although they may have been following different rules, responding to slightly different incentives, and speaking very different languages, they were headed in the same general direction.

The same cannot be said of campaign finance reform, which is an example of a *deconstructive* pattern. Far from building on and fortifying each other's work – in this area the court pulled out bricks laid by Congress, replacing them with different bricks, in different patterns. But the process did not end there. After the Court certified some but not other parts of the complex and interdependent Campaign Finance Reform Act of 1974, Congress responded not by fighting back nor by starting over from scratch. Instead, members of Congress built on the gutted structure left by the Court. And the process continues, with each side leaping over the other, as one poorly designed fix and bandage are applied over yet another inopportune judicial adjustment or renovation. Far from removing money and the taint of corruption from politics, these moves have spawned features that may well be worse than the initial problem that triggered this effort in the first place. And because this was a question not only of public policy but also of the very structure of the political process that would have to be relied on to revise, correct, and implement any policy that emerged, it took on even more profoundly deconstructive elements, discussed in Chapter 6.[72]

Why one and not the other? Why do some of these iterated, layered patterns follow a constructive pattern, whereas others end up following a deconstructive pattern? Part of the answer is relatively easy. We could call it *institutional alignment* – which is another way to say that, when the federal judiciary is in general ideological and/or partisan agreement with the dominant political coalition in the elected branches (or at least with Congress), there is at least a better chance of a constructive pattern.[73] This certainly was the case with the environment. Federal judges like Gerhard Gesell, who found in the NEPA statute an implied right to challenge environmental impact statements in court, were well in tune with the congressional majority of the time. And the environment (at least initially) was an exceptional case in which important and natural cross-party coalitions were possible, as some Republican conservationists lined up with some environmentalists in the Democratic party. By contrast, the reform-minded Democratic Congress that swept into office in the wake of the Watergate scandal was not exactly in line with a federal judiciary that had begun a wrenching turn away from the Warren Court, on its way eventually to becoming the far more assertively conservative Rehnquist and then the Roberts Court. That important reform legislation might run into a deconstructive pattern should not be terribly surprising. We might also expect that, as Congress itself becomes more bitterly divided and less capable of unified action, not only in regard to the executive

---

72 The effort, initially instigated by the Court, to command that states reapportion their districts, ultimately insisting on a standard as mathematically close to one-person-one-vote as possible, has shaped our political institutions, influenced political campaigns, and spilled over into areas as far reaching as racial discrimination and federalism because it structures the institutions that ultimately develop and implement public policy generally.

73 Institutional alignment fits well with what some refer to as the "regime theory" of judicial decision making. See Cornell Clayton and J. Mitchell Pickerill, *The Supreme Court in the Political Regime: How Politics Structures the Exercise of Judicial Review*, Chicago: University of Chicago Press, forthcoming. See also Jack Balkin and Sanford Levinson, "The Processes of Constitutional Change: From Partisan Entrenchment to the National Surveillance State," 75 *Fordham Law Review* 489 (2006).

branch but also within its own body and even within its own party caucuses, the Court becomes a staunch ally for some and a clear enemy for others, making constructive patterns less and less likely.[74] Divided government and fractured political coalitions also appear likely to encourage ever more space in which an aggressive Court might be able to set or reset agendas. As Keith Whittington argues, if political coalitions "are fragmented or insecure or if coalition partners disagree [about] myriad issues" courts can become increasingly useful. And, as he notes, "when the signals about constitutional priorities" coming from the leaders of fractious political coalitions become increasingly weak, even more space opens for the courts to becoming increasingly independent agents.[75]

Party cohesion and institutional alignment tell an important part of the story. Unfortunately, the more important part of the story is the one far less easily observed, measured, and counted. The other part of the explanation for why some issues end up in a constructive pattern and others in a deconstructive pattern is that, although Court and Congress may be speaking about the same issues, they see those issues in very different ways. Even in eras of unified government, the way judges articulate, explain, and rationalize their choices and the way earlier decisions influence, shape, and constrain later judicial decisions are distinctly different from the patterns, practices, rhetoric, internal rules, and driving incentives that operate in the elected branches and among bureaucrats. Legalistic policy may produce similar results in the short term, but it can limit, direct, shape, and constrain those policies in the longer run in ways quite different from what might have been expected by those who chose a legalistic route in the first place (see Chapter 3).

We cannot yet predict when policy will be more or less skewed or when law will save politics or undermine it, but we can identify conditions that are likely to produce higher and lower risks of each situation happening. Although neither politicians nor policy entrepreneurs can fully control who takes a case to court, they certainly can decide if they will join in that effort wholly, in part, or not at all. Ultimately, policy entrepreneurs have to judge for themselves if these are risks worth taking, and this judgment should be driven by an evaluation of the alternatives that are available, the incentives and motives to embrace juridification in the first place, and the pattern that effort will follow.

---

74 See Polsby, *How Congress Evolves*; Sarah Binder, *Minority Rights, Majority Rule: Partisanship and the Development of Congress*, New York: Cambridge University Press, 1997; Jon R. Bond and Richard Fleisher, *Polarized Politics: Congress and the President in a Partisan Era*, Washington, DC: CQ Press, 2000; Barbara Sinclair, *Party Wars: Polarization and the Politics of National Policy Making*, Norman: Oklahoma University Press, 2006; David Mayhew, *Divided We Govern: Party Control, Lawmaking and Investigations, 1946–2002* (2nd ed.), New Haven: Yale University Press, 2005.
75 Whittington, *Political Foundations*, p 274.

2 WHY NOW?

From May and May Not – To Must

THE AMERICAN SYSTEM is remarkably legalistic and has been from the start. In a constitutional system of limited government, someone or some institution is needed to define and interpret those limits. And in a complex federal system, in which power is fragmented among national, state, and local governments, and subdivided again within each into executive, legislative, and judicial institutions, the power to say what is – and what is not – allowed is far from trivial. Though not explicitly provided for in the Constitution and, with only a few exceptions, not widely debated in the Constitutional Convention in 1787 nor in the ratification debates, the courts were well designed to assume this role: to exercise a *blocking* function, saying what the government *can* and what it can *not* do.

The utility of the blocking function is not limited to one faction, one party, or one ideological strain: It has been a great source of central power and nationalization in many eras – and of recalcitrance, resistance, and decentralization in others. Among other things, the Court blocked: states from taxing the national bank,[1] African Americans from full use of the judicial system,[2] the national government from imposing an income tax,[3] national antitrust measures,[4] national efforts to curb child labor,[5] presidential orders seizing steel mills in time of war,[6] prayer in schools,[7] and the use of quotas in affirmative action,[8] to name just a few rulings.

---

1 *McCulloch v. Maryland*, 17 U.S. 316 (1819).
2 *Dred Scott v. Sandford*, 60 U.S. 393 (1857).
3 *Pollack v. Farmer's Loan & Trust*, 157 U.S. 429 (1895).
4 *U.S. v. E.C Knight*, 156 U.S. 1 (1895).
5 *Hammer v. Dagenhart*, 247 U.S. 251 (1918),
6 *Youngstown Sheet and Tube v. Sawyer*, 343 U.S. 579 (1952).
7 *Abington School Dist. V. Schempp*, 374 U.S. 203 (1963).
8 *Regents of the University of California v. Bakke*, 438 U.S. 265 (1978).

The eight Supreme Court Justices appointed by Franklin Roosevelt[9] during the Great Depression may have abandoned the Court's effort to block economic regulation, but neither they nor any other Supreme Court after that time would forswear the blocking function itself. Although the Court indicated in 1938 that it would be far more deferential to the elected branches when it came to blocking economic regulation, the Justices were equally clear that this would not be the case where "legislation on its face" appears to violate "a specific prohibition of the Constitution, such as those of the first ten Amendments" nor would the Court abandon its blocking function when confronting legislation that "restricts those political processes which can ordinarily be expected to bring about repeal of undesirable legislation." The Court, Chief Justice Harlan Fiske Stone made clear in 1938, also would actively review statutes that might tend to seriously "curtail the operation of those political processes ordinarily to be relied upon to protect minorities," which, he said, may "call for a correspondingly more searching judicial inquiry."[10]

Blocking – saying what the government *can* and what it can *not* do – remains the Court's primary function. By the mid-1960s, however, the Court increasingly was willing to say not only what the government could and could not do – but also to tell the government what it *must* do as well. This was not then nor is it today primarily a story of judicial imperialism (although there is certainly some of that going on); nor is it a story of legislative abdication or strategic maneuvering by litigators and lobbyists (although these are part of the story as well). The command function evolved, slowly and somewhat haphazardly.[11] This new path expanded

---

9 Roosevelt nominated eight Associate Justices to the U.S. Supreme Court and elevated Harlan Fiske Stone from Associate to Chief Justice, ultimately nominating all nine members of the court.

10 *United States v. Carolene Products Co.*, 304 U.S. 144 (1938). This signal was sent in what has come to be known as the most famous footnote in American law – footnote four in this very same case.

11 The massive resistance to the end of segregation ratcheted up the Court's insistence on compliance with its commands, ultimately coming to a peak in *Cooper v. Aaron* 358 U.S. 1 (1958), and in *Green v. New Kent County* 391 U.S. 430 (1968). In *Cooper*, facing direct defiance by the governor of Arkansas, the Supreme Court unanimously held that "the federal judiciary is supreme in the exposition of the law of the Constitution," noting that this principle is "a permanent and indispensable feature of our constitutional system." It follows, the Court added, "that the interpretation of the Fourteenth Amendment enunciated by this Court in the *Brown* case is the supreme law of the land," and Article VI of the Constitution makes it of binding effect on the States "any Thing in the Constitution or Laws of any States to the Contrary notwithstanding." In *Green*, the Court no longer left any doubt about its command: "Delays are no longer tolerable," the Court held. "The burden on a school board today is to come forward with a plan that promises realistically to work, and promises realistically to work now." This is not to say that the notion of the Supreme Court as the supreme interpreter of the Constitution was a product of the Warren era – it assuredly has a far longer provenance, as Keith Whittington demonstrates in *Political Foundations of Judicial Supremacy: The*

law's allure, offering an alternative route, and some felt a normatively superior route, for policy entrepreneurs to press for their desired goals.

If the emergence, the evolution of a new command function expanded law's allure, the steady erosion of Americans' faith in their political process accelerated its appeal and extended its reach from the judicialization of policy to efforts to construct legalistic solutions for the flaws and failures of politics and the political process itself. In the wake of an inability to end the war in Vietnam; the assassinations of John F. Kennedy, Martin Luther King Jr., and Robert F. Kennedy; the urban riots of Watts, Newark, and Detroit; and the abject and explicit rejection of the political process embodied in the riots outside the Democratic National Convention in Chicago in 1968, law's allure grew – reaching something of a zenith in the aftermath of Watergate, as members of Congress increasingly sought not only to involve the courts in the policy process, but more frequently sought to substitute the precision, the black-and-white of what some thought and hoped was the clarity of law in place of the frustrating and prone-to-corruption gray of politics. This trend fed into what John Hibbing and Elizabeth Theiss-Morse suggest is America's simultaneous desire for procedural efficiency and procedural equity.[12] In an era in which politics had been so deeply corrupted, judges and the seeming clarity of law promised to deliver both equity (which many, rightly or wrongly, believed the courts had done so effectively during the civil rights struggle) and efficiency (one case, one decision, one winner, one loser – no negotiation, no endless adjustment, and no visible horse trading).[13] Abraham Chayes labels this hope the "traditional conception of adjudication."

Understanding the expansion and then the acceleration of law's allure requires a look at three important areas – school integration, reapportionment, and criminal procedure – in which the Warren Court and key judges in the federal circuit courts, *together with* politicians, policy entrepreneurs, lobbyists, and lawyers, tentatively and incrementally built a new path.

Madison's Machine Meets Linda Brown

The Rev. Oliver Brown did not like the fact that his young daughter, Linda, had to walk through the dangerous Rock Island Railroad's train

---

Presidency, the Supreme Court and Constitutional Leadership in U.S. History, Princeton: Princeton University Press, 2007.

12 John Hibbing and Elizabeth Theiss-Morse, *Congress as Public Enemy: Public Attitudes toward American Political Institutions*, New York: Cambridge University Press, 1995, pp 14–15.

13 Abraham Chayes goes a bit further, suggesting that what once had been done in the political arena moved over to the legal arena, where the trial judge increasingly became "the creator and manager of complex forms of ongoing relief," requiring the judge's "continuing involvement in administration and implementation." Abraham Chayes, "The Role of the Judge in Public Law Litigation," 89 *Harvard Law Review* 1281, 1284 (1976).

yards in Topeka, Kansas, to get to a bus stop where she – and other African-American children – would be picked up every day, driven across town, and deposited miles away at the Monroe Elementary School. Monroe was not the closest elementary school; the Sumner Elementary School was just a few blocks from their home. But the Sumner School – ironically named for abolitionist Charles Sumner – was segregated and its enrollment limited to white students only.[14]

Topeka was hardly unique. Public school segregation was widespread in the United States, both North and South. Even Princeton, New Jersey, home to the Continental Congress, a critical Revolutionary War battlefield, and an Ivy League university, formally segregated elementary schools as late as 1948, when a change in the New Jersey State Constitution led to the end of de jure – though not de facto – school segregation.[15] And though there was a growing national consensus to end school segregation in the wake of a world war fought, in part, to repudiate the racist ideologies of Nazi Germany, this impulse was far from universal and certainly had not spread to Kansas, never mind the states of the Old Confederacy. But even if a national consensus could be mustered and even if it could be motivated to strike at segregation, it still faced huge road blocks, because education was very much considered a state responsibility and something over which the national government had virtually no control. This meant that if the Brown family and 16 million other African Americans wanted access to the same educational opportunities as Caucasians in 1954, they would have to find another way.

If "one arm of government cannot or will not solve an insistent problem," Archibald Cox argues, "the pressure falls upon another."[16] In this

14 The whites-only Sumner School – originally built for black students, but later upgraded, improved, and reassigned to white students only – was named for radical abolitionist Charles Sumner who served as an attorney in one of the earliest challenges to school segregation, *Sarah Roberts v. City of Boston*, 59 Mass. 198 (1849). Benjamin Roberts wanted to enroll his five-year-old daughter, Sarah, in a primary school near their home. The school committee refused and assigned her to a segregated school for blacks twice as far from her home. Charles Sumner, representing Roberts and his daughter, argued that "according to the spirit of American institutions, and especially the Constitution of Massachusetts, all men, without distinction of color or race, are equal before the law" and that the "exclusion of colored children from the public schools, which are open to white children is a source of practical inconvenience to them and their parents to which white persons are not exposed, and is, therefore, a violation of equality." But Sumner and Roberts lost their case, with Chief Justice Lemuel Shaw ruling that the school committee was operating within the parameters of its legal discretion and that segregation did not infringe on the equal rights to which they were entitled.

15 See: *The Princeton Packet*, June 8, 1999, available at http://www.pacpubserver.com/new/news/6-9-99/princetonplan.html. Also note that among Princeton University's more distinguished graduates were James Madison (class of 1771), Aaron Burr (class of 1772), and Woodrow Wilson (class of 1879). Wilson, of course, went on to serve as Princeton's president before moving to the White House.

16 Lucas Powe, Jr., *The Warren Court and American Politics*, Cambridge: Harvard University Press, 2000, p 48.

case, the other arm was the judicial branch. And although "the judiciary was constrained," Lucas Powe, Jr., notes, it was not constrained in ways "that precluded action."[17] *Plessy v. Ferguson* was the main doctrinal constraint for the courts. In 1896, *Plessy* held that the Fourteenth Amendment's equal protection clause required equal treatment and that separate facilities – provided they were roughly equal – were enough to satisfy this constitutional mandate. Some wanted to attack the inequity of segregation by focusing on the obvious material inequalities. However, to attack segregation itself, litigants would have to argue that there was a fundamental flaw in the assumption undergirding *Plessy*. This would mean arguing that, regardless of any material equality, separating one group from the other on the basis of race was itself a denial of equal protection, that a segregated classroom inherently meant an unequal education in violation of the Constitution.

It is one thing to state that separate is inherently unequal. But why? Judicial practice requires judges to give reasons.[18] What is it about this separation that makes it unconstitutional? What, precisely, is the violation that is being asserted? If a court is asked to provide a remedy, it needs to identify the wrong, the violation that this remedy is designed to fix. If the violation is that a government may not prevent students of different skin colors from attending school together, then perhaps the remedy could be as simple as a blocking order telling the government to stop, telling the government what it may *not* do. By contrast, if the problem is not simply the action of government, but that a segregated education is, by definition, a denial of equal protection of the law, then merely telling the government to stop will not do the job. The Court would have to tell the government what it *must* do; the Court would have to order the government to act, require it to provide students with an *integrated* education.

For young Linda Brown and millions of African Americans living in states, counties, and towns with formal, government-imposed segregation, this distinction was irrelevant – they were receiving a segregated education mandated and enforced by government. But this question would become increasingly central as those favoring segregation found ever more inventive ways to remove the state from segregation without actually integrating their schools. For those living where segregation was the result of migration, residential poverty, and a host of less explicitly formal restrictions rather than the product of formal government rules, this question would be critical: Does the Constitution *permit* government at the state,

---

17 Powe, Jr., *The Warren Court*, p 48.
18 Martin Shapiro, *The Supreme Court and Administrative Agencies*, New York: Free Press, 1968; Martin Shapiro, *Who Guards the Guardians: Judicial Control of Administration*, Athens: University of Georgia Press, 1988; Martin Shapiro, "The Giving Reasons Requirement," in Martin Shapiro and Alec Stone Sweet, *On Law, Politics and Judicialization*, New York: Oxford University Press, 2002.

local, or national level to segregate public schools on the basis of race? The Warren Court unanimously ruled that it did not and that it may not. But why? Was the problem the legally mandated segregation of these students? Or was the problem the separation itself?

The *Brown* ruling suggests that it was a little bit of both. To separate children "from others of similar age and qualifications solely because of their race generates a feeling of inferiority as to their status in the community that may affect their hearts and minds in a way unlikely ever to be undone,"[19] the Court ruled. "Separate educational facilities are inherently unequal."[20] Is the government action the key or is it the reality of separate educational facilities? On this narrow, seemingly semantic difference, much depends. "If segregation meant forced separation by law, then it could be remedied by the removal of the law. But if segregation meant one-race schools (or classrooms), then it could be remedied only by racial mixing."[21] The decision suggests both, though the bulk of the ruling focuses on the fact that the separation was mandated by explicit laws "requiring or permitting segregation according to race."[22] This is hardly surprising, as all of the cases consolidated under the *Brown* banner involved state laws requiring or allowing formal segregation.[23]

The Court did not provide a clear answer in 1954, nor has it provided a definitive answer in the years since. Fifty-eight years after *Brown*, the new John Roberts-led Supreme Court split on this very question. When asked to rule on the use of race in school-assignment integration plans in Seattle and Louisville, four of the Justices insisted that *Brown* unequivocally stood for the proposition that "legally separating children on the basis of race" was the evil the Constitution forbade.[24] Four other Justices, however, declared that the hope, and "promise of *Brown*," was "true racial equality – not as a matter of fine words on paper, but as a matter of everyday life in the Nation's cities and schools ... not simply as a matter of legal principle but in terms of how we actually live."[25]

Both sides had a point in 2007. The effect of separating students "from others of similar age and qualifications solely because of their race,"

---

19 *Brown v. Board of Education*, 347 U.S. 483, 494 (1954).
20 *Brown*, 347 U.S. at 495.
21 Powe, Jr., *The Warren Court*, p 50.
22 *Brown*, 347 U.S. at 488.
23 *Belton v. Gebhardt (Bulah v. Gebhardt)* (Delaware); *Briggs v. Elliott* (South Carolina), and *Davis v. Prince Edwards County School Board* (Virginia). A fifth case, *Bolling v. Sharpe*, had to be disposed of separately because it involved the District of Columbia and, therefore, the federal government rather than a state government. This meant that the case had to be considered under something other than the Fourteenth Amendment alone, which is explicitly directed at the states and not the national government.
24 *Parents Involved in Community Schools v. Seattle School Board* and *Joshua Ryan McDonald v. Jefferson Country Board of Education*, 551 U.S. case 05-908 (2007); (Roberts, C.J., joined by Alito, J., Scalia, J., and Thomas, J.).
25 *Parents Involved*, 551 U.S. (Breyer, J., joined by Ginsburg, J., Souter, J., and Stevens, J.).

the unanimous *Brown* court held in 1954, would be to severely limit
their educational opportunities. To support this argument, the Supreme
Court quoted one of the findings of fact in the district court's decision
in the case that the Supreme Court was reviewing. "Segregation of white
and colored children in public schools has a detrimental effect upon the
colored children," the lower court stated in Finding 8. "*The impact is
greater*," the lower court continued, "*when it has the sanction of the law*;
for the policy of separating the races is usually interpreted as denoting
the inferiority of the Negro group." Segregation "with the sanction of
law, therefore, has a tendency to [deprive Negro children] of some of the
benefits they would receive in a racial[ly] integrated school system."[26] So,
mere separation *is* a problem, made *worse* by state sanction.

The judiciary initially had dockets full of cases arising in states with
formal, legally mandated systems of segregated schools, and it would not
be until the early 1970s that the Supreme Court would be forced to confront the problem of de facto segregation in northern cities like Denver.[27]
But almost immediately after the *Brown* decision, federal court judges
began to split on the question of just what the Supreme Court was ordering. The battleline was drawn in a South Carolina case, *Briggs v. Elliott*,
which had been one of several cases decided together with *Brown*. When
the case returned to South Carolina, the district court judges insisted that
the Supreme Court has "not decided that the states *must* mix persons of
different races in the schools or *must* require them to attend schools or
must deprive them of the right of choosing the schools they attend." If
schools "are open to children of all races, no violation of the Constitution is involved even though the children of different races voluntarily
attend different schools, as they attend different churches. Nothing in
the Constitution or in the decision of the Supreme Court takes away
from the people freedom to choose the schools they attend." To clar-
ify this point, the district court insisted, "The Constitution, in other
words, does not *require* integration. It merely *forbids* discrimination.
It does not forbid such segregation as occurs as the result of voluntary
action. It merely forbids the use of governmental power to enforce segregation. The Fourteenth Amendment is a limitation upon the exercise of
power by the state or state agencies, not a limitation upon the freedom of
individuals."[28]

This assertion would be widely quoted – favorably by judges who
insisted that courts should merely tell the government what it could and
could *not* do, and derisively by those judges who understood one of
the core holdings of *Brown* to be that "in the field of public education

---

26 *Brown*, 347 U.S. at 494, *emphasis added*.
27 *Keyes v. School District No. 1, Denver, Colorado*, 413 U.S. 189 (1973).
28 *Briggs v. Elliott*, 132 F. Supp. 776, 777 (1955), *emphasis added*.

the doctrine of 'separate but equal' has no place. Separate educational facilities are inherently unequal."[29]

For those who saw a broader, affirmative requirement in *Brown*, the claim in *Briggs* was entirely out of step with *Brown* and with a proper reading of the Constitution. In a 1961 decision that was one of the first to deal with separate schools in the North, Judge Irving R. Kaufman insisted that the "benefits inherent in an integrated education are essential to the proper development of all children"[30] But Kaufman went further. Although acknowledging that *Brown* applied to cases in which the state had played a role in establishing segregated schools, Kaufman insisted that its application could not be limited to explicit, formal, state-mandated segregation. There is "no basis to draw a distinction, legal or moral, between segregation established by the formality of a dual system of education, as in *Brown*, and that created by gerrymandering of school district lines," he argued. Kaufman insisted that his reading was not only a reasonable interpretation of *Brown*, but also one mandated by the Supreme Court's own ruling.[31]

Judges in the Eighth Circuit insisted in 1965 that the *Briggs* interpretation "is logically inconsistent with *Brown* and subsequent decisional law on this subject."[32] On the Fifth Circuit Court of Appeals, Judge Minor Wisdom held in 1966 that the *Brown* case "is misread and misapplied when it is construed simply to confer upon Negro pupils the right to be considered for admission to a white school."[33] Noting that the Supreme Court never used either the words "desegregation" or "integration" in the first *Brown* decision, Wisdom argued that decision making in this important area of the law "cannot be made to turn upon a quibble devised over ten years ago" by the South Carolina court in *Briggs*, a court that "misread *Brown*, misapplied the class action doctrine in the school desegregation cases, and did not foresee the development of the law of equal opportunities."[34] As we see it, Judge Wisdom wrote for the Circuit Court,

The law imposes an absolute duty to desegregate, that is, disestablish segregation. And an absolute duty to integrate, in the sense that a disproportionate concentration of Negroes in certain schools cannot be ignored; racial mixing of students is a high priority educational goal. While that does not mean that there needs to be a perfect balance or a precise reflection of the community population in every school, it does require more than simply lifting existing barriers, it requires not only the end of segregation, but it requires some measure of integration.[35]

29 *Brown*, 347 U.S. at 495.
30 *Taylor v. Board of Education of City of New Rochelle*, 191 F.Supp. 181, 192 (1961).
31 *Taylor*, 191 F.Supp. at 192.
32 *Kemp v. Beasley*, 352 F.2d 14, 21 (1965).
33 *U.S. v. Jefferson County Board of Education* 372 F.2d 836, 846 (1966).
34 *U.S. v. Jefferson County*, 372 F.2d at 847.
35 *U.S. v. Jefferson County*, 372 F.2d at 847.

When this same case returned to the Fifth Circuit the next year, the judges ruled that "public schools in this circuit have the *affirmative duty* under the Fourteenth Amendment to bring about an integrated, unitary school system in which there are no Negro schools and no white schools – just schools." They then made it clear that any distinctions between integration and desegregation that the court may have made in earlier decisions "must yield to this *affirmative duty* we now recognize."[36]

That same year, in what legal scholar Alexander Bickel labeled "a jeremiad,"[37] J. Skelly Wright – a D.C. Circuit Court of Appeals judge – ruled that an equal educational experience for school children in Washington, D.C., was mandated not only by the Constitution, but also by Supreme Court precedent. Not only did he cite *Brown*, but he turned to *Plessey v. Ferguson* as well, transforming the Court's infamous shield protecting "separate but equal" into a weapon – insisting that even if it was true that there were not enough Caucasian students in the city to fully integrate its schools (in 1966, the African-American public school population "reached 90.2% with every indication of a further rise"),[38] it would have to compensate for this with other resources. Wright ordered that, when "the density of residential segregation" made it impossible to provide "the benefits of an integrated education," the court would "require" that the Washington D.C. school system provide "compensatory education sufficient at least to overcome the detriment of segregation and thus provide, as nearly as possible, equal educational opportunity to all school children."[39]

Who was right? The South Carolina District Court or Judges Kaufman, Wisdom, Wright and their colleagues?[40] The Supreme Court never really said. A docket overflowing with direct challenges from jurisdictions in which districts continued to sponsor or support state-imposed dual-systems of education left little time or room for the Supreme Court to more fully answer this question.[41] This silence provided an opportunity for the lower courts to develop their own answers. Because the Supreme Court was not issuing definitive rulings that were directly on point, there should be little surprise that lower court judges might use a wider net in looking for cases that could provide more authoritative guidance in filling in the blanks. Federal Judge J. Skelly Wright looked back to *Plessy*, which was also about segregation. But he did not limit himself to what might be thought of as direct, lineal precedents – cases speaking to the

---

36 *U.S. v. Jefferson County*, 380 F.2d at 385 (emphasis added).
37 Alexander Bickel, "Skelly Wright's Sweeping Decision," *New Republic*, July 8, 1967, p 11.
38 Clement Vose, "School Desegregation: A Political Scientist's View," 2 *Law & Society Review* 1 (November 1967), p 144.
39 *Hobson v. Hansen*, 269 F.Supp. 401, 515 (1967).
40 For a full discussion of how unanimity was achieved in *Brown*, see S. Sidney Ulmer, "Earl Warren and the Brown Decision, 33 *Journal of Politics* 3, 689–702 (1971).
41 *Cooper v. Aaron*, 358 U.S. 1 (1958), is but one example.

same or very similar questions, in the same or a very similar area of law. He also looked for what might be called *lateral* precedents as well – cases from what appeared to be quite different streams of precedent that might illuminate, extend, and support his interpretation of the Supreme Court's somewhat ambiguous ruling.

The central issue in the Washington, D.C., case – *Hobson v. Hansen* – was not whether de facto segregation was itself unconstitutional, but whether equal educational opportunity "required equality when schools were racially separate for whatever reason."[42] *Brown*, of course, did not settle this debate, and so, like any trained lawyer, Judge Wright looked to other cases, other policy issues the Supreme Court had decided to see if there was a parallel or lateral track that would help him decide the case before him (or, if you prefer, would help him build ammunition to support the result he sought)[43] – and indeed, he believed there was.

At first glance, one might not think to look at a case about drawing legislative district lines in Tennessee for guidance in a school segregation/ integration case, but Wright saw in the Tennessee districting case of *Baker v. Carr* language and arguments that might help settle the questions in his school case. Though *Baker* was not about race, it was a case about the equal protection clause of the Constitution, and clearly the equal protection clause was implicated in questions about school segregation/integration. Wright argued that there is a right to equal protection, and that if this right is infringed or denied, it makes no difference whether the denial was the intentional work of the government or not. Either way – intentional or not, explicit or coincidental – individuals are entitled to equal protection, and the government is *required* to provide it. The notion that "no violation of equal protection vests unless the inequalities stem from a deliberately discriminatory plan is simply false," Wright held, turning to *Baker v. Carr* for support. In *Baker*, he said, Justice Brennan ruled that discrimination is a problem even when it "reflects *no* policy," but rather represents "simply arbitrary and capricious action" (Justice Brennan's emphasis). Whatever the law may once have been, Wright insisted, "we now firmly recognize that the arbitrary quality of thoughtlessness can be as disastrous and unfair to private rights and the public interest as the perversity of a willful scheme."[44]

---

42 Beatrice A. Moulton, "*Hobson v. Hansen*: The De Facto Limits on Judicial Power," 20 *Stanford Law Review* 1249, 1253 (1968).

43 Consider, as just a starting point on this subject, Martin Shapiro, *Law and Politics on the Supreme Court: New Approaches to Political Jurisprudence*, New York: Free Press, 1964; Walter Murphy, *Elements of Judicial Strategy*, Chicago: University of Chicago Press, 1970; Lee Epstein and Jack Knight, *Choices Justices Make*, Washington, D.C.: CQ Press, 1997; Jeffrey A. Segal and Harold J. Spaeth, *The Supreme Court and the Attitudinal Model*, Cambridge: Cambridge University Press, 1993; and Forrest Maltzman, James Spriggs, and Paul Wahlbeck, *Crafting Law on the Supreme Court: The Collegial Game*. Cambridge: Cambridge University Press, 2000.

44 *Hobson*, 269 F.Supp. at 497.

The turn to *Baker* certainly was facilitated by the ambiguity of *Brown*. Was the ambiguity in *Brown* the result of a strategic choice? Was it necessary to ensure unanimity on the Court? Or was it the product of genuine and sincere confusion? One might have expected this ambiguity to be clarified as the Supreme Court developed its doctrine in other cases, but the Court's docket was filled with cases that *did* involve legislatively mandated segregation, leaving the resolution of cases involving de facto segregation to later Supreme Court rulings and to the lower courts.

In what he labeled a "parting word" in *Hobson v. Hansen*, Judge Wright said that it "would be far better indeed for these great social and political problems to be resolved in the political arena by other branches of government." But in dealing with "social and political problems which seem at times to defy such resolution," the American system requires the judiciary to "accept its responsibility to assist in the solution where constitutional rights hang in the balance." This was the case in *Brown*, he wrote, in *Bolling v. Sharpe* "and *Baker v. Carr*."[45]

Baker v. Carr illuminated, shaped, and informed Wright's understanding of (and application of) *Brown*, and so we need to turn to the case Chief Justice Warren himself insisted was "the most important case of my tenure on the Court."[46]

Legal Rules and Political Power

Although just 9.7 percent of Tennessee's population lived in the state's three most urban counties in 1900, by 1960 those same counties accounted for almost 36 percent of the state's population – and yet their representation in the Tennessee legislature did not increase. Arguing that Tennessee's failure to reapportion political power for more than sixty years meant that the state's urban residents were unfairly underrepresented (and those in shrinking rural districts were increasingly overrepresented), Charles Baker sued Joe C. Carr, the Tennessee Secretary of State. The Tennessee courts were unwilling to intervene, insisting that this was a question for the political branches to resolve and not something that was – or ought to be – subject to judicial control. Relying on the political branches to fix this problem was, of course, a very bad bet. Reapportionment, in fact, was a political problem that the political process really could not be expected to solve. This was not because legislators lacked the formal power to make these changes, but because politically and institutionally they had nothing to gain, and everything to lose, if they did.[47]

---

45 *Hobson*, 269 F.Supp. at 517.
46 Earl Warren, *The Memoirs of Earl Warren*, Garden City: Doubleday, 1977, p 306.
47 Archibald Cox, "The Supreme Court – 1965 Term," 80 *Harvard Law Review* 91, 122 (1966).

Tennessee law required any reapportionment to originate in the State Assembly, but it was hardly realistic to imagine that an institution dominated by representatives from rural districts would champion a cause that would put some of them out of office and slash their constituents' relative power. Theoretically, the U.S. Congress might attempt to intervene, but as U.S. Supreme Court Justice Tom Clark noted in his concurrence in *Baker*, "from a practical standpoint this is without substance. To date Congress has never undertaken such a task in any state." Therefore, Clark wrote, "The people of Tennessee are stymied and without judicial intervention will be saddled with the present discrimination in the affairs of their state government."[48] In *Baker*, Abner Mikva argues, the Court acted when the Court and only the Court had the capacity to act and, by so acting, brought about "massive, nationwide political reform where before prospects for change had been hopeless."[49]

Baker was a broadly popular decision. At a press conference, President John Kennedy endorsed the Court ruling, saying, "The right to fair representation and to have each vote count equally is, it seems to me, basic to the successful operation of a democracy."[50] Two Supreme Court Justices vehemently disagreed. In his dissent, Justice Harlan insisted that the federal Constitution did nothing to prevent a state "from choosing any electoral legislative structure it thinks best suited to the interests, temper, and customs of its people," provided the division is not wholly irrational.[51] In a separate dissent, Justice Frankfurter lamented the Court's decision to enter into what he had labeled the "political thicket" in a 1946 case called *Colegrove v. Green*. Frankfurter argued that *Colegrove* had sealed the Court's doors to questions dealing with the political process.

"The remedy for unfairness in districting," Frankfurter insisted in *Colegrove*, "is to secure State legislatures that will apportion properly, or to invoke the ample powers of Congress" These political choices, he said, "cannot be challenged in the courts." The answer, he insisted, was to recognize that the Constitution leaves "the performance of many duties in our governmental scheme to depend on the fidelity of the executive and legislative action and, ultimately, on the vigilance of the people in exercising their political rights."[52]

However, there was a fundamental problem with Frankfurter's prescription: The people of Tennessee could only change matters by convincing legislators to surrender the advantages that accrued to them and to their disproportionately powerful constituents. Possible? Perhaps. Likely?

---

48 *Baker v. Carr*, 369 U.S. 186, 259 (1962).
49 Abner J. Mikva, "Justice Brennan and the Political Process: Assessing the Legacy of *Baker v. Carr*," 1995 *University of Illinois Law Review* 683, 685 (1995).
50 John F. Kennedy press conference, quoted in Powe, Jr., *The Warren Court*, p 204.
51 *Baker v. Carr*, 369 U.S. at 334.
52 *Colegrove v. Green*, 328 U.S. 549, 556 (1946).

Not at all. Frankfurter might not disagree – but in his *Baker* dissent, he made clear that his worry centered on the risk to the Court, that its own authority and legitimacy might be tarnished by getting involved in what he called "the essentially political conflict of forces by which the relation between population and representation has time out of mind been and now is determined."[53]

In a dissent in the 1964 districting case of *Reynolds v. Sims*, Justice John Harlan focused more on the political system and less on the Court's authority. Harlan noted that "the vitality of our political system, on which in the last analysis all else depends, is weakened by reliance on the judiciary for political reform; in time a complacent body politic may result." The Court, he added, "does not serve its high purpose when it exceeds its authority, even to satisfy justified impatience with the slow workings of the political process."[54]

Despite the dissents, *Baker v. Carr* was a monumental decision tightly wound into a narrow ruling – much as *Brown v. Board of Education* had been a few years earlier. In *Baker*, the Justices limited themselves to answering only two basic questions: Did the Court have constitutional jurisdiction to hear this case? And was this, in principle, a question courts *could* resolve? The majority answered yes to both questions. The Supreme Court made no final determination and issued no orders. The appropriate relief, Justice Douglas noted, can readily be constructed "in the light of well-known principles of equity,"[55] but that would have to be done by the lower courts – not by the Supreme Court. At least not yet; at least not in this case. Noting their confidence that "the District Court will be able to fashion relief if violations of constitutional rights are found," the majority ruled – much as it had in *Brown* – that "it is improper now to consider what remedy would be most appropriate if appellants prevail at the trial."[56]

The Court stepped lightly as well because there was an explicit hope, even expectation, that the Court's ruling, its "assertion of power," as Justice Brennan put it, "will cause the Tennessee legislature to act." In other words, once the question had been constitutionalized, the legislature would prefer to work out its own political compromise, rather than risk the imposition of a less optimal result through a judicial decree over which they would have no control – a hope shared by Chief Justice Warren – and thus law might actually *save* politics.[57] *Baker* itself was an exercise

53 *Baker v. Carr*, 369 U.S. at 267.
54 *Reynolds v. Sims*, 377 U.S. 533, 624–625 (1964) (Harlan, J., dissenting). My thanks to Gary Jacobsohn for pointing me to this passage.
55 *Baker v. Carr*, 369 U.S. at 250.
56 *Baker v. Carr*, 369 U.S. at 198.
57 Richard L. Hasen, *The Supreme Court and Election Law: Judging Equality from Baker v. Carr to Bush v. Gore*, New York: New York University Press, 2003, p 52, citing Justice Brennan's conference notes on *Baker v. Carr* (William J. Brennan, Jr., Papers, Manuscript Division, Library of Congress. Container I:60, Folder 6).

of the Court's traditional blocking function, with the Justices ruling that the Tennessee government could *not* apportion its legislature in such an unbalanced fashion. It would take a number of cases before the Court would be willing to take the full leap and exercise its command function, telling state governments that they *must* reapportion to achieve the near-mathematical precision of one-person-one-vote.

In 1963, in a case concerning Georgia's method for counting votes in Democratic primary elections, the majority held that giving one person "ten times the voting power of another person" violates the equal protection of law guaranteed by the Fourteenth Amendment. "The conception of political equality from the Declaration of Independence, to Lincoln's Gettysburg Address, to the Fifteenth, Seventeenth, and Nineteenth Amendments," Justice Douglas wrote for the majority, "can mean only one thing – one person, one vote."[58] Finally, in 1964, the Court enshrined the rule in a case concerning national congressional elections: "We hold that... as nearly as practicable, one man's vote in a congressional election is to be worth as much as another's."[59] The frame was set, and the federal courts were now telling states not only that they *should*, but that they *must* reapportion their legislative districts, and they needed to do so in a way that would meet a standard articulated by the Court, interpreting the U.S. Constitution.

This, Justice Harlan reminded his brethren in a bitter dissent, was precisely what they had assured him would not happen. "State legislatures, it was predicted, would be prodded into taking satisfactory action by the mere prospect of legal proceedings," Harlan wrote. But within months of the ruling in *Baker*, "the apportionment of seats in at least 30 state legislatures had been challenged in state and federal courts," and ten other "electoral cases of one kind or another are already on this Court's docket."[60] Legislative districting, which had been seen as exclusively the province of political struggle, was now on its way to being fully judicialized. Samuel Issacharoff notes that the Supreme Court initially seemed to leave "open the possibility that alternatives to the one-person, one-vote rule might satisfy constitutional norms, [but] the logic of judicial review inexorably pushed the equipopulation principle to the fore." This was because the "very qualities of objectivity and manageability that made the equipopulation strategy appealing" Issacharoff writes, soon made it the "sole arbiter of political fairness."[61] *Baker* ultimately led to the

---

58 *Gray v. Sanders*, 372 U.S. 368, 381 (1963). This phrase first appears in *Gray v. Sanders* and *not* in *Baker v. Carr* as is often assumed. The next year, in *Wesberry v. Sanders*, it becomes "as nearly as is practicable one man's vote in a congressional election is to be worth as much as another's" (376 U.S. 1, 8 (1964)), and does not appear as "one man, one vote" in these cases.

59 *Wesberry v. Sanders*, 376 U.S. at 8.

60 *Gray v. Sanders*, 372 U.S. at 382.

61 Samuel Issacharoff, "Judging Politics: The Elusive Quest for Judicial Review of Political Fairness," 71 *Texas Law Review* 1643, 1651 (1993).

constitutionalization of the right to an equal vote under the equal protection clause. But *Baker* did more than that. It opened the Court's doors to a broad range of demands that the Court tell the government what it must do in policy and in managing the political process itself.

Crime – Where Law and Politics Meet

In politics and policy, the Warren Court signaled there might be a new path; in criminal law, the Court constructed that path. Crime straddles the worlds of politics and law. A crime is a crime because legislators make it so. The range of punishments for crimes are set by politicians, through legislation. And the choices of which cases to prosecute and when and how to do so are political choices made by prosecutors who are either popularly elected or appointed by those who were. Criminals are investigated, arrested, interrogated, and incarcerated by officers who serve elected officials. But the admission of evidence and the determination of guilt and innocence – those belong to the judicial branch. In short, the substantive choices of what is a crime and what is to be done about it belong to politics, whereas traditionally, the choices about the process by which trials are conducted and resolved are judicial matters. It makes sense, then, that the Court's opening of a new *command* path would be reflected in, and shaped by, decisions in this literally pivotal arena.

The Constitution deals with criminal procedure in three of the amendments that make up the Bill of Rights. The Fourth Amendment prohibits unreasonable searches and seizures and requires the government to demonstrate probable cause before a warrant will be issued – and even then, warrants must be limited, defined, and specific. The Fifth Amendment requires indictment by a grand jury for major crimes; prohibits the government from trying the same person more than once for a crime (no double jeopardy); requires due process for anyone at risk of losing "life, liberty or property"; and guarantees that no one can be compelled to be a witness against him- or herself in a criminal trial. Finally, the Constitution provides a set of rules about trials in the Sixth Amendment, including provisions requiring speedy and public jury trials as well as the right to be informed about the nature and cause of the accusation, to confront witnesses, to compel witnesses to testify, and "to have the assistance of counsel" for their defense. These rights clearly apply to federal prosecutions. Some actually require the government to act, and these the Court had long been willing to enforce, even in the pre-Warren era. But these rights did not apply so clearly to state prosecutions (where the bulk of criminal law and criminal trials take place) and only would do so as the Court expanded its understanding and application of the Fourteenth Amendment's due process and equal protection clauses.

Well before Earl Warren's tenure, the Supreme Court exercised a command function in criminal procedure in *Powell v. Alabama* (the Scottsboro Boys case), a 1932 case involving nine poorly educated African-American teenagers who were accused of raping two Caucasian girls in a open boxcar in which they were traveling through Alabama. After a fight broke out between the African Americans and seven Caucasian boys who were riding in the same boxcar, the conductor sent a message ahead to the next station, and a sheriff's posse met the train before it reached Scottsboro: the African Americans were arrested and charged with assault.

The case was riddled with problems – the local judge not only failed to provide the defendants with legal counsel, but the defendants also were never given a chance to contact counsel or even their families until the trial began. The case wound up at the Supreme Court where the Justices ultimately ruled that the accused were entitled to "reasonable time and opportunity to secure counsel" and that the failure to provide this time and opportunity "was a clear denial of due process."[62]

This ruling was, however, far from a mandate for the provision of legal counsel. The Court went out of its way to make clear that this was a narrow and extraordinarily limited intervention. Speaking for the majority, Justice George Sutherland made clear that the decision was driven not by a general principle of what states were obliged to do for criminal defendants, but rather the extraordinary facts of this particular case. The "ignorance and illiteracy of the defendants, their youth, the circumstances of public hostility . . . the fact that their friends and families were all in other states and communication with them necessarily difficult and above all that they stood in deadly peril of their lives" – it took all of this to add up to a violation of the Fourteenth Amendment's requirement of due process. All we decide, Sutherland wrote, "is that in a capital case, where the defendant is unable to employ counsel, and is incapable adequately of making his own defense because of ignorance, feeble-mindedness, illiteracy, or the like, it is the duty of the court" to assign counsel for him. In other words, this was a very limited holding and one directed at the courts, not at the executive branch nor its direct agents, the police and prosecutors.

The Scottsboro case involved a state trial, but even in cases at the federal level – where the requirements of the Fourth, Fifth, and Sixth Amendments clearly apply – the pre-Warren Court tended to focus any mandates at courts and judges, not at elected officials or their agents. For example, consider the 1935 counterfeiting case involving John Johnson and an accomplice named Monroe Bridwell. Accused of counterfeiting U.S. currency, a federal crime, Johnson and Bridwell were taken to court two days later where they were told of their indictment for the first time and were

---

62 *Powell v. State of Alabama*, 287 U.S. 45, 71 (1932).

then immediately "tried, convicted and sentenced that day...without assistance of counsel."[63] The question was whether the Sixth Amendment *required* the government to provide counsel for this trial. Federal law had, since 1790, provided for the appointment of legal counsel in all *capital* trials, but that was a statute, not a constitutional mandate interpreted and enforced by the Supreme Court. Would this privilege extend to noncapital cases?[64]

In a ruling by Justice Hugo Black, the Supreme Court used the *Johnson* case to extend the requirement for the appointment of counsel to all federal trials. But the Court did this *not* by commanding legislators or the executive branch to provide counsel, but rather by instructing the lower courts to simply terminate any and all prosecutions where this requirement was not met. In other words, the Court was *not* telling the elected branches what *they* must do, but rather articulating a rule of procedure for the lower courts. This would, of course, have the same effect, but it was also much more in line with the traditional blocking function. "If this requirement of the Sixth Amendment is not complied with," Justice Black held, "the court no longer has jurisdiction to proceed." And any conviction "pronounced by a court without jurisdiction is void."[65]

A few years later, in 1942, the Court had an opportunity to revisit the counsel requirements at the state level. Far from building on or expanding the limited requirements coming out of the *Scottsboro* case, the Court actually narrowed its holding, closing the door that it had barely cracked open with that decision. It ruled in *Betts v. Brady* that the Fourteenth Amendment only requires states to provide legal counsel in extraordinary cases in which the lack of counsel would constitute a denial of "fundamental fairness, shocking to the universal sense of justice."[66] In other words, the Court made clear that it would intervene in situations like *Scottsboro* – and only those like *Scottsboro* – where not only were lives on the line, but the circumstances also were so extraordinary that extraordinary provisions would be needed to assure a fair process.[67] Lacking circumstances that shocked the conscience, the Court ruled, the question of the provision of counsel was something that must be left to state legislators. It is a matter, Justice Owen Roberts insisted, that "has generally been deemed one of legislative policy."[68]

---

63 *Johnson v. Zerbst*, 304 U.S. 458, 460 (1938).
64 18 U.S.C. 563 (originally passed in 1789).
65 *Johnson v. Zerbst*, 304 U.S. at 468.
66 *Betts v. Brady*, 316 U.S. 455, 462 (1942).
67 In his concurrence in *Gideon v. Wainwright*, Justice Harlan made particular note that *Betts v. Brady* focused on the need for "special circumstances" before the Fourteenth Amendment might be read to require the provision of counsel in criminal trials. *Gideon v. Wainright*, 372 U.S. 335, 350 (1963) (Harlan, J., concurring).
68 *Betts v. Brady*, 316 U.S. at 471.

This was the state of affairs in 1963 when the Warren Court seized an opportunity to revisit the question of the constitutional mandate for legal counsel in state trials in *Gideon v. Wainwright*, in which it reversed the Court's 1942 ruling by requiring courts to appoint counsel for all felony trials, with or without special circumstances, whether for a capital crime or not. As significant as *Gideon* was, it was relatively noncontroversial. Twenty-two states signed an *amicus* brief urging the Court to extend the right-to-counsel provisions, and just three registered official opposition.[69] The Court commanded in *Gideon*, but it still was a command aimed at judges. The political reaction would be dramatically different when the Court began issuing mandates to executive agents – to police and prosecutors – telling them not what only they could and could *not* do, but also what they *must* do.

Just one year after *Gideon*, the Supreme Court took up an Illinois case asking if the right to legal counsel extended beyond the courtroom and into the police station. In *Escobedo v. Illinois*, the Supreme Court ruled that those being interrogated in criminal investigations could not be denied access to legal counsel. In this case, the Court took another step, ruling that the Sixth Amendment (applied to the states through the due process clause of the Fourteenth Amendment) embodied an *affirmative* obligation, a mandate *requiring* police to "effectively" warn a suspect "of his absolute constitutional right to remain silent."[70] In dissent, Justice Stewart insisted that this "court has never held that the Constitution requires the police to give any 'advice' under circumstances such as these."[71] Stewart might have been right in 1964 – but by 1966, this clearly was no longer the case. In *Miranda v. Arizona*, decided in 1966, the Supreme Court explicitly instructed the police in what they needed to say, what they *must* say if they wanted any statements or confessions they were able to get to be admitted as evidence in court. The Court even suggested specific words – words Hollywood has now burned into the minds of just about everyone in the United States and around the world. Writing for the Court, Chief Justice Warren ruled that "the following measures are *required*. Prior to any questioning, the person must be warned that he has a right to remain silent, that any statement he does make may be used as evidence against him, and that he has a right to the presence of an attorney, either retained or appointed."[72]

In *Miranda*, the Court unquestionably told executive branch agents what they *must* do and even suggested *how* they were to do it. This was not a case in which the Supreme Court was attempting to substitute its

---

69 These were cited by Justice Harlan in his dissent in *Miranda v. Arizona*, 384 U.S. 436, 520 (1966) (Harlan, J., dissenting).
70 *Escobedo v. Illinois*, 378 U.S. 478, 491 (1964).
71 *Escobedo v. Illinois*, 378 U.S. at 494.
72 *Miranda v. Arizona*, 384 U.S. at 447, *emphasis added*.

view, its policy, its judgment for that of legislators and executives. Rather it was a case in which the Court quite explicitly instructed the government to set policy – provided that policy met minimum standards set by the Court. The Court explicitly encouraged "Congress and the States to continue their laudable search for increasingly effective ways of protecting the rights of the individual while promoting efficient enforcement" of criminal laws. "However," the majority insisted, "unless we are shown other procedures which are at least as effective" as those spelled out by the Court, then the Court's specific safeguards "must be observed."[73]

In *Miranda*, the Court made two important moves. First, the majority shifted from a focus on what government could, and could not do, to what the government, prosecutors, and police were *required* to do. Second, it moved from a case-by-case analysis of the sort of legal process required in a courtroom in particular cases to a far broader statement about the absolute rights commanded by the Fifth and Fourteenth Amendments – affirmative rights *required* by the Constitution. The Court in no way cut off or blocked legislative authority to revise and reform the rules for police and prosecution. Instead, the Court paved a new, alternative path for those seeking these reforms. Politicians and policy entrepreneurs alike could continue to push for them through the political process, of course, but politics is slow, and battling entrenched interests can sometimes pose extraordinary burdens. *Miranda* suggested an alternative, one that was likely to be faster and with lower political costs, because blame could be deflected to the courts. Where before policy entrepreneurs were forced into the political process, now they might have a choice, turning instead to the courts as a legal route to a policy goal.

Violations and Remedies

American judges have no problem telling people what they must do, and have done so for generations, although mostly in disputes dealing with property and contract claims. In areas concerning broader public policy claims, the shift from can and cannot to *must* represents an important break with past practice, though it followed quite logically from the American legal tradition.

"The judicial power," Article III of the U.S. Constitution says, "shall extend to all cases, in law and equity, arising under this Constitution, the Laws of the United States and treaties made or which shall be made under their authority."[74] Assigning both types of cases – both cases in law and cases in equity – to the same court was a break with English tradition. Cases in law are fairly obvious – these are cases that arise under

73 *Miranda v. Arizona*, 384 U.S. at 468.
74 U.S. Constitution, Article III, section 2, paragraph 1.

specific statutes, regulations, and legal provisions. The law says stealing is a crime. You are charged with stealing. A trial determines if, indeed,
you have broken the law. But a case in equity is a far murkier thing. A
case in equity is a case in which the law as written is not quite adequate or
perhaps too rigid. It is a case in which justice, if it is to be done, requires
flexibility, adjustment, and compulsion and a range of remedies, orders,
and commands.

Equity has a long, distinguished provenance, reaching back to Rome
and, ultimately, to Athens where Aristotle distinguished equity as "justice that goes beyond the written law."[75] English judges traditionally
divided these functions into two types of courts. Common courts served
as increasingly independent dispensers of the forms and formalities of the
science of the common law, whereas equity courts were something of an
extension of the king's prerogative (and grace). In America, this separation made far less sense – no king, no prerogative, no real need to separate
two sides of the same coin. Judges were supposed to be involved not only
in the technical application of statutes and regulations, but also they
were charged with settling disputes, making wrongs right, and generally
delivering some form of justice.

But old traditions die hard. Some states, particularly in the South, maintained two separate courts for these different functions.[76] And although
the Constitution seems to promise to blend these functions, American
politicians, lawyers, and judges were wary from the start and quickly
began to build distinctions between the two. In the Judiciary Act of 1789,
Congress "established a firm rule as to when causes in equity could and
could not be sustained."[77] And in 1792, Congress made clear that equity
cases would be handled "according to the principles, rules and usages
which belong to a court of equity as contradistinguished from a court of
common law."[78] Justice Joseph Story, who came to the Supreme Court in
1812, fortified the American tradition of separating the functions of law
from those of equity, establishing different rules of procedure, different
forms, and different precedents.[79]

The Warren Court, however, took seriously its charge to hear and
decide both types of cases – and decisions in the areas of race, redistricting,

---

75 Aristotle, *The Rhetoric*, quoted by Gary McDowell, *Equity and the Constitution: The
    Supreme Court, Equitable Relief and Public Policy*, Chicago: University of Chicago
    Press, 1982, p 5.
76 And still do – a fact that was critical in the strategy to use the courts to shape tobacco
    policy in the 1990s. See Chapter 9.
77 McDowell, *Equity and the Constitution*, p 7.
78 McDowell, *Equity and the Constitution*, p 7.
79 Joseph Story, *Commentaries on Equity Jurisprudence as Administered in England and
    America*, Boston: Hilliard, Gray & Co, 1836, and Joseph Story, *Commentaries on
    Equity Pleadings and the Incidents Thereto according to the Practice of the Courts of
    Equity of England and America*, Boston: C.C. Little and J. Brown, 1838.

and criminal procedure all suggested that equitable remedies, orders from the court, orders to government, mandates of what government *must* do as well as what it can and cannot do, would be an option. It should hardly be surprising that many who came of age in the Warren Court era increasingly came to think of the courts as a place to go, not only to stop the government, but also to force the government to act. Law's allure expanded when the Warren Court opened a new avenue for policy change, and it accelerated as Watergate capped two decades of frustration with the traditional political tools of negotiating, bargaining, organizing, electioneering, and persuading. But a turn to the courts and a reliance on more formal, less malleable rules and automated procedures were not merely alternative routes to the same goals – juridification matters because law is different, because law shapes and constrains politics and policy in important ways. And that is the subject of the next chapter.

3 LAW IS DIFFERENT

The Power of Precedent

F OR POLICY ENTREPRENEURS AND POLITICIANS DETERMINED to advance their cause, it would seem that the choice of a judicial route rather than using the traditional political tools of bargaining, persuading, negotiating, and running election campaigns should simply be guided by matters of efficiency – which path will get me closer to my goal at the lowest cost? But law is different, and choosing a legal path generates risks that need to be considered. Judicial decisions may be political, but judicial decision making follows different rules and is driven by different incentives, limited by different constraints, and addressed to different audiences in a different language than is the political process. The way judges articulate, explain, and rationalize their choices and the way earlier decisions influence, shape, and constrain later judicial decisions are distinctly different from the patterns, practices, rhetoric, internal rules, and driving incentives that operate in the elected branches and among bureaucrats. These differences suggest that, although a legal strategy may be relatively successful in the short term, the judicial decisions and legal forms on which it relies can limit, direct, shape, and constrain those policies in the longer run in ways quite different from what might have been expected by those who embraced this approach in the first place.

After outlining a three-dimensional view of precedent, this chapter uses examples from cases involving slavery, religious liberty, racial discrimination, representation, and voting rights to illustrate both the ways in which legal decision making is different from ordinary political bargaining and how and why judicial precedent shapes and constrains policymaking and the political process itself.

Presidents have a vast bureaucracy and armies at their command. Members of Congress can turn funds on (and off). But not the courts. Federal judges, Alexander Hamilton assured his skeptical readers in 1788, would have "no influence over either the sword or the purse," but merely the power to exercise judgment, the power to persuade. And how does one persuade? By giving reasons.[1]

Like presidents, members of Congress, governors, and mayors, judges might choose outcomes they prefer for ideological or partisan reasons.[2] Unlike their elected counterparts, judges – and particularly the judges on the U.S. federal courts – almost always give reasons for their votes. This means that, unlike a vote in Congress, which can be ad hoc and responsive to quick and unexpected changes, the structure and style of legal decision making emphasize explanations for how and why legal decisions hew to or differ from a long line of established cases. In their explanations, judges may try to show how and why a ruling is or should be seen as exceptional[3] or how and why that long line of reasoning is now – or has always been – wrong. In building these explanations, judges may well cynically hunt for useful existing lines of reasoning, or they may sincerely struggle to fit their interpretation as tightly as possible within the scope and limits of an existing line of reasoning that they believe appropriate.

The language of policymaking is a language of preferences and choices and power; the language of law is precedent. Judges are not bound by earlier decisions, but earlier decisions structure the dimensions and language of new decisions. Judges work within a professional syntax, and they are trained (and have been well rewarded) to use that language – to reason by analogy, to think "like a lawyer," to build decisions not simply to resolve a particular case, but as part of a far more complex tapestry of reasons and reasoning that might stand for, influence, and shape other cases and other claims. In his book of advice to new law students, which is still regularly assigned in many schools, Karl Llewellyn writes that the first year of legal training is designed to get a student "thinking like a lawyer." The program is designed to "lop off your commonsense, to knock your ethics into *temporary* anesthesia. Your view of social policy, your sense of justice – to knock these out of you along with woozy thinking." In their place, he assures the aspiring attorney, you will acquire the "ability to think precisely, to analyze coldly, to work within a body of materials

---

1 Martin Shapiro explores the critical role of requirements to give reasons in controlling administrative discretion in "The Giving Reasons Requirement," in Martin Shapiro and Alec Stone Sweet, *On Law, Politics and Judicialization*, New York: Oxford University Press, 2002.

2 There is extensive scholarship in political science on both the attitudinal and strategic models of judicial decision making. On the attitudinal model, see Jeffrey A. Segal and Harold J. Spaeth, *The Supreme Court and the Attitudinal Model*, New York: Cambridge University Press, 1993, and the special issue of the *American Journal of Political Science*, (volume 40, number 4), 1996. On the strategic approach, see Forrest Maltzman, James Spriggs, and Paul Wahlbeck, *Crafting Law on the Supreme Court: The Collegial Game*, Cambridge: Cambridge University Press, 2000.

3 "Our consideration [of the equal protection claims] is limited to the present circumstances." *Bush v. Gore*, 531 U.S. 98, 109 (2000) (*per curiam*).

that is given, to see, and see only, and manipulate the machinery of the law." In the second year, Llewellyn says, law students will revive their ethics, but this time "in a better guise," as a body of ethics "no longer at war with law," but one that will inform the law, "helping you solve and criticize; no longer impeding your techniques, but furthering them."[4]

Judicial opinions, not who won or lost, are what matters, Martin Shapiro writes, "since it is the opinions which provide the constraining directions to the public and private decision makers who determine ninety-nine percent of conduct that never reaches the courts."[5] One of the most important effects of precedent, then, "is to be found in the structures the justices create to guide future decision making" – not only decision making on their own court, but also, perhaps more importantly, the decision making by "lower courts and that of nonjudicial political actors."[6] It follows, then, that the more heavily reliant legislators and administrators are on judicial decision making, the more their own future interests and policy preferences will also be influenced, shaped, and constrained by the frames and arguments and reasons given by the judges.

It makes far more sense for legislators, litigators, and policy entrepreneurs (not to mention judges) to follow the path already laid down, to fit their claims inside the frames that are more likely to win favor in court rather than to press new or different frames. Building on existing foundations certainly is more promising than trying directly to challenge the frame, the analogy, the path that already has garnered at least five votes on the U.S. Supreme Court. The more heavily dependent on judicial decision making the policy might be, the more compelling is the argument to hew to the line, the frame, the path that seems more, rather than less, promising.

Rational lobbyists, legislators, and concerned citizens alike pay close attention to the Supreme Court. When crafting legislation and litigation, they will look backward in retrospective efforts to identify well-trod paths that will make it more likely that the judges will accept and reinforce these legislative decisions. But they will likely look forward as well, prospectively trying to anticipate where the Court is headed, where the justices are willing or even inclined to take the Court and the country. Legislative and executive choices – influenced by the choices judges already

---

4 Karl Llewellyn, *The Bramble Bush: On Our Law and its Study*, Dobbs Ferry: Oceana, 1960, pp 102–8. In John Jay Osborn's *The Paper Chase* (New York: Houghton-Mifflin, 1971), the fictional Professor Kingsfield tells his students: "You teach *yourselves* the law. I train your *minds*. You come in here with a *skull full of mush*, and if you survive, you'll leave *thinking like a lawyer*."
5 Martin Shapiro, *The Supreme Court and Administrative Agencies*, New York: Free Press, 1968, p 39.
6 Mark Richards and Herbert Kritzer, "Jurisprudential Regimes in Supreme Court Decision Making, 96 *American Political Science Review* 2, 306 (2002).

have made – constrain the next round of Court decisions. And those, in turn, shape and direct any legislative and executive choices that follow.[7]

As powerful an influence as precedent might be when the primary concern is that the Court may say no or may block particular policy preferences, it is likely even more significant when the Court is willing to command as well as block. When policy bounces from Congress to courts, to the administration, and back again, not once but many times, the influences become more complex and often more constraining. We might think of a game of *Scrabble*, a game in which players often end up where none had originally planned or imagined. In a game of *Scrabble*, players start with a blank board, and the first player can head off in any direction he or she chooses. But slowly, over the course of the game, the players often end up in one corner of the board, whereas another part of the board is totally empty. No one quite knows how or why he or she ended up playing in such a constricted space. In theory, it is still possible to move the game off in a radically different direction, but it becomes increasingly difficult (and unlikely) for that to happen.[8]

Defining Precedent

Many in political science who study the courts and precedent have done a commendable (albeit contested) job of demonstrating that holdings in past cases do not *control* judicial decisions in later cases.[9] But the method these scholars have used in their analyses implies that cases, holdings, dissents, and concurrences are no more than "the stuff of insincere

---

7 Lee Epstein and Joseph Kobylka, *The Supreme Court and Legal Change: Abortion and the Death Penalty*, Chapel Hill: University of North Carolina Press, 1992; Jack Greenberg, *Crusaders in the Court*, New York: Basic Books, 1994; Clement Vose, *Caucasians Only: The Supreme Court, the NAACP and the Restrictive Covenant Cases*, Berkeley: University of California Press, 1967

8 See Paul Pierson, "Increasing Returns, Path Dependence, and the Study of Politics," 94 *American Political Science Review* 2, 251–67 (2000).

9 Attitudinalist studies (see, e.g., Jeffrey A. Segal and Harold J. Spaeth, *The Supreme Court and the Attitudinal Model*, Cambridge: Cambridge University Press, 1993, and later work by Segal and Spaeth) have been challenged from within the behavioral camp and from the recent work in new institutionalism. See Richard Brisbin, "Slaying the Dragon: Segal, Spaeth and the Function of Law in Supreme Court Decision-Making," 40 *American Journal of Political Science* 4, 1004–17 (1996); Saul Brenner and Charlotte Mare Stier, "Retesting Segal and Spaeth's Stare Decisis Model," 40 *American Journal of Political Science* 4, 1036–48 (1996); Donald Songer and Stefanie Lindquist, "Not the Whole Story: The Impact of Justices' Values on Supreme Court Decision Making," 40 *American Journal of Political Science* 4, 1049–63; Cornell Clayton and Howard Gillman (eds.), *Supreme Court Decision-Making: New Institutionalist Approaches*, Chicago: University of Chicago Press, 1999; Howard Gillman and Cornell Clayton (eds.), *The Supreme Court in American Politics: New Institutionalist Interpretations*, Lawrence: University Press of Kansas, 1999; Rogers Smith, "Political Jurisprudence, the 'New Institutionalism,' and the Future of Public Law," 82 *American Political Science Review* 1, 89–108 (1988).

rationalization of mere political ends."[10] To say that precedent does not *control* future holdings does not mean that earlier holdings, legal arguments, dissents, and concurrences cannot or do not *influence* and even constrain the development and interpretation of law within the courts.[11] As they respond to or anticipate court decisions, these rulings and their rationale also influence and constrain politicians and policy entrepreneurs alike. For judges, Cass Sunstein argues, precedent may not determine the right answer, but it does remove "certain arguments from the legal repertoire" – or, at the very least, raises the costs of choosing a discredited or long-ignored path and lowers the costs of extending or expanding existing paths.[12] As Karl Llewellyn puts it, precedent does not determine the outcome of a particular case, and "legal rules do not lay down any *limits within* which a judge moves. Rather, they set down *guidelines from* which a judge proceeds toward a decision."[13]

Part of the confusion about the role of precedent stems from a tendency to conflate precedent – previous examples used to support current choices – with the legal doctrine known as *stare decisis*, which is a rule for the application of precedent. In their influential work on judicial decision making, Harold Spaeth and Jeffrey Segal start with the assumption that "precedent, or *stare decisis*, quite simply means adherence to what has been decided."[14] This conflation is no surprise; even the 1992 edition of *Black's Law Dictionary* leaves some ambiguity about the distinction between these concepts, linking the two definitions. But a careful examination of the definitions of each offers a clear distinction that is essential if we are to understand the full function of legal precedent in the political process.

A legal precedent is a case or ruling or holding "which *may* be taken as an example or rule for subsequent cases," or a ruling or holding that *can* be used to support or justify a similar act or circumstance.[15] *Stare decisis*, in contrast, describes a *rule* for the *application* of precedent.

10 Epstein and Kobylka, *The Supreme Court and Legal Change*, p 310.
11 Mark J. Richards and Herbert M. Kritzer offer compelling empirical evidence for one way in which precedent shapes and constrains judicial decision making on the U.S. Supreme Court (Richards and Kritzer, "Jurisprudential Regimes"). See as well Herbert M. Kritzer and Mark J. Richards, "Jurisprudential Regimes and Supreme Court Decision Making: The Lemon Regime and Establishment Clause Cases," 37 *Law & Society Review* 4, 827–40 (2003), and Herbert M. Kritzer and Mark J. Richards, "The Influence of Law in the Supreme Court's Search-and-Seizure Jurisprudence," 33 *American Politics Research* 1, 33–55.
12 Cass Sunstein, *One Case at a Time: Judicial Minimalism on the Supreme Court*, Cambridge: Harvard University Press, 1999, p 42 (cited in Richards and Kritzer, "Jurisprudential Regimes," p 306).
13 Karl Llewellyn, *The Case Law System in America*, Chicago: University of Chicago Press, 1989, p 80, emphasis in original.
14 Segal and Spaeth, *The Supreme Court and the Attitudinal Model*, p 44.
15 *Oxford English Dictionary Online Edition*, 2001, emphasis added.

Stare decisis is the doctrine that previous decisions (precedents) should govern like cases in the future. As *Black's Law Dictionary* puts it, s*tare decisis* means "to abide by, or adhere to, decided cases. [It is a] policy of courts to stand by precedent and not to disturb settled points."[16] *Stare decisis* is a method for the application of *precedent*; the two are not the same thing.[17]

Stare decisis typically functions in a lineal fashion, where there is a direct line of descent in which precedent set by one case – in one doctrinal area of the law – is upheld, reversed, or parsed by a second case in the same doctrinal line. For example, Free Speech Case A sets a precedent that decides Free Speech Case B, or Free Speech Case A establishes a precedent that is discarded and replaced by an alternate reading of the doctrine in Free Speech Case B.

In addition to this more familiar lineal form of precedent there is another, one that is missed or explicitly excluded from the dominant studies of precedent. This other form of precedent is what might be called *lateral* precedent – in which precedent from one doctrinal area is used to frame and even decide a case in what would seem to be a different doctrinal arena. Perhaps the easiest way to think about the lateral function of precedent would be to imagine two parallel sets of train tracks, each representing a preexisting set of lineal precedents. A lateral move might occur when a judge jumps from one track to another. A case concerning the constitutionality of a legally enforced, mandatory flag salute, for example, clearly raises free speech concerns. But it just as clearly might be thought of as a burden on religious liberty for those who object to saluting inanimate objects or those who object to being required to participate in an exercise celebrating the role of a deity in "one nation under God." Thought of as a religious liberty case, this issue raises one, distinct stream of lineal precedent. Thought of as a question of free speech, it raises an entirely different *lateral* stream of precedent. One stream might lead to only four votes on the Supreme Court, whereas the other could secure five.

For lawyers and legal academics alike, one of the most important tasks is to persuade a judge to see a case from the proper vantage point – to

---

16 *Black's Law Dictionary*, St. Paul: West Group, 1992, p 1406.
17 Blackstone's classical assumption that in the Anglo-American Common Law system, precedent controls legal decisions through the mechanism of *stare decisis* (William Blackstone, *Commentaries on the Laws of England*, Chicago: University of Chicago Press, 1979 [1765]) was challenged by the legal realist movement of the 1930s and 1940s (Llewellyn, *The Case Law System*; John Chipman Gray, *The Nature and Sources of the Law*, Boston: Beacon Press, 1963; William Fisher, Morton Horowitz and Thomas Reed (eds.), *American Legal Realism*, New York: Oxford University Press, 1993) and later by the behavioral revolution in the social sciences (e.g., Segal and Spaeth, *The Supreme Court and the Attitudinal Model*). The attitudinal model has been challenged by some in political science (see footnote 9) and from the legal academy (Dworkin 1986; Ackerman 1991; Rosenberg 1991; Perry 1991; Scalia 1997; Gerhardt 1991; Cooper 1988; Maltz 1988). But it continues to generate impressive data and further empirical evidence (Brenner and Spaeth 1995; Spaeth and Segal 1999).

properly frame a set of facts within a line of precedent or reasoning that will convince the judge to support one's argument.[18] In his first meetings with new law clerks, Justice Brennan was said to have held up his hand with his fingers spread wide apart. This, he would say, is the most important rule in constitutional law. "Some clerks understood Brennan to mean that it takes five votes to do anything, others that with five votes you could do anything," but what mattered was getting to those five votes.[19]

Political psychology teaches us that decisions are powerfully influenced by the "formulation of the problem," by the way in which we understand the problem we face.[20] By their choices "of which arguments to tender and which to ignore," Lee Epstein and Joseph Kobylka argue, litigators and interest groups "influence legal outcomes."[21] How a case is framed, understood, and explained is critically important in determining who gets those five votes. With each run through the courts, litigators learn from past behavior, past signals that strategic framing of one sort works or fails. Later litigants (and later judges) will incorporate those lessons as they move on to new disputes, to new cases. The decisions reached in earlier cases and the frames in which those decisions were set, Alec Stone Sweet writes, are "likely to generate powerful pedagogical (or positive feedback) effects, to be registered on subsequent exchange and dispute resolution."[22]

Here we can begin to see path dependence emerging in the legal realm. A reinforcing series of framing choices begins to construct a well-worn path – if you are more likely to win your case by making it look like a free speech case, you will do so, and success with that strategy encourages the development of one path and the abandonment of another.[23] Path dependence has come to mean many things, Paul Pierson writes, but in simple terms it tends to refer to the argument that "we cannot understand

---

18 This effort extends as well to lower courts. As one writer argues, anticipation about the use of precedent combined with retrospective evaluation of existing precedent is used by lower courts as well: Lower courts often try to anticipate where the Supreme Court is heading and the sorts of arguments that might be appealing to the Justices of the Court. They do this by examining existing doctrine and by examining doctrine in related cases – in other words, by examining both lineal and lateral precedent. An expectation that the Court might be willing to move in directions that are *not* suggested by the dominant lineal precedent is often anticipated by lower courts that explicitly reject the Supreme Court's lineal precedent. Consider, for example, the Fifth Circuit's decision to ignore the Supreme Court's doctrine in affirmative action set down in *Regents of the University of California v. Bakke* (1978), which was effectively overturned by the Fifth Circuit's ruling in *Hopwood v. Texas* (1996).

19 Mark Tushnet, "Themes in Warren Court Biographies," 70 *New York University Law Review* 748, 763 (1995).

20 Amos Tversky and Daniel Kahneman, "The Framing of Decisions and the Psychology of Choice," 211 *Science* 453 (January 30, 1981). See also Erving Goffman, *Frame Analysis: An Essay on the Organization of Experience*, New York: Harpers, 1974.

21 Epstein and Kobylka, *The Supreme Court and Legal Change*, p 307.

22 Alec Stone Sweet, *Governing with Judges: Constitutional Politics in Europe*, London: Oxford University Press, 2000, p 18.

23 Pierson, "Increasing Returns."

the significance of a particular social variable" without understanding the path that brought it to that point. "Previous events in a sequence influence outcomes and trajectories but not necessarily by inducing further movement in the same direction."[24] Pierson has shown that political decision making and policy formation often are path dependent: When we are dealing with judicialized policy, we are looking at precedent as a significant influence on the construction, direction, and boundaries of that path.

The more legalistic the policy and the more dependent it is on judicial decision making, of course, the more significant is the role of judicial precedent in shaping and framing the path followed by elected officials and administrators. Once policymakers have "started down a track," Margaret Levi writes, "the costs of reversal are very high. There will be other choice points, but the entrenchments of certain institutional arrangements obstruct an easy reversal of the initial choice."[25] Because judges must give reasons, because they are trained to "think like lawyers," trained to make their arguments analogically and (whether cynically or sincerely) to use precedent to bolster, defend, and support those reasons, this observation has even more bite when we are talking about judicial decision makers or legally trained executives or agents in the administration and the legislature alike.[26]

Before turning to the more complicated ways in which precedent can spiral through all three branches of government, a close examination of a stream of cases concerning the free exercise of religion will illustrate the ways in which framing and path dependence can work within the Supreme Court itself. The ways in which precedent paths led to the odd marriage of hamburgers and human rights in American law in 1964, and the trail that led from the Court's command to Tennessee to reapportion its political election districts to the legalistic rules and procedures of the Voting Rights Act of 1965 will help explain the interbranch effects of precedent.[27] Both will illuminate ways in which judicial precedent spirals through all three branches of government, shaping and influencing the course of American politics and American public policy.

---

24 Pierson, "Increasing Returns," p 252.
25 Margaret Levi, "A Model, a Method, and a Map: Rational Choice in Comparative and Historical Analysis," in *Comparative Politics: Rationality, Choice and Structure* (Mark Lichbach and Alan Zuckerman, eds.), Cambridge: Cambridge University Press (1997), cited in Pierson, "Increasing Returns," p 252.
26 We are long past the day when it is plausible to imagine that a president might appoint someone to the federal bench who was not a trained lawyer. And that training is designed in large part, as Professor Karl Llewellyn wrote (and the fictional Professor Charles W. Kingsfield insisted in *The Paper Chase*) to get them to think in a very particular way. See note 4.
27 See Mark C. Miller and Jeb Barnes, *Making Policy, Making Law: An Interbranch Perspective*, Washington, DC: Georgetown University Press, 2004.

Religious Liberty and Free Speech: The Power of an Effective Frame

The First Amendment instructs that "Congress shall make no law respecting an establishment of religion, or prohibiting the free exercise thereof." But would a law be constitutional if it required religiously observant children to violate the tenets of their faith and pledge allegiance to an inanimate symbol of secular authority? When the Jehovah's Witnesses first brought this question to the Supreme Court in 1940, Justice Felix Frankfurter rejected the claim that the free exercise clause required an exemption for the Gobitis family from a mandatory schoolhouse flag salute in Minersville, Pennsylvania. In his majority opinion (which drew only one dissenting vote), Frankfurter held that the Court's task was to balance "the right to freedom of religious belief" and the need to enforce behavior that "society thinks necessary for the promotion of some great common end."[28] Yet, just three years later, in *West Virginia State Board of Education v. Barnette*, the U.S. Supreme Court held that a virtually identical flag salute requirement in West Virginia violated the First Amendment. The difference was that in 1943 the Court decided that a compulsory flag salute was a form of coerced speech – meaning the First Amendment problem was one involving free speech, not the free exercise of religion.[29]

"There is no doubt," Justice Jackson wrote for the 8–1 majority in 1943, that "the flag salute is a form of utterance" and that "to sustain the compulsory flag salute we are required to say that a Bill of Rights which guards the individual's right to speak his own mind, left it open to public authorities to compel him to utter what is not in his mind."[30] Justice Jackson insisted that religion was not even a consideration in the 1943 case:

While religion supplies appellees' motive for enduring the discomforts of making the issue in this case, many citizens who do not share these religious views hold such a compulsory rite to infringe constitutional liberties of the individual.... The question which underlies the flag salute controversy is whether such a ceremony so touching matters of opinion and political attitude may be imposed upon the individual by official authority under powers committed to any political organization under our Constitution.

28 *Minersville School District v. Gobitis*, 310 U.S. 586, 593–4 (1940). It should be noted that the words "under God" had not yet been inserted in the pledge. The religious objection was in requiring students to pledge allegiance to an inanimate object, in direct contravention to the tenets of the Jehovah's Witnesses.

29 Robert Tsai argues that the Court actually borrowed much of its new approach to the First Amendment from speeches and arguments advanced by the executive branch, demonstrating the interactive nature of the development of constitutional doctrine. Robert L. Tsai, "Reconsidering Gobitis: An Exercise in Presidential Leadership," 86 *Washington University Law Review* 2 (2008).

30 *West Virginia v. Barnette*, 319 U.S. 624, at 632, 634 (1943). *Rosenberger v. University of Virginia*, 515 U.S. 819 (1995) is another, more recent example of the link between speech and religion.

Did precedent matter here? In terms of strict, traditional precedent – what might be called *lineal* precedent – in which Religious Liberty Case A determines the result in Religious Liberty Case B – it did not. In doctrinal terms, these cases had nothing to do with one another; one was about religious liberty and the other about free speech. And yet the 1943 case reversed the practical result of the 1940 case.[31] One might conclude that this was merely an episode in which changing personnel, combined with the lessons learned from fighting fascism in World War II had produced a different result.[32] But if that was the case, why not simply overrule *Gobitis* on free exercise grounds? Shifting to free speech did not spare the Justices from the need to overrule their earlier decision that had said the Constitution provides no shield from a mandatory flag salute.

If we use a more three-dimensional view of precedent, it becomes clear that precedent shapes and constrains litigators, legislators, and judges in a variety of ways beyond the classic, lineal form of precedent. Precedent also can influence and shape cases when it comes from another stream of cases, what might be called lateral precedent. In this example, the Justices in the second case shifted their frame of analysis; they jumped from one path (religious liberty) to another, lateral path (free speech). Once they switched paths, the outcome switched as well. These switches might be conscious and considered; they might be the product of the historic context in which the cases arise. They might even be something of a matter of chance. As Lon Fuller notes, the order in which cases arise is "a matter of chance" as is "the doctrinal connection . . . between the cases which do arise and those already decided."[33]

If the only impact of these lateral switches was the outcome in this individual case, the use of lateral precedent would be interesting but hardly significant. But because law is different, because the rationale used in legal decisions can shape and influence future litigation as well as legislation, this switch had far more significance. Those interested in expanding or protecting religious liberty now had two choices – they could follow this new path, putting their arguments in a free speech frame, focusing on claims they might be able to link to free speech, or they could continue to press the Court to articulate a more favorable religious liberty doctrine that would stand on its own.

Tying claims to free speech required a tradeoff – it was an efficient and promising means to achieve many important objectives these litigants

---

31 "The decision of this Court in *Minersville School District v. Gobitis* and the holdings of those *per curiam* decisions which preceded and foreshadowed it are overruled" (*Barnette*, 319 U.S. at 642).

32 Mary L. Dudziak, *Cold War Civil Rights: Race and the Image of American Democracy*, Princeton: Princeton University Press, 2002.

33 Lon Fuller, *American Legal Realism*, 82 *University of Pennsylvania Law Review* 429 (1934), cited and discussed at length in Malcolm M. Feeley, "The Black Basis of Constitutional Development," in Harry Schreiber (ed.), *Earl Warren and the Warren Court: The Legacy in American and Foreign Law*. New York: Lexington Book, 2007. pp 53–5.

sought in the short term, but one with real long-term risks for future religious claims that might not be so easily linked to speech. Conversely, asking the Court to revisit and reopen its doctrine on religious liberty might support a wide range of religious claims in the long run, but there was little reason to believe it would succeed in the short term. No surprise then that lawyers and litigants tied their arguments to speech and not religion. And so one path became more clearly defined and the other even less likely to be used in the future.

The Jehovah's Witnesses were frequent litigants before the U.S. Supreme Court – and they were extraordinarily successful. Between 1938 and 1944, the Witnesses were party to sixteen Supreme Court cases, losing only four – two of which were reversed within three years.[34] The first two Supreme Court cases the Witnesses won involved the distribution of handbills explaining their doctrine and beliefs, and both "were decided under the free speech and free press clauses rather than the free exercise clause."[35] This was not a random bit of good fortune. By dismissing the case of *Coleman v. Griffin* in 1937, when it was cast as a free exercise case and then the next year striking down an almost identical statute in *Lovell v. Griffin* in 1938, when it was challenged as a violation of free speech and free press, the Court itself had signaled both an unwillingness to expand the free exercise doctrine and an open door for arguments that might link to free speech and press.[36] The handwriting was on the wall, but the Witnesses failed to fully see it right away, arguing religious liberty again in the *Gobitis* case (which they lost) and yet again three years later in *Barnette*. It was the Supreme Court that jumped tracks in *Barnette*. The Court shifted the frame from religion to speech and in so doing not only handed the Witnesses a victory, but also finally made clear to them the utility of putting their claims in a free speech frame. The Witnesses finally got the point. Hitching their free exercise wagon to the horse of the rest of the First Amendment, and to free speech in particular, the Witnesses began to enjoy great success in Court.[37]

The Court's sympathy for free exercise claims wrapped in the mantle of free speech and free press continued long after World War II had passed into memory. Between 1944 and 1961, the Justices dismissed a number of cases that were appealed on free exercise grounds alone, and

---

34 William Chase Parsons, *A Secular Faith: The Supreme Court and the Free Exercise Doctrine*, unpublished Senior Honors Thesis, Harvard College, 1989 (available from Harvard University Libraries, Harvard Archives), p 29.

35 Leo Pfeffer, "The Supremacy of Free Exercise," 61 *Georgetown Law Journal* 1115, 1125 (1973), discussing *Lovell v .Griffin*, 303 U.S. 444 (1938), and *Schneider v. New Jersey*, 308 U.S. 147 (1939).

36 Pfeffer, "The Supremacy of Free Exercise," p 1125.

37 See Shawn Francis Peters, *Judging Jehovah's Witnesses: Religious Prosecution and the Dawn of the Rights Revolution*, Lawrence: University Press of Kansas, 2002, and Merlin Newton, *Armed with the Constitution: Jehovah's Witnesses in Alabama and the U.S. Supreme Court, 1939–1946*, Tuscaloosa: University of Alabama Press, 1995.

"of the six non-secular cases the Court did hear, it sided favorably with religionists only three times" but "none of those three decisions turned on Free Exercise protection."[38] More recently, a number of religious litigants used the lateral free speech path to try to actually force the government to take affirmative steps to accommodate religious practice – shifting ground from asking the Court to tell the government what it *may* and may *not* do to what it *must* do. When student groups at the University of Missouri, Kansas City, sought to use that public institution's facilities to "engage in religious worship and discussion," the Court ruled that, although these cases might bump into the establishment clause, the free speech demands of the First Amendment trumped those concerns. Although religious in substance, the Court held, these "are forms of speech protected by the First Amendment."[39]

In 1990, Justice Scalia argued that when it comes to the claims of religious liberty, precedents from the lineal track of free exercise have mattered far less than has the doctrine developed in the lateral streams of free speech, free press, and the right of assembly.[40] "The only decisions in which we have held that the First Amendment bars application of a neutral, generally applicable law to religiously motivated action," he wrote, "have involved not the free exercise clause alone, but the free exercise clause in conjunction with other constitutional protections, such as freedom of speech and of the press."[41] Some of the cases that prohibit compelled expression, he wrote, were "decided exclusively upon free speech grounds," although they have "also involved freedom of religion."[42] It is easy, he added, "to envision a case in which a challenge on freedom of association grounds would likewise be reinforced by Free Exercise clause concerns."[43] But, as Scalia commented in another case, "a free exercise claim unconnected with any communicative activity or parental right" does not have the same constitutional protection.[44] For Justice Douglas, "full and free discussion has indeed been the first article of our faith."[45] Faith is important, but in the Supreme Court, real power attaches to faith in speech, not religious liberty.[46]

38 Parsons, *A Secular Faith*, p 50.
39 *Widmar v. Vincent*, 454 U.S. 263 (1981).
40 *Employment Division, Department of Human Resources of Oregon v. Smith*, 494 U.S. 872 (1990).
41 *Cantwell v. Connecticut*, 310 U.S. 296 (1940); *Follett v. McCormick*, 321 U.S. 573 (1944); *Pierce v. Society of Sisters*, 268 U.S. 510 (1925); *Wisconsin v. Yoder*, 406 U.S. 205 (1972).
42 *Wooley v. Maynard*, 430 U.S. 705 (1977), and *Barnette*.
43 *Roberts v. United States Jaycees*, 468 U.S. 608 (1984).
44 *Employment Division v. Smith*, 494 U.S. at 881, 882. *In Smith*, the Court denied an exemption to otherwise reasonable drug laws in Oregon on grounds of religious practice.
45 *Dennis v. United States*, 341 U.S. 494, 494 (1951).
46 Congress did struggle to revive the independent authority of the free exercise clause in the Religious Freedom Restoration Act (1993), but the Court swatted down that

Scalia's comments came in his majority opinion for the Court in a 1990 case called *Employment Division of Oregon v. Smith* in which the Court was asked to reinstate a public employee who was fired for breaking drug laws by ingesting peyote as a part of a Native American religious ritual. Here was an example of a case that would be difficult to hitch to free speech. The peyote was ingested in a private ceremony, in the woods. It had nothing to do with speech, and, therefore, this claim could not easily build on the path of cases that had expanded religious liberty to that point. Scalia, writing for the Court, said that framed as a religious claim, on its own, the right of free exercise of religion could not trump the legislature's authority to pass and enforce public health and safety regulations. The *Smith* case made clear that, although the lateral move – from religious liberty to free speech – may have generated great success, there might be a cost for this move as well, a cost in terms of the atrophy of the free exercise doctrine, possibly making it harder for many religiously observant people to extend and expand free exercise in areas that had no plausible link to speech.[47]

The religious liberty cases stretched out over many decades, involving a range of judges, litigators, advocates, and interest groups. They illustrate the ways in which legal decision making works, the importance of framing, and, once framed, the power of that frame to influence and constrain future choices. These patterns and paths are not limited to litigants and judges, but powerfully influence and shape policy choices in the other branches as well. Legalistic solutions – built on frames constructed by legal decisions – generate real opportunities, but they are constrained and bounded opportunities. No set of cases better illustrates both the success and the constraints than the unlikely marriage of civil rights to the commerce clause of the U.S. Constitution.

Hamburgers, Human Rights, and the Commerce Clause

To end racial discrimination nationally, supporters not only had to find the votes and political will to do so, but these advocates also had to find

---

invasion of what the Justices thought to be their exclusive preserve in *City of Boerne v. Flores*, 521 U.S. 507 (1997).

47 The *Smith* case finally set off a rather dramatic backlash in Congress, which attempted to reverse the *Smith* decision with the passage of the Religious Freedom Restoration Act of 1993. In this law, Congress attempted to legislate a "compelling state interest" test for laws that burden religious practices – and attempted to blunt any Supreme Court criticism that such a law might run afoul of the establishment clause. Although this bill might well have produced a terrific discussion about religious liberty, instead, it generated a blunt and unequivocal statement by the Court focused on the question of separation of powers and judicial authority – the main thrust of the Court's opinion in *City of Boerne v. Flores*, 521 U.S. 507 (1997), the case in which the Supreme Court struck down much of the Religious Freedom Restoration Act.

a constitutional path that would allow the national government to exercise power in an area traditionally assumed to rest with the states. The seemingly obvious constitutional path would have been the Fourteenth Amendment's mandate that no state infringe the "privileges and immunities" of American citizens and that same amendment's assurance of the "equal protection of the laws" combined with its explicit authorization that "the Congress shall have power to enforce, by appropriate legislation, the provisions of this article." These mandates appear to offer a promising path for national legislation to assure civil rights: Among the "privileges and immunities" of citizenship, one might argue, are the rights to the full use of, and to benefit from, government programs and freedom from harassment, arrest, incarceration, and fines for participating in the social and political life of the nation. A guarantee of the "equal protection of laws" would assure that law itself would not be employed to bring advantage to one group or disadvantage to another on the basis of their race.

But, when first proposed, these legal arguments were foreclosed by the Supreme Court shortly after the ratification of the Fourteenth Amendment. An 1872 Court ruling in *The Slaughterhouse Case* severely circumscribed the reach of the privileges and immunities clause.[48] A few years later, in 1883, the Court struck down a set of civil rights laws that would have forbidden discrimination in transportation, restaurants, hotels, parks, and other forms of public accommodation, arguing that Congress lacked the power to pass these laws.[49] The Court insisted that the Fourteenth Amendment's protection extended only to public, rather than private discrimination, and then defined the arena of private discrimination to include just about any and all social interaction. Arguing that discrimination in transportation, hotels, restaurants, and bars was the product of private choices made by private individuals, and, therefore, not subject to constitutional limits, the Court threw up serious impediments to any future effort to break down Jim Crow and end segregation.[50]

Advocates and legislators pushing for more aggressive civil rights legislation in the 1950s and 1960s certainly could have asked the Court to

---

48 A detailed account of that case and the Court's interpretation of the privileges and immunities clause can be found in Charles Black, *A New Birth of Freedom: Human Rights Named and Unnamed*, New Haven: Yale University Press, 1997.

49 *The Civil Rights Cases*, 109 U.S. 3 (1883), striking down the *Civil Rights Act of 1875*.

50 Pamela Brandwein makes a compelling case that, although the Court struck down these laws, it did not close the door on the possibility of federal intervention or the possibility of aggressive legislation under the Fourteenth Amendment and, more particularly, the Fifteenth Amendment. See: Pamela Brandwein, "A Judicial Abandonment of Blacks? Rethinking the 'State Action' Cases of the Waite Court," 41 *Law & Society Review* 4, 997 (2007) and Pamela Brandwein, "The *Civil Rights Cases* and the Lost Language of State Neglect," in Ronald Kahn and Ken Kersch (eds.), *The Supreme Court and American Political Development*, Lawrence, Kansas: University Press of Kansas, 2006.

reverse itself on these precedents. However, even a sympathetic Court might have been reluctant to do so because that would generate significant ripple effects through all sorts of doctrine in a wide array of cases and rulings that had long been built on those decisions. Instead, legislators, litigators, and judges alike made a lateral move, jumping to another well-developed and long-established path that did not pose the same constraints. Instead of asking the Court to undo one hundred years of Fourteenth Amendment doctrine, advocates instead simply asked the Court to widen the existing, well-paved, and much traveled road of the commerce clause of the U.S. Constitution.

Arguing that racial discrimination impedes interstate commerce (those discriminated against are unlikely to travel, unlikely to establish new businesses, and unlikely to expand current businesses into segregated cities and states), advocates could suggest that, because the national government has the power to "regulate commerce with foreign nations and among the several states" (U.S. Constitution, Article I, section 8) surely it must have the authority to remove racial barriers to the smooth functioning and growth of interstate commerce.[51] Unlike the Fourteenth Amendment, the Justices had spent more than 170 years expanding (albeit in fits and starts) the powers of the national government under the commerce clause. Faced with a choice between the philosophically consistent but doctrinally constrained lineal foundation of the Fourteenth Amendment and the wide lateral path offered by commerce clause precedents, "both the administration and ultimately Congress made the safer choice" to base the new 1964 Civil Rights Act on the commerce clause.[52]

Given how hard they knew it would be to win passage of any civil rights bill, the last thing they wanted was to risk having the Court overturn their work, forcing them to return to Congress, break through what would undoubtedly be yet another filibuster, and win passage of a revised Civil Rights Act. The government's chief litigator testified at congressional hearings that a majority on the Supreme Court would not support desegregation built on the Fourteenth Amendment. Solicitor General Archibald Cox said that "if we went for all or nothing, it would have been nothing." In his Supreme Court brief defending the constitutionality of the law in test cases from Georgia and Alabama in 1964, Cox wrote, "We stake our case on the Commerce Clause."[53]

---

51 Additionally, it was argued that discrimination was likely to draw protests, picket lines, and boycotts and that these, in turn, would have an adverse effect on interstate commerce – discouraging consumers or impeding the flow of commerce; see Richard Cortner, Richard Cortner, *Civil Rights and Public Accommodations: The Heart of Atlanta Motel and McClung Cases*, Lawrence: University Press of Kansas, 2001, p 129.
52 Richard Cortner, *Civil Rights and Public Accommodations*, p 18.
53 Cortner, *Civil Rights and Public Accommodations*, p 6. The cases were *Heart of Atlanta Motel v. United States*, 379 U.S. 241 (1964), and *Katzenbach v. McClung*, 379 U.S. 294 (1964).

Although many Republicans initially resisted yet another expansion of national power under the commerce clause, the tide turned "in favor of the commerce clause as the basis" of the law during Senate Commerce Committee hearings on the Civil Rights Act in 1963. Experts from the Justice Department, the Congressional Research Service, and the ranks of legal academe all insisted that the commerce clause presented a clear and open constitutional path to the legislative objective of ending segregation in public accommodations, whereas the Fourteenth Amendment path was strewn with doctrinal barriers. Even though the Fourteenth Amendment provided the most coherent foundation for the law, they all testified that this path had been significantly limited almost at birth by Court decisions that "have never been questioned in subsequent opinions of the Court." Pointing to recent Court decisions in racial sit-in protests, the Justice Department lawyers said they felt there were likely to be "serious problems" in building a public accommodations law on a Fourteenth Amendment foundation and that to do so "would jeopardize civil rights by taking an unnecessary risk of unconstitutionality."[54]

Harvard Law Professor Paul Freund agreed, arguing that the Supreme Court had ruled on almost precisely the same issues in the 1883 *Civil Rights Cases* and "[t]hat decision has not been overturned." The commerce power "is clearly adequate and appropriate," Freund said. Whether the Supreme Court "would sustain the legislation under the Fourteenth Amendment," he added, "is more uncertain."[55] Vincent Doyle, from the Legislative Reference Service of the Library of Congress, echoed this view, saying that the Fourteenth Amendment was highly problematic because of the existing precedent. By contrast, "from the cases decided it seems clear that under the Commerce Clause, Congress can prohibit racial discrimination."[56]

Supporters of the civil rights bill recognized how hard it would be to achieve cloture and defeat a certain filibuster from the Senate's southern Democrats. Winning would require the cooperation and support of key Republicans, including the GOP's initially reluctant Senate minority leader, Everett Dirksen of Illinois. Ultimately, it required California Senator Clair Engle, unable to speak because of recent brain surgery, to be helped to the floor where he cast his "Aye" vote by pointing to

---

54 Department of Justice, "The Constitutionality of the Public Accommodations Provisions of Title II," in *Hearings Before the Committee on Commerce, United States Senate, 88th Congress, 1st Session on S. 1732, part 2*, Washington, DC: U.S. Government Printing Office, 1963, p 1301.

55 Paul Freund, "Constitutional Bases for the Public Accommodations Bill – A Brief on the Constitutional Issues," in *Hearings Before the Committee on Commerce*, p 1187, 1190.

56 Vincent Doyle, "The Power of Congress to Prohibit Racial Discrimination in Privately Owned Places of Public Accommodation," in *Hearings Before the Committee on Commerce*, pp 1304–1305, 1313.

his eye and nodding when his name was called.[57] Unwilling to gamble, the Johnson administration, along with congressional sponsors, built their legislation on the least assailable constitutional (and, therefore, most efficient) foundation possible. As Everett Dirksen put it on the Senate floor, if the commerce clause "provides a source of authority for us to act, we should use it." Though many in Congress recognized that the commerce path was neither the most logical nor coherent route to follow, it certainly seemed the most viable option.

Congress clearly paid attention to judicial precedent and judicial preferences. But this was very much a two-way street, with the Justices paying equally close attention to Congress, weighing legislative choices that had influenced earlier judicial choices. The Justices took explicit note of the fact that neither the legislature nor the administration had chosen to confront key Fourteenth Amendment cases from the years after the Civil War, instead framing their new law in the commerce clause, a frame that a majority of the Justices were willing to accept. During oral argument, Justice Harlan insisted that "it is perfectly clear that the government is arguing only that this act . . . is a constitutional exercise of the Commerce Clause power, and that's all we've got." This other Fourteenth Amendment debate "may be interesting," he added, but it "hasn't anything to do with this lawsuit." Justice Black also paid close attention to what he perceived to be congressional preferences: He "would have preferred," he said, "to have rested the decisions of the Court on the Fourteenth Amendment," but it seemed clear that Congress had "relied primarily on the Commerce Clause."[58]

In their conference after oral argument, Chief Justice Warren started the discussion by noting. "We should not concern ourselves with the Fourteenth Amendment. Congress need make no findings. The commerce power is adequate."[59] Next in seniority, Justice Black made clear his preference for the Fourteenth Amendment, but noted that "Congress limited the act to the Commerce Clause." Otherwise, Black added, "I would be for overruling the *Civil Rights Cases*." Justice Harlan suggested that Solicitor General Cox, the administration, and Congress had probably been correct in a pragmatic sense. "I would stand by the *Civil Rights Cases*," Harlan said, "and hold this act unconstitutional" if it were before the Court as a Fourteenth Amendment case. But, he added, "I have no problem under the Commerce Clause." Justice Stewart made clear that

57 Marjorie Hunter, "Packed Senate Galleries Tense; 10 Minute Vote Makes History," *New York Times*, June 11, 1964, p 21. Senator Engle died on July 30, 1964, just six weeks after the final passage of the Civil Rights Act.

58 Cortner, Civil Rights and Public Accommodations, p 102, 145.

59 Chief Justice Warren, Supreme Court Conference of October 5, 1964. Quoted in Del Dickson (ed.), *The Supreme Court in Conference: 1940–1985*, New York: Oxford University Press, 2001, p 726.

"resting on the Commerce Clause" he would uphold the law – a position Justice White said that he would join.[60]

Justices William O. Douglas and Arthur Goldberg fought for a shift to a Fourteenth Amendment frame, but to no avail. The majority rested on the commerce clause. No doubt this frame significantly expanded civil rights, but it was an expansion of a particular sort. Just as religious liberty became tightly interwoven with free speech, so the expansion of civil rights would become dependent on the continued expansion of national power under the commerce clause. It would allow significant growth in national guarantees for civil rights in the short and medium term, but there was a risk that future efforts to expand protections might be skewed, or limited, or simply not imagined. Future cases, Justice Douglas warned, would now turn not on questions of fundamental human rights, but rather "over whether a particular restaurant or inn is within the Commerce definitions of the Act or whether a particular customer is an interstate traveler."[61] In a draft concurrence, Justice Goldberg reminded his brethren that "the primary purpose of the Civil Right Act of 1964 is the vindication of human dignity and not mere economics."

Two separate cases were joined together that day, testing the reach and limits of the 1964 Act. One, *Heart of Atlanta Motel v. United States*, seemed to be easy to link to commerce. The motel was located at a key intersection of a federal interstate highway; it advertised widely, not only in Georgia, but also across the Eastern Seaboard; and a large proportion of its customers came from other states. The other case, *Katzenbach v. McClung*, was a tougher sell: Much further from the highway, the back-country barbeque restaurant served an almost purely local clientele and engaged in no out-of-state advertising. But there was a link to commerce – much of the meat they used for their burgers was not from Alabama, but arrived there from other states. That was enough for the majority, although it led Justice Goldberg to pass a note to Justice Douglas during the formal reading of the Court's opinions in these two cases: "It sounds like hamburgers are more important than human rights."[62]

The commerce path was a wide one indeed, but not without its limits. The worries expressed by Goldberg and Douglas began to manifest themselves as early as 1969, when Hugo Black sent an ominous warning that the commerce clause could stretch just so far and no further. After the Court upheld the 1964 Civil Rights Act, Euell Paul and his wife decided to turn their segregated amusement park on the outskirts of Little Rock, Arkansas, into a "private" club. Membership in the new Lake Nixon Club

---

60 Supreme Court Conference of October 5, 1964. Quoted in Dickson, *The Supreme Court in Conference*, p 726.
61 *Heart of Atlanta Motel*, 379 U.S. at 280 (Douglas, J., dissenting).
62 Cortner, *Civil Rights and Public Accommodations*, p 108, 169, 180.

could be had on a seasonal basis on payment of a 25-cent membership fee, limited to those eligible for membership – Caucasians. Writing for the Court, Justice Brennan had no trouble extending the commerce path, suggesting at least two ways in which this soon-to-be private club was linked to interstate commerce: The club leased fifteen paddleboats from a company based in Oklahoma (from which it purchased one boat), and the club operated a jukebox that, along with the records played on it, was manufactured in states other than Arkansas. Justice Black's discomfort level had been reached. To apply these rules to a recreation center in the Arkansas hills, "miles away from any interstate highway," Black wrote, "would be stretching the Commerce Clause so as to give the Federal Government complete control over every little remote country place of recreation in every nook and cranny of every precinct and county in every one of the 50 States." This, he concluded, "goes too far for me."[63] In a footnote, he added that this reasoning was precisely what he had been worried about in the 1964 cases, when he had warned that "every remote, possible, speculative effect on commerce should not be accepted as an adequate constitutional ground to uproot and throw into the discard all our traditional distinctions between what is purely local, and therefore controlled by state laws, and what affects the national interest and is therefore subject to control by federal laws."[64]

Was this Hugo Black returning to his Alabama roots, preparing to say of civil rights thus far and no farther? No. Hugo Black was saying that the Court and Congress had built this important enterprise on the wrong foundation, that they had selected the wrong path. In 1969, in *Daniel v. Paul*, Justice Black wrote,

I could and would agree with the Court's holding in this case, had Congress in the 1964 Civil Rights Act based its power to bar racial discrimination at places of public accommodations upon [Section] 5 of the Fourteenth Amendment. But Congress in enacting this legislation did not choose to invoke this broad Fourteenth Amendment power to protect against racial discrimination; instead it tied the Act and limited its protection to congressional power to regulate commerce among the States.[65]

If the Court did not draw the line somewhere, Black was suggesting, stretching the commerce clause to accommodate desegregation would, inevitably, spill over as legislators and litigators interested in expanding national power in other realms saddled up and rode off down that same commerce clause trail. This suggests, of course, that those concerned about the power of precedent to shape, frame, push, and influence would

63 *Daniel v. Paul*, 395 U.S. 298, 315 (1969) (Black, J., dissenting).
64 *Heart of Atlanta Motel*, 379 U.S. at 275 (Black, J., concurring).
65 *Daniel v. Paul*, 395 U.S. at 309 (Black, J., dissenting).

have to think about checking this expansion in areas they favored so as to prevent its expansion in areas they did not.

Hugo Black's misgivings in *Daniel v. Paul* and in other cases,[66] as well as those of Douglas and Goldberg, flowered twenty-five years later when the Rehnquist Court finally insisted that the commerce path went only so far and no further. In 1987, Justice Scalia issued a sobering warning. "Some distance down that path," Scalia wrote, "there comes a point at which a later incremental step, again rational in itself, leads to a result so far removed from the statute that obedience to text must overcome fidelity to logic."[67] And this is precisely what happened when Congress tried to ban the possession of handguns near schools in 1990 and when it passed a law to curtail violence against women in 1994 – building both on the commerce clause.[68]

Trying to limit the possession of firearms near schools and yet lacking the clear constitutional authority to do so, Congress, quite logically and unsurprisingly, built a new law banning gun possession near schools on the commerce clause path. Struggling to demonstrate a link to the commerce clause, Justice Breyer outlined a House-that-Jack-Built scenario to link firearms near schools to interstate commerce. Guns near schools, he noted, would intimidate students and teachers; that would scare them into poor attendance and weak performance; weak performance in school would generate a poorly trained work force; unable to hire well-trained employees in the area, employers would go out of business, move, or never consider starting up in the first place – and that would damage the national economy. But Breyer was in dissent. This time five Justices said no. This time a majority said so far and no farther down this path.[69] And lest anyone think this ruling was an aberration or something unique about guns, the Court reiterated its limit to the commerce clause five years later by striking down the Violence Against Women Act, another statute built on the commerce clause path.

The problem of course is, What then? What next? The costs of returning to the Fourteenth Amendment at this late date have only gone higher. It is still not impossible to do so, of course, but those costs are a clear disincentive to legislators and judges alike. Congress had a chance in the 1960s to press the Court to reinvigorate the Fourteenth Amendment, to jump out of the corner of the *Scrabble* board within which civil rights was

66 Cases including *Bell v. Maryland*, 378 U.S. 226 (1964), as well as in *Heart of Atlanta Motel* and *Katzenbach v. McClung*.
67 *NLRB v. Intl. Brotherhood of Electrical Workers*, 481 U.S. 573, 598 (1987) (Scalia, J. concurring), cited in Monaghan 1988, footnote 203.
68 The stretching of the commerce clause would eventually snap, in *United States v. Lopez*, 514 U.S. 549 (1995), and again in *United States v. Morrison*, 529 U.S. 598 (2002), where the Court struck down efforts to extend the reach of the commerce clause to cover laws banning handguns near schools and violence against women.
69 *United States v. Lopez*.

being defined. There were risks in that strategy, and so Congress, along with the executive branch and key interest groups, chose the safer path. This choice proved a successful one in the short term, but as the Warren Court gave way to the increasingly conservative Burger, Rehnquist, and then Roberts Courts, the consequences of this choice became more apparent. Future legislators and policy entrepreneurs now have two dead ends that are even more atrophied than ever before. Did the benefit exceed the cost? Possibly. But there were risks. There are risks. Law is different. Precedent matters.

Baker v. Carr – From Should to Must: From Apportionment to Voting Rights

Baker v. Carr, the case Chief Justice Earl Warren insisted was "the most important case of my tenure on the Court," made clear that the Constitution mandates a fair allocation of political power.[70] But how and why? The constitutional route that emerged would not only shape and constrain the allocation and distribution of political power in every state in the Union, but it also would influence the Voting Rights Act of 1965, which, in turn, would trigger a long series of court cases that, in turn, would be reflected in the revisions to the Voting Rights Act, which would shape and frame later court challenges, moving judges and legislators, litigators and advocates, candidates and voters farther and farther toward one corner of the *Scrabble* board. *Baker*, one might say, was the first set of tiles placed on the *Scrabble* board, but the choices made in that case very much shape, frame, and constrain the options available to the Court and Congress today.

In *Baker*, the Supreme Court broke through an institutional catch-22: As the population shifted in Tennessee from the farms and into the cities, the allocation of legislative seats was not keeping pace. The only way it might would be if the legislators themselves reapportioned power – but, of course, that would mean that some sitting legislators might have to give up their rural seats to create new urban districts – not a likely prospect.[71] For the majority in the *Baker* case, it was clear that this degree of unequal representation based on malapportioned legislative electoral districts violated the Constitution, but the explicit constitutional foundation for this conclusion was less clear. At first glance, there would appear to be at least five constitutional provisions that one could conceivably link to equality of representation: (1) the rules for the allocation of legislative seats in Article I, section 2; (2) the Constitution's guaranty clause – which

---

70 Earl Warren, *The Memoirs of Earl Warren*, Garden City: Doubleday, p 306.
71 Archibald Cox, "The Supreme Court – 1965 Term," 80 *Harvard Law Review* 91, 122 (1966).

guarantees "to every state in this union a republican form of government" (Article IV, section 4); (3) the rights provisions of the First Amendment (speech, association, and the right to petition for the redress of
grievances); (4) the Fifteenth Amendment, which gives Congress broad
power to enforce the right to vote; and (5) the equal protection clause of
the Fourteenth Amendment itself.

Each of these choices would have different consequences – building
election law on the First Amendment would set up a very different conception of what the right to vote entailed and what was required to make
it effective; building on the Fifteenth Amendment or the guaranty clause
might well have allowed the Justices to think about voting far less as a
question of individual property or individual rights and far more as a
question of effective representation. Any of these could conceivably have
supported a ruling that would strike down the state of Tennessee's particularly egregious apportionment scheme, in which 37 percent of the voters
of Tennessee elected more than 60 percent of the state's Senate.[72] So why
opt for the equal protection clause? And with what risks?

The why is easy: expediency. Just as had been the case with desegregation, there was a logical path that was blocked by an earlier Court ruling,
and there was a relatively unobstructed path that had no major doctrinal
impediments. The guaranty clause was the logical path in this case – as
then law professor and now Federal Judge Michael McConnell wrote. "A
districting scheme so mal-apportioned that a minority faction is in complete control, without regard to democratic sentiment, violates the basic
norms of republican government," and surely one cannot consider this a
republican form of government if a "majority has no means of overturning it."[73] But the guaranty clause was one of the routes into the "political
thicket" that Justice Frankfurter had warned his brethren against in his
1946 majority opinion in *Colegrove v. Green*.[74] A guaranty clause ruling
in *Baker* also would have required overturning two extremely venerable
decisions – *Luther v. Borden* from 1849 and *Pacific States Tel. & Tel. v.
Oregon* from 1912,[75] which, together, essentially ruled the guaranty
clause nonjusticiable.

The *Baker* case was terribly divisive for the Supreme Court. One of
the Justices, Charles Evans Whittaker, ultimately recused himself. And

---

72 The malapportionment in Tennessee "permits a minority of about thirty-seven percent
   of the voting population of the State to control twenty of the thirty-three members of
   Tennessee's Senate, and a minority of forty percent of the voting population to control
   sixty-three of the ninety-nine members of the House." *Baker v. Carr*, 369 U.S. 186, 274
   (1962).
73 Michael McConnell, "The Redistricting Cases: Original Mistakes and Current Consequences," 24 *Harvard Journal of Law and Public Policy* 103, 105–6 (2000).
74 *Colegrove v. Green*, 328 U.S. 549 (1946).
75 *Luther v. Borden*, 48 U.S. 1, 42 (1849); *Pacific States Tel. & Tel. v. Oregon*, 223 U.S.
   118, 151 (1912).

although the final vote was 6–2, the critical decision that the Court could, constitutionally, take the case was said to have been decided on a vote of 5–4, with Potter Stewart casting the decisive vote. Stewart "was absolutely unwilling to overrule any precedent," according to one of Justice Brennan's clerks. And that was a problem because to get to *Baker* – or so it seemed – the Court would almost certainly have to reverse *Colegrove v. Green*, the Illinois malapportionment case in which Frankfurter's plurality opinion so forcefully insisted the Court had no authority to intervene.

The Court found a way. Or, rather, Justice Brennan found a way. Frankfurter, as it happens, had not actually ruled that the Court lacked jurisdiction over all malapportionment cases in *Colegrove*. Rather, Frankfurter had affirmed a lower court's statutory interpretation of a 1911 federal law.[76] Frankfurter then explained why he was not going to discuss the constitutional claims the petitioners had made, and it was in that context that he invoked the political question doctrine and warned his brethren to avoid the "political thicket." Thus, when the Court came to *Baker v. Carr* in 1962, it did not actually have to reverse or overturn *Colegrove*. The constitutional foundation on which the *Baker* decision – and its progeny – would rest would be the equal protection clause. And because Frankfurter never reached the constitutional claims in *Colegrove*, never discussed or even mentioned the equal protection clause, doing so in *Baker* did not require the Court to reverse or overturn *Colegrove* or any other existing precedent.[77]

Baker itself was a fairly limited ruling – it simply held that the case was justiciable because the equal protection clause entitled the appellants to bring their case in federal court – and remanded the case to the district court for a trial and ruling. *Baker* opened a door, but it opened a particular door, shaped and constrained by precedent and internal needs to build a coalition that would allow the Court to hear the case.

As was the case with *Brown*, this seemingly modest initial decision was hugely important. In dismissing the *Colegrove* case, Justice Frankfurter noted in passing that, even if the Court were to accept the case, there was little that the Court realistically could accomplish: "Of course," he wrote for a three-Justice plurality, "no court can *affirmatively* remap the Illinois districts. At best we could only declare the existing electoral system invalid."[78] Sixteen years later, however, the *Baker* ruling signaled that the Court might, indeed, *affirmatively* command a new map, specifying with mathematical precision the numbers of constituents in each district. This

---

76 § 3 of the Reapportionment Act of August 8, 1911, 37 Stat. 13 as amended, 2 U.S.C. § 2a.
77 Equal protection, it should be noted, had been discussed in *Colegrove* – and in the dissent by Justice Black, who insisted that the equal protection clause claim was valid and that it should govern. His arguments would reemerge in *Baker* and its progeny.
78 *Colegrove v. Green*, 328 U.S. at 553 (emphasis added).

would not happen in *Baker*, of course, but *Baker* paved the way, built on the foundation of the equal protection clause. No doubt, it was an efficient and, perhaps, essential way around an institutional flaw in the system. But it had risks.

If we think about voting under the heading of equal treatment of the law, we begin to think about it as something that belongs to individuals, and the test is likely to be whether or not like individuals are being treated alike. "With respect to the allocation of legislative representation," McConnell argues, "all voters, as citizens of a State" should get the same rights and privileges, "regardless of where they live."[79] The problem with this approach is that legislative districts are put together for many different (political) reasons and with many different (political) objectives. Some states have clear urban/rural, manufacturing/farming divisions; others are divided between coastal and mountainous regions; some, like Oregon, contain defoliated deserts along with virtual rainforest conditions elsewhere. These and so many other ways to think about how to appropriately distribute political power do not lend themselves well to a clear, uniform, national, predictable, transparent, and replicable standard. Politics traditionally is fairly good at compromise and adjustment town-by-town, region-by-region, state-by-state – in contrast, judicial decision making, particularly on issues of fundamental rights, is not nor can it be.[80] And so the "logic of the equal protection argument, and the need for judicially manageable standards, thus drove the Court to ever more radical insistence on precise mathematical equality" in the cases following *Baker*.[81]

Having opened the door, the Court would now confront a series of cases that would more deeply involve the Justices in defining just how much latitude each state might have in drawing its districts. In a Georgia case, the Court held that giving one person "ten times the voting power of another person" violates the equal protection of law guaranteed by the Fourteenth Amendment and announced the appropriate standard: "The conception of political equality from the Declaration of Independence, to Lincoln's Gettysburg Address, to the Fifteenth, Seventeenth, and Nineteenth Amendments," Justice Douglas wrote for the majority, "can mean only one thing – one person, one vote."[82]

---

79 McConnell, "The Redistricting Cases," pp 105–106.
80 Jacob Hacker and Paul Pierson explore the reasons why politicians of late have become less skilled in the art of compromise. It might be worth considering, however, the degree to which juridification and a growing reliance on courts may have facilitated or hastened this trend. See: Jacob S. Hacker and Paul Pierson, *Off Center: The Republican Revolution and the Erosion of American Democracy*, New Haven: Yale University Press, 2005.
81 McConnell, "The Redistricting Cases," p 108.
82 *Gray v. Sanders* , 372 U.S. 368, 381 (1963).

By 1964, the Court was fully engaged in determining what met the one-person-one-vote standard and what did not. In *Wesberry v. Sanders*, the Court ruled that one person's vote in a congressional election had to be worth as much as the vote of any other.[83] *Reynolds v. Sims* struck down the state of Alabama's decision to have one house of its legislature reflect geographic districts (much as does the U.S. Senate), whereas the other would be population based. Electing state senators by county in Alabama meant that, whereas one senator might represent 10,726 people, another would represent 634,864. Insisting that the equal protection clause of the Fourteenth Amendment *affirmatively requires* "that the seats in both Houses of a bicameral state legislature must be apportioned on a population basis,"[84] the Court struck down Alabama's plan, telling the state that it *must* design a different system.

One-Person-One-Vote Means One-Person-One-Vote: Law as Rules

In *Baker*, Justice Brennan expressed the hope that the Court's mere "assertion of power will cause" legislatures to act so that the Court might avoid engaging in precise boundary drawing, and vote weighting.[85] But although the Court initially "left open the possibility that alternatives to the one-person, one-vote rule might satisfy constitutional norms, the logic of judicial review inexorably pushed the equipopulation principle to the fore. The very qualities of objectivity and manageability that made the equipopulation strategy appealing" soon made it "the sole arbiter of political fairness."[86] And, by 1968, the Court was exercising a very precise metric indeed, striking down a districting plan from Missouri in which the most populous district was 3.13 percent "above the mathematical ideal, and the least populous was 2.84 percent below."[87] As time ground on, the Court's mathematical demands became ever more precise. By 1983, the Court would reject a discrepancy that was actually less than 1 percent from the ideal, overturning a districting plan in New Jersey in which the difference between the largest and smallest districts would have been 0.6984 percent.[88] In effect, the Court had now framed the issue of fair

---

83 *Wesberry v. Sanders*, 376 U.S. 1 (1964).
84 *Reynolds v. Sims*, 377 U.S. 533, 568 (1964), *emphasis added*.
85 Justice Brennan's conference notes on *Baker v. Carr* (William J. Brennan, Jr., Papers, Manuscript Division, Library of Congress, Container I:60, Folder 6), cited in Richard L. Hasen, *The Supreme Court and Election Law: Judging Equality from* Baker v. Carr *to* Bush v. Gore, New York: New York University Press, 2003, p 52.
86 Samuel Issacharoff, "Judging Politics: The Elusive Quest for Judicial Review of Political Fairness," 71 *Texas Law Review* 1643, 1651 (1993).
87 *Kirkpatrick v. Preisler*, 394 U.S. 526, 528–9 (1969).
88 *Karcher v. Daggett*, 462 U.S. 725 (1983). The districting plan that was rejected by the Supreme Court in *Karcher* included a population deviation between the largest district (with 527,472 people) and the smallest, with a population of 523,798 – yielding a difference of 0.6984 percent.

political participation as something largely, if not exclusively, determined by precise equivalence in terms of population: The "one-person, one-vote rule became increasingly reified as the functional definition of what it meant for an electoral process to be politically fair."[89]

That the Court would rapidly move to an ever narrower, ever more specific set of rules should not be surprising, for two reasons. The first is practicality. Just as it was pragmatic need (working around Justice Stewart's refusal to overturn precedent) that led Justice Brennan to the Fourteenth Amendment's equal protection clause, which, in turn, helped frame the issue as one of mathematical equality, so too are there practical reasons why – where possible – judicial decision makers tend to embrace more explicit rulings. The most prominent reason is that, of the thousands of cases submitted, the U.S. Supreme Court decides just eighty to ninety cases a year.[90] In selecting and deciding cases and in writing opinions, the objective is to provide guidance to the lower courts, so that the Supreme Court does not have to weigh in on every case, over and over. Where explicit rules are not possible, the Court might favor somewhat broader standards to be followed in applying general rules to specific cases.[91] But rules and procedures, even watered down to broader standards, are something that decision makers aim to create. Rules, procedures, and standards are also very much in keeping with the universal assumption that if the rule of law means anything, it means uniformity of application, a commitment that is deeply chiseled in marble high above the brass doors of the U.S. Supreme Court building in Washington, D.C., in bold, capital letters: EQUAL JUSTICE UNDER LAW.

The other problem is what might be called the *Lochner* problem. There are a number of ghosts that stalk the U.S. Supreme Court – including *Dred Scott*, *Plessy v. Ferguson*, *Korematsu* – and *Lochner v. New York*. This labor case, in which the Court struck down a New York State effort to regulate wages, hours, and working conditions for bakers, is typically thought of as a cautionary tale teaching the lesson that the Court should not impose one set of economic preferences in place of another favored by elected officials. But that is not *Lochner's* only legacy.[92] We think of the Court of that era as being uniformly opposed to Progressive legislation and then the New Deal. And it was opposed – but not uniformly. And

89 Issacharoff, "Judging Politics," p 1650.
90 In fact, the Court issued final decisions in just seventy-four cases in 2005–2006, John Roberts' first year as Supreme Court Chief Justice, and seventy-three in the 2006–2007 term.
91 The distinction between rules and standards is well developed in Kathleen Sullivan, "The Supreme Court 1991 Term, Foreword: The Justices of Rules and Standards," 106 *Harvard Law Review* 22 (1992–1993).
92 Howard Gillman, *The Constitution Besieged: The Rise and Decline of Lochner Era Police Powers Jurisprudence*, Durham: Duke University Press, 1993.

that, one might argue, is *Lochner's* other shadow, a second reason why the Court might move to an ever narrower, ever more specific set of rules. In an era of divided Courts, with a profusion of dissent-in-part and concurrence-in-part rulings, it is little wonder that we see far fewer examples of courts working *together with* Congress and the president and far more instances of *deconstructive* patterns of interaction between the judicial and the elected branches.

Congress *Together with the* Court: Precedent in Action

Baker was about equal protection, equal rights, and political rights, but it was not about race, at least not in any direct sense. The primary division in Tennessee was between rural and urban – with the rural districts simply holding onto political power long after economic patterns had shifted population off the farms and into the cities. And although *Baker* led, eventually, to a strict metric of one-person-one-vote, it did not say anything about various voter qualifications. The idea was that each qualified and legitimate voter was entitled to an equally weighted vote. But who was a legitimate and qualified voter?

The Fifteenth Amendment, passed in the wake of the Civil War, explicitly extended the franchise to former slaves and gave Congress broad power to pass laws needed to make sure that the right to vote was not denied on the basis of "race, color, or previous condition of servitude." Though far from aggressive, the Court had over the years been willing to use the Fifteenth Amendment to strike down some explicit barriers to black voters, such as the white primaries in the Deep South.[93] But the Court was quite clear that, although the Fifteenth Amendment gave Congress the power to regulate some explicit barriers to voting, it did not constitutionally ban qualifications like literacy tests that could be shown to have some rational basis. This ruling, another of the precedents Justice Stewart refused to overturn, came in a 1959 case, in which the Court upheld literacy tests used in North Carolina. These were, as Justice Douglas put it, "applicable to members of all races," and this requirement was not, he wrote, "unrelated to the desire of North Carolina to raise the standards for people of all races who cast the ballot." Although a literacy test, "fair on its face, may be employed to perpetuate that discrimination which the Fifteenth Amendment was designed to uproot," he said, this did not appear to be the state's objective in this case. The right of suffrage "is established and guaranteed by the Constitution," but "it is subject to the imposition of state standards which are not discriminatory and which

---

93 *Nixon v. Herndon*, 273 U.S. 536 (1927); *Nixon v. Condon*, 286 U.S. 73 (1932); *Smith v. Allwright*, 321 U.S. 649 (1944); and *Terry v. Adams*, 345 U.S. 461 (1953).

do not contravene any restriction that Congress, acting pursuant to its constitutional powers, has imposed."[94]

That last sentence is worth some attention. In the North Carolina case (*Lassiter v. Northampton Election Board*), the Justices were asked if this test was forbidden by the Constitution, and they ruled that it was not, that the government *could* impose this requirement. Nevertheless, *Lassiter* does suggest that, although the Constitution does not ban literacy tests, it was plausible that Congress had the power, under the Constitution, to do so by statute. *Lassiter* said what the national government *could* do – did not *have* to do, was not forbidden to do – but was *allowed* to do.[95] That was an invitation for politics and for politicians to work *together with* the courts. Led, inspired, and organized by Martin Luther King and other key civil rights leaders along with the nameless thousands who had been viciously attacked by state troopers on the Edmund Pettus Bridge in Selma, Alabama, and across the South during voter registration drives in the 1950s and early 1960s; prodded, pushed, and strong-armed by Lyndon Johnson; Congress took up the Court's invitation on August 6, 1965.[96]

The Voting Rights Act of 1965 put enormous reliance on the courts and on judicial process to define, expand, and enforce voting rights. The words *court* or *courts* appear forty-six times in the statute's eight pages. The attorney general was instructed to institute court proceedings to enforce the provisions of Section 2 of the act, which says, "No voting qualification or prerequisite to voting, or standard, practice, or procedure shall be imposed or applied by any State or political subdivision to deny or abridge the right of any citizen of the United States to vote on account of race or color." Courts are empowered to appoint federal examiners; courts "shall determine"; courts that find violations of the Fifteenth Amendment may grant "equitable relief." A three-judge panel of the U.S. District Court in Washington D.C., "shall retain jurisdiction of any action pursuant to this subsection for five years after judgment.... The Attorney General may forthwith file with the District Court.... The District Court shall hear and judge" – and on and on and on.

---

94 *Lassiter v. Northampton Election Board*, 360 U.S. 45, 53 and 51 (1959).
95 *Lassiter* was fairly explicit on this point, but in a series of cases stretching back to at least 1927, the Court had ruled that the Fifteenth Amendment would not permit explicit racial bans on participation in primary elections. *Nixon v. Herndon*, 273 U.S. 536 (1927); *Nixon v. Condon*, 286 U.S. 73 (1932); *Smith v. Allwright*, 321 U.S. 649 (1944); and *Terry v. Adams*, 345 U.S. 461 (1953). This point is more fully developed in an article written by Louis H. Pollak in the wake of *Baker*, but before the Voting Rights Act, "Judicial Power and 'the Politics of the People,'" 72 *Yale Law Journal* 81 (1962).
96 "Bill Moyers, then a young White House staff assistant, is said to have called President Johnson to congratulate him on this triumph. Silence ensued; then LBJ replied: 'Bill, I think we just delivered the South to the Republican Party for a long time to come.'" Tom Wicker, "Remembering the Johnson Treatment," *New York Times*, May 9, 2002, p 39.

Clearly, the Voting Rights Act would go nowhere without the courts. Step one, of course, was to test whether the hint in the 1959 *Lassiter* case was understood correctly – would the Supreme Court validate the law as something the government *could* do? Indeed, it did in a case challenging a literacy test – *South Carolina v. Katzenbach*.[97] In an opinion by Chief Justice Earl Warren, the Court made clear that the "language and purpose of the Fifteenth Amendment, the prior decisions construing its several provisions, and the general doctrines of constitutional interpretation, all point to one fundamental principle. As against the reserved powers of the States, Congress *may use* any rational means to effectuate the constitutional prohibition of racial discrimination in voting."[98] Literacy tests, on their face, may not violate the Constitution, but where there is a statute banning those literacy tests, the question then becomes whether Congress has the power to ban them – rather than the question of whether the Constitution itself forbids or allows them.

Without the Voting Rights Act, the Court may well have more fully constitutionalized voting rights on its own, but it likely would have done so ever more narrowly focused on the rights of an individual not to be deprived of his or her vote, as the Court had ruled just a few years before *Baker* in a case about redistricting from Tuskegee, Alabama.[99] But this time the Court invited, Congress accepted, and both participated. On the one hand, it certainly provided a means around the institutional barriers facing any effort to more fairly ensure that each citizen was fairly represented in the legislature. On the other hand, it has also produced some rather noxious unintended consequences, ranging from intensely partisan gerrymanders (that maintain the mathematical obligation of one-person-one-vote) and some intensely racial gerrymanders that have guaranteed seats for minority-group politicians, but may have sacrificed their power to actually effect change and influence policy.[100]

Because law functions through the language of precedent and because judges and lawyers are steeped in this tradition, legal decision making is different from the electoral political process. Using the courts can be a more efficient and, at least in the short term, more effective means to

---

97 *South Carolina v. Katzenbach*, 383 U.S. 301 (1966).
98 *South Carolina v. Katzenbach*, 383 U.S. at 324, *emphasis added*.
99 *Gomillion v. Lightfoot*, 364 U.S. 339 (1960).
100 See, among many, Samuel Issacharoff, "Gerrymandering and Political Cartels," 116 *Harvard Law Review* 593 (2002); Nathaniel Persily, "Reply: In Defense of Foxes Guarding Henhouses: The Case for Judicial Acquiescence to Incumbent-Protecting Gerrymanders," 116 *Harvard Law Review* 649 (2002); Bruce Cain, "Assessing the Partisan Effects of Redistricting," 79 *American Political Science Review* 2, 320–33 (1985); David Canon, *Race, Redistricting and Representation: The Unintended Consequences of Black Majority Districts*, Chicago: University of Chicago Press, 1999; David Lublin, *The Paradox of Representation: Racial Gerrymandering and Minority Interests in Congress*, Princeton: Princeton University Press, 1999.

desired ends. But it can skew, shape, and constrain future decisions. There are risks that need to be understood and calculated by policymakers, politicians, and advocates alike. Where law has skewed results, the answer tends to be a demand for more law, more legal process.[101]

The "power of precedent, when analyzed," Justice Cardozo writes, "is the power of the beaten track."[102] The path does not, of course, determine the result. Once chosen, there is nothing formally to stop us from reversing course and trying another path. It is possible to return another day and try a different path but, as Robert Frost famously reminds us, that is not likely. Facing the choice of two paths in the yellow woods of New England, Frost wrote,

> *And both that morning equally lay*
> *In leaves no step had trodden black.*
> *Oh, I kept the first for another day!*
> *Yet knowing how way leads on to way,*
> *I doubted if I should ever come back.*
> *Robert Frost, 1915*[103]

What is hard to imagine for a poet in the New England woods is harder still for politicians and administrators – and even more difficult to fathom by trained lawyers and judges responding to their own professional norms and expectations. Precedent may not control, but it does influence, shape, and constrain.

The consequences of this apparent reality are explored through the rest of this book. Chapter 1 outlined a road map by which to consider and evaluate the relative risks of various modes of judicialization and legalization. Chapter 2 tried to explain why law's allure accelerated and expanded in the last half of the twentieth century. Now, with an understanding of just how and why legal decision making is different, the book turns to a series of case studies to illuminate and illustrate the different levels of risk that can be generated by the various patterns and processes that legalistic solutions tend to generate.

---

101 As Karl Llewellyn reminds his novice law students, there is "no cure for law but more law." Llewellyn, *The Bramble Bush*, pp 102–8.
102 Benjamin Cardozo, *The Growth of the Law*, New Haven: Yale University Press, 1924, p 62, cited in Barry Cushman, *Rethinking the New Deal: The Structure of a Constitutional Revolution*, New York: Oxford University Press, 1988, p 216.
103 Robert Frost, "The Road Not Taken," Mountain Interlude, New York: Henry Holt and Company, 1920: "Two roads diverged in a yellow wood, / And sorry I could not travel both / And be one traveler, long I stood / And looked down as far as I could / To where it bent in the undergrowth; / Then took the other, as just as fair, / And having perhaps the better claim, / Because it was grassy and wanted wear. / Though as for that the passing there / Had worn them really about the same, / And both that morning equally lay / In leaves no step had trodden black. / Oh, I kept the first for another day! / Yet knowing how way leads on to way, / I doubted if I should ever come back. / I shall be telling this with a sigh / Somewhere ages and ages hence: / Two roads diverged in a wood, and I – / I took the one less traveled by, / And that has made all the difference."

Part II

Law's Allure: Patterns, Process,
and Cautionary Tales

4 POVERTY AND ABORTION

The Risks and Rewards of a Judicial Strategy

J URIDIFICATION COMES in two basic flavors: attempts to accomplish policy and political goals by relying on judicial decisions and attempts to reform, control, automate, proceduralize, formalize, and depoliticize political institutions, politics, and the political process itself. Each involves courts and judicial rulings to some degree. Sometimes, these rulings shape choices by saying no. Sometimes, the courts *together with* the elected branches engage in something like a game of leap-frog, with each jump moving the players along an unpredictable path, in which legislation builds on judicial rulings and the next round of judicial rulings pivot on the previous round of legislation. Poverty and abortion are cases in which the law and the courts seemed to offer a substitute for the political process. The motives and incentives in these cases, however, were different, as were the results. Although the juridification of abortion was very much an example of relying on the court's classical blocking function, juridification in the poverty case was an early and ultimately unsuccessful effort to use the Court's new command function to work around a political process that had lost its appeal.

Poverty and the Allure of the Court's Commands

Brown v. Board of Education and *Baker v. Carr*[1] paved what seemed a more efficient, more effective, even morally superior path for advocates and entrepreneurs to follow in pursuit of their policy goals. And policy advocates, entrepreneurs, and a small army of young, low-paid, progressive lawyers were ready to march down that path.[2]

---

1 347 U.S. 483 (1954) and 369 U.S. 186 (1962), respectively.
2 Michael McCann carefully details the development and expansion of public interest litigation in *Taking Reform Seriously: Perspectives on Public Interest Liberalism*, Ithaca: Cornell University Press, 1986.

Just ten months after *Baker v. Carr* the Supreme Court put the finishing touches on its invitation for public interest litigation in a case called *NAACP v. Button*, in which the Court explicitly linked litigation to political advocacy.[3] Virginia law banned the "improper solicitation of any legal or professional business," and the state argued that the NAACP Legal Defense Fund's efforts to identify and support legal test cases ran afoul of this ban. The Court disagreed, saying the Virginia law unconstitutionally infringed First Amendment freedoms of expression and association. "In the context of NAACP objectives," the Court ruled, "litigation is not a technique of resolving private differences; it is a means for achieving the lawful objectives of equality of treatment by all government, federal, state and local, for the members of the Negro community in this country. It is thus a form of political expression. Groups that find themselves unable to achieve their objectives through the ballot frequently turn to the courts," the majority ruled, and "under the conditions of modern government, litigation may well be the sole practicable avenue open to a minority to petition for redress of grievances."[4] Upholding the law, of course, would have made it extraordinarily difficult for any public interest litigation organization to spearhead a legal campaign for social reform.

In the wake of *Brown* and *Baker,* the court's ruling was an invitation to politicians, lawyers, policy advocates, and entrepreneurs to turn to the courts, to pursue a judicial path to their policy goals. Building on their landmark decision in *Brown v. Allen* (1953), the Court added *Fay v. Noia* and then *Townsend v. Sain* in 1963,[5] making the invitation even more appealing, substantially easing access to the federal courts for a writ of habeas corpus to challenge state convictions. These, in turn, would lead to a series of cases in which the Supreme Court "reinterpreted the Constitution, applying to the states the criminal procedure provisions of the Bill of Rights" and opening the way for a wide range of commands to the states involving search and seizure, interrogation, and prison conditions.[6] Together, these cases and others gilded the invitation that the Court had extended in *Brown* and in *Baker.*

The invitation was enthusiastically accepted by a number of groups and individuals, including Jean and Edgar Cahn, a young husband-and-wife team of legal scholars who saw a new, efficient, and powerful pathway to force change in policies for dealing with poverty in the United States.

---

3 Although originally argued in November 1961, *Button* was reargued seven months after the Court's ruling in *Baker* and handed down three months after that.

4 *NAACP v. Button*, 371 U.S. 415, 429–430 (1963).

5 *Brown v. Allen*, 344 U.S. 443 (1953), *Fay v. Noia*, 372 U.S. 391 (1963) and *Townsend v. Sain* 372 U.S. 293 (1963).

6 Robert A. Kagan, *Adversarial Legalism: The American Way of Law*, Cambridge: Harvard University Press, 2001, p 77.

In a 1964 *Yale Law Journal* article (which they began to circulate in 1963), the Cahns laid out a blueprint for a new judicial approach to the policy problems and consequences of poverty in America. Building on a wide set of Supreme Court rulings from lateral arenas, including race, criminal procedure, voting, and districting cases, the Cahns mapped out a new strategy to fight for changes in poverty policy. Malapportionment cases like *Baker v. Carr* are critically important to the urban poor, the Cahns wrote, but "the process of enfranchisement must not cease with the composition of the legislature; it must take place in all the organs of government – both public and private – where law is made."[7] That sounds like a political strategy, but they made it clear that there were many forums of representation and that representation in the courts might actually be as important if not more important than representation in the legislature.

Courts had long been a place to go to fight for the enforcement of work and economic regulations. The National Consumers League (NCL), for example, started litigating to improve working conditions in the 1900s, but like others that turned to the courts for public ends in that period, it usually asked the courts to enforce existing statutes or common law rulings, offering arguments for why the courts should resist business groups that were challenging these rules and laws in court.[8] The NCL "employed the test case approach and the pioneering Brandeis brief," tactics that would later come to be used by civil rights litigators for the NAACP Legal Defense Fund, the American Jewish Congress's Committee on Law and Social Action, and the American Civil Liberties Union.[9] To the extent the NCL was asking the Court to intervene with the government, however, the NCL was asking the Court to say "thou *may*" or "thou may *not*," and *not* thou *must*.

The Cahns built their argument on the lateral foundations established in criminal procedure cases, and particularly on *Gideon v. Wainright*, a widely popular Supreme Court decision holding that the Sixth Amendment requires states to provide legal counsel for those accused of crimes, but who could not afford to hire legal representation on their own. The Cahns wrote that Gideon's case – which had been decided shortly before they began their article – removed "one form of disenfranchisement by providing a forum of representation in another law-making organ." Giving the accused "the right to representation by counsel was in effect giving him the power to change the law by objecting to and eliminating a body

7 Edgar Cahn and Jean Cahn, "The War on Poverty: A Civilian Perspective," 73 *Yale Law Journal* 1317, 1333 (1964).
8 Karen O'Connor and Lee Epstein, "Rebalancing the Scales of Justice: Assessment of Public Interest Law," 7 *Harvard Journal of Law & Public Policy* 483, 484 (1984). See also the sources cited there.
9 O'Connor and Epstein, "Rebalancing the Scales," p 484.

of improper practices by police officers, magistrates, and prosecuting attorneys which had, for all intents and purposes, assumed the status of law."[10]

Arguing that the "case and controversy focus of legal activity can provide one possible alternative to middle class forms of organization and protest," the Cahns insisted that a lawyer's approach to these problems might be far quicker and more effective. It may "take less time and effort" for a lawyer "to articulate a concern than to press the same demand by organizing citizens groups."[11] The Cahns played an important role in crystallizing the turn to the courts to battle against poverty, but they were not alone. As they were working on their 1964 article, Attorney General Robert F. Kennedy focused on similar themes in a speech at the University of Chicago Law School. Kennedy urged a focused strategy of developing "new kinds of legal rights in situations that are not now perceived as involving legal issues." Kennedy insisted that there was a need to "convert" the many responsibilities of America's vast bureaucracy "into legal obligations."[12]

The idea that there might be certain positive rights to basic economic necessities was very much a part of the law-school-driven intellectual climate of the early 1960s. More particularly, it was the subject of a tremendously influential article by Charles Reich that appeared in the same journal as the Cahns' article. In "The New Property,"[13] Reich proposed that certain economic rights were every citizen's entitlement and that welfare rights in particular were not only statutorily assured – initially in the Social Security Act of 1935 – but constitutionally grounded as well.[14] Traditional, negative-rights approaches, of course, fit well with the Court's traditional *blocking function*, but if the "new property" approach were to have an impact, it would require something more – it would rely in large measure on the Court's new *command function*.

In their article, the Cahns insisted – as Kennedy hinted – that this "power to create legal relationships" is a "form of political power" and its use by those in America's slums "is one way of revitalizing the democratic

10 Cahn and Cahn, "The War on Poverty," p 1333, footnote 22.
11 Cahn and Cahn, "The War on Poverty," p 1335.
12 Robert F. Kennedy, "Address on Law Day," May 1, 1964 at the University of Chicago Law School, quoted in Cahn and Cahn, "The War on Poverty," pp 1336–7, footnote 27.
13 Charles A. Reich, "The New Property," 73 *Yale Law Journal* 733 (1964); see also "Individual Rights and Social Welfare: The Emerging Legal Issues," 74 *Yale Law Journal* 1245 (1965).
14 A more extensive discussion and debate about Reich's article and its influence can be found in Elizabeth Bussiere, *(Dis)Entitling The Poor: The Warren Court, Welfare Rights and the American Political Tradition*, University Park: Pennsylvania State University Press, 1997. See as well, Elizabeth Bussiere, "The 'New Property' Theory of Welfare Rights; Promises and Pitfalls," 13 *The Good Society: A PEGS Journal* 2, 1–9 (2004).

process."[15] The goal, they insisted, was to take cases that were "representative of larger social ills," which were "sufficiently representative and symbolic so that vigorous advocacy would alter the pattern of official, civic private response in a way deemed desirable." Reich's arguments about the "new property" were tangled and torn between the individualist claims for property rights he advocated and the broad, group-, and even class-based strategies his arguments inspired in cases such as *Goldberg v. Kelly*. In that case, the Supreme Court ruled that New York State was required to provide welfare recipients with a hearing at which they could provide evidence before the state could terminate their benefits. Although the Court refused to label welfare a right, it did signal a movement in that direction, calling these payments a statutory entitlement rather than a mere privilege.[16]

The courts seemed to be ready; the lawyers were ready.[17] Even the administration was ready, as Lyndon Johnson became increasingly committed to making the war on poverty a signature policy for his administration. To push this movement to the next stage, however, would require both popular and financial support. The financial support, and with it the blessing of wealthy and well-connected leaders in the business and policy community, quickly came from the Ford Foundation, one of the most important players in the nongovernmental, philanthropic world of policy advocacy.

The notion of providing free legal services to the indigent was not new – the American Bar Association had been sponsoring legal aid for decades, and most major law firms contributed some of their time pro bono for indigent cases. But the Ford Foundation began to pour money into a new initiative, one that had been "conceived and led by youthful lawyer-politicians and dedicated to some vaguely conceived goal of social reform."[18] Lyndon Johnson's War on Poverty would embrace this initiative and, through the new Office of Economic Opportunity, would attempt to bridge these two approaches – the bar's traditional commitment of aid to help with the day-to-day legal needs of impoverished individuals and a new strategy of using litigation to advance broad social reform. The idea was to wed these two approaches, to knit "these two divergent movements" into "a single crusade."[19]

It was an uncomfortable marriage at best. At one extreme were those who "did not even want to talk of the program in terms of law and

15 Cahn and Cahn, "The War on Poverty," p 1339.
16 *Goldberg v. Kelly*, 397 U.S. 254 (1970). See Bussiere, "The 'New Property' Theory."
17 See Martha Davis, *Brutal Need: Lawyers and the Welfare Rights Movement, 1960–1973*, New Haven: Yale University Press, 1995.
18 Earl Johnson, *Justice and Reform: The Formative Years of the OEO Legal Services Program*, New York: Russell Sage Foundation, 1974, p 39.
19 Johnson, *Justice and Reform*, p 39.

justice [in individual cases] but purely as an instrument of social change."
This faction insisted that there had to be a focus on the "law to be
developed."[20] The idea here was that individual claims were merely the
instrument that would help develop new law, new rulings that would
make broader social change not only possible but also mandatory.

It was a radical goal, but one that could take advantage of the skills
of a largely conservative profession. Attorneys, after all, had long experience in working the halls of political power on behalf of their clients.
The only difference here would be the clients – and their causes. The
ABA's own Code of Professional Responsibility, which came into effect
in 1970, provided "a pre-existing conservative, well-accepted rationale
for law reform," and advocates insisted that those who opposed these
reforms, who objected to the use of legal means to accomplish political
ends, would find it hard "to challenge the right of lawyers to pursue
their client's interests in the appellate courts or legislative chambers."[21]
It was an efficient strategy. As Earl Johnson, then director of the Legal
Services Program in the Office of Economic Opportunity, told a conference audience at Harvard in 1967, law reform is "the means by which
we can provide more for the poor than in almost any other way with less
expenditure of time and money. Law reform can provide the most bang
for the buck."[22]

Law reform – legal advocacy for broad social objectives that would benefit the poor – seemed to make a lot of sense. If a legal strategy could work
for the disenfranchised or those subject to discrimination, surely it could
work for the poor who, by definition, lack the votes to force change and
"lack the money to buy change."[23] But this was also a group that lacked
the funds to pay for legal services. Using the courts for significant social
change seemed promising as long as the government, combined with phi-
lanthropies such as the Ford Foundation, paid the bills. The problem was
that building a social and political movement primarily on the financial
support of philanthropic organizations is not a long-term strategy for
success. Foundations very much want to be part of new initiatives – they
rarely want to become the sole source of support for long-term commitments. A joint American Bar Association/Ford Foundation report in 1976
put the problem bluntly: Public interest law holds great promise, but new
sources of support would be required for a more long-term, comprehensive effort. Those firms "now heavily dependent on foundation support
cannot remain so," the report concluded, "if for no other reason than

---

20 Johnson, *Justice and Reform*, p 48. Two of the leading voices in this faction were Ed
  Sparer and Nancy LeBlanc.
21 Johnson, *Justice and Reform*, p 131.
22 Johnson, *Justice and Reform*, p 131.
23 Johnson, *Justice and Reform*, p 258.

that most foundations are reluctant to tie up their resources in long-term commitments."[24]

Politics Defeats the Legal Strategy Meant to Replace Politics

Public interest lawyers would have to figure out how to "earn their way from the people they seek to serve."[25] This could be done through government support, of course, and initially that avenue seemed promising. The Johnson administration embraced the Legal Services Program's mission, funding it out of the Office of Economic Opportunity. But ironically, for a program that was attempting to use legal means to achieve policy ends, it would be the politics that would be its undoing.

There are three basic ways for public interest law to earn its way. One way is through foundation support and public subsidies. A second – which has become more viable in recent years – is to rely on huge damage awards or statutorily guaranteed awards of attorneys' fees for those who win these cases.[26] The third is for these firms, and their small armies of dedicated, committed young lawyers, to focus litigation on issues and policies near and dear to those who actually can pay for these services. This might jeopardize the widely shared assumption among those who embraced the legal route to change in the poverty area that public interest law would serve only those who could not otherwise afford legal services. As Justice Thurgood Marshall put it in his foreword to the 1976 ABA/Ford Foundation report on public interest law, "Almost by definition, public interest lawyers represent persons or groups who cannot easily compete in the ordinary market for legal services."[27]

Marshall was wrong. Although initially applied to questions of race, criminal procedure, and poverty, public interest law by no means was logically limited to litigation on behalf of the poor. There were and are many middle-class public concerns that might be well served by litigation. When the Warren Court signaled the availability of a judicial path to policy goals, it was not an invitation necessarily or even logically limited to poverty alone nor simply to questions concerning political disenfranchisement, political participation, or racial discrimination. It was an invitation that could and would be just as eagerly embraced by those concerned with a wide range of public causes, some of which – many of which – were core concerns for the middle class and the well off. Although Edgar and

---

24 Ford Foundation and American Bar Association, *Public Interest Law: Five Years Later*, New York: Ford Foundation, 1976, p 33.
25 Ford Foundation and ABA, *Public Interest Law*, p 33.
26 Paul Frymer, *Black and Blue: African Americans, the Labor Movement and the Decline of the Democratic Party*, Princeton: Princeton University Press, 2008.
27 Foreword by Justice Thurgood Marshall, in Ford Foundation and ABA, *Public Interest Law*, p 7.

Jean Cahn had started the movement with an almost-exclusive focus on poverty concerns, others – like Ralph Nader – saw the power of litigation to advance public interests ranging from consumer protection to the environment. Unlike poverty and disenfranchisement, these concerns had a far broader potential base of support – one with far deeper pockets.

While one arm of the Ford Foundation was funding pilot projects to focus litigation efforts on poverty, another of its arms was equally committed to pressing for the use of litigation to advance a broad agenda of more middle-class public policy objectives. The cauldron of the mid-1960s, combined with the Court's new path to accomplishing policy goals, produced "a new breed of liberal litigators" with Ralph Nader at its core. Very quickly, a network of groups "dedicated to using the courts for reform of corporate practices and/or social change" grew up around Nader. But that was not all. At the same time, "environmentalists began to resort to litigation to challenge other kinds of business practices."[28] And they all tapped into Ford Foundation support. These groups quickly exploded in size, scope, number, and influence. One study, Michael McCann notes, revealed that the number of public interest law firms doubled in just five years, expanding from forty-five in 1969 to more than ninety by 1975.[29]

The Ford Foundation and other private groups provided critical financial support for public interest litigation. Intellectual capital came from the law schools and from the government itself. The courts not only opened their doors, but they also forged and authorized critical legal tools. Before most public interest claims could have their day in court, a judge would have to actually give someone standing to argue the case. The problem was that, traditionally, the standing doctrine made it very hard to bring general assertions or broad public policy demands to court. Starting in 1966, however, the federal courts loosened those rules in a decision by then-Circuit Court Judge Warren Burger in a contentious set of cases in which blacks in Mississippi challenged the federal broadcast license of the dominant, white-owned television station in Jackson, the state capital.[30] NBC affiliate WLBT not only refused to present both sides of the integration story, but it also consistently editorialized against integration – and this despite the fact that about 40 percent of the station's audience was African American. When these editorials led to complaints being filed

---

28 O'Connor and Epstein, "Rebalancing the Scales," p 485.
29 McCann, *Taking Reform Seriously*, p 46. The study he mentions can be found in Jeffrey Berry, *Lobbying for the People: The Political Behavior of Public Interest Groups*, Princeton: Princeton University Press, 1977, p 34, and in the Council for Public Interest Law, *Balancing the Scales of Justice: Financing Public Interest Law in America*, Washington, D.C., 1976, p 29.
30 Please see Kay Mills, *Changing Channels: The Civil Rights Case That Transformed Television*, Jackson: University Press of Mississippi, 2004, for a full discussion of these cases and their backgrounds.

with the Federal Communications Commission (FCC), asserting that this violated the federal "fairness doctrine" for broadcast licensees, the FCC investigated, but did nothing. This inaction left frustrated viewers with little choice. Under the then-current law, only those with a direct financial stake could formally challenge federal broadcast license renewals, and the FCC ruled that the United Church of Christ, which had petitioned to challenge the license, lacked standing and so would not be heard. The church group challenged this ruling in court, and in one of his final opinions for the D.C. Circuit Court of Appeals before joining the U.S. Supreme Court, Warren Burger ruled that public interest groups were entitled to standing to challenge administrative rulings. There is "nothing unusual or novel in granting the consuming public standing" in these cases, he held. The "gradual expansion and evolution of concepts of standing in administrative law attests that experience rather than logic or fixed rules has been accepted as the guide."[31]

Burger's decision in *United Church of Christ v. FCC*, the Ford Foundation reported, "asserts the right of public groups to separate representation in the proceedings of government agencies."[32] As Michael McCann notes, "From the late 1960s federal courts began to recognize various collective environmental, consumer, aesthetic and recreational interests as valid legal claims for review."[33] This expanded the new judicial path to public policy for a much wider range of groups. Groups "sharing interests that cut across ethnic or economic considerations – environmental, consumer and health issues, for example – began to make claims on an economic and political system they believed to be unresponsive to their concerns." The 1966 *Church of Christ* decision "affirmed the need for representation of the noncommercial interests of large groups of citizens in the proceedings of regulatory agencies."[34]

So far so good. The courts certainly seemed to provide an opportunity. A court strategy, however, also entailed risk. One risk was that there were no assurances that the tools developed and refined to fight one battle might not be hijacked to fight another. A second risk is that legal arguments in court may change the minds of a few key federal judges – but that's not the same as changing public opinion.[35] That change is far more likely to be the product of traditional political tools that focus on convincing people to shift their position and adopt another. There is a third risk to a legal strategy as well: Although the public interest lawyers

---

31 *United Church of Christ v. FCC*, 359 F.2d 994, 1002, 1004 (1966).
32 Ford Foundation, *The Public Interest Law Firm: New Voices for New Constituencies*. New York: Ford Foundation, 1973, p 9.
33 McCann, *Taking Reform Seriously*, p 64.
34 Ford Foundation and ABA, *Public Interest Law*, p 11.
35 See Nathaniel Persily, Jack Citrin, and Patrick Egan (eds.), *Public Opinion and Constitutional Controversy*, New York: Oxford University Press, 2008.

were dedicated and willing to work for salaries far below what they might earn in the corporate sector, and although a litigation strategy was far less expensive than a full-scale political campaign, it was still not free of charge. With Lyndon Johnson's White House committed to a war on poverty, government subsidies and philanthropic grants might well fund these operations. But what happens if you rely on government subsidies and they are terminated? What happens when the foundations move on to new projects?

Richard Nixon took over the White House in 1969, putting Donald Rumsfeld in charge of the Office of Economic Opportunity. It should come as no surprise that Nixon and Rumsfeld were far from convinced of the utility and importance of continuing to offer administrative and government support for public interest law and litigation. On October 9, 1970, the Internal Revenue Service (IRS) announced that it no longer would allow public interest law firms to operate as tax-exempt organizations. In its ruling, the IRS distinguished the new public interest law from the traditional, charitable legal aid approach. The latter was fine, the IRS ruled, and there would be no loss of tax-exempt status for organizations providing counsel for "specifically identified persons or groups, such as poor and underprivileged people that are traditionally recognized as objects of charity."[36]

The IRS ruling set off a political firestorm – but again, not over the question of poverty abatement, nor over any particular policy question, but rather over restrictions on the use of litigation to advance these causes. Two months later, on November 12, 1970, the IRS reversed itself. The administration now announced that it would allow public interest firms to be treated as tax-exempt organizations – but not without some strict guidelines and limits that actually defined the parameters of public interest law, its direction, and trajectory. Here again, we can see some degree of what Paul Pierson identifies as path dependency as a function of increasing returns.[37] The IRS ruling may actually have unintentionally accelerated the turn to law and courts and away from the political arena. Public interest law firms could accept tax-free donations, but only if they restricted their efforts to the courtroom. In other words, they could pursue legal strategies to accomplish policy objectives – and *only* legal strategies to accomplish policy objectives: Their tax status would be jeopardized if they engaged in lobbying or other political strategies. The new rules left the path to the courthouse intact, but actually blocked state-funded public interest lawyers from using the traditional path to legislation and reform through political advocacy.

36 Ford Foundation, *The Public Interest Law Firm*, p 10.
37 Paul Pierson, "Increasing Returns, Path Dependence, and the Study of Politics," 94 *The American Political Science Review* 2, 251–67 (2000).

The administration was not quite yet done. In May 1971, President Nixon proposed shifting the Legal Services Program from the Office of Economic Opportunity to the newly created separate and semi-autonomous Legal Services Corporation. The move was driven by several conservative governors – led by California's Ronald Reagan – who claimed that the program had become a government-funded hotbed of political activism, rather than an instrument to provide the indigent with basic legal services. The Nixon reform appeared to be a boon for the agency – removing it from the political fray. In fact, it was a Trojan horse. Although the new agency would be an independent corporation, all eleven members of the independent board of directors for this independent agency would be appointed by the president. As Walter Mondale told the *New York Times*, "A board totally controlled by the President is likely to create precisely the same political problems which exist in the present program."[38] Congress tried to amend the president's proposal, limiting executive appointees to just six of seventeen slots, with the others to be selected from a list provided by various professional groups and organizations. But Nixon vetoed the legislation, arguing that it would be worse to have a legal services corporation that was "so irresponsibly structured" than not to have one at all.[39]

Nixon tried to push his version of reform again in 1972, but the bill died in committee. This time, critics had a smoking gun, documents showing that the administration was eager to block efforts by the legal services attorneys "to help the poor as a class through changes in judicial interpretations of the law and through administrative and legislative reforms."[40] Despite this revelation, the proposal finally passed in 1973. Nixon would appoint all eleven board members, and restrictive amendments from the House would ban legal services lawyers from policy advocacy and legislative lobbying. This was not the end of public interest law or the use of the courts to advance public interest policy causes, but it did suggest that the continuation of this project would now have to depend on financial support from the private sector. Middle-class public interest causes like the environment would have no problem securing financial support. But the brief window that had opened in the 1960s, a political window in which there was real support for using government to combat poverty, was now largely shut.

Much was and still is being accomplished by litigation in this area, but was the emphasis on law and the bypassing of the political avenues

---

38 Jack Rosenthal, "Nixon Proposes New Legal Aid Unit," *New York Times*, May 16, 1971, p 1.
39 Jack Rosenthal, "President Vetoes Child Care Plan as Irresponsible," *New York Times*, Dec 10, 1971, p 1.
40 John Morris, "Memos Show New Plans to Narrow U.S. Legal Aid," *New York Times*, Feb 19, 1972, p 16.

worthwhile?[41] Important gains were achieved through litigation, to be
sure: For example, when the Court struck down Alabama's presumption
that the presence of an adult male made a family ineligible for welfare
benefits, it opened up welfare access to something like 500,000 children.[42]
These and a series of other statutory and procedural rulings, Robert
Kagan notes, "had genuine substantive consequences." But, Kagan also
notes, these "victories in court often triggered political or administrative
reactions that eroded or reversed the apparent gains."[43] Were the risks
properly considered and properly calculated?

Legal Dreams, Political Nightmares?

The Cahns' 1960s dream of using the courts to force fundamental reforms
that might end poverty eventually came full circle, turning into a 1970s
nightmare: The courts now offered a viable alternative route to public
policy – but not for those seeking to attack the structural causes and
consequences of poverty. Instead, the strategy built to combat poverty
in America would now largely serve a host of more middle-class public
purposes, ranging from the environment to health care, from labor to the
protection of endangered species and a wide array of consumer interests.
Although most of these causes were no doubt worthy – and many advocated policies with which the Cahns no doubt agreed – the goals they had
in mind for the juridification of social policy were skewed and even their
antipoverty agenda was largely left behind in the process.

The Cahns themselves had seen the writing on the wall three years
before Nixon's victory in the struggle over the legal services agency.
Returning to the pages of the *Yale Law Journal* in 1970, the publication in which they had launched the poverty law strategy in 1964, the
Cahns lamented what happened to their movement. "Our society," they
wrote, "seems to be possessed of a sudden anal-retentive compulsion
to scrub clean our skies, our rivers and our streets – perhaps because
our souls have become ineradicably sullied with the stains of racism and

---

41 Consider the Court's ruling in *King v. Smith*, which struck down Alabama's presumption
   that if there was an adult male as part of the household, it could and would deny
   welfare benefits to that household. This ruling, Martha Davis notes, opened up welfare
   access to something like 500,000 children (Davis, *Brutal Need*). These and a series of
   other statutory and procedural rulings, Robert Kagan notes, "had genuine substantive
   consequences" (Kagan, *Adversarial Legalism*, p 173). But, Kagan also notes, these
   "victories in court often triggered political or administrative reactions that eroded or
   reversed the apparent gains." For a more complete treatment of the litigation successes
   in this period, see R. Shep Melnick, *Between the Lines: Interpreting Welfare Rights*,
   Washington, DC: Brookings Institution Press, 1994, among others.
42 Davis, *Brutal Need*.
43 Kagan, *Adversarial Legalism*, p 173. For a more complete treatment of the litigation
   successes in this period, see R. Shep Melnick, *Between the Lines: Interpreting Welfare
   Rights* (Brookings Institution, 1994).

poverty." They agreed with Mayor Richard Hatcher of Gary, Indiana – one of the nation's first African American mayors of a major city – who lamented that the environmental issue "may have done what Alabama's George Wallace had not been able to do – 'distracted the attention of the nation from the pressing problems of the Black and poor people of America.'" The problem, they said, was that "given the current unresponsiveness of the political system to ethnic minorities, the allocation of public interest law resources to majoritarian, middle-class, white concerns is contrary to the public interest." They insisted that the "political system can respond to these [middle-class] concerns without siphoning off the limited, special and constitutionally distinctive resources of the legal profession."[44] But they were very much swimming against the tide.

As early as 1969, Geoffrey Hazard had noted that there were real problems with relying on the courts for positive rights, particularly economic rights, or rights of social justice. Robert Kagan summarizes the problem this way: "After all, whom can [the courts] hold legally responsible for systemic inequalities in income? How can a court remedy those inequalities, short of massive redistributions of money and power that are well beyond the authority and competence of judges to order?"[45] If the motive to turn to the courts was purely one of efficiency and effectiveness, these questions would be central, and yet, they were not fully developed in those heady days. Efficiency was not the only motive – it seems clear that the broad gains of the civil rights movement and the powerful example set by *Brown v. Board of Education* combined to increase the normative preference for judicial decisions, for the black-and-white of law and rights to substitute for the ambiguous, negotiated, and compromised approach of politics. Were the courts the only option, this risk might have been more tolerable. But this was not the case for the antipoverty movement.[46]

At the very least, the Cahns and the poverty law movement provide a cautionary tale for others who may see the courts as a full-scale substitute for the political process. The poverty experience illustrates some of the risks inherent in this choice: Even if courts were receptive to these demands for command rulings, there was no sure way to provide the

44 Edgar Cahn and Jean Cahn, "Power to the People or the Profession? The Public Interest in Public Interest Law," 79 *Yale Law Journal* 1005, 1005 (1970).
45 See Kagan, *Adversarial Legalism*, p 173, and Geoffrey Hazard, "Social Justice through Civil Justice," 36 *University of Chicago Law Review* 699 (1969).
46 To the degree the courts were important and effective, they were because of their interpretations of the broad language of statutes such as the Aid to Families with Dependent Children (AFDC). Statutes, of course, can be changed. And although the courts had issued generous readings of statutes such as AFDC, eventually politics would control. Welfare advocates went to court, Robert Kagan notes, but state governments responded "by appealing to Congress, and Congress eventually amended the AFDC law to rein the courts in" (*Adversarial Legalism*, p 173). See also Melnick, *Between the Lines*, pp 104–8, and R. Shep Melnick, "Federalism and the New Rights," 14 *Yale Law & Policy Review* 325 (1996), pp 346–7.

resources and support for this strategy without the government, without political support. There also was nothing to guarantee that the method (relying on the courts) would always be focused on the issues that motivated these advocates. Public interest litigation efforts could as easily focus on consumers' rights and the environment as they could on poverty. And, in fact, it was more likely they would because those who cared most about these middle-class concerns were in a position to fund and support the litigation effort.

Although some Court rulings expanded access to welfare payments, the doctrinal frame in which these decisions were set limited their reach and scope. Far from asserting a positive right to subsistence, one of the Court's key rulings on access to welfare payments – *Shapiro v. Thompson* – assured that access not as a fundamental right to subsistence, but rather as the byproduct of a constitutional right to free movement between and among the states.[47] The Court never ordered the states to provide welfare payments, but rather ruled that should the states choose to offer these payments, it could not discriminate against new arrivals.[48] In *Goldberg v. Kelly*, the Supreme Court ruled that New York State was required to provide welfare recipients with a hearing before it could terminate their benefits, but the U.S. Supreme Court refused to label welfare a right, calling these payments a statutory entitlement.[49] And in a case challenging the way Texas funded public education (largely through local property taxes) – which produced significant gaps between the amount of public money spent on education in poor districts compared with wealthy districts – the Court toyed with, but ultimately rejected the claim that these discrepancies violated constitutional guarantees of equal protection. The Court refused to assert a constitutional right to education and upheld the Texas school financing system.[50]

47 *Shapiro v. Thompson*, 394 U.S. 618 (1969).
48 This ruling would be reaffirmed by the Supreme Court in 1982 (*Zobel v. Williams*, 457 U.S. 55) and again in 1999 in *Saenz v. Roe* (526 U.S. 489), in which the Court went beyond the right to travel, invoking (for only the second time in the 131 years since the ratification of the Fourteenth Amendment) the privileges and immunities clause of the Fourteenth Amendment. It argued that a federal statute that allowed states to pay new residents no more than they had received in their previous state of residency violated the privileges and immunities clause, arguing that law would permit long-term state residents to enjoy different and superior privileges than those allowed to recent state residents. But again, the Court said nothing about what sorts of economic subsistence any resident was entitled to enjoy – simply ruling on the question of how these benefits might be allocated differently among more recent and more established state citizens.
49 *Goldberg v. Kelly*, 397 U.S. 254 (1970). See Bussiere, "The 'New Property' Theory."
50 *San Antonio School District v. Rodriguez*, 411 U.S. 1 (1973). The *San Antonio* case challenged a state education financing plan under which wealthy communities were able to raise far more funds for education than were poor communities. This was because the funding formula was based on the tax rate allowed on property – communities with high property values, therefore, could raise far more revenue than could those that, even if they taxed at a higher rate, did not have the property base needed to match the revenue

The Cahns were right to be disappointed, but they should not have been surprised. Law's allure was indeed strong. But in their case, there were viable political alternatives, and a near-exclusive reliance on a judicial strategy never came close to forcing the government to do what politicians and public opinion did not support. Accomplishing this goal through a political strategy or, at the very least, a strategy of courts *together with* electoral politics was institutionally and politically possible, if not easy. With hindsight, it certainly appears a more promising path than the legal one the Cahns and those in sympathy with them pursued.

Abortion: Different Motives, Different Risks

Roe v. Wade, Justice David Souter wrote in 1992, was one of only two instances "in our lifetime" when a Supreme Court ruling would call on "the contending sides of a national controversy to end their national division by accepting a common mandate rooted in the Constitution." The other, Souter said, was *Brown v. Board of Education*.[51] Pairing *Brown* and *Roe* actually puts in sharp relief the contrast between two very different patterns of juridification. The Supreme Court played a critical role in both, but its intervention played out dramatically differently in each. Both decisions were greeted with significant criticism, not only by policy opponents, but even by some who supported the policy objective and yet still found the Court's logic, reasoning, or argument far from convincing and far from clearly grounded in the Constitution itself.[52]

Wealthy, educated, and well-connected women generally could obtain an abortion in the United States in the 1960s, but it was illegal under nearly all circumstances. Obtaining an abortion required women and their physicians to break the law or required women to flee overseas to countries where it was legal. Rapidly liberalizing social attitudes and the changing role of women in education, medicine, law, and politics,

---

of the wealthier communities. The Court was asked to rule education a fundamental right and one that could not therefore be inequitably allocated, but it declined. For a full treatment of this case and issue, see Douglas Reed, *On Equal Terms: The Constitutional Politics of Educational Opportunity*, Princeton: Princeton University Press, 2001.

51 *Planned Parenthood of S.E. Pennsylvania v. Casey*, 505 U.S. 833, 867 (1992) (Souter, J., concurring). If we stretch the timeline out, he might have noted that there have been really just three such cases in the history of the U.S. Supreme Court – *Roe*, *Brown* and *Dred Scott v. Sandford*. See Mark A. Graber, *Dred Scott and the Problem of Constitutional Evil*, New York: Cambridge University Press, 2006.

52 On *Roe*, see Jack Balkin (ed.), *What* Roe v. Wade *Should Have Said*, New York: New York University Press, 2005, and Jack Balkin (ed.), *What* Brown v. Board of Education *Should Have Said*, New York: New York University Press, 2002. On *Brown*, see as well Herbert Wechsler, "Toward Neutral Principles of Constitutional Law. 73 *Harvard Law Review* 1 (1959). On public opinion and the Court's abortion decision, see Samantha Luks and Mike Salamone, "Abortion," in Nathaniel Persily, Jack Citrin, and Patrick Egan (eds.), *Public Opinion and Constitutional Controversy*, New York: Oxford University Press, 2008.

however, began to shift public opinion, suggesting that there was growing support for the liberalization of abortion laws: A December 1965
National Opinion Research Center (NORC) poll showed that 71 percent of those surveyed believed that "it should be possible for a pregnant
woman to obtain a legal abortion if the woman's own health is seriously
endangered by the pregnancy," whereas 56 percent indicated that abortion should be possible for a woman who had become pregnant as the
result of rape.[53] This same survey showed far less support for abortion
for which financial concerns or family planning preferences were the reason. Nevertheless, this survey led the Catholic weekly *America* to observe
in an editorial that "if three-quarters of the American people seriously
want broader grounds for abortion written into the law, their wishes will
eventually prevail."[54]

Reform was not necessarily what all abortion rights advocates sought,
however. Reform meant compromise. Reform meant that there were conditions and times when the state would be allowed to regulate, limit, and
control a woman's choices about reproduction and about her body. For
those who saw the right to choose abortion as a fundamental, core right
of individual liberty, reform was not enough – they wanted repeal. They
wanted an end to all government intervention in a woman's reproductive
choices, from conception to delivery. Yet, unlike the reform movement
for which there was growing political support, the repeal movement was
not making dramatic political strides. Those who sought repeal had good
reason to believe that – far from undermining their ultimate objective –
the courts might actually offer the only way to accomplish a goal that
faced a profound political barrier.

These two groups – those seeking repeal and those seeking reform –
faced different risks. Those seeking repeal might well have concluded that
there were profound political barriers that might justify a far higher risk
strategy of relying on the courts. For those seeking reform, however, Justice Ruth Bader Ginsburg might well have been right when – before she
joined the Supreme Court – she wondered in print whether *Roe* might not
have "halted a political process that was moving in a reform direction."[55]
For those seeking reform, the legal path – a reliance on the courts – may
have diffused or diluted the impetus for political persuasion. Rather than

53 The health exceptions, Mark Graber argues, would effectively legalize abortion for any-
    one with a private doctor who would certify that the conditions had been met. See:
    Mark A. Graber, *Rethinking Abortion: Equal Choice, the Constitution and Reproduc-
    tive Politics*, Princeton: Princeton University Press, 1999.
54 David J. Garrow, *Liberty and Sexuality: The Right to Privacy and the Making of* Roe
    v. Wade, Berkeley: University of California Press, 1998, p 303.
55 Judge (now Justice) Ruth Bader Ginsburg, "Speaking in a Judicial Voice," 67 *New York
    University Law Review* 1185, 1208 (1992). But see Rosemary Nossiff, "Why Justice
    Ginsburg Is Wrong about States Expanding Abortion Rights," 27 *PS: Political Science
    and Politics* 2, 227–31 (1994).

capitalizing on the jumpstart the Court's dramatic decision in *Roe* provided, Ginsburg argues that there was a tendency to focus on a defensive judicial strategy. The problem with that approach, of course, is what would happen if and when the Court's personnel changed – particularly when this change was not simply the product of the natural replacement of retiring Justices, but rather was influenced powerfully by the political alignment that might control that nomination process, a political alignment that could – and was – significantly shaped by politically active opponents of the judicially protected right to choose.

Unlike in Western Europe, where abortion rights – pursued through the political process – are now deeply entrenched, the seemingly more efficient judicial route was followed in the United States.[56] Despite the favorable polling trends, even reformers in the late 1960s and early 1970s could be excused for thinking they faced an uncertain future. Although thirteen states had passed "what was for them a liberalized abortion statute" in the years between January 1967 and June 1970,[57] some already were attempting to revoke these changes, and other reform efforts were stumbling. In 1970 alone, although South Carolina did enact a statue that eased restrictions on abortion in the event that a woman's life or health was threatened by the pregnancy, Vermont reformers got an abortion rights bill through the state House, but lost in the state Senate; in Massachusetts, reform lost by a vote of 184 to 32 in the state House; a reform bill in Iowa never got out of committee; Arizona's repeal law got through its House, but did not reach the state Senate floor; and a proposed Michigan law made no progress. Hawaii, however, became the first state to pass something closer to a repeal of abortion restrictions.[58]

And in April 1970, a dramatic abortion reform measure passed in New York State. But this was far from the leading edge of a sweeping political movement toward reform. As David J. Garrow explains, the bill fell two votes short of the 76 needed to pass in the New York State Assembly. Just as the clerk was about to announce that the measure had failed, something exceedingly rare happened. George Michaels, an obscure Assembly member from a heavily Catholic upstate New York district, "rose to his feet and struggled to get the attention" of the Assembly Speaker, Republican Perry Duryea.[59] With "hands trembling and tears welling in his eyes," Michaels said, "I realize, Mr. Speaker, [that I am] terminating my

---

56 It is worth considering here the contrast between the United States – where the legal route was dominant – and Western Europe, where the political path was followed, and abortion rights are far more deeply entrenched. See Mary Ann Glendon, *Abortion and Divorce in Western Law*, Cambridge: Harvard University Press, 1989.

57 James B. Kahn, Judith Bourne, and Carl W. Tyler, Jr., "The Impact of Recent Changes in Therapeutic Abortion Laws," 14 *Clinical Obstetrics and Gynecology* 1130, 1131 (December 1971).

58 Garrow, *Liberty and Sexuality*, p 412.

59 Garrow, *Liberty and Sexuality*, p 420.

political career, but I cannot in good conscience sit here and allow my vote to be the one that defeats this bill – I ask that my vote be changed from 'no' to 'yes.'"[60]

Michaels' switch made the vote 75–73. But in New York, the rules required 76 votes to pass the law. There was, however, one member who had not voted: Assembly Speaker Duryea, following a longstanding tradition. Unknown to most everyone in the room, Duryea had pledged reform supporters that he *would* vote for this bill, but *only* if his vote would be the deciding vote – the 76th vote. Michaels' reversal meant that Duryea would, indeed, have the deciding vote. In "the confusion that followed" Michaels' switch, "few people saw Mr. Michaels slump in his chair holding his head in his hands, or heard Speaker Perry B. Duryea ask that his name be called so that he, as Speaker, could provide the final vote for passage."[61] Duryea cast the 76th and decisive vote. The State Senate that, earlier, had passed an even more liberal repeal measure, approved the Assembly version, and it was signed into law by Governor Nelson Rockefeller two days later, on April 11, 1970. (Michaels was right – his vote terminated his political career. Defeated in the next election, Michaels returned to Auburn, New York, to practice law with his son until his death in 1992.)

Those who look back at the New York reform as a sign of a significant trend do not typically dwell on how extraordinarily close this vote was. The legislative route to reform was viable – but it was far from anything approaching an onrushing train, speeding down the tracks. In fact, almost as soon as the New York law was signed, there were major political efforts undertaken to reverse the reforms. Just two years after Michaels' remarkable act of political courage, an effort to reverse that vote and revive more stringent abortion restrictions passed in the Assembly by a vote of 79–68 and, more surprisingly, was approved by the Senate, 30–27. Were it not for a veto from Governor Nelson Rockefeller, even New York's reform movement not only would have been knocked off the tracks in 1972 – it would have been significantly reversed.[62]

Yet, if reform was moving forward in the early 1970s – albeit haltingly – repeal was not moving at all. Surveys between 1962 and 1972 show that there was growing support for some liberalization of abortion laws – even by Catholics – but only in very specific circumstances.[63] According to the December 1965 study for the National Opinion Research Council, 64 percent of Catholics favored liberalized abortion rules when the health

60 Bill Kovach, "Abortion Reform Is Voted by the Assembly, 76 to 73," *New York Times*, April 10, 1970, p 1.
61 Kovach, "Abortion Reform."
62 Garrow, *Liberty and Sexuality*, p 546.
63 Lee Epstein and Joseph Kobylka, *The Supreme Court and Legal Change: Abortion and the Death Penalty*, Chapel Hill: University of North Carolina Pres, 1992, pp 147–8, 152, 187–8.

of the mother was in danger.[64] However, when abortion was sought because a woman felt she could not afford additional children, national support dropped to just 21 percent and to just 15 percent when the reason was that a married woman simply did not want additional children. These findings certainly suggested "how greatly different were the political prospects for [reform] as opposed to more far-reaching repeal."[65]

In 1970 there were four states that came close to the repeal of government restrictions on abortion – New York, Washington, Hawaii, and Alaska.[66] But that seemed to be as far as the repeal movement could go – at least along the legislative path. By 1970 "it became apparent that pro-choice forces had reached an impasse; no other states were willing to repeal their restrictive laws. Indeed, in 1971, thirty-four states considered – and rejected – repeal.[67] "While pro-choicers were lobbying for repeal, most politicos, simply reflecting the views of their constituents, would go only as far as 'reform.'"[68]

Before 1970, Mark Graber notes, the abortion rights movement was really a wide collection of rather disorganized groups and individuals.[69] Some pressed for liberalization, which would acknowledge that the government could legitimately intervene in a woman's choice about abortion, whereas others headed to court to build a constitutional shield that would accomplish by law what they could not, at that point, accomplish by legislation. Writing in the *New York Times Magazine* in January 1970, Linda Greenhouse noted that reformers "throughout the country" were beginning "to look to a new forum; the courts. As 1969 drew to a close, their efforts had been startlingly effective. By the end of 1970," she noted, "they may be rewriting history."[70]

The turn to the courts was not simply a strategic means to the same ends. For those who wanted repeal, who believed that a fundamental right was at stake and not simply a preferred policy, the judicial path not only looked more inviting but it also seemed the only way to go. Legislative reform required compromise. Reform of any sort, they feared, would deflate the repeal movement; it would make it easier for the courts to leave the issue to legislatures and easier for legislatures to stop short

---

64 Garrow, *Liberty and Sexuality*, p 303.
65 Garrow, *Liberty and Sexuality*, p 303.
66 Repeal bills already "had gone down to defeat in Illinois, Maine, Ohio and North Dakota, and prospects looked bleak even in Michigan, which repeal proponents had once counted as perhaps their best prospect for a 1971 victory." Garrow, *Liberty and Sexuality*, p 496.
67 Epstein and Kobylka, *The Supreme Court and Legal Change*, p 151, citing Lynn Wardle and Mary Anne Wood, *A Lawyer Looks at Abortion*, Provo: Brigham Young University Press, 1982, p 43.
68 Epstein and Kobylka, *The Supreme Court and Legal Change*, p 152.
69 Mark A. Graber, *Rethinking Abortion*, Princeton: Princeton University Press, 1999.
70 Linda Greenhouse, "Constitutional Question: Is There a Right to Abortion?" *New York Times Magazine*, January 25, 1970, p 20.

of repeal as the reforms would inevitably undercut the political demand for more complete repeal.

Richard Lamm (a state legislator who would later serve as governor of Colorado) made it clear that, for many in the abortion rights movement, legislative compromise that might lead to reform "would be counterproductive to... the goal of abortion law repeal." Lamm insisted that if a reform bill were to be "introduced by compromise-minded politicians, it should be fought." The best bet, he said, was to turn to the courts. Key lawyers in the fight for abortion rights "are doing more today through the courts," Lamm noted, "than any legislator can do in the state capital. If I read the cases and trends correctly," he added, "the major wave of future change lies with the courts."[71]

It was a sentiment that was endorsed by many politicians. For some, the courts offered a way to dodge the political cost of casting a vote for or against repeal *or* reform. In Texas, one abortion reform supporter noted that "some members of the Legislature would love to have the Supreme Court decide this for us."[72] New York Assemblyman Albert Blumenthal told Linda Greenhouse in 1970 that "repeal is the correct route now, and if the courts could solve the problem it would be both preferable and faster."[73] Other New York legislators said they sensed an unwillingness on the part of their colleagues "to become embroiled in the issue." As the *New York Times* headline on January 26 noted, "Opponents of the Abortion Law Gather Strength in the Legislature: But Many Lawmakers Would Prefer to Let the Courts Settle Controversy."[74] U.S. Senator Bob Packwood insisted that "most of the legislators in the nation I have met and certainly many members of Congress would prefer the Supreme Court to legalize abortion, thereby taking them off the hook and relieving them of the responsibility for decision-making."[75] For those favoring total repeal, relying on the courts certainly seemed to be the best (possibly the only) viable path in the short run.

The Judicial Path to Repeal

Privacy was a well-developed judicial doctrine in 1969. It was not, however, a path that had been built *together with* state legislatures or Congress. On the contrary, the Court nearly always invoked the right

---

71 Richard D. Lamm, "Therapeutic Abortion: The Role of State Government," 14 *Clinical Obstetrics and Gynecology* 4, 1205 (1971).
72 Texas State Rep. Sam Coats, quoted in Garrow, *Liberty and Sexuality*, p 491.
73 Greenhouse, "Constitutional Question," p 20.
74 William E. Farrell, "Opponents of the Abortion Law Gather Strength in the Legislature but Many Lawmakers Would Prefer to Let the Courts Settle Controversy," *New York Times*, Jan. 26, 1970, p 19.
75 U.S. Senator Bob Packwood, "The Role of the Federal Government," 14 *Clinical Obstetrics and Gynecology* 4, 1213 (1971).

of privacy as a trump to block or stop government action – or to protect an individual from unjustified intrusion whether by government or
employer. In 1891, the Court refused to allow the Union Pacific Railroad
to force a woman who was suing them for injuries sustained on one of
their trains to submit to a physical examination by a railroad company
physician. "No right is held more sacred, or is more carefully guarded
by the common law," Justice Gray wrote for the Court, "than the right
of every individual to the possession and control of his own person, free
from all restraint and interference of others, unless by clear and unques-
tionable authority of law." To support this assertion, Gray quoted from
the then-standard text – *Cooley on Torts* from 1888 – in which Michigan
Supreme Court Justice Thomas M. Cooley plainly stated that "the right
to one's person may be said to be a right of complete immunity: to be let
alone."[76]

The importance of the right to be let alone surfaced again in 1928,
in a U.S. Supreme Court case testing whether government wiretaps on
telephones were constitutional. The claim was that the government was
secretly forcing defendants to bear witness against themselves, because
the government would use their own words and speech to convict them.
A divided Court ruled 5–4 that using wiretap evidence did not violate the
Fifth Amendment. However, the case is at least as well remembered for a
dissent by Justice Brandeis, in which he argued that, although the Framers
could not have imagined telephones when they wrote the Constitution,
nevertheless, their commitment to guarantee "the right of the people to
be secure in their persons, houses, papers and effects, against unreasonable searches and seizures" surely applied to this modern extension of
personal property. The Framers, Brandeis wrote, "conferred, as against
the Government, the right to be let alone – the most comprehensive of
rights and the right most valued by civilized men."[77]

In a separate dissent, Justice Holmes endorsed the Brandeis opinion,
but did not fully embrace its reasoning. Although he agreed that "courts
are apt to err by sticking too closely to the words of a law where those
words import a policy that goes beyond them," he was not quite ready
to join Brandeis in arguing that "the penumbra of the Fourth and Fifth
Amendments covers the defendant."[78] Holmes seemed to recognize there
was some sort of a penumbra of rights woven from the textually explicit

76 *Union Pacific Railroad Co. v. Botsford*, 141 U.S. 250, 251 (1891). Clara Botsford was
suing the railroad after an upper berth in the sleeping car collapsed and fell on her head,
an injury for which the jury awarded her $10,000.
77 *Olmstead v. United States*, 277 U.S. 438, 478–9 (1928) (Brandeis, J., dissenting). This
dissent echoed "The Right to Privacy," a law review article written by Samuel Warren
and Louis Brandeis in 1890 (4 *Harvard Law Review* 193), two years after this concept
appeared in *Cooley on Torts* by Michigan Supreme Court Justice Thomas Cooley.
78 *Olmstead*, 277 U.S. at 469 (Holmes, J., dissenting).

provisions of Constitution, but it would be thirty-seven years before another Supreme Court Justice would assert that this penumbra included a right of privacy, woven not only from the Fourth and Fifth Amendments but also from the First Amendment's guarantees of free speech and the right of assembly; the Third Amendment's protection against government quartering of troops in a person's home; and the broad instruction of the Ninth Amendment that "the enumeration in the Constitution of certain rights, shall not be construed to deny or disparage others retained by the people."[79]

By the late 1960s, it was widely accepted that there was a long and deep commitment to privacy embedded in American culture, American history, and American law. Not only was there the tradition – stretching back at least to Cooley – of the notion of a right to be let alone, but there also were a string of cases dealing with parental rights: the right to educate children in a foreign language from a case in 1923, the right to send children to private schools from a 1925 case. In addition, there were cases that established basic liberties involved in procreation, including those that prohibited mandatory sterilization laws in 1942 and then, in 1965's *Griswold* decision, a ruling that allowed married couples to decide about the use of contraceptive devices.[80] Two years later, the Court added the right to be free in the choice of whom one married, regardless of race, striking down a Virginia statute prohibiting interracial marriage.[81] Clearly, privacy had a fairly solid foundation – at least in judicial doctrine. But would this foundation support an additional right, the right not simply to be left alone, but the right to choose to have medical professionals terminate a pregnancy in their offices or at a hospital without state restrictions or prohibition?

The first tentative answer to that question came not from the U.S. Supreme Court, but from California's State Supreme Court. Leon Phillip Belous, a Beverly Hills doctor, was convicted for "conspiracy to commit an abortion" and sentenced to two years probation and fined $5,000 under California's 1850 abortion statute. That statute made it a crime for anyone – a doctor or the patient herself – to induce a miscarriage unless this procedure was "necessary to preserve her life." This law was revised in 1967, when then-Governor Ronald Reagan reluctantly signed a new statute adding a few exceptions to the law, allowing abortions when there was "substantial risk that continuance of the pregnancy would gravely impair the physical or mental health of the mother," when the pregnancy

---

79 The penumbra argument was developed by Justice Douglas in his opinion for the court in *Griswold v. Connecticut*, 381 U.S. 479, 484–6 (1965).
80 Foreign language, *Meyer v. Nebraska*, 262 U.S. 390 (1923); schools, *Pierce v. Society of Sisters*, 268 U.S. 510 (1925); sterilization, *Skinner v. Oklahoma*, 316 U.S. 535 (1942); contraception, *Griswold v. Connecticut*, 381 U.S. 479 (1965).
81 *Loving v. Virginia*, 388 U.S. 1 (1967).

"resulted from rape or incest," or when the woman was under fifteen years of age. But this revision also required that all abortions had to take place in accredited hospitals with the approval of a hospital committee "consisting of at least three licensed physicians and surgeons."[82]

In *Belous*, the California court ruled that the laws – both the original 1850 statute and the revised and somewhat liberalized 1967 law – could not stand because both turned only on what might constitute measures that were "necessary to preserve" the life of the mother. Because a doctor faced criminal sanctions for abortions that did not meet this test, the court held that this phrase had to be clear and unambiguous. But just what did "necessary" or "preserve the life" mean? At one extreme, of course, one would assume this wording meant that abortion was only to be allowed when a woman would almost certainly die without the procedure. But reading the statute strictly, the court said, would violate the "fundamental right of the woman to choose whether to bear children" – a right, the justices argued, that "follows from the Supreme Court's and this court's repeated acknowledgment of a 'right to privacy' or 'liberty' in matters related to marriage, family and sex."[83]

Belous was handed down on September 5, 1969. Just two months later, on November 10, 1969, the federal district court in Washington, D.C., echoed the California court with a very similar decision in a very similar case called *United States v. Milan Vuitch*.[84] Again, a doctor was indicted for abortion, but this time under a federal statute, because the District of Columbia is a federal enclave. This 1901 statute made it a crime to participate in an abortion "on any woman, unless the same were done as necessary for the preservation of the mother's life or health and under the direction of a competent licensed practitioner of medicine." The penalty for this felony included prison sentences of from one to ten years.

The district court considered both of these provisions – finding no problem with the requirement for medical supervision, but finding a serious flaw with the "life or health" exception, much as had the California court. The word "health," Judge Gerhard Gesell wrote for the district court, "is not defined," and there "is no clear standard to guide either the doctor, the jury or the Court." This phrase, "preservation of the mother's life or health," which had been part of the law for nearly seventy years, Gesell ruled, "will not withstand [constitutional] attack for it fails to give that certainty which due process of law considers essential in a criminal statute."[85]

82 The Therapeutic Abortion Act (Health & Safety Code sections 25950–25954), quoted in *People v. Belous*, 71 Cal. 2d 954, 960 (1969).
83 *People v. Belous*, 71 Cal. 2d at 963.
84 *United States v. Vuitch*, 305 F. Supp. 1032 (DC 1969).
85 *United States v. Vuitch*, 305 F. Supp. at 1033.

That, of course, was more than enough to dispose of Dr. Vuitch's conviction and to overturn the law. Gesell went on, however, to discuss the question of a right to choose abortion – sending a powerful signal to abortion rights advocates that unlike the legislative path, where profound political barriers meant that incremental reform was the most they were likely to achieve, a judicial path might lead to full-scale prohibition of government restrictions on a woman's right to make this choice. The ambiguities of the phrase, Gesell noted, "are particularly subject to criticism for the statute unquestionably impinges to an appreciable extent on significant constitutional rights of individuals."[86] Gesell then pointed to the same stream of precedents as had the California court. There has been, he wrote, "an increasing indication in decisions of the Supreme Court of the United States that as a secular matter a woman's liberty and right of privacy extends to family, marriage and sex matters and may well include the right to remove an unwanted child at least in early stages of pregnancy."[87]

This was, of course, dicta – judicial opinion unnecessary to the resolution of the case itself. But it certainly was a potent signal. The next day the *New York Times* reported that for abortion rights advocates, the judicial route – which had until then been seen as a supplement to the political – now appeared to be a far more promising, more efficient, and more effective alternative or even substitute. "Civil liberties groups, birth control organizations, physicians and feminist groups that had only modest success with a legislative campaign to change the laws," the *Times* reported, "are now turning increasingly to court action attacking their constitutionality." This stress on litigation reflected "rising optimism among these lawyers that they will win in the Supreme Court."[88]

The rights path was further bolstered a few months later by a federal district court ruling in Wisconsin in which the judges insisted that "recent Supreme Court pronouncements regarding the Ninth Amendment compels our conclusion that the State of Wisconsin may not... deprive a woman of her private decision whether to bear her unquickened child."[89] Citing the same cases as had been cited by the California court, as well as those cited by the U.S. Supreme Court in the 1965 *Griswold* case, the federal district court in Wisconsin insisted that although, "the sanctity of the right to privacy in home, sex and marriage" was of fairly recent vintage,

---

86 *United States v. Vuitch*, 305 F. Supp. at 1034.
87 *United States v. Vuitch*, 305 F. Supp. at 1035.
88 Fred Graham, "Court Fight for Legal Abortions Spurred by Washington Ruling," *New York Times*, Nov. 12, 1969, p 30.
89 *Babbitz v. McCann*, 310 F. Supp. 293, 299 (ED Wis. 1970). Quickening traditionally was said to take place when a woman could first feel a kick or independent movement of the fetus in her uterus.

"the concept of private rights, with which the state may not interfere in the absence of a compelling state interest, is one of long standing."[90] This was not an absolute right, the court made clear, but one that required "a balancing of the relevant interests," including the state's interest in protecting the embryo as well as a woman's rights. This balance, the judges ruled, led them to conclude that "a woman's right to refuse to carry an embryo during the early months of pregnancy may not be invaded by the state without a more compelling public necessity than is reflected in the statute in question."

The doors to the courthouse were very much open. There were other paths available, even other judicial paths, but the privacy path was well paved, clear, and accessible. Looking back almost a decade later, abortion rights advocates such as Laurence Tribe argued that it appeared to be "a logical extension" of the existing doctrine and, "far from creating some novel and unprecedented liberty, simply recognized and extended some deeply felt and well-established principles about the limits of governmental power."[91] For others, of course, abortion was distinctly different from these other rights, but there certainly was a coherent precedent path on which abortion rights advocates now could travel – one certified, in a sense, by these more recent rulings. Precedent would not, of course, determine the result, but it powerfully shaped choices, political and legal alike.

An Alternate Path? The Judicial *Together with* the Political/Legislative Path

Of the plausible judicial paths, privacy was the one least likely to generate movement *together with* the legislatures of the states and Congress: It was the path most likely to remain exclusively judicial. One alternative path would press the courts to strike down abortion laws as vague or lacking clear direction for doctors and pregnant women alike. This would have built on the California decision in *Belous*, and it would have required a dialogue of Congress (and state legislatures) *together with* the courts, as phrases, terms, limits, and conditions that might pass the vagueness requirement were developed and tested. In his *Vuitch* decision, striking down the 1901 Washington, D.C., abortion law, District Court Judge Gesell extended an explicit invitation to Congress: The courts, Gesell concluded, "cannot legislate." But a "far more scientific and appropriate

---

90 *Babbitz v. McCann*, 310 F. Supp. at 299.
91 Laurence Tribe, testifying before the Senate Committee on the Judiciary, "Constitutional Amendments Relating to Abortion – Hearings Before the Subcommittee on the Constitution," 97th Congress, 1st sess., October 5, 1981, p 77, quoted in Garrow, *Liberty and Sexuality*, p 615.

statute could undoubtedly be framed than what remains of the 1901 legislation."[92]

John Hart Ely, who served as a clerk for Earl Warren the year *Griswold* was decided, pressed the Chief Justice to consider an alternative precedent path on which to build decisions involving reproductive choice. Ely argued that the Connecticut contraception restriction at issue in *Griswold* should be thought of as a violation not of privacy rights, but of the equal protection clause because the statute effectively treated poor women differently from those who were better off. Wealthy women had no great difficulty in securing contraception, and, therefore, the law unfairly discriminated, preventing the operation of birth control clinics for the poor. Here Ely turned to an 1886 Court decision, *Yick Wo v. Hopkins*, in which the Supreme Court struck down a municipal ordinance in San Francisco designed to limit and even shrink the city's growing Chinese population by making it illegal to operate a laundry in a wooden building without a special permit. Because virtually all of the housing in the city's Chinatown area was made of wood, this would disproportionately affect the Chinese population. In *Yick Wo*, the Court had ruled that though "the law itself be fair on its face and impartial in appearance, yet, if it is applied and administered by public authority with an evil eye and an unequal hand, so as practically to make unjust and illegal discriminations between persons in similar circumstances, material to their rights, the denial of equal justice is still within the prohibition of the Constitution."[93]

Justice Ginsburg also has suggested that equal protection might have made a more credible foundation on which to build the right to choose abortion. This argument was spelled out in a 1977 article by Kenneth Karst in the *Harvard Law Review*, which argues that the concern should not have been one of "recognizing a woman's interest in controlling the use of her body," but rather a focus on a "woman's claim of the right to control her own social roles." The abortion issue is not merely a question of "women versus fetuses," Karst argues; it is also an issue "going to women's position in society in relation to men." The right in question, he suggests, is "not a right to access to contraceptives, or a right to an abortion, but a right to take responsibility for choosing one's own future."[94]

---

92 *United States v. Vuitch*, 305 F. Supp. at 1035.
93 Quoted in Garrow, *Liberty and Sexuality*, p 237. The Supreme Court would later agree that, although the Constitution blocked the government from banning abortions, at least in the first trimester, the equal protection clause did not command the government to provide all women with equal access to this choice. Beal v. Doe, 432 U.S. 438 (1977), Maher v. Roe, 423 U.S. 464 (1977), and *Harris v. McRae*, 448 U.S. 297 (1980).
94 This argument is, as Karst acknowledges, dependent "on the assumption that a fetus is not a 'person' protected by the fourteenth amendment – an assumption which the Court made explicit in *Roe v. Wade*." Kenneth Karst, "The Supreme Court 1976

Far more likely to generate a *together with* solution, a more embedded outcome, Ginsburg argues, would be an incremental strategy much as the Court actually followed in striking down a number of laws that permitted and even required gender discrimination. In this arena, Ginsburg notes, the Court "overturned several state and federal laws, for example, laws exempting all women from jury service, and laws declaring the husband 'head and master' of the household." Here, she writes, "the Supreme Court wrote modestly; it put forward no grand philosophy, but by forcing legislative reexamination" of these statutes, the Court "helped ensure that laws and regulations would 'catch up with a changed world.'"[95] The Court's dramatic ruling in *Roe*, Ginsburg argues, "left virtually no state with laws fully conforming to the Court's delineation of abortion regulation still permissible" and called into question "the criminal abortion statutes of every state, even those with the least restrictive provisions"[96] The Court would have been far wiser to have adopted a more modest approach, Ginsburg writes, one that would have struck down abortion laws one at a time as unconstitutionally vague or perhaps for creating unequal conditions. This approach likely would have produced a series of court cases and very well may have generated something of a dialogue, with state legislatures building off court rulings and later courts building on both. Far from a dialogue, Ginsburg argues, "the sweep and detail of the [*Roe*] opinion stimulated the mobilization of a right-to-life movement and an attendant reaction in Congress and State legislatures" that "adopted measures aimed at minimizing the impact of the 1973 rulings, including notification and consent requirements, prescriptions for the protection of fetal life, and bans on public expenditures for poor women's abortions."[97]

But what about *Brown*? Surely, that was at least as bold a step as *Roe*. Would school desegregation have been possible – let alone more successful – if the Court had taken the modest approach used in gender discrimination? Actually, Ginsburg argues that the Court *did* follow the more modest path in desegregation. As bold and stunning as the *Brown* decision may have been, it did not strike down segregation across the board. The decision explicitly was limited to education, and even there, the Court asked for reargument – a year later – before requiring the end of segregation in public education but again not immediately or across the board, but "with all deliberate speed." In fact, it would not be until 1968 – more than a dozen years after *Brown II* – that the Court would

Term – Foreword: Equal Citizenship under the Fourteenth Amendment," 91 *Harvard Law Review* 1, 57–8 (1977).
95 Ginsburg, "A Moderate View on *Roe*," *Constitution*, p 17.
96 Ginsburg, "Speaking in a Judicial Voice," p 1205; Ginsburg, "Some Thoughts on Autonomy and Equality," p 382.
97 Ginsburg, "Some Thoughts on Autonomy and Equality," pp 381–2.

insist that school boards come forward with plans designed to realistically work and "realistically to work now."[98] *Brown*, Ginsburg notes,

> launched no broadside attack on the Jim Crow system in all its institutional manifestations. Instead, the Court concentrated on segregated schools; it left the follow-up for other days and future cases. *Brown* did not strike down segregation. *Brown* said that segregation in public education, and in public education alone, was unconstitutional. A burgeoning civil rights movement – which *Brown* helped to propel – culminating in the Civil Rights Act of 1964, set the stage for the Court's ultimate total rejection of Jim Crow.[99]

Roe v. Wade was different. At least in the first three months of pregnancy, it required no compromise; it "invited no dialogue with legislators. Instead, it seemed entirely to remove the ball from the legislators' court."[100] As a normative matter, this is entirely appropriate, of course, for those who saw abortion as a question of fundamental rights. But relying on a judicial strategy alone is particularly risky when opponents are using those same rulings to galvanize and mobilize their own political power, which might eventually enable them not only to influence and persuade voters, but through those voters to influence the courts themselves through the selection of judges to replace those who eventually retire or those, as all must eventually, pass on.

Had the Court in *Roe* opted for one of the other paths – vagueness or perhaps equal protection – it is plausible that abortion repeal advocates might have been more inclined, indeed compelled, to maintain and expand their political efforts, rather than relying so heavily on judicial rulings. They certainly could have used the court rulings as a weapon in this struggle, as they worked to persuade majorities in the states or on the

---

98 In the original *Brown* case, the Court held, "We conclude that in the field of public education the doctrine of "separate but equal" has no place. Separate educational facilities are inherently unequal." *Brown v. Board of Education of Topeka, Kansas*, 347 U.S. 483, 494 (1954). A year later, in *Brown II*, the Court ruled that the District Courts should enter orders and decrees necessary "to admit to public schools on a racially nondiscriminatory basis with all deliberate speed the parties to these cases." *Brown v. Board of Education of Topeka, Kansas*, 349 U.S. 294, 301 (1955). It would be nine more years, in 1964, when the Court would declare that there had been "too much deliberation and not enough speed in enforcing the constitutional rights which we held in *Brown*" in *Griffin v. County School Board of Prince Edward County*, 377 U.S. 218, 229 (1964). And it would be four more years (1968) before the Court unequivocally insisted that school boards were required to fulfill an "affirmative duty to take whatever steps might be necessary to convert to a unitary system in which racial discrimination would be eliminated root and branch." The burden on the school board, the Court insisted, "is to come forward with a plan that promises realistically to work, and promises realistically to work now." *Green v. County School Board of New Kent County, Virginia*, 391 U.S. 430, 434 and 439 (1968).
99 Ginsburg, "Speaking in a Judicial Voice," p 1207. See as well Michael Klarman, *From Jim Crow to Civil Rights*, New York: Oxford University Press, 2006, pp 363–85.
100 Ginsburg, "Speaking in a Judicial Voice," p 1205.

national level that theirs was the correct view of the matter.[101] As Barbara Ehrenreich noted in 1989, by turning to the courts, not *together with* the legislatures but independently, using judicial rulings as a shield against all attacks, abortion rights advocates stepped back from a national effort to "reach out to, and *convince* the undecided public of the justice of what [they] called abortion rights."[102]

Women certainly have an easier time obtaining abortions today than they did in 1972. But are abortion rights advocates really better off then they might have been had they focused on a different precedent path or fortified their legal gains with more traditional political measures, passing statutes and constitutional amendments in each state and at the national level and, in the process of that debate, embedding their policy and their preferences? Did the turn to the courts short-circuit a political process that might have better, and more deeply, embedded itself into the political and social consciousness of the nation?

This question first flared into conventional wisdom in the late 1970s as the Court failed to extend its holding in *Roe* to insist on state or federal financing of what had been asserted to be a constitutional right to choose.[103] The Supreme Court decision allowing the government to pay for obstetrical and childbirth services for poor women, but to ban the use of government funds, including Medicaid, for abortion provoked the *New Republic* to editorialize that "pro-abortion forces, have brought this disaster upon themselves.... By relying on the courts to do their job for them, they loftily have abandoned the processes of democracy to the ardent right-to-lifers." *Roe v. Wade*, they insisted, "killed off the movement for abortion reform, by making it seem superfluous."[104] It was a sentiment echoed by Barbara Ehrenreich, writing just after a massive march on Washington in 1989, when 300,000 rallied for abortion rights.[105] The odd thing about the march in 1989 is that the protestors were not there to put pressure on the president or Congress – they were there to send a message to the U.S. Supreme Court that was about to hear oral argument in *Webster v. Reproductive Services*,[106] a case challenging a series of restrictions on abortion that had been legislated by the state

---

101 Although it is worth asking just how hard they would have worked for these rights – once reform had been secured for women able to afford private medical care, would they have pressed the case to cover all women? On the other hand, the judicial strategy that, in principle generated a rights-based claim that was open to all regardless of income ultimately hit a wall when the Supreme Court made clear that the right to choose abortion was actually the right not to have the government ban abortions, rather than any sort of affirmative right to actually have an abortion. See *Beal v. Doe* 432 U.S. 438 (1977) and *Maher v. Roe*, 432 U.S. 464 (1977).
102 Barbara Ehrenreich, "Mothers Unite," *New Republic*, July 10, 1989, p 30.
103 *Beal v. Doe*, 432 U.S. 438 (1977); *Maher v. Roe*, 423 U.S. 464 (1977).
104 *The New Republic* editorial, "The Unborn and the Born Again," July 2, 1977, p 5.
105 R.W. Apple Jr., "Justice and the Public," *New York Times*, April 10, 1989, p B6.
106 *Webster v. Reproductive Health Services*, 492 U.S. 490 (1989).

of Missouri. One of the most common complaints at the "mega-march for abortion rights," Ehrenreich wrote, had been "too bad we have to do this all over again." The truth, she added, "is that we had not done 'this' in the first place."[107]

The sentiment that abortion rights advocates had not "done 'this' in the first place" was echoed in a mildly bitter comment by Governor Rockefeller, noted by David Garrow. When Planned Parenthood's president, Alan Guttmacher, came to lobby Rockefeller in 1973 to oppose yet another legislative effort to overturn New York's 1970 abortion reform law, the governor made it clear that his position on this issue was set, but wanted it to be known that he had "felt very lonely" a year earlier when he vetoed a previous attempt at revocation "because there was no public evidence of grass roots support" for his veto.[108] Whereas those favoring abortion rights shifted their focus away from the political realm, those opposed used the abortion rulings to galvanize and consolidate a political movement. Abortion became an important issue that brought evangelical Americans into the political process and into a coalition with the Republican Party.[109]

Abortion: The High Political Cost of Legal Success?

Twenty years after it was handed down, *Brown v. Board of Education* had become so deeply embedded that Supreme Court Justice William Rehnquist went out of his way to distance himself from a memo he had written as a clerk during the Court's consideration of the *Brown* case, laying out the doctrinal framework for a ruling that would uphold segregation. Rehnquist's 1952 memo to Justice Robert Jackson offered a legal argument against *Brown*, concluding that it may be "an unpopular and unhumanitarian position" but the Court's separate-but-equal doctrine articulated in *Plessy v. Ferguson* "was right and should be reaffirmed."[110]

Whether the memo reflected Rehnquist's personal views (he later denied that it did), it certainly was well within the ambit of mainstream legal argument in the early 1950s. But when this memo surfaced during Rehnquist's 1972 confirmation hearings, these views were no longer anywhere near that mainstream. In a letter to Senate Judiciary Committee Chairman James Eastland, Rehnquist stated "unequivocally that I fully support the legal reasoning and the rightness from the standard of fundamental

107 Ehrenreich, "Mothers Unite," p 30.
108 Garrow, *Liberty and Sexuality*, p 578.
109 Saletan, *Bearing Right*.
110 "A Random Thought on the Segregation Cases," a memo from William Rehnquist (clerk) to Justice Robert Jackson. Printed in *New York Times*, Dec. 9, 1971, p 26.

fairness of the *Brown* decision."[111] *Brown* was indeed deeply embedded: Rehnquist's letter of contrition and clarification was addressed to Mississippi Democrat James Eastland, who had once been a bitter and vocal opponent of the *Brown* ruling, telling his constituents at the time *Brown* was decided that "you are not required to obey any court which passes out such a ruling. In fact, you are obligated to defy it."[112]

Twenty years after *Roe*? It was anything but embedded. "At least half a million people" – a crowd, the *New York Times* reported, that was "perhaps the largest ever to march on Washington" up until that day – swept from the White House to the steps of the Capitol Building on April 5, 1992, much as many of them had marched just three years before.[113] Again, they gathered in Washington from across the nation on a bright spring day to influence the votes of the nine members of the U.S. Supreme Court, who were about to hear oral argument in *Planned Parenthood v. Casey*, a case many thought would mark the end of the road for *Roe v. Wade*.[114]

Casey did not, formally, end *Roe*. Those in the majority insisted that "the essential holding of *Roe v. Wade*" was retained and reaffirmed, whereas the dissents made clear they were ready to reverse *Roe* as soon as they could secure a fifth vote. *Roe*, they announced, "was wrongly decided, and it can and should be overruled."[115] Justice Scalia was even more explicit: The *Casey* decision, he wrote, "merely prolongs and intensifies the anguish" of the Court and the nation. "We should get out of this area," Scalia said, "where we have no right to be, and where we do neither ourselves nor the country any good by remaining."[116]

Unlike *Brown*, which came to be unassailable in the nation's law schools, attacking *Roe* helped establish the analytic credentials of many an aspiring law professor and continues to be a law review staple even now, more than thirty years later.[117] *Roe's* failure to embed itself intellectually

111 Letter from William Rehnquist to Senator James Eastland. Printed in *New York Times*, Dec. 9, 1971, p 26.

112 Senator James Eastland, quoted in Klarman, *From Jim Crow to Civil Rights*, p 413.

113 Karen de Witt, "Huge Crowd Backs Right to Abortion in Capital March," *New York Times*, Apr 6, 1992, p A1.

114 And it wasn't the first time they did this. Just three years earlier (nearly to the day), around 300,000 marchers had walked the same route, for the same reason – to influence the U.S. Supreme Court just weeks before oral argument in a critical abortion case many feared would result in a reversal of the Court's *Roe v. Wade* abortion ruling. R.W. Apple Jr., "Justice and the Public," p B6.

115 *Planned Parenthood v. Casey*, 505 U.S. at 944 (Rehnquist, C.J., concurring in part, dissenting in part, joined by White, J., Scalia, J., and Thomas, J.).

116 *Planned Parenthood v. Casey*, 505 U.S. at 1002 (Scalia, J., dissenting).

117 John Hart Ely, "The Wages of Crying Wolf: A Comment on *Roe v. Wade*," 82 *Yale Law Journal* 920 (1973); Michael Stokes Paulsen, "The Worst Constitutional Decision of All Time," 78 *Notre Dame Law Review* 995 (2003); Michael Stokes Paulsen, "Abrogating *Stare Decisis* by Statute: May Congress Remove the Precedential Effect

was more than matched by its failure to embed itself politically or even jurisprudentially within the walls of the Supreme Court itself. In 1989, Justice Blackmun, the author of the Court's opinion in *Roe v. Wade*, wrote that the 1973 ruling in *Roe* and "the fundamental constitutional right of women to decide whether to terminate a pregnancy, survive, but are not secure."[118] Three years later, he was even more resigned to seeing *Roe* reversed. Noting that he was eighty-three years old, Blackmun wrote, "I cannot remain on the Court forever, and when I do step down, the confirmation process for my successor well may focus" on abortion.[119]

Blackmun retired in 1994. With Bill Clinton in the White House and the Senate under Democratic Party control, the fight was deferred for another eleven years, but flared up just as Blackmun predicted when President George W. Bush was forced to withdraw his nomination of Harriet Miers to replace Sandra Day O'Connor, under intense pressure from conservatives in his party, particularly those concerned that Miers might not be a reliable anti-abortion vote.[120] Bush's next two nominees – John Roberts and Samuel Alito – were thought far more dependable on that question. Indeed, within two years of his confirmation, Alito would cast the decisive fifth vote to uphold a law criminalizing a specific late-term abortion procedure in 2007 – the first criminal statute on abortion to survive Court scrutiny since 1972.[121] It was a scenario that Justice Blackmun feared and expected.

Brown and *Roe*. Why the different outcomes? Both were constitutional interpretations, and both spawned decades of litigation and further court rulings. But *Brown* served as a powerful *legislative* as well as judicial precedent. Legislative and judicial precedent were used to open the door for even more dramatic legislation and further judicial rulings that, *together* ultimately changed behavior, public perception, and public acceptance of *Brown's* once-controversial holding.[122] *Brown* was a case of law *together with* politics – the Court did not end segregation, but judicial rulings enforced statutes that had been made politically possible

of *Roe* and *Casey*?", 109 *Yale Law Journal* 1535 (2000); Jack Balkin (ed), *What* Roe v. Wade *Should Have Said*, New York: New York University Press, 2005, among many others.

118 *Webster v. Reproductive Health Services*, 492 U.S. at 538, 560.
119 *Planned Parenthood v. Casey*, 505 U.S. at 943.
120 Todd Purdum, "Potentially, the First Shot in All-Out Ideological War," *New York Times*, November 1, 2005, p 22; Amy Goldstein and Charles Babington, "Miers Once Vowed to Support Ban On Abortion; But Conservatives Still Question Nominee's Views," *Washington Post*, October 19, 2005, p 1.
121 See, for example, *Gonzales v. Carhart*, 550 U.S. ____ (2007), in which the Court upheld a congressional statute criminalizing a particular abortion procedure.
122 Michael Murakami, "Desegregation," in Nathaniel Persily, Jack Citrin, and Patrick J. Egan (eds), *Public Opinion and Constitutional Controversy*, New York: Oxford University Press, 2008 pp 34–8.

in part thanks to *Brown* and its progeny – which, together, brought an end to state-sanctioned segregation.[123]

Two dramatic instances of juridification, but in one case – *Brown* – intransigent resistance to the ruling ultimately lost public respectability. Combined with massive political efforts that culminated in the Civil Rights Act of 1964 and the Voting Rights Act of 1965, *Brown* and its holding are now deeply embedded. In the other case – *Roe* – resistance only grew in the wake of the ruling. Far from energizing legislative efforts, *Roe* seems to have taken the wind out of what limited sails there had been for legislative reform. Rather than using the Court as a sword with which to fight for legislative reform, many abortion rights advocates embraced *Roe* as a judicial shield that would assure women a right to choose abortion. But, more than thirty-five years later, *Roe* and its holding are anything but deeply embedded.

---

123 Michael Klarman notes that *Brown* had a powerful effect, even if it failed to accomplish the objectives set out in the decision itself. *Brown* put racial segregation, and segregation in public schools in particular, on the national agenda, front and center. Klarman, *From Jim Crow to Civil Rights*, p 364.

5 ENVIRONMENTAL REGULATION

A Constructive Pattern

NINE DAYS AFTER RICHARD M. NIXON'S INAUGURATION on a cold, cloudy day in January 1969, an oil well blew off the coast of Southern California, pumping about 200,000 gallons of oil onto the popular beaches of Santa Barbara, killing thousands of birds and fish. Just two months later, sparks from a freight train trundling over an aging trestle in the industrial Flats section of Cleveland set the Cuyahoga River on fire. It was not a large fire. It was not the first time the Cuyahoga had burned, and it was far from the first time flames had leapt from rivers running through America's industrial cities.[1] But the Cuyahoga fire, coming so soon after the oil spill, accelerated what the *New York Times* noted was a rising concern about the "environmental crisis," a crisis that seemed to be "sweeping the nation's campuses with an intensity that may be on its way to eclipsing student discontent over the war in Vietnam."[2] The crisis generated an extraordinary leap-frog of legislation and court rulings, which led to more legislation with ever more reliance on litigation and more legislation that, in turn, guaranteed easier access to the courts for yet more litigation.

There can be no question that America's air and water are cleaner today than they were in 1969.[3] Judges and courts certainly did not effect this change alone, but just as certainly the environment would look dramatically different today had the courts and key federal judges not played critical roles, shaping environmental policy *together with* politicians, interest groups, lobbyists, and lawyers alike. Gerald Rosenberg argues that courts deserve little credit for a cleaner environment, pointing instead to the growth and empowerment of an environmental movement that led

1 Jonathan Adler, "Fables of the Cuyahoga: Reconstructing a History of Environmental Protection," 14 *Fordham Environmental Law Journal* 89 (2002).
2 Gladwin Hill, "Environment May Eclipse Vietnam as College Issue," *New York Times*, Nov. 30, 1969. p 1.
3 Gregg Easterbrook, *A Moment on The Earth: The Coming Age of Environmental Optimism*, New York: Viking, 1995.

to the passage of key legislative initiatives; he insists that "politicians reacted to the power of a political movement, not the command of a court decision."[4] Indeed, Rosenberg is right: There was no single command, ruling, or judicial decision in state or federal courts that brought about this change, but there certainly was enormous activity in those courts, activity reflected in the legislation he applauds. To say the courts were not solely responsible is not the same as saying that courts, judges, and judicial decision making played no role.

If we insist on a simple scorecard with just two choices – did the courts control or not – then indeed we would have to agree court decisions were not the controlling element. But if we look at the courts, not alone or as an adversary, but *together with* Congress, each building on what the other had done, each anticipating what the other might need, each shaping and constraining the direction and scope of the policy, the judicial role appears far more significant. This was a *constructive* process, in the sense that for a twenty-year period starting in 1969, the courts – *together with* legislators, some administrators, lobbyists, litigators, and interest groups – pursued the same general objectives and policy goals. These objectives and goals were shaped and constrained by this iterated process itself, as court decisions framed legislation that triggered judicial interpretation that was reflected in later legislation. Juridification offered great advantages for policy entrepreneurs interested in improving the environment, but these advantages were not without risks and costs. They may well have been worth the risk – but we need to understand how these iterative processes work, both when they function in a *constructive* pattern – as they appear to have done with the environment (explored in this chapter) – or a *deconstructive* pattern, illustrated by campaign finance reform, which is examined in the next chapter.

There have been two related, but distinctly different environmental movements in the United States. The first, the conservation movement, fought to protect natural resources that were already owned by the federal government. Its objective was to tell government what it could and could not do with the land that it held in trust for the nation. This movement produced legislation "favoring governmental retention, conservation and, increasingly, preservation of natural resources as part of the nation's heritage" ranging from national parks legislation in 1916 to the Wilderness Act of 1964.[5] The second environmental movement was quite different and was very much a product of its time. Coming on the heels of the civil rights movement and born as the struggle over the Vietnam War was

---

4 Gerald Rosenberg, *The Hollow Hope: Can Courts Bring about Social Change?*, Chicago: University of Chicago Press, 1991, p 292.
5 Richard Lazarus, *The Making of Environmental Law*, Chicago: University of Chicago Press, 2004, p 49.

accelerating, the newer movement no longer was content to focus solely on the conservation of existing government lands, but rather sought to "regulate private activities that adversely affect public health and welfare."[6] To achieve that aim would require regulating what private business and even private landowners could do on and with their property because those private choices were increasingly understood to have unavoidable consequences for the air and water, flora and fauna far beyond their property lines. The 1962 publication of biologist Rachel Carson's best seller, *Silent Spring*, helped expand the popular reach of this movement, sparking an intense battle over the use of pesticides. Three years later, a federal court in New York made an important move in what would be a decades-long pattern of courts working *together with* legislators and administrators, opening a new path for those seeking changes in the nation's environmental policy.

The 1965 case in New York stemmed from efforts by a conservationist group, the Scenic Hudson Preservation Conference, to stop a government agency – the Federal Power Commission – from approving a license to build a massive hydroelectric project on Storm King Mountain, beside the Hudson River in Cornwall, New York. Scenic Hudson's arguments about the beauty of the Hudson River and the environmental risk posed by this project were profound, but those alone were not enough to secure their day in court. For that, the group first had to establish that it had standing to bring this case, that it had a sufficient, particularized interest to allow the federal courts, under the Constitution's case and controversy clause, to decide the legal issue in question.

One potential obstacle was a 1923 case (*Frothingham v. Mellon*) in which the Supreme Court had made it very difficult for individuals to meet this burden. To get their day in court, an individual would have to show that he or she "has sustained or is immediately in danger of sustaining some direct injury as the result" of the enforcement of the statute or ruling, "and not merely that he suffers in some indefinite way in common with people generally."[7] This standard, Justice William O. Douglas would later insist, would mean that the Constitution was "not adequate to protect the individual against the growing bureaucracy in the Legislative and Executive Branches." The individual, in these circumstances, was "almost certain to be plowed under, unless he has a well-organized active political group to speak for him." And if a powerful political sponsor is lacking? Then, Douglas said, under this doctrine "individual liberty withers."[8]

Article III of the Constitution allows Congress to expand (or contract) standing by statute – but the Court has also developed its own rules

---

6 Lazarus, *The Making of Environmental Law*, p 50.
7 *Frothingham v. Mellon*, 262 U.S. 447, 488 (1923) (Sutherland, J.).
8 *Flast v. Cohen*, 392 U.S. 82, 111 (1968) (Douglas, J., concurring).

and interpretations of standing. If Congress could not be relied on to pave the way to court, Justice Douglas argued that the courts ought to independently give individuals the authority to bring suits in the public interest, in effect, to serve as "private attorneys general." Douglas said it was folly to wait for Congress "to give its blessing to" this sort of expansion of the standing to sue. To wait for Congress in this way, he insisted, "is to allow important constitutional questions to go undecided and personal liberty unprotected."[9]

The law that established the Federal Power Commission states that any party that is "aggrieved by an order issued by the Commission" was entitled to "obtain a review of such order in the United States Court of Appeals."[10] This meant that the key issue would be determining what exactly was required to show that a party was "aggrieved." Would the party have to make a "claim of personal economic injury resulting from the Commission's action," as the FPC argued?[11] The appeals court said it did not. All that was needed, the court ruled, was a showing of "a direct personal interest." In this case, the court noted, the law itself required the FPC to serve the "aesthetic, conservational, and recreational aspects of power development," giving those bringing the case a clear individual interest.[12] The courthouse doors were open.

Once inside, however, things were less promising. Scenic Hudson might have standing to sue, but would the court consider reversing the Commission's decision? Scenic Hudson could argue no more than that the FPC had failed to follow its own rules or had not followed the proper procedures in reaching its conclusions. It could not challenge the substantive conclusions themselves. The court would "decide whether the Commission has correctly discharged its duties," including making sure "that the record is complete." The court would be willing to decide whether the FPC had executed its "affirmative duty to inquire into and consider all relevant facts."[13] Although the court could and would order the Federal Power Commission to "include as a basic concern the preservation of natural beauty," keeping in mind that "the cost of a project is only one of several factors to be considered," the final decision, if reached through the proper process, would be left to the FPC.[14] "This court," the judges ruled, "cannot and should not attempt to substitute its judgment for that

9 *Flast v. Cohen*, 392 U.S. at 112 (Douglas, J., concurring). A more developed consideration of the significance of standing in policy litigation can be found in Karen Orren, "Standing to Sue: Group Conflict in the Federal Courts," 70 *American Political Science Review* 723 (1976).
10 16 U.S.C. § 825l(b).
11 *Scenic Hudson Preservation Conf. v. Federal Power Commission*, 354 F.2d 608, 615 (1965).
12 *Scenic Hudson v. FPC*, 354 F.2d at 615.
13 *Scenic Hudson v. FPC*, 354 F.2d at 612.
14 *Scenic Hudson v. FPC*, 354 F.2d at 624.

of the Commission."[15] The courthouse doors were open to environmental interest groups, but achieving substantive policy objectives would require more than litigation. Scenic Hudson won a crucial battle, but it had not won the war.

Six years later, the war looked very different. The Cuyahoga had burned, Santa Barbara had been despoiled, millions had gathered to mark the first Earth Day,[16] and the White House was paying attention, eager to seize an issue that might otherwise have redounded to the benefit of Edmund Muskie, Nixon's most likely Democratic challenger in the next election. The twin environmental crises in California and Ohio offered the newly inaugurated and politically astute Richard Nixon a chance to work with young protestors instead of against them. Unlike the war in Vietnam, which was "physically remote" and would "be liquidated in due course," the *New York Times* reported, the "deterioration of the nation's 'quality of life' is a pervasive, here-and-now, long-term problem that students of all political shadings can sink their teeth and energies into. And they are doing it." Here was a protest movement with a conservative "aura," one with "coats and ties as conspicuous as beards and blue jeans."[17] Even Keith Lampe, one of the co-founders of the Yippie movement, saw "a role for everybody in ecology"; it was a movement, Lampe said, in which people "with widely different styles and politics can talk to each other with no more tension than a Presbyterian talks with a Methodist."[18]

Within a week of the oil spill in Santa Barbara, Maine's Democratic Senator Edmund Muskie who, the *New York Times* reported, "has been making laconic Yankee President noises of late" presided over Senate hearings on the oil crisis.[19] Nixon rushed to stake his claim to the environmental movement, loath to cede the issue to the Democrats and particularly to Muskie. Nixon quickly embraced the National Environmental Protection Act (NEPA), signing it into law on January 1, 1970; endorsed the creation of the Environmental Protection Agency; and signed off on the Clean Air Act Amendments of 1970 that authorized private citizens to sue state agencies and the federal government in federal court for not adhering to its various action-forcing provisions.[20]

The first of Nixon's actions was signing NEPA into law, a bill that flew through the House after being approved on a voice vote: House debate on

15 *Scenic Hudson v. FPC*, 354 F.2d at 612.
16 April 20, 1970.
17 Hill, "Environment May Eclipse Vietnam," p 1.
18 Hill, "Environment May Eclipse Vietnam," p 1.
19 Warren Weaver, "Pollution: The Oil Threat to the Beaches," *New York Times*, Feb. 9, 1969, p E2.
20 See Robert A. Kagan, *Adversarial Legalism: The American Way of Law*, Cambridge: Harvard University Press, 2001, pp 46–8, 193–4 and 221–4.

the conference report was brief, taking up just "six pages in the *Congressional Record.*"[21] And no wonder – on its face, the legislation provided a good opportunity for environmentalists to claim credit with their supporters without actually requiring very much from recalcitrant agencies save another stack of reports to add to their blizzard of paperwork.

NEPA provided a broad declaration of policy objectives, stating that the federal government was to use "all practicable means and measures" to "create and maintain conditions under which man and nature can exist in harmony." To do that, the government would undertake to "use all practicable means, consistent with other essential considerations of national policy," to fulfill its responsibilities as "trustee of the environment." Agencies were now required to consider health, productivity, aesthetics, and cultural heritage in their decisions. But how? The only concrete requirements in NEPA were in Section 102 in which Congress ordered "all agencies of the Federal Government" to develop methods that would "insure that presently unquantified environmental amenities and values may be given appropriate consideration in decision making along with economic and technical considerations." Section 102 also required every government agency that proposed legislation or federal actions that might "significantly" affect the "quality of the human environment" to include "a detailed statement" on the "environmental impact of the proposed action" and the "alternatives to the proposed action." Finally, Section 102 required federal officials to "consult and obtain the comments" of other relevant agencies. And that was about it. The government was on record that the environment mattered – though not precisely how much. All that NEPA required was that an environmental impact report be attached to each new project proposal.

Although it had few concrete requirements, NEPA did make clear that the national government – president and Congress together – sought to give environmental concerns a higher priority. The legislative record on NEPA was fairly thin and rather ambiguous – an ambiguity that would generate an invitation for the next players in this game: interest groups (who now had greater access to the courts in environmental matters) and the judges who might hear those cases.[22] D.C. Circuit Court of Appeals Judge J. Skelly Wright was eager to accept the invitation. It remains to be seen, Judge Wright noted, "whether the promise of this legislation will become a reality. Therein lies the judicial role." The courts, he wrote,

21 Richard A. Liroff, *A National Policy for the Environment: NEPA and its Aftermath*, Bloomington: Indiana University Press, 1976, p 10, 30.
22 NEPA did not make clear that any private citizen or environmental group could sue an agency for not preparing an environmental impact statement or for preparing an inadequate one. And this certainly is not absolutely necessary – in fact, as Robert Kagan makes clear, many countries today have environmental impact statement requirements but they are not justiciable. See Kagan, *Adversarial Legalism*, p 221.

have a duty "to see that important legislative purposes, heralded in the halls of Congress, are not lost or misdirected in the vast hallways of the federal bureaucracy."[23]

Wright's 1971 ruling took the next step in this iterated, constructive process, building on the expanded standing opportunities heralded by *Flast v. Cohen* and extended to environmental groups in *Scenic Hudson*.[24] In *Calvert Cliffs Coordinating Committee v. U.S. Atomic Energy Commission*, Wright put some substantive teeth into the procedural developments that preceded him. Although Judge Wright acknowledged that NEPA "may not require particular substantive results," he found in its procedures a strict requirement that all federal agencies take the environmental impact statement requirements seriously. "These provisions are not highly flexible," he wrote. "Indeed, they establish a strict standard of compliance."[25] NEPA, he argued, "was meant to do more than regulate the flow of papers in the federal bureaucracy." The requirement for an impact statement "must not be read so narrowly as to make [it] ludicrous."[26] Expanded standing, along with signals that the courts would not necessarily accept just any impact statement an agency chose to attach, provided litigators with another signal that the courts could, at a minimum, significantly slow projects that raised environmental concerns – and in many cases slowing these projects was the next best thing to stopping them.[27]

Judge Wright knew full well that his expansive reading of the ambiguous requirements of the NEPA statute might be paving a major new pathway for public policy. "These cases," he wrote in the opening line of his majority opinion in *Calvert Cliffs Coordinating Committee v. U.S. Atomic Energy Commission*, "are only the beginning of what promises to become a flood of new litigation – litigation seeking judicial assistance in protecting our natural environment."[28]

---

23 *Calvert Cliffs Coordinating Committee v. U.S. Atomic Energy Commission*, 449 F.2d 1109, 1111 (1971).
24 In *Flast v. Cohen*, 392 U.S. 83 (1968), the Court authorized taxpayers to sue the government when there was an allegation that government spending was in violation of the prohibitions of the establishment clause of the First Amendment (see below).
25 *Calvert Cliffs v. U.S. Atomic Energy Commission*, 449 F.2d at 1112.
26 *Calvert Cliffs v. U.S. Atomic Energy Commission*, 449 F.2d at 1117.
27 Serge Taylor offers a great deal of evidence that the demand for environmental impact statements made some incremental improvements in the degree to which agencies actually thought about and paid attention to environmental concerns. In *Making Bureaucracies Think: The Environmental Impact Statement Strategy of Administrative Reform* (Stanford: Stanford University Press, 1984), Taylor argues that the requirement forced agencies to employ scientists and some of the methods of science inside their agencies, and these practices and practitioners had some effects on pressing agencies to take environmental concerns into account. The impact was limited, but to the degree it succeeded, it also had a lot to do with the dual pressure from the inside, reinforced by external pressures brought by interest groups that could litigate and demand more and better impact statements.
28 *Calvert Cliffs v. U.S. Atomic Energy Commission*, 449 F.2d at 1111.

Scenic Hudson extended standing to environmental interest groups, and now *Calvert Hills* made clear that courts might insist on more than simple procedural paper pushing, demanding that agencies perform an in-depth analysis of environmental risks and alternatives, forcing them to justify their decisions with hard data. Judge Wright certainly had made a jump – but not nearly as dramatic a jump as one might imagine. Not because there were other judicial cases on which Wright built, but because there was another, related statute that had passed through Congress and been signed by the president in the interim – the Clean Air Amendments of 1970. Signed into law less than four months before oral argument in the *Calvert Cliffs* case, the Clean Air Act was far more explicit than NEPA. The Clean Air Act authorized "any citizen" to bring suit in federal district courts to force the Environmental Protection Agency to perform its duties – duties spelled out in the legislation. And to put some real muscle into this enforcement provision, the law encouraged these suits by authorizing courts to award attorneys' fees to the plaintiff.[29]

The idea of empowering "private attorneys general" was hardly new in 1970. As the administrative state grew, as Congress delegated more power and discretion to federal agencies, the need to patrol these agencies grew as well. One answer that emerged was the possibility of allowing individual citizens to bring suits against government agencies that were failing to perform their functions or were overstepping their bounds. Although the Supreme Court had, since 1923, maintained that simply paying taxes did not give individual citizens standing to bring suit against the government, the Court has long allowed Congress to authorize private parties to bring suits as a means of enforcing statutes (something Congress *may* do).[30] In 1943, a circuit court held that equity courts "may, and frequently do, go much further both to give and withhold relief in furtherance of the public interest than they are accustomed to go when only private interests are involved."[31] Constitutionally, the circuit court said, there was no barrier "prohibiting Congress from empowering any person" to bring suit against officials allegedly acting in violation of their statutory powers, even where the "sole purpose is to vindicate the public interest. Such persons, so authorized, are, so to speak, private Attorneys General."[32]

---

29 Richard B. Stewart, "The Development of Administrative and Quasi-Constitutional Law in Judicial Review of Environmental Decisionmaking: Lessons from the Clean Air Act," 62 *Iowa Law Review* 713, 724 (1977).

30 In *Frothingham v. Melon*, 262 U.S. 447 (1923), the Court ruled that taxpayers do not have standing to bring suits over federal spending programs simply because they pay taxes. In 1968, however, the Court ruled that when there was an explicit constitutional prohibition that might concern the expenditure of federal funds (such as the establishment clause of the First Amendment), paying taxes might be enough to allow a citizen's suit to be heard. *Flast v. Cohen*, 392 U.S. at 111.

31 *Associated Industries of New York State v. Ickes*, 134 F.2d 694, 703 (1943) citing *Virginian Railway. Co. v. System Federation*, 300 U.S. 515, 522 (1937).

32 *Associated Industries v. Ickes*, 134 F.2d at 703, cited and discussed in Liroff, *A National Policy for the Environment*, p 145, 252 (fn 5).

Judge Jerome Frank, who wrote the 1943 circuit court opinion assuring standing for "private attorneys general," was interpreting a provision in the Bituminous Coal Act of 1937 that authorized suits by "any person aggrieved by an order issued by the [Coal Commission] in a proceeding in which such a person is a party."[33] His conception of a private attorney general using the courts to vindicate the public interest was an attempt to put flesh on the bones of just what constituted an "aggrieved" person who is an appropriate party to this sort of proceeding. The courts slowly developed this concept, and Congress happily added similar provisions to various statutes.

The phrase "private attorneys general" is a notoriously slippery term. In 1998, Jeremy Rabkin noted, "It is revealing that there is still no legal definition, nor any well-established pattern of usage, which precisely identifies a litigant as a private attorney general."[34] But although its meaning remains elusive, William Rubenstein writes, the fact that it is "employed so frequently suggests its utility as a concept." Rubinstein notes that the concept slipped into the Supreme Court reports in 1942, in a dissenting opinion by Justice William O. Douglas, who indicated a cautious acceptance of this new concept. Douglas noted that, though he had earlier expressed "concern" with the "constitutionality of a statutory scheme which allowed one who showed no invasion of a private right to call on the courts to review" an administrative ruling,[35] he was now of the opinion that if the Court were to "accept as constitutionally valid a system of judicial review invoked by a private person who has no individual substantive right to protect, but who has standing only as a representative of the public interest," then the Court must be "exceedingly scrupulous to see to it that his interest in the matter is substantial and immediate." In a footnote, Douglas cited the Jerome Frank opinion and its use of the phrase "private attorneys general" to capture this function.[36]

The phrase turns up a few times in the 1940s, but appears with greater frequency after 1968, when Justice Douglas used the phrase again in his concurrence in *Flast v. Cohen*, in which the Court ruled in favor of a group of taxpayers led by Florence Flast, who sued to stop the government from providing textbooks for parochial schools. Flast argued that this action violated the First Amendment's prohibition of an establishment of religion. The Supreme Court case, however, turned on the question of

33 William B. Rubenstein, "On What a 'Private Attorney General' Is – And Why it Matters," 57 *Vanderbilt Law Review* 2129, 2134 (2004).
34 Jeremy Rabkin, "The Secret Life of the Private Attorney General," 61 *Law & Contemporary Problems* 179, 194–195 (1998). See as well Rubenstein, "On What a Private Attorney General Is."
35 *Scripps-Howard Radio, Inc. v. Federal Communications Commission*, 316 U. S. 4, 20–21 (1942).
36 *FCC v. National Broadcasting Corporation*, 319 U.S. 239, 265 (1943).

standing – could taxpayers sue the government? In an 8–1 decision, the Court said yes, although it set some clear requirements that had to be met.[37]

Taxpayer suits certainly contributed to the growing frequency with which the phrase "private attorneys general" was used in the 1970s: Appearing just 7 times in American legal cases in the 1940s, it was mentioned 56 times in the 1960s, and then turned up everywhere – showing up 705 times in case law in the 1970s.[38] However, although the phrase became common, its meaning was never perfectly clear. In some legal arenas, such as civil rights law, the idea was to use fee-shifting provisions to encourage individual victims to bring suit. Although broad public interests could be advanced, they would be incidental to the individual claim. In other cases – including many environmental laws and regulations – private attorneys general were authorized to serve as a supplemental means of enforcement. In these cases, the primary objective would be to serve the broader public interest. But even in these cases – thanks to Supreme Court doctrine and rules – these attorneys still must show that they are in court to demand redress for a particular client's actual interests and not purely to advance a public goal.[39] This means that the Court's willingness to raise (or lower) the threshold of what would and what would not meet the standing requirement could be critical.[40]

As long as the courts were working *together with* Congress, liberal private attorneys general provisions, along with fee shifting, certainly made the judicial path to policy goals appear quite attractive. Going along this path could even be more efficient, particularly in the face of an administration that was not eager to enforce restrictive statutes. As Michael McCann notes, "Liberal judicial interpretations of standing as well as of statutory rights to direct participation have enabled the reformers to initiate litigation challenging agency action on the vague provisions of the NEPA, FOIA, OSHA, Clean Air Act, Water Pollution Control Act, and other statutory programs to a degree never before paralleled."[41]

---

37 *Flast v. Cohen.*
38 Rubenstein, "On What a "Private Attorney General' Is," p 2135 (fn 32), who notes that the terms appears 949 times in the case law in the 1980s and 1,035 times in the case law of the 1990s. Much of that growth came thanks to a number of civil rights provisions, in which the phrase, "private attorney general" often appeared.
39 Rubenstein, "On What a "Private Attorney General' Is," p 2156.
40 Indeed, in *Lujan v. Defenders of Wildlife*, 504 U.S. 555, 560 (1992), the Court insisted that there was a need to demonstrate that the plaintiff has suffered an "injury in fact," calling this an "irreducible constitutional minimum of standing." See Pamela Karlan, "Disarming the Private Attorney General," 2003 *University of Illinois Law Review* 183 (2003), who argues that the Court's has significantly tightened the standing requirement making it far more difficult to pursue litigation as a private attorney general, and Cass Sunstein, "What's Standing after *Lujan*? Of Citizen Suits, 'Injuries' and Article III," 91 *Michigan Law Review* 163 (1992).
41 Michael McCann, *Taking Reform Seriously: Perspectives on Public Interest Liberalism*, Ithaca: Cornell University Press, 1986, p 64.

Section 304 of the 1970 amendments to the Clean Air Act authorized suits by "any citizen" to force compliance with the mandatory duties laid out by the law. To encourage these actions, Section 304 also authorized the courts to award attorneys' fees to those who brought these actions. A few members of Congress, like Senator Roman Hruska, a Republican from Nebraska, did insist that this provision was "predicated on the erroneous assumption that officials of the Executive Branch of the United States Government will not perform and carry out their responsibilities under the Clean Air Act."[42] But most in the Senate, on both sides of the aisle, understood these provisions to be a supplement, a way to protect the new agency from being captured by the industry it was supposed to regulate, or a way to help supervise an enormous volume of regulations without actually having to expand the staff of administrative agencies.

In a "truly extraordinary surge of activity," Robert Kagan writes, Congress "passed twenty-five major environmental and civil rights acts" between 1964 and 1977. Yet, at the same time, "Congress was reluctant – for political, fiscal and constitutional reasons – to create huge federal bureaucracies" to enforce these regulations. Legislators, therefore, assigned enforcement to state and local government, but to make sure these regulations actually were enforced, they wrote these statutes in ways that would encourage and authorize private attorneys general to take up the enforcement fight in courts.[43]

Despite President Nixon's early reputation "as a strong supporter of environmental protection," his interest was "surprisingly short-lived." Early in 1971, "Nixon began to change course," becoming increasingly annoyed with his inability to gain political advantage from his embrace of environmentalism. This changing attitude in the White House actually made the role of the courts all that much more important for environmentalists. What had been included initially as a means of keeping new agencies and bureaucrats from being captured by the industry they regulated became a vital weapon to battle an administration increasingly committed to trimming back on environmental protection. Instead of being a supplement to a political strategy, litigation rapidly became central to the effort.[44]

---

42 U.S. Senate Committee on Public Works; "A Legislative History of the Clean Air Amendments of 1970." 93d Congress, 2d Session, Serial no. 93–18, Volume 1, January 1974, p 277.
43 Kagan, *Adversarial Legalism*, p 47.
44 In other contexts, Tom Ginsburg and Ran Hirschl have developed arguments that politicians will empower courts as they are slipping from power – or fear the loss of power. Ginsburg talks of "political insurance," whereas Hirschl refers to this as "hegemonic protection." See: Tom Ginsburg, *Judicial Review in New Democracies: Constitutional Courts in Asian Cases*, New York: Cambridge University Press, 2003, and Ran Hirschl, *Towards Juristocracy: The Origins and Consequences of the New Constitutionalism*, Cambridge, MA: Harvard University Press, 2004.

The White House tried to use its budgetary authority to limit the reach and scope of environmental regulation, trying to make sure that the Environmental Protection Agency and other agencies – staffed as they were by people with strong environmental interests – would respond to White House orders. To do that, "Nixon strengthened the Office of Management and Budget and selected sub-cabinet officials on the basis of ideological consistency with the administration." The goal was clear: "to ensure that the bureaucracy would take its orders from the White House, not congressional subcommittees." Congress fought back, becoming more and more "inclined to encourage litigation," adding explicit authorization for "suits by private parties to enforce regulatory requirements" and expand and ease standing requirements in environmental laws, not only to avoid the expense and challenges of building up an administrative apparatus, but also as an end run around an administrative apparatus that was increasingly deployed against them.[45]

The branches were working *together with* each other in a basically constructive manner: Congress was adding more detailed and prescriptive provisions in statutes like the Clean Air Act and the Clean Water Act, thereby making it easier for litigants and judges alike to build substantive outcomes out of procedural requirements.[46] Judge Wright's *Calvert Cliffs* decision was the boldest statement on this subject in 1971, but it was not the only one that year. Six months before Wright handed down his decision, his D.C. Circuit Court of Appeals colleague David Bazelon announced that the nation was standing on "the threshold of a new era in the history of the long and fruitful collaboration of administrative agencies and reviewing courts." And although traditionally courts had "treated administrative policy decisions with great deference," they had done so at a time when these decisions focused on "the economic interests at stake in a ratemaking or licensing proceeding." The new environmental regulations, in contrast, touch on "fundamental personal interests in life, health and liberty," Bazelon wrote. Interests that "have always had a special claim to judicial protection," he added, may require more than simple "strict judicial scrutiny of administrative action"[47] particularly at a time when "the character of administrative litigation is changing" – a change he attributed in part to *Scenic Hudson*, decided six years earlier. "As a result of expanding doctrines of standing and reviewability" and

45 R. Shep Melnick, *Between the Lines: Interpreting Welfare Rights*, Washington, DC: Brookings Institution Press, 1994, p 34. "The Voting Rights Act, the Endangered Species Act, the Clean Air Act, the Federal Water Pollution Control Act and the Futures Trading Act all explicitly authorize suits by private parties.... The Toxic Substances Control Act, the Consumer Product Safety Act and the Occupational Safety and Health Act create liberal standing requirements for those challenging agency rules."

46 Robert Kagan offers a number of examples that illustrate this in *Adversarial Legalism*, Chapters 3 and 10.

47 *Environmental Defense Fund v. Ruckelshaus*, 439 F.2d 584, 596–9 (D.C. Cir. 1971).

new statutory causes of action, he added, "courts are increasingly asked to review administrative action that touches on fundamental personal interests in life, health, and liberty."[48]

In March 1971, in a case concerning plans to build a new highway (*Citizens to Preserve Overton Park v. Volpe*), the U.S. Supreme Court noted that it was "not empowered to substitute its judgment for that of the agency." However, in that same opinion, the High Court also insisted that federal courts could, would, and should enforce strict procedural requirements and standards, making it that much easier for courts to reverse agency policy decisions.[49] Four months later, Judge Wright's *Calvert Cliffs* opinion did just that, skillfully acknowledging and endorsing a distinction between the administrative flexibility that was necessary in reaching substantive conclusions in these cases and the procedural requirements that, he ruled, "are not highly flexible." These requirements and standards "establish a strict standard of compliance." But then, the rest of his opinion "proceeded to blur the very line he had created."[50]

Despite the degree to which Wright and a number of other judges blurred the line between process and substance, they agreed that the line was there, that it was distinct, and that it was to be maintained. And although it did not seem to matter a great deal in the early years, this line – which no one denied – most certainly would make a difference later. Because law is different, because precedent shapes and constrains decisions even when it does not determine their outcomes, this line should have been the subject of close attention. But, for litigators, policy entrepreneurs, and politicians interested in the most direct, most efficient means to their short-term policy ends, these caveats were easy to ignore.

Citizen suits and an active role for the courts may initially have served to protect against agency capture by those the law sought to regulate, but as the Nixon administration lost its enthusiasm for environmental regulation and, more important, as the power struggle between the White House and Congress escalated, these provisions became weapons in a very different struggle. Those who favored environmental regulation well understood that citizen suits and liberal standing rules were effective tools to protect their legislation. "One way to force administrators to execute laws faithfully is to allow public interest groups to sue them when they do not. Thus, when the Nixon administration tried to remove the 'citizen suit' provision from the Clean Air Act, it met defeat after bitter partisan

---

48 *Environmental Defense Fund v. Ruckelshaus*, 439 F.2d at 598, citing *Scenic Hudson v. FPC.*
49 *Citizens to Preserve Overton Park v Volpe*, 401 U.S. 402, 416–17 (1971).
50 David Trubeck, "Environmental Defense I: Introduction to Interest Group Advocacy in Complex Disputes," in Burton Weisbrod, Joel Handler and Neil Komesar (eds), *Public Interest Law: An Economic and Institutional Analysis*, Berkeley: University of California Press, 1978, p 172.

debate."[51] Though citizen suits initially were seen "as a way to speed up enforcement of the Act," disputes between the White House and Congress turned these provisions "into a mechanism not for facilitating enforcement, but for forcing the EPA to institute new programs."[52] They were transformed from tools to tell government what it could and could not do into tools to force the government to act, to tell the government what it *must* do. The expectation was that sweeping environmental statutes would give agencies such as the Environmental Protection Agency (EPA) not only broad authority, but *together with* the courts, it might force the EPA to use that authority in ways that would advance the broader legislative agenda on the environment, even in the face of White House opposition.

Nixon's divorce from the environmental movement became official in the wake of the 1972 elections. Environmental regulation takes a long time to produce tangible results – too long to make much of a difference in the elections that mattered to Nixon. Moreover, despite his administration's supportive role in creating the EPA and in passing critical legislation such as NEPA and the Clean Air Act, voters who did care about the environment tended to vote Democratic for other reasons. At the same time, Nixon's frustrations dealing with a Congress controlled by Democrats began to be expressed in more and more aggressive refusals to spend money that Democrats appropriated for programs Nixon wanted to cut.[53] Nixon's response was to announce that he had the executive authority to "impound" those funds – to order his agencies and officers to simply refuse to spend the funds appropriated for them. This tactic extended to the environmental realm. "By 1974, Nixon had become one of environmental law's harshest critics. He advised his cabinet to "[g]et off the environmental kick."[54]

Nixon's resignation in August 1974 did nothing to end this executive-legislative struggle. When the Clean Air Act came up for significant revision in the summer of 1977, Congress relied on expansive court rulings and decisions to support arguments for even greater reliance on courts and judicial decision making, expanding standing and providing ever more provisions to enhance access to the courts for citizen suits. In its

51 R. Shep Melnick, *Regulation and the Courts: The Case of the Clean Air Act*, Washington, DC: Brookings Institution Press, 1983, p 8.
52 Melnick, *Regulation and the Courts*, p 57.
53 Of course, Nixon hardly limited his impoundments or his refusal to comply with congressional mandates exclusively to the environmental arena. By the summer of 1974, his impoundments so infuriated Congress that both Houses voted to override Nixon's veto and pass the Budget Control and Impoundment Act of July 12, 1974, in an effort to end them. This struggle is discussed in greater detail in Chapter 7.
54 Lazarus, *The Making of Environmental Law*, p 78, citing J. Brooks Flippen, *Nixon and the Environment*, Albuquerque: University of New Mexico Press, 2000, p 214, as the source of the Nixon quote.

report on the 1977 legislation, the House Commerce Committee "paraphrased the *Overton Park* opinion to explain the role it envisioned for judicial review under the Clean Air Act." The committee report said that the law was intended to "endorse the court's practice of engaging in searching review without substituting their judgment for that of the Administrator and *to assure that no retreat to a less searching approach take place.*"[55]

Congress, Shep Melnick reports, authorized three different types of suits in 1977: "challenges to EPA rules and regulations; citizen suits seeking the performance of nondiscretionary duties by the EPA; and enforcement suits against polluters." In addition, the 1977 Clean Air Act provided "greater specificity to these judicial review provisions, incorporating into the act major court rulings issued between 1971 and 1976."[56] This was a case of courts building on Congress and Congress in turn building on judicial rulings. Congress had turned to the courts in 1972 primarily to speed regulation and to avoid agency capture. Since then, the growing struggle with the White House and the apparently supportive, even enthusiastic embrace that environmental legislation had received from the federal courts suggested that, although they had lost the White House, legislators could fall back on the courts to accomplish what had become politically more difficult. Rather than investing in costly and increasingly unpromising political battles, policy advocates put their faith – and effort – into ever greater reliance on the courts.

The belief that the courts would serve as a substitute for the political process was predicated on another assumption: that the courts would continue to work in a constructive sense with the legislature – or, even if the legislature should go the way of the White House and become unsympathetic to environmentalists, the courts might just be able *and willing* to soldier on indefinitely. These, it turns out, were not good assumptions.[57]

Shifts in interpretation began to appear in Supreme Court rulings in the late 1970s, in which the Justices returned to the task of defining and enforcing the line between process and substance that had never been fully erased, eliminating the blur that had been exploited by policy entrepreneurs and facilitated by earlier judicial rulings. The High Court began to focus more explicitly on the text of the statutes, moving away from default assumptions that tended to enforce the implied legislative intent, and it increasingly insisted that courts enforce the letter and not

---

55 Melnick. *Regulation and the Courts*, p 54, quoting from *Clean Air Act Amendments of 1977*, H. Rept. 95-294, 95 Cong. 1st Sess. (1977), p 323 (emphasis added).
56 Melnick, *Regulation and the Courts*, p 55.
57 Some might argue that the use of the courts was an instrumental choice and that legal advocates had carefully built in a number of provisions that, once accepted by the courts, would be very difficult to dislodge or reverse – fortifying the argument advanced in Chapter 3 that precedent matters. See Kagan, *Adversarial Legalism*, pp 215–18.

the presumed spirit of the legislation. The Supreme Court shifted from reading broad substantive goals into procedural requirements to rejecting lower court efforts to impose stricter procedural requirements than those required by the clear text of the statutes. This move was not limited to the environment – it was a shift in interpretation that applied to (and was drawn from) lateral cases and that created precedent that would, in turn, influence, shape, and constrain other lateral areas of doctrine.

The first clear hint of this shift in the environmental realm came in a case challenging the issuing of a license to the Vermont Yankee nuclear plant on the Connecticut River, just north of the Vermont-Massachusetts border. Justice Rehnquist's majority opinion in *Vermont Yankee v. Natural Resources Defense Council* in 1978 rejected procedural barriers that had been erected by the lower courts. The Supreme Court insisted that, although NEPA "does set forth significant substantive goals for the Nation...its mandate to the agencies is essentially procedural."[58] And those procedures are fairly explicit and fairly limited: The "only procedural requirements imposed by NEPA," Rehnquist held, "are those stated in the plain language of the Act."[59] To transform NEPA's substantive goals and limited procedural requirements into a mandate for administrative requirements not included in any of the relevant statutes is something the U.S. Supreme Court no longer was willing to tolerate. NEPA's mandate, Rehnquist wrote, "is to insure a fully informed and well-considered decision, not necessarily a decision the judges of the Court of Appeals or of this Court would have reached had they been members of the decision-making unit of the agency."[60] It was a clear warning to the lower courts, to those who might still be inclined to build on the arguments first articulated by Judge Bazelon or Judge Wright. If Congress wanted to continue to force government action in environmental protection, then Congress would have to write more explicit and more comprehensive standards into its legislation, rather than relying on the courts to work *together with* the legislature.

Vermont Yankee was not unique. In another environmental case, one having nothing to do with nuclear power, the Supreme Court handed down an even more explicit warning that the default assumption that had once favored legislative intent might now have fundamentally shifted. In a decision for a short-handed Court in *Chevron v. Natural Resources Defense Council*, Justice Stevens held that henceforth the Supreme Court would defer to administrative agencies *unless* those agencies were making choices that had been *explicitly* foreclosed by the text of the legislation

---

58 *Vermont Yankee Nuclear Power Corp. v. Natural Resources Defense Council (NRDC)*, 435 U.S. 519, 558 (1978).
59 *Vermont Yankee v. NRDC*, 435 U.S. at 548.
60 *Vermont Yankee v. NRDC*, 435 U.S. at 558.

itself.[61] In short, where before courts had been using a default assumption in favor of what Congress *likely intended* (as the judges understood that intent), now they should assume that an agency's interpretation of a law would be valid unless that interpretation contradicted the clear text of the statute.[62]

In one way, nothing had changed – from the earliest post-New Deal days of the Administrative Procedures Act, the Court had made a clear distinction between substantive discretion (in which the default assumption was to accept an agency's interpretation) and procedural requirements (in which the default was to favor legislative intent). And that still held after *Chevron*. But in another way, much had changed. The environmental cases of the 1970s had suggested that, although agencies would have discretion on substantive choices, that discretion was to be guided by the ambiguous goals and objectives that lay behind the procedural requirements of laws like NEPA. This interpretation had invited legislators, lobbyists, and policy entrepreneurs alike to put more reliance on the courts; it built in more provisions for judicial review, provided more opportunities for citizen suits, and led to looser standing requirements. In the process, they would spend far less time battling the White House directly or using the blunt and less reliable political tools at their disposal.

Now, the Court was signaling an important shift, not in the rules of the game or the game itself, but in the default assumption about how umpires should decide close calls. Where before, the umpire would award a tie to Congress, now a tie would more likely go to the administration. To win, Congress would now need to be clear and specific. It would have to anticipate the loopholes and exceptions that might come up; legislators would have to plug those holes, dot their *i*s, and cross their *t*s, rather than count on judges and private attorneys general to do that for them. If they did not, the administration would be more likely to prevail in court.

Where Congress "has directly spoken to the precise question" in dispute, where "the intent of Congress is clear," the Court held, that would be "the end of the matter; for the Court, as well as the agency, must give effect to the *unambiguously expressed* intent of Congress."[63] And if not?

---

61 *Chevron v. Natural Resources Defense Council*, 467 U.S. 837 (1984). Justices Marshall, Rehnquist and O'Connor did not participate in the 6–0 decision.
62 See Gordon Silverstein, "Statutory Interpretation and the Balance of Institutional Power," 56 *Review of Politics* 3, 475–503 (1994). Robert Kagan notes that the *Chevron* analysis was so complicated that it gave judges on the Courts of Appeals leeway to interpret and apply the doctrine so as to fortify their own policy leanings, leading ultimately to inconsistency. See Frank Cross and Emerson Tiller, "Judicial Partisanship and Obedience to Legal Doctrine: Whistleblowing on the Federal Courts of Appeals," 107 *Yale Law Journal* 2155 (1998); and Peter Schuck and E. Donald Elliott, "To the Chevron Station: An Empirical Study of Federal Administrative Law," 1990 *Duke Law Journal* 984 (1990).
63 *Chevron v. NRDC*, 467 U.S. at 842–3 (emphasis added).

Where Congress is less than "unambiguously" explicit or fails to anticipate a new problem or a new variation on an old problem, then judges
must make a choice: Either they defer to the agency's interpretation, or
a court would have to "impose its own construction" of what the judges
can, at best, only guess was intended by Congress.[64] But that is something
judges "who have no constituency" should not do.[65] Instead, they should
defer to the agency, which ultimately answers to the elected president,
until such time as Congress sees fit to pass a less ambiguous statute.[66]

As Justice Antonin Scalia would write more than a decade after
Chevron (a case decided before he joined the Court), Congress "now
knows that the ambiguities it creates, whether intentionally or unintentionally, will be resolved, within the bounds of permissible interpretation,
not by the courts but by a particular agency, whose policy biases will
ordinarily be known."[67] If that interpretation does violence to what a
majority in Congress would like to see done, well, the answer is simple
enough: They can pass a new statute.[68]

But the answer really is not quite that simple. Congress is a flowing
stream, which new members join from time to time and (occasionally)
incumbents leave. Although it is theoretically easy for Congress to correct
any mistaken deference to administrative interpretations, institutionally,
it can be extraordinarily difficult.[69] For a variety of reasons – the com-
plexity of the American legislative process; the many veto points that can
block legislation because Madison brilliantly set up a system in which it
was hard (not impossible, but very hard) to pass legislation and very easy
to block it; because when Congress and the White House are controlled by
different parties, it takes a simple majority in Congress to hand power to
the president, but thanks to a near-certain veto, it would take 67 percent
to override a veto and get that power back; and more – it is in fact very
difficult for Congress to make these corrections. Changing this default
assumption, then, can profoundly shift the balance of power between
Congress and the executive, particularly in periods of divided control.

---

64 *Chevron v. NRDC*, 467 U.S. at 843.
65 *Chevron v. NRDC*, 467 U.S. at 866–867.
66 It is worth mentioning that this default tells us nothing about whether or not policy
   advocates would benefit under the *Chevron* default – in the environmental case, for
   example, those favoring stricter environmental regulation might embrace this default in
   the event that there was a president in the White House sympathetic to their cause. The
   point here is to understand the risks involved in engaging in *constructive* juridification.
67 Antonin Scalia, "Judicial Deference to Administrative Interpretations of Law," 1989
   Duke Law Journal 511, 517 (1989).
68 This is, of course, not quite what Scalia has said in one of the Court's most recent cases
   dealing with the reach of federal law – see *Rapanos v. United States*, 547 U.S. 715
   (2006).
69 These implications are more fully developed in Silverstein, "Statutory Interpretation and
   the Balance of Institutional Power."

Chevron seemed an object lesson in one of the risks of juridification – at least until 2001, when the Supreme Court significantly softened *Chevron*'s seemingly draconian shift in the default assumption. In an 8–1 decision in *U.S. v. Mead*, the Supreme Court ruled that courts should defer to agency interpretations only "when it appears that Congress delegated authority to the agency generally to make rules carrying the force of law, and that the agency interpretation claiming deference was promulgated in the exercise of that authority." Justice Scalia (offering the lone dissent in this case) was appalled at what he claimed was a stark reversal. "What was previously a general presumption of authority in agencies to resolve ambiguity in the statutes they have been authorized to enforce has been changed to a presumption of no such authority," Scalia insisted, adding that *Mead* "today replaced the *Chevron* doctrine." His brethren, however, sternly and explicitly disagreed, in an opinion joined by all eight of Scalia's fellow Justices (without any separate concurrences). There are, the eight held, a "great variety of ways in which the laws invest the Government's administrative arms with discretion, and with procedures for exercising it, in giving meaning to Acts of Congress." Justice Scalia, the majority states, "would pose the question of deference as an either-or choice." It is, the majority held, "simply implausible that Congress intended such a broad range of statutory authority to produce only two varieties of administrative action, demanding either *Chevron* deference or none at all." The wide range of "statutory variation has led the Court to recognize more than one variety of judicial deference, just as the Court has recognized a variety of indicators that Congress would expect *Chevron* deference."

Mead in no way struck down or reversed *Chevron*, although it did suggest that courts might now insist on clear indications that there was a congressional intent to give wide deference to agency interpretation. This suggestion very well may help legislators who are eager to hold onto legislative priorities and authority, although even this aid is a bit questionable, given how institutionally and politically difficult it is for Congress to be specific and anticipate future developments. But even if *Mead* significantly waters down *Chevron*'s default assumption, it simply reinforces the broader cautionary story of the *Chevron* case: To rely on constructive juridification is risky – for as easily as one Court can build *Chevron*, another can trim it, and yet another can build it back and stronger the next time.[70]

---

70 Note well that this could prove to be a case of two steps forward for every one step backward – *Mead* does not return the Court to its pre-*Chevron* default assumptions. If *Chevron* moved the Court two steps in one direction, and *Mead*, one step back, the Court may well remain one step beyond where it was before *Chevron*. This is also, of course, another demonstration that law and judicial decision making are different. The Court is free to reverse precedent, free to reverse earlier decisions. In this case, there were eight Justices who agreed that the *Chevron* deference principle should not apply as a simple either-or proposition. But they were in no way prepared to reverse or strike it down. The Court will typically go well out of its way to preserve what it can of earlier

Although *Mead* may well remove risk in any effort by Congress to work *together with* the courts, there remain two other great risks to this reliance on juridification to advance environmental (or any other) policy goals. The second risk is posed by the ways in which judicial decision making is different and can skew and shape preferences and priorities as policy bounces from court to legislature to agency and back again. And the third, perhaps most risky of all concerns is this: What happens when the judges, on whom one has relied so heavily, reinterpret what they have said and done in the past or when, as inevitably they must, the judges change and are replaced by new judges appointed by new and different presidents? *Chevron* (and now *Mead*) suggest one way in which these changes can matter – but not the only one.[71]

In 1990, the U.S. Supreme Court also returned to where the whole pattern had begun, revisiting the initial, broad interpretation of NEPA in a case called *Lujan v. National Wildlife Federation*.[72] In this case, the Supreme Court was asked to consider, again, the standing requirements for lawsuits under NEPA. Writing for a narrow 5–4 majority, Justice Scalia held that NEPA has no "private right of action" in its text, and therefore injured parties must rely on the traditional fallback statute, the Administrative Procedures Act (APA). The APA, he said, requires plaintiffs to demonstrate that the government's actions have a direct effect, that the person bringing a suit suffered a legal wrong resulting from the agency's choices.

At first, this ruling seems consistent with the Court's decisions in the 1970s – at no time did the Court ever eliminate the requirement that environmental groups needed to show, as the Court put it in a 1972 decision, that "the party seeking review be himself among the injured."[73] But the difference was that in 1972 the Court was quite willing to turn to NEPA's substantive clauses to expand the sorts of injuries that might constitute the ground for a lawsuit under the APA. "The trend of cases arising under the APA and other statutes authorizing judicial review of federal agency action," the 1972 Court decision held, "has been toward recognizing that injuries other than economic harm are sufficient to bring a person within the meaning of the statutory language, and toward discarding the notion that an injury that is widely shared is *ipso facto* not an injury sufficient

decisions – often in the process damping or trimming, skewing or framing its newer doctrine to allow the Justices to avoid direct reversal. This was the case, for instance when *Flast v. Cohen* appeared to all but reverse *Frothingham v. Melon* – all but, but not, much to the chagrin of Justice Douglas.

71 Only one of the Justices who participated in the *Chevron* decision in 1984 also participated in the *Mead* case in 2004 – and that was Justice Stevens, *Chevron*'s author. The other five – Blackmun, Burger, Brennan, Powell, and White – had all left the Court, two replaced by Bill Clinton and the others replaced by Republican presidents.

72 *Lujan v. National Wildlife Federation*, 497 U.S. 871 (1990).

73 *Sierra Club v. Morton*, 405 U.S. 727, 734–5 (1972).

to provide the basis for judicial review." In its 1972 decision, the Court insisted that one might legitimately suffer injuries to "aesthetic, conservational, and recreational as well as economic values" and that this might be quite sufficient to meet the statute's requirements.[74]

In 1990, however, with a different Court in place, and after nearly twenty years of increasingly conflictual relations between Congress and the White House, the same statute (NEPA) would be read quite differently. In *Lujan v. National Wildlife Federation*, Justice Scalia said that because NEPA authorized no private right of action, plaintiffs would have to rely on the APA – and if they rely on the APA, they would have to show that the agency action complained of affects them directly. But just what might constitute a direct effect? Would it be a simple matter of extrapolating from the legislative intent seemingly embodied in the substantive clauses of NEPA and a host of other environmental legislation (built on a host of judicial rulings) that had passed in the meantime – as the courts had done in the 1970s? No. Not now. In 1990, Justice Scalia rejected signed affidavits from two plaintiffs who claimed that the Bureau of Land Management's plans to allow mining on public lands would threaten their "recreational use and aesthetic enjoyment of federal lands." This claim was no longer enough to constitute a direct injury.[75]

Two years later, Justice Scalia reinforced his narrower interpretation of standing in environmental cases, this time in interpreting a provision of the Endangered Species Act of 1973 that requires federal agencies to "insure that any action authorized, funded or carried out" would not be "likely to jeopardize the continued existence of any endangered species or threatened species or result in the destruction or adverse modification of the habitat of such species."[76] How might one show direct injury in many of these cases, because so many animal species were located in such distant and remote locations?

One answer was to persuade the Court to move away from its *Chevron* deference to agencies and back to its pre-*Chevron* deference to legislative intent as expressed by the objectives embedded in NEPA (and illustrated in cases such as the 1972 *Calvert Cliffs* decision). Not only did *Chevron* and its related cases seem to provide a barrier to this argument, at least in 1992, but the Court's earlier decision in the 1990 *Lujan* case also suggested the futility of this approach. A second option might have been to convince an increasingly skeptical Supreme Court majority to develop or adopt a rather novel and creative interpretation of direct injury. One that was suggested was something called an "animal nexus" in which anyone who has a professional or avocational interest in studying or seeing an

---

74 *Sierra Club v. Morton*, 405 U.S. at 738.
75 *Lujan v. National Wildlife Federation*, 497 U.S. at 886 (1990).
76 *Lujan v. Defenders of Wildlife*, 504 U.S. at 558.

endangered animal would be granted standing.[77] But this and other novel theories, Justice Scalia said in 1992, were "beyond all reason." Standing, he said (quoting an earlier case), is not "an ingenious academic exercise in the conceivable," but, requires "a factual showing of perceptible harm."[78]

This argument, combined with *Chevron*, would suggest the answer would simply be that Congress needs explicitly to authorize far broader criteria for citizen suits. But here Scalia suggested that even this authorization might not be enough. Not any longer. Courts, he insisted, cannot ignore "the concrete injury requirement described in our cases," Scalia ruled, whether they do so "on their own, or at the invitation of Congress."[79] To "permit Congress to convert the undifferentiated public interest in executive officers' compliance with the law into an 'individual right' vindicable in the courts," Scalia wrote, "would enable the courts, with the permission of Congress, 'to assume a position of authority over the governmental acts of another and coequal department,' and to become 'virtually continuing monitors of the wisdom and soundness of Executive action' " – even if Congress wants them to do so. We have, Scalia insisted, "always rejected that vision of our role."[80]

There were some strongly worded dissents in this 5–4 decision. Justice Blackmun argued that the real threat in this case was to Congress – that it would put Congress into an impossible box. "We have long recognized that the non-delegation doctrine does not prevent Congress from seeking assistance, within proper limits, from its coordinate Branches," Justice Blackmun wrote. "The Court's intimation today that procedural injuries are not constitutionally cognizable threatens this understanding upon which Congress has undoubtedly relied."[81]

The *Lujan* cases – both from 1990 and 1992 – have not had the effect of significantly restricting the judicial role in environmental regulation, because there is no shortage of cases in which real people have been able to establish easily that they have suffered real harm. But the *Lujan* cases are a clear signal that there are risks in the juridification of public policy – even in the most *constructive* patterns.

As Robert Kagan notes, in a nation that increasingly "expects and demands comprehensive governmental protections from serious harm, injustice, and environmental dangers" and yet builds government institutions "that reflect mistrust of concentrated power and hence that limit and fragment political and governmental authority,"[82] it should hardly

77 *Lujan v. Defenders of Wildlife*, 504 U.S. at 566.
78 Lujan v. Defenders of Wildlife, 504 U.S. at 566.
79 *Lujan v. Defenders of Wildlife*, 504 U.S. at 576.
80 Lujan v. Defenders of Wildlife, 504 U.S. at 576–7.
81 *Lujan v. Defenders of Wildlife*, 504 U.S. at 604–605 (Blackmun, J., dissenting).
82 Kagan, *Adversarial Legalism*, p 15.

surprise us to see policy advocates turn to the courts and come to rely upon creative and constructive judicial rulings. "The attractions of the judicial forum are obvious," David Trubeck notes. "The judiciary seems to be more neutral than legislative and administrative bodies where (at least in low-visibility disputes) the advantages of organization are substantial. Moreover, the techniques of advocacy in the courts are well understood and, for public interest law firms at least, relatively inexpensive in comparison with legislative or administrative lobbying activities and media campaigns."[83] But it is a strategy with real risks as well.[84]

Environmentalists and members of Congress alike came to rely on the courts, and that was fine as long as the courts were working *together with* them, all moving in roughly the same direction. This reliance is, however, a multi-edged sword. Those who were not enamored of this constructive pattern came to understand that, for their policy preferences to prevail, they would need not only to win the debate over the policy question, but also to secure changes in judicial doctrine or, failing that, to force changes in judicial personnel. New judges, and new doctrine, would, of course, erode the value of juridification. But this is not the only risk. Even if courts could be relied on to remain consistent and constructive partners, never changing, there are risks that "the energies invested in litigation" are energies that might otherwise have been "devoted to direct efforts to increase the political resources available for the environmental cause." There is also the risk that litigation in some cases may discourage direct political action "since it initially looked like the courts would 'take care of things.'" Litigation also tends to force the debate "to concentrate on narrow issues" such as compliance with particular statutes rather than encouraging debate (and persuasion) "on the values and priorities" that are the "real issues at stake."[85]

The environment today is not what it was in 1970.[86] Parents bring their children to play and swim again on the beaches of Santa Barbara; not only are there no fires on the Cuyahoga River, but it is open for fishing and its shores are lined by expensive restaurants and attractive parks; and public health officials no longer have to insist on giving a tetanus shot to anyone who falls into Boston's Charles River.[87] In part these changes have something to do with what Richard Lazarus refers to as the "greening of the nation's economy," as well as a great deal to do with social pressures, education, and public awareness, all of which seem

---

83 Trubeck, "Environmental Defense I," p 215.
84 Trubeck, "Environmental Defense I," p 215.
85 Trubeck, "Environmental Defense I," p 214.
86 Easterbrook, *A Moment on The Earth*.
87 Made infamous in the lyrics of the Standells 1966 hit song, "Dirty Water": " . . . down by the river, down by the banks of the river Charles . . . That's where you'll find me . . . Well I love that dirty water, Oh, Boston, you're my home."

to make it impossible to imagine that anyone could really roll back these reforms.[88] The constructive pattern of juridification in environmental policy may well have played an important role in these changes, but it was not – and is not – a pattern without risks. These may be risks worth taking, but they are risks that need to be fully understood and carefully weighed.

88 Lazarus, *The Making of Environmental Law*, pp 149–65. Neil Gunningham, Robert A. Kagan, and Dorothy Thornton argue that it was, in fact, the complex interaction of regulation and social pressure from community and environmental activists, along with serious economic constraints and internal corporate management, that made the difference, at least for the paper pulp mill operators studied in their book, *Shades of Green: Business, Regulation and Environment*, Stanford: Stanford University Press, 2003.

6   CAMPAIGN FINANCE

A Deconstructive Pattern

COURTS AND CONGRESS, working *together with* each other – each building on the other, and both heading roughly in the same direction – can engage in *constructive* juridification, pushing policy in directions favored by politicians and policy entrepreneurs alike. But when, far from building and fortifying each other's work, judges and legislators intentionally, inadvertently, or unavoidably work at cross-purposes; when the courts pull out bricks laid by Congress or replace them with different bricks, in different patterns; when one side tears down part of the foundation laid by the other, rebuilding on top of what is left, limiting, construing, and misconstruing the actions of the other; the result actually may generate new problems as bad or worse than those that inspired the move to juridify in the first place. Consider campaign finance reform as such an example of what might be called *deconstructive* juridification.

Few would argue that a vibrant democracy can long endure rampant political corruption. Even the mere appearance of corruption can have a corrosive effect, suppressing voter turnout and undermining political claims to legitimacy and authority. This lesson was raw and fresh when Congress set out to debate amendments to the Federal Elections Campaign Act in the shadow of the Watergate scandal in 1974. The legislators produced an extremely complex set of rules, regulations, and bureaucratic and criminal enforcement mechanisms designed to generate transparency and to limit the importance of money – and, therefore, the temptation and even the appearance of political corruption. When the law finally got to the Supreme Court in the midst of the 1976 election campaign, the Justices struck down key parts of the statute. Severing limits on contributions from those on expenditures, and ruling that independent expenditures could not be limited without violating the First Amendment, the Court also held that individuals were free to use their own funds without limitation to support their own campaigns and that the way in which commissioners were named to the Federal Election Commission violated the Constitution's separation of powers. This patchwork ruling led Chief

Justice Burger, in a partial concurrence, to argue that "the Court's result does violence to the intent of Congress in this comprehensive scheme of campaign finance. By dissecting the Act bit by bit, and casting off vital parts, the Court," Burger argued, "fails to recognize that the whole of this Act is greater than the sum of its parts."[1]

In response, rather than challenging the Court's fundamental assertions that money was inherently an aspect of free speech, Congress took the Court's premise as a given and tried to work around it or make adjustments that would be compatible with it – despite the fact that the Court itself was hardly unequivocal about the connection between money and speech.[2] Rather than taking a fresh swing at campaign finance or challenging a divided Court and its complex opinion, many in Congress and the broader public largely internalized the Court's ruling, accepting its patchwork rulings as the new baseline, the new foundation on which any effort at regulation would have to be built. By 2001, when Senators John McCain and Russ Feingold sponsored another attempt at comprehensive campaign finance reform, they accepted the Court's framework as a given. The question no longer was, "Is money speech?" Instead, the starting point was more like this: "*Given* that money is speech, when and why is it acceptable to restrict and regulate that speech?"

Each iteration of this process moved the participants into an ever narrower corner of the *Scrabble* board: The 1974 law was unbuilt and reconstructed by the 1976 Court decision, on which were built the 2001 McCain-Feingold reforms. When the 2001 law bounced across the street to be tested in the Supreme Court in *McConnell v. FEC*, the Justices simply built on the congressional construction, itself built atop what the judges themselves had left standing in the 1974 law. "We are also mindful" the Court wrote, that "Congress properly relied on the recognition of its authority contained in *Buckley* and its progeny."[3] The tight corner that the *McConnell* case left on the board became even more limited in 2006, when the new Roberts Court struck down Vermont's very strict limits on both contributions and expenditures for campaigns.[4]

---

1 *Buckley v. Valeo*, 424 U.S. 1, 235–236 (1976) (Burger, C.J., concurring in part and dissenting in part).
2 The phrase "money is speech" seems to have appeared for the first time during oral argument in the *Buckley* case. Oddly enough, though this phrase perfectly captures the frame in which a majority of the Court ultimately saw the limits on campaign spending, it appears just once in the Court's opinions in the case, on page 263 of a 295-page set of complicated opinions, concurrences, and dissents – in a partial *dissent* by Justice Byron White. Nevertheless, the Court's emphasis on the First Amendment came to frame and dominate all discussion of the issue. For a rather strongly worded rejection of the 'money-is-speech' trope, see *Nixon v. Shrink Missouri*, 528 U.S. 377, 398–9 (2000) (Stevens, J., concurring).
3 *McConnell v. FEC*, 540 U.S. 93, 137 (2003).
4 *Randall v. Sorrell*, 438 U.S. 230 (2006). A year later, the Court reinstated a suit by a Wisconsin right to life organization seeking to challenge and further narrow the application

Efforts to regulate campaign finance go back at least to the Pendleton Act of 1883, which banned government officials from requiring employees to provide political services or make political contributions. In 1907, the Tillman Act was designed to stop large corporations from using money to influence federal elections.[5] The year 1925 brought the Federal Corrupt Practices Act, which set spending limits for parties in congressional elections and imposed the first rules for public disclosure in national elections. The Hatch Act in 1939 put limits on some contributions by government employees,[6] whereas Taft-Hartley in 1947 limited contributions by labor unions as well as corporations.[7]

Needless to say, each law produced loopholes demanding new rules. Some thought that this piecemeal approach was part of the problem. In vetoing a 1970 effort to limit the amount of money candidates could spend on broadcast (radio and television) advertising, Richard Nixon argued that the law was too selective and too narrow. "If, indeed, there is merit in limiting campaign expenditures," Nixon wrote to Senate Minority Leader Hugh Scott in November, 1970, "the problem should be dealt with in its entirety." Any measure "must also provide a meaningful mechanism for enforcement," he added.[8]

The next year, Congress put together a slightly more comprehensive approach in the Federal Election Campaign Act of 1971 (FECA), which Nixon signed into law in February 1972. This time, the law limited spending on advertising generally, placed formal limits on what candidates and their families were allowed to contribute to their own campaigns, and imposed a number of other reporting and disclosure rules.

Concerns about the First Amendment were raised when Congress was first drafting the legislation. However, after reviewing the legal precedents, the Senate Commerce Committee reported in May 1971 that earlier cases had "established the right of Congress to protect the integrity of Federal elections," leaving open the question of whether the limitations proposed by Congress might be seen as "reasonably related to the evil sought to be remedied, i.e., the spiraling cost of election campaigns and the attendant difficulty of candidates of obtaining access to the media." The committee concluded that these limitations were reasonably related, and "its judgment in this respect is concurred in by the great majority of the experts

---

of McCain-Feingold, asking the Court to revisit and refine its *McConnell* decision. See *Federal Election Commission v. Wisconsin Right to Life*, 551 U.S. ___ (2007).

5 Tillman Act (January 26, 1907), 34 Stat. 864, now a part of 18 U.S.C. 610.
6 5 U.S.C. 7324–7.
7 29 U.S.C. 141–97.
8 Richard Nixon, letter to Hugh Scott (R-PA), November 20, 1970, reproduced in Federal Election Commission, *Legislative History of the Federal Election Campaign Act of 1971*, Washington, DC: Government Printing Office, 1981, p 77.

who testified."[9] In the floor debates, Rhode Island Democrat John Pastore noted that, although "the Supreme Court has never ruled on this precise point, the Committee believes that what the Court has said on the First Amendment generally and in an analogous situation – the Federal Corrupt Practices Act – fully supports the constitutionality of the limitations in Title I of the amendment."[10] Republican Peter Dominick of Colorado added that there had been "very little Supreme Court activity in this area" largely because "of the ineffectiveness of present campaign restrictions."[11]

The 1971 debate and legislation predated Watergate, which broke in full fury in the months following the 1972 presidential election, providing significant public pressure to press for and impose new and even more comprehensive campaign finance reform. But, as Rebecca Curry persuasively demonstrates, Watergate was not the only impetus for this new legislation – in addition to the political demands for reform, there were real legal threats as well.[12] Just weeks after House and Senate conferees signed off on the 1971 Federal Elections Campaign Act (FECA), the district court in Washington, D.C., issued a ruling allowing the public interest group, Common Cause, to pursue a class action lawsuit against the national Democratic and Republican parties. This suit alleged that the parties' failure to abide by the 1948 Hatch Act rules – which put limits on political contributions and expenditures[13] – could "undermine and perhaps even nullify [plaintiffs] right to vote" and that the plaintiffs who were the intended beneficiaries of these statutes "comprise a class whose interests may be protected by a private civil action."[14] Sections 608 and 609 of the Hatch Act, the court ruled, were intended "not to punish otherwise illegal activities, but rather to protect the plaintiffs' interests as voters, campaign workers and contributors" by limiting otherwise acceptable practices. If the facts are as alleged, the court said, "This is a flagrant and irreparable erosion of the right to an effective vote, and, in the absence of an express statutory provision to the contrary, clearly warrants immediate judicial relief."[15]

---

9 "Promoting Fair Practices in the Conduct of Election Campaigns for Federal Elective Offices and for other Purposes," Report of the Senate Commerce Committee on S. 382, May 6, 1971, 92nd Congress, 1st Session, Senate Report 92-6, p 32 (cited in FEC, *Legislative History*, p 86).

10 John Pastore (D-RI), *Congressional Record*, August 2, 1971, p 28794.

11 Peter Dominick (R-CO), *Congressional Record*, December 14, 1971, p 46947.

12 I want to thank Rebecca Curry for sharing her research findings as she was preparing her PhD dissertation, "Legislatures, Lawsuits and Loopholes: The Politics of Judicial Review in U.S. Campaign Finance Policy," in the Jurisprudence and Social Policy Program at the University of California, Berkeley.

13 18 U.S.C. 608–9.

14 *Common Cause et al v. Democratic National Committee et al*, 333 F. Supp. 803, 812 (D.D.C. 1971).

15 *Common Cause v. DNC*, 333 F. Supp. at 814.

Would this ruling be caught up in the "political thicket" and, therefore, left to be resolved by the political and not the judicial branch? No longer. The authority for that change was *Baker v. Carr*, which the district court cited a number of times in this opinion. Again, we can see the inwardly turning juridification spiral in play – after the Court opened new paths in *Brown* and *Baker*, lobbyists and politicians alike turned to the courts, and then court rulings shaped and influenced the next round of legislation.

The *Common Cause* ruling, Curry argues, was a fire bell in the night, a dramatic warning to incumbents and political insiders that the courts might exercise their command function, providing for campaign and election rules and policy. In the short term, the easy answer was to get rid of the two troublesome provisions in the Hatch Act – and this was quickly accomplished as part of the 1971 FECA, which was coincidentally being debated at the very time this case went to court. Repealing those provisions took the immediate pressure off, but Curry argues, it suggested to legislators that they might not be able to maintain exclusive control over these regulations.[16] Curry notes that, before 1974, campaign finance rules were what she calls instances of "direct legislation," in which Congress set the rules and then controlled the interpretation, application, and enforcement of those rules. The Senate voted to approve the establishment of a separate and autonomous bureaucracy to enforce the new election laws – a Federal Election Commission – which would have changed this characteristic of the finance rules. However, the House version rejected this approach, "insisting that congressional campaign records should be kept by congressional employees," and reports of presidential campaign spending "would go to the Controller General." In conference, the House version won out. Under heavy political pressure in the wake of Watergate, however, Congress agreed to give an independent and separate bureaucratic agency the power to supervise the new and far more comprehensive Federal Election Campaign Act of 1974.[17]

The 1974 act was not strictly a product of Watergate. However, Watergate was widely understood to have been in large measure a product of the corruption of the political process in general and of campaign finance abuse in particular. Just weeks after Richard Nixon took the oath of office for the second time, the Senate voted 77–0 to set up a Select Committee on Presidential Campaign Activities. Chaired by North Carolina's Sam Ervin, the committee's hearings, along with a steady flow of media reports, leaks, and criminal investigations, generated a wide

16 With the repeal of the legislation, the case "was dismissed as moot after FECA went into effect on April 7, 1972." Joel L. Fleishman and Carol Greenwald, "Public Interest Litigation and Political Finance Reform," 425 *Annals of the American Academy of Political and Social Science* 1, p 121 (1976).

17 Warren Weaver, "Campaigning Bill Passed by House," *New York Times*, December 1, 1971, p 1.

and deep demand for significant reform. In floor debates on the 1974 proposed amendments to FECA, Democratic Senator Claiborne Pell of Rhode Island insisted that although we "may not eradicate all future Watergates," legislation certainly could "discourage the perpetuation of a climate in which power is abused by the clever at the expense of the unwary, where power is perverted by a calculated deception which – in Richard Sheridan's words – we might call a 'school for scandal.'"[18]

The 1974 amendments stitched together a number of reforms, including more extensive reporting and public disclosure requirements, contribution and spending limits, public financing of campaigns, and the establishment of a separate agency to administer and enforce these provisions – one that would formally, and officially, and legally be beyond the control of elected officials, an agency that would look more like a legal institution and less like a political agent. Of all of these provisions, floor debates suggest that the one members of Congress thought would be most likely to generate constitutional controversy was public financing. Tennessee's Howard Baker, the ranking Republican on the Senate Watergate committee, (the Select Committee on Presidential Campaign Activities), noted that in the "wake of Watergate and the events of the past year, it is not surprising that considerable support has developed within the Congress for new concepts," including "public financing of campaigns for Federal office. In fact, having listened to months of testimony about abuse and circumvention of existing statutes, I can sympathize with the temptation to abandon that system altogether in favor of some other approach." But was public financing the right way to go? "Public financing," Baker said, "is definitely new, and it appears pure and absolute; but is it right?"[19]

"Because it appeared that many of the alleged wrongdoings associated with Watergate were tied to the raising of campaign funds," Nebraska Republican Roman Hruska insisted, "the idea occurred to alter the basis by which candidates receive funds to run their campaigns. Public financing became the banner for those who sought to reform the system."[20] Hubert Humphrey agreed, insisting that public finance was the "most important feature in this legislation."[21] New York's Conservative Party Senator, James Buckley – who would later lend his name to the case that upended the campaign finance reform legislation the Senate was then debating – said that both those "in and out of Congress who advocate public financing are selling it as a cure-all for our national and political ills." That

18 Sen. Claiborne Pell (R-RI), *Congressional Record*, March 26, 1974, p 8184.
19 Sen. Howard Baker (R-TN), *Congressional Record*, March 26, 1974, p 8202.
20 Sen. Roman Hruska (R-NE), *Congressional Record*, March 27, 1974, p 8443.
21 Sen. Hubert Humphrey (D-MN), *Congressional Record*, March 27, 1974, pp 8452–3.

group, Buckley noted, included "the Senator from Massachusetts."[22] It was a charge Edward Kennedy accepted readily. "Just as Watergate and private campaign contributions have mired the executive branch in its present quicksand of corruption," Kennedy responded, "so, I am convinced, the present low estate of Congress is the result of the ingrained corruption and appearance of corruption that our system of private financing of congressional elections has produced."[23]

In the end, the 1974 amendments to the 1971 Federal Election Campaign Act produced a broad, complicated, and interwoven set of rules to combat some of the abuses that had been revealed by the Watergate investigations. The amended act was a comprehensive attempt to further formalize, more tightly legalize, and focus attention not on political incentives and disincentives, but rather on legal and even criminal regulations, black-letter law, and clear, independent regulatory enforcement mechanisms. It included limits on contributions to political campaigns, limits on what individuals or groups could spend to support any individual candidate, limits on what a candidate might spend on his or her own campaign; it required detailed record keeping along with the filing of quarterly reports and disclosure of the names of donors and the amounts of contributions; and finally it established a complex system to create an eight-member commission charged with administering "record keeping, disclosure and investigatory functions," as well as being responsible for issuing new rules and enforcing those rules. Two commissioners would be picked by the president, two by the Speaker of the House, and two by the President pro tempore of the Senate; the final two positions would be held by the Secretary of the Senate and the Clerk of the House – who would both serve as ex officio, nonvoting commissioners. Finally, the 1974 amendments established an elaborate method of public financing for political campaigns.[24]

This is where the federal courts came into the picture – expeditiously. Signed by Gerald Ford on October 15, 1974, the law authorized the new Federal Election Commission, the national committee of any political party, or "any individual eligible to vote in any election for the office of President of the United States" to challenge the "constitutionality of any provision of this Act." The district court, the law stated, "immediately shall certify all questions of constitutionality" to the U.S. Court of Appeals, which "shall hear the matter sitting *en banc.*" "Notwithstanding any other provision of law, any decision on a matter certified" to the circuit court, "shall be reviewable by appeal directly to the Supreme

---

22 Sen. James Buckley (C-NY), *Congressional Record*, March 27, 1974, p S 8455.
23 Sen. Edward M. Kennedy (D-MA), *Congressional Record*, March 28, 1974, p 8772.
24 This is drawn from the syllabus of the Supreme Court decision in *Buckley v. Valeo*, 424 U.S. 1 (1976).

Court of the United States." Such appeal, the law said, "shall be brought no later than 20 days after the decision of the Court of Appeals." And if that was not enough to move this legislation directly from Congress to the U.S. Supreme Court, the law made it clear that "it shall be the duty of the Court of Appeals and of the Supreme Court of the United States to advance on the docket and to expedite to the greatest possible extent the disposition of any matter certified" for their resolution by the district court.

This extraordinary set of provisions meant that there was no decision reached at the district court level – the district court judges' function was to pull together the evidentiary record and then develop and certify what they ruled were the essential constitutional questions. The entire record, along with twenty-eight certified constitutional questions, was then sent to the Court of Appeals for the District of Columbia, sitting *en banc*. The circuit court proceeded to pare those twenty-eight questions down to just nine. It then issued a *per curiam* decision in which the judges announced: "After subjecting the issues to 'exacting judicial scrutiny,' the court today upholds the core provisions of the legislative scheme, holds one incidental provision unconstitutional, and declines to rule on other provisions for lack of a ripe controversy." In short, they found very little to be constitutionally objectionable in the law and sent the package a few blocks east to the U.S. Supreme Court.[25]

The Supreme Court did not agree – at least not on all nine of the remaining certified questions (and a few subsidiary questions). The High Court ultimately produced a 295-page *per curiam* decision upholding some, but not all, of the contribution limits, striking down some, but not all, of the expenditure rules, upholding most of the public financing provisions, and rejecting the rules for the selection of election commissioners to staff the newly created Federal Election Commission, giving Congress just thirty days to develop a constitutionally acceptable selection procedure.[26]

Although the Court issued a unanimous *per curiam* decision, there was little on which the Justices unanimously agreed, other than the fact that the case warranted judicial review and that the method for the appointment of commissioners for the Federal Election Commission violated the separation of powers. Only Justices Brennan, Stewart, and Powell joined in full. Justice Marshall joined in all but Part I-C-2, Justice Blackmun in all but Part I-B, Justice Rehnquist in all but Part III-B-1, Chief Justice Burger in Parts I-C and IV (except insofar as it accorded de facto validity for the FEC's past acts), and Justice White only in Part III. Justice White,

---

25 *Buckley v. Valeo*, 519 F.2d 821 (D.C. Cir. 1975).

26 The urgency was real. Despite the extraordinarily expeditious journey this bill had taken from Capitol Hill to the district court, through the appeals court, and onto the Supreme Court docket, the final decision was handed down on January 30, 1976 – less than ten months before a presidential and full national election would be held.

just to be clear, concurred in the Court's answers to the lower court's certified constitutional questions 1, 2, 3 (b), 3 (c), 3 (e), 3 (f), 3 (h), 5, 6, 7 (a), 7 (b), 7 (c), 7 (d), 8 (a), 8 (b), 8 (c), 8 (d), 8 (e), and 8 (f), but chose to dissent from the Court's answers to questions 3 (a), 3 (d), and 4 (a), although he did "join in Part III of the Court's opinion and in much of Parts I-B, II, and IV."[27]

The Court had unstitched a complicated and interdependent quilt of laws. It was – as are most complicated pieces of public policy – a set of compromises that ultimately left loopholes and a trailing set of unintended consequences. There had been a clear understanding expressed in the legislation and debates that any attempt to contain and control any risk of corruption in campaigns would have to address the problem of money in politics from two equally important but opposite directions: It would have to limit contributions (the source of the funds), and it would have to regulate expenditures. Any law that only addressed half this equation (as was the case with the 1971 statute) was unlikely to have much effect. The Court's deconstruction of the complex law led Chief Justice Warren Burger to conclude that the "statute as it now stands is unworkable and inequitable."[28] The Court's "piecemeal approach," Burger added, "fails to give adequate consideration to the integrated nature of this legislation." When central elements of the law, when "key operative provisions [of] this Act are stricken, can what remains function in anything like the way Congress intended?"[29]

"The incongruities are obvious," Burger wrote. "The Commission is now eliminated, yet its very purpose was to guide candidates and campaign workers – and their accountants and lawyers – through an intricate statutory maze where a misstep can lead to imprisonment." Candidates, he added "can now spend freely; affluent candidates, after today, can spend their own money without limit; yet, contributions for the ordinary candidate are severely restricted in amount – and small contributors are deterred. I cannot believe that Congress would have enacted a statutory scheme containing such incongruous and inequitable provisions."[30]

The Court could have agreed with Burger and struck down the full package of amendments, arguing that what was left simply could not advance the goals Congress had in writing the law in the first place. The Court could have done that – but it did not have to, because there was a severability clause (as is often the case in most pieces of complex modern legislation) designed to allow the Court to pick and choose, leaving some parts of a law intact even as it struck down others.

27 *Buckley v. Valeo*, 424 U.S. at 257 (White, J., concurring in part and dissenting in part).
28 *Buckley v. Valeo*, 424 U.S. 1 at 252.
29 *Buckley v. Valeo*, 424 U.S. 1 at 255.
30 *Buckley v. Valeo*, 424 U.S. at 255.

Severability clauses have become standard items in our modern world of omnibus legislation. These clauses say something like the following: "If any provision of this Act, or the application thereof to any person or circumstance, is held invalid, the validity of the remainder of the Act and the application of such provision to other persons and circumstances shall not be affected thereby."[31] They are designed to ensure that some parts of a law can survive even if other parts are stricken by the courts. In many cases, these clauses are vital, allowing a complex law to stand even if a minor technical aspect is knocked out.

Even if Congress failed to write a severability clause into a bill, the Supreme Court has indicated that its own canons of interpretation might allow and even compel the Justices to act as if one were there – absent explicit statutory language to the contrary. In its 1976 *per curiam* decision in the *Buckley* campaign law case, the Court cited a 1932 case indicating its own longstanding assumption that the "unconstitutionality of a part of an Act does not necessarily defeat or affect the validity of its remaining provisions." Unless it is evident that the legislature would not have enacted the remaining, constitutional part of the law "independently of that which is not [constitutional] the invalid part may be dropped if what is left is fully operative as a law."[32]

However, what is "fully operative as a law" is a matter of interpretation. Chief Justice Burger clearly did not think that what was left after the Supreme Court ruled was even close to what Congress had meant to achieve with this set of laws. A severability clause, Burger insisted, "is not an inexorable command," and to "invoke a severability clause to salvage parts of a comprehensive, integrated statutory scheme, which parts, standing alone, are unworkable and in many aspects unfair, *exalts a formula* at the expense of the broad objectives of Congress."[33]

---

31 2 U.S.C. 454 (1970 ed., Supp. IV).
32 *Champlin Refining Co. v. Corporation Commission of Oklahoma*, 286 U.S. 210, 234 (1932), cited and quoted in *Buckley v. Valeo*, 424 U.S. 1, 109 (1976). It is worth noting the layered, *together with* quality of this ruling. In *Champlin*, the Court asserts the general interpretive principle of severability. ("Unless it is evident that the Legislature would not have enacted provisions which are within its power, independently of that which is not, the invalid part may be dropped if what is left is fully operative as law.") The 1932 Court then listed a series of supporting cases – *Connolly v. Union Sewer Pipe Co.*, 184 U.S. 540 (1902); *Pollock v. Farmers' Loan & Trust Co.*, 158 U.S. 601 (1895); *Reagan v. Farmers' Loan*, 154 U.S. 362 (1894); *Field v. Clark*, 143 U.S. 649 (1892) – suggesting that this was a judicial canon of interpretation. But immediately after this, the Court notes that in the case before them, Congress had, in fact, put in place a severability clause: "Section 10 declares that the invalidity of any part of the Act shall not in any manner affect the remaining portions." That, the Court concluded, "discloses an intention to make the Act divisible and creates a presumption that, eliminating invalid parts, the legislature would have been satisfied with what remained and that the scheme of regulation derivable from the other provisions would have been enacted" regardless of the Court's decision. 286 U.S. at 235.
33 *Buckley v. Valeo*, 424 U.S. 1, 255 (1976), emphasis added.

It is not beyond reason to think that the deconstructive story of campaign finance might have played out differently. The laws tested by the Court in 1976 actually were amendments to a statute originally passed in 1971 – which contained the severability clause. But there was, in fact, a dispute about the sort of severability clause to include in the 1971 legislation. The House version (H.R. 11060) contained the familiar blanket severability clause, but the Senate version (S. 383) did not. Instead, the only severability clause in the Senate version applied exclusively to the reporting requirements of Title III of the act – and not to the rest of the law. The House amendment "was similar" to that of the Senate, according to the Joint Explanatory Statement of the Committee of Conference, "except that it extended the application of the separability provision to any provision of the House [bill] and was not limited to the provisions relating to disclosure of Federal campaign funds." The committee reported that "the conference substitute is the same as the House amendment."[34]

That seemingly innocuous change may have made a significant difference. Had the Senate version prevailed instead of the version from the House, the Supreme Court in 1976 would not have had a statutory green light to unstitch the quilt – instead, the Justices might have felt compelled to say yes or no: all or nothing. If the Court had said no, Congress might well have been forced to engage in an immediate and full debate about campaign finance. Instead, responding to the patchwork charge it was given by the Court, congressional debate dealt with the immediate requirements of the Court decision, with little time (and less political inclination) to address the more comprehensive problem of campaign finance. As then-Assistant Attorney General Antonin Scalia put it, in the aftermath of the *Buckley* case, Congress faced two sets of decisions, one of which, Scalia said "is extraordinarily difficult, and the other extraordinarily urgent." The urgent decision concerned the appointments to the Federal Election Commission: The Court ruling gave Congress just thirty days to fix the one thing everyone on the Court seemed to agree was unconstitutional – the method to be used to appoint members of the FEC.[35] This left little time to reconstruct a complex and comprehensive set of elections laws before Congress would have to leave town to start campaigning.

---

34 Conference Report to accompany S. 382, "Federal Election Campaign Act of 1971," 92d Congress, 1st Sess., House Report 92–752, Joint Explanatory Statement of the Committee on Conference, p 37.

35 The problem was that the Commission had been given rule-making as well as adjudicative and even enforcement authority. These functions, the Court argued, made the commissioners "officers of the United States," which, according to Article II of the Constitution, could only be appointed by the president – after confirmation by the U.S. Senate. But the selection process in the election law gave the legislature the authority to select four of the six members without any executive role – and then gave to the House as well as the Senate the authority to approve the president's two appointees.

The "extraordinarily urgent" concern actually stole the spotlight from what Scalia called the "extraordinarily difficult" decision. Congress, Scalia said, "will have to decide if the "elimination of certain features that were the quids or the quos in a long debated and carefully crafted legislative package, leaves a residue which is still an approximation of legislative will." The likely effects of the Court-ordered changes, "limiting contributions but *not* limiting expenditures on the part of candidates who have received no Federal funding," are to increase the importance of a candidate's personal wealth and to create a distinction between independent expenditures and those coordinated by campaigns that "may be impossible to administer." Perhaps most important of all, "by enabling contributions above the established limits to be funneled into campaigns only through organizations separate from the candidate himself, the [post-*Buckley v. Valeo*] law may sap the strength of our 'political party' system, and foster elections whose major themes are selected by issue-oriented or narrowly factional groups, rather than by the candidate or even the candidate's political party."[36] In sum, Scalia noted, the "total system which now exists is one which, in substantial and important respects, has been designed by no Congress and approved by no President."[37]

Ira Glasser, director of the New York Civil Liberties Union – which joined Senator Buckley in his challenge of the campaign finance laws – agreed that what was left of the bill "can fairly be called a wreckage." If it had been submitted initially as a proposed bill, Glasser said, "nobody would have supported it." The answer, Glasser said, was to "begin from scratch, to take the Court decision as a signal to go back and do it right this time, and to separately address each of the problems which the legislation sought to address the first time, but this time within the limits set by the Court."[38]

But of course, that is not at all what happened. It was too hard to pass the original bill, the political pressure to juridify too great, and the urgency imposed by the looming national election too significant. Once the path had been paved, it would be too difficult to abandon it and start a new one. Yet, few were willing to simply accept the status quo. Another option might have been to require full disclosure – placing no limits on expenditures or contributions, but requiring full and very public disclosure that then would have given voters a chance to make a fully informed decision. Among other problems, however, that approach

---

36 Antonin Scalia in prepared testimony, "Federal Election Campaign Act Amendments of 1976," Hearings before the Subcommittee on Privileges and Elections of the Committee on Rules and Administration, U.S. Senate, 94th Congress, 2d Session, February 18, 1976, pp 104–105, 108.
37 Scalia in prepared testimony, "Federal Election Campaign Act Amendments of 1976," p 109.
38 Ira Glasser, in "Federal Election Campaign Act Amendments of 1976," p 187.

had been endorsed by many who had opposed the 1971 and 1974 laws, putting the disclosure option in a poor light for reformers. Their concerns were real: What sort of mechanism could ensure full disclosure and how could it be enforced? The nation's experience with disclosure laws seemed to prove they were easily evaded, as Nixon's Committee to Re-Elect the President demonstrated quite clearly in 1972. There may have been other options to consider, but members of Congress had no real need to try, because the Court's *Buckley* decision left a few of the reforms in place, relieving pressure to rethink the effort in a comprehensive fashion. Instead, the Court pulled out some of the bricks Congress had put in place, and legislators would now respond, piece by piece and, together with the Court, pave the deconstructive path that emerged. And the path they paved clearly was labeled, "Money Is Speech."

Money Is Speech?

The free speech argument was not something the Supreme Court discovered on its own. Free speech concerns certainly came up in the original 1971 debates, but they were far from a central issue, as expressed in the thousands of pages of hearings, committee reports, expert testimony, and congressional debates.[39] The Senate Commerce Committee reported that two witnesses "expressed their view that any limitation on media spending violates the First Amendment because it limits a candidate's right of expression as well as the right of those who wish to support him,"[40] but it dismissed this concern. Turning to judicial precedent from two U.S. Supreme Court cases that, the committee asserted, stood for the proposition that Congress has the power to safeguard elections "from the improper use of money to influence the result" of that election, the committee concluded that the proper legal test was a balancing one. Was there an evil "which may validly be prevented," and was there a "reasonable relationship of the regulation to the evil"? If so, then there needed to be a "balancing of the limited effect upon free speech as against the substantiality of an evil to the prevention of which a regulatory statute is reasonably addressed."[41] Were the regulations reasonably related to the evil – to "the spiraling cost of election campaigns and the attendant difficulty of candidates of obtaining access to the media"? The committee

---

39 A fairly representative sample of which can be found in the Federal Election Commission, *Legislative History of the Federal Election Campaign Act of 1971*.
40 U.S. Senate Committee on Commerce, "Promoting Fair Practices in the Conduct of Election Campaigns for Federal Elective Offices," 92d Congress, 1st Session, report No. 92–96, p 30.
41 U.S. Senate Committee on Commerce, "Promoting Fair Practices," p 31, citing *Burroughs and Cannon v. United States*, 290 U.S. 534, 545 (1934), *Stephenson v. Binford* 287 U.S. 251, 272 (1932), and *Konigsberg v. State Bar*, 366 U.S. 36, 50–1 (1961).

"believes they are, and its judgment in this respect," they concluded, "is concurred in by the great majority of the experts who testified."[42]

Only two senators focused on the First Amendment objections – Republican Minority Leader Hugh Scott from Pennsylvania and Colorado Republican Peter Dominick. But even Dominick recognized that his own constitutional interpretation had very little Supreme Court precedent behind it. "Because of the ineffectiveness of present campaign restrictions," he noted in Senate debate, "there has been very little Supreme Court activity in this area, and no freedom of speech precedent has been set."[43] And none, it should be noted, was added in the two years between Dominick's speech and the Court case testing the 1974 amendments. In the 1974 debates over the amendments to the 1971 act, speech, money, and the First Amendment were more commonly linked and discussed,[44] but the constitutional question that occupied members of Congress was less about speech and more about the constitutionality of public financing for campaigns.

When the U.S. Court of Appeals for the District of Columbia took up the case of *Buckley v. Valeo* in April 1975, the judges were writing on a fairly clean slate – there was no clear Supreme Court frame to either confirm, or reject, or revamp, nor was there a clear set of lower court rulings that might point to the logical path to follow. The D.C. appeals court had a number of viable frames at its disposal. It could be a case that had nothing to do with speech – money, after all, is inanimate. Money makes no speeches and expresses no ideas on its own, but is merely a means to other ends. Money is property, to be sure, and property is protected by the Constitution – but at a level far below the protection afforded to free speech, particularly in the post-New Deal era. Alternatively, the court could have argued that money is a means of expression, that campaign contributions of money, like contributions of labor, were a clear demonstration of support for a set of political ideas and arguments and that one could not separate the money from the message.

Two paths, two roads "diverged in a yellow wood" and "both that morning equally lay, In leaves no step had trodden black" – but that choice, difficult as it might be, was not the only choice the judges had to make.[45] If the court opted to see money as either wholly or partially linked to speech, then the judges would be traveling a very different doctrinal path, a lateral path paved by decades of cases, arguments, and understandings about when and why it might or might not be acceptable

---

42 U.S. Senate Committee on Commerce, "Promoting Fair Practices," p 32.
43 Senator Peter Dominick (R-CO), *Congressional Record*, December 14, 1971, p 46947.
44 See Rebecca Curry, "Legislatures, Lawsuits and Loopholes: The Politics of Judicial Review in U.S. Campaign Finance Policy," a doctoral dissertation, the University of California, Berkeley, in preparation.
45 "The Road Not Taken" by Robert Frost (1915).

for the government to limit or infringe free speech. If money is property, the court could travel a "property path" and not a "First Amendment path." What restrictions on the use of property would the Constitution tolerate? By 1974, a great deal. And this was the path that one might have expected the courts to follow – at least in the early 1970s.

The circuit court recognized that the law might bump into the First Amendment, but the majority found no problem working around that, handling the speech concern much as members of Congress had expected. In an explicitly lateral move, the D.C. Appeals Court ruled that "the pertinent standard is that set forth by the Supreme Court, *albeit in another context*." In a case concerning a free speech challenge to a law banning the burning of draft cards (*U.S. v. O'Brien*), the Appeals Court argued that "when 'speech' and 'non-speech' elements are combined in the same course of conduct, a sufficiently important governmental interest in regulating the nonspeech element can justify incidental limitations on First Amendment freedoms."[46] *O'Brien*, however, was not the only lateral speech precedent it might have considered. The appeals court also cited the very same cases Congress relied on in 1971, suggesting that Congress had done a reasonable job of prospectively anticipating where the courts would go when faced with a question of first impression, that is a doctrinal question that had not yet been considered by the Supreme Court.[47] The government "has a clear and compelling interest in safeguarding the integrity of elections and avoiding the undue influence of wealth," the circuit court ruled, and both the "reality and appearance of electoral corruption," the judges insisted, "justify congressional intervention."[48] If the law, "in service of the compelling governmental interest in insuring the integrity of federal elections against undue influence" imposed "incidental restrictions on First Amendment freedoms, these constraints, broadly considered, are necessary to assure the integrity of federal elections."[49]

O'Brien suggested one lateral stream of free speech cases that the courts could build on, but on June 9, 1969, the Supreme Court had handed down another, very different free speech case – *Brandenburg v. Ohio*. This case struck down an Ohio law that had been used to prosecute members of the Ku Klux Klan for "advocating . . . the duty, necessity, or propriety of crime, sabotage, violence, or unlawful methods of terrorism as a means of accomplishing industrial or political reform." In a landmark free speech ruling, the Supreme Court held 7–1 that "mere advocacy" was not the same as "incitement to lawless action." Laws that aimed to

---

46 *Buckley v. Valeo*, 519 F.2d at 840, citing *United States v. O'Brien*, 391 U.S. 367, 376–377 (1968), emphasis added.
47 U.S. Senate Committee on Commerce, "Promoting Fair Practices," p 31.
48 *Buckley v. Valeo*, 519 F.2d. at 835.
49 *Buckley v. Valeo*, 519 F.2d. at 842.

repress "mere advocacy" could not withstand constitutional challenge. *Brandenburg* suggested a far higher bar for laws that infringed on free speech, and it was *Brandenburg*, Judge David L. Bazelon wrote in his appeals court dissent in *Buckley*, that ought to suggest the free speech test in this case: The majority's approach, Judge Bazelon wrote, "stands First Amendment jurisprudence on its head. To justify infringing freedom of speech, a danger must be 'present' or 'imminent,' not hypothetical. The crucial issues at stake in this case call for strengthening, not relaxing, that requirement."[50] Although Bazelon and his *Brandenburg* test for speech restrictions were relegated to a single footnote in one of three dissents (against five appeals court judges in the majority), speech would take center stage when the case moved up to the Supreme Court.

The phrase "money is speech" seems to have appeared for the first time in the *Buckley* case during oral argument before the U.S. Supreme Court, in an exchange between Justice Stewart and Deputy Solicitor General Daniel Friedman. Pressing the congressional understanding, Friedman "contended that the law regulates money, not speech." Whether money was used to buy television time, or radio or newspaper advertising, "or even buying pencils and a microphone," Stewart argued that in the context of a political campaign at least, "money is speech." It proved to be a powerful framing concept. Minutes later, Justice Blackmun indicated that he was warming to the idea, telling Friedman that "part of your opponents' argument is very forceful on that. It [money] does produce speech."[51]

Oddly enough, though Stewart's phrase perfectly captures the frame in which a majority of the Court ultimately saw the limits on campaign spending, it appears just once in the Court's opinions in the case, on page 263 of a 295-page set of complicated opinions, concurrences, and dissents. Not only that, but the phrase appears not in support of the majority's conclusions, but in a partial *dissent* by Justice Byron White. The argument that "money is speech," Justice White writes, is one that "proves entirely too much," because there are so many activities that the government regulates that do, in some sense, have an effect on speech. Federal taxes paid by newspaper owners, for example, is money that might otherwise "be spent on larger and better newspapers." Add to that compulsory bargaining and a federally enforced right to strike, which have "increased the labor costs of those who publish newspapers" and have been "an important factor in the recent disappearance of many daily papers." Not to mention antitrust laws and even price control laws that

50 *Buckley v. Valeo*, 519 F.2d. at 911–912.
51 Lesley Oelsner, "High Court's Queries Hint Doubt on Parts of New Election Law." *New York Times*, November 11, 1975, p 1.

have, from time to time, "been applied to the newspapers or other media." No one, White insisted, would argue that these laws "and many others, are invalid because they siphon off or prevent the accumulation of large sums that would otherwise be available for communicative activities."[52]

But the majority rejected Deputy Solicitor General Friedman's argument that the law regulated money, not speech, and rejected as well the appeals court majority's insistence that a simple balancing test would permit a law designed to advance a compelling government interest in fair elections to impose incidental limits on free speech. Instead, the Supreme Court adopted a very different view of speech, arguing that money donated or spent in a political campaign could not be separated from the message the money was used to promote. In other words, to limit donations and expenditures in political campaigns would be akin to limiting what could be said and how much speech would be allowed. As the *Wall Street Journal* put it, "The Justices held, in effect, that money talks and, thus, spending limits impose 'a substantial restraint on the ability of persons to engage in protected First Amendment expression.'"[53]

To choose the free speech path is not to determine the fate of any and all campaign finance regulations, but it does powerfully frame that debate, raising significant barriers to future legislation. Congress was (and is) free to take another swing at expenditure limits, but this was not a high priority in January 1976. The priority was to reconstitute the Federal Election Commission, thereby satisfying the Court's concerns about a perceived violation of the separation of powers. Far from challenging a divided Court and its complex opinion, many in Congress almost immediately began to internalize the Court's ruling, echoing the sentiments of representatives such as Wisconsin Republican William Steiger, who, in complaining of one proposed restriction on what noncandidates might spend in support of those running for office, said that the "Supreme Court said we cannot write such a law. If there were any one message in the *Buckley versus Valeo* decision," Steiger argued on the House floor, "it was that we cannot – cannot underlined – by an act of Congress inhibit the ability of the American people to spend money freely in elections."[54] In fact, of course, the *Buckley* decision upheld contribution limits, but the point here is the degree to which many in Congress had already (less than three months after the case had been handed down) internalized the Court's free speech frame and the doctrinal path on which it was built. It is also a powerful reminder of the degree to which members of Congress had come to fully accept and even embrace the idea that the Supreme

---

52 *Buckley v. Valeo*, 424 U.S. at 262–263 (White, concurring in part, dissenting in part).
53 "Top Court Upholds Most of Election-Financing Law but Finds Flaws in Makeup of the Enforcement Panel," *Wall Street Journal*, February 2, 1976, p 3.
54 William Steiger (R-WI), *Congressional Record*, April 1, 1976, p 9097.

Court was and ought to be the final and infallible oracle of constitutional finality.[55]

McCain-Feingold and the Power of the Beaten Path

James Buckley largely rested his free speech arguments on the writing of two academic lawyers, Ralph Winter of Yale Law School and Northwestern's Martin Redish.[56] Winter's writing was cited numerous times in the congressional debates in 1974.[57] By the time Wisconsin's Democratic Senator Russ Feingold and Arizona Republican John McCain began to push a major campaign finance reform bill in Congress in 2001, the free speech frame was deeply entrenched. Supreme Court Justice John Paul Stevens had tried valiantly, but in vain, to move the Court off the path he helped pave, but by 2000 the money-is-speech trope was so widely accepted that Justice Stevens was reduced to offering a 511-word (including footnotes) plea to his colleagues on the Court to abandon what he saw as a false and misleading link between campaign finance and free speech in *Nixon v. Shrink Missouri*. It was, he argued, time for a fresh start on campaign finance, time for a "fresh examination of the constitutional issues raised by Congress's enactment of the Federal Election Campaign Acts of 1971 and 1974 and this Court's resolution of those issues in *Buckley v. Valeo*." And that new beginning, Stevens argued, could be summed up in one simple phrase: "Money is property; it is not speech." Our Constitution, "and our heritage properly protect the individual's interest in making decisions about the use of his or her own property," Stevens wrote. This raises "important constitutional concerns," but they are "unrelated to the First Amendment." The "right to use one's own money to hire gladiators, or to fund 'speech by proxy,' certainly merits significant constitutional protection," Stevens wrote, but these "property rights are not entitled to the same protection as the right to say what one pleases."[58]

Justice Stevens was swimming against a powerful tide. Not only did courts at the federal and state levels by then seem to start with the

---

55 For a comprehensive history and analysis of the emergence of the doctrine of judicial supremacy, and its embrace by elected officials see Larry D. Kramer, *The People Themselves: Popular Constitutionalism and Judicial Review*, New York: Oxford University Press, 2004, and Keith Whittington, *Political Foundations of Judicial Supremacy: The Presidency, the Supreme Court and Constitutional Leadership in U.S. History*, Princeton: Princeton University Press, 2007.

56 Ronald Reagan nominated (and the Senate confirmed) Winter as a judge on the Second Circuit Court of Appeals in 1981.

57 Senator Buckley's most extensive speech on the subject was delivered on the Senate floor on April 10, 1974, and included 21 footnotes added to the *Congressional Record* version of his speech.

58 *Nixon v. Shrink Missouri*, 528 U.S. 377 (2000).

assumption that money is speech – but so did legislators, both those favoring stronger campaign finance rules and those opposed. When Senators McCain and Feingold joined together in 2001 to press for a new bill, the Bipartisan Campaign Reform Act (BCRA), there was a fight, of course, but not over the doctrinal foundation; the fight was over how and when it is permissible to restrict speech.[59] The BCRA took aim primarily at two major problems that had developed largely as the product of loopholes and unintended consequences of the 1971 and 1974 laws and the amendments to those laws and regulations imposed by the Federal Election Commission in response to court rulings. One of BCRA's targets was what had come to be known as "soft money," funds donated to the national political parties that could then be deployed to help candidates. Because the money had been donated to the party and not the candidate directly, it was unregulated and there were no limits on how much could be raised or spent. The other target was the proliferation of what were called "issue ads" – advertisements that supported (and more often attacked) the positions of individual candidates, but that were paid for by others – including the national political parties, unions, corporations, and other ostensibly independent groups and not part of a candidate's formal organization. Because the ads were not paid for by a candidate running for office, there were no limits or restrictions on the funds that could be raised or spent on these efforts.

One could certainly imagine a robust claim that the Court was, in fact, wrong and that money was not speech, but rather a form of property. The speech frame, however, was not seriously contested, even by strong supporters of campaign finance controls. Those favoring limits started by essentially conceding the frame, arguing, explaining, and justifying when and why it was constitutionally permissible to *restrict* free speech. "It simply cannot be said," Senator John Kerry insisted on the floor, "that the First Amendment provides an absolute prohibition of any and all restrictions on speech. When state interests are more important than unfettered free speech, speech can be narrowly limited."[60]

West Virginia's Robert Byrd noted the limited range of options the Court had left to Congress. "The current system is rotten, it is putrid, it stinks," he said. But, unfortunately, "the Supreme Court has given this kind of campaign system First Amendment protection." And, by "equating campaign expenditures with free speech, the Supreme Court has made it all but impossible for us to control the ever-spiraling money chase."[61] Those opposed to the 2001 reforms raised the Constitution, the Supreme Court, and the First Amendment incessantly, leading Congressman

---

59 *Nixon v. Shrink Missouri*, 528 U.S. at 398–399 (Stevens, J., concurring).
60 Sen. John Kerry (D-MA), *Congressional Record*, April 3, 2001, p S 3334.
61 Sen. Robert Byrd (D-WV), *Congressional Record*, March 26, 2001, pp 4512–13.

Barney Frank to note that he found it quite interesting to see "Members that I have served with for a very long time who for the first time in their careers have become champions of free speech." Legislators who have "supported virtually every restriction on free speech," now "when it comes to the power of money to swamp" our political system, "suddenly they become advocates of free speech."[62]

"On Thursday afternoon," Republican Senator Arlen Specter noted on the floor, "we had an extensive debate with the Senator from Kentucky, Mr. McConnell, the Senator from Delaware, Mr. Biden, the Senator from Tennessee, Mr. Thompson, and I, and we were pontificating – I was pontificating, they were giving legal arguments – about what was constitutional and what was not constitutional; what is a bright line to satisfy *Buckley v. Valeo.*" Supreme Court decisions, Specter insisted, are merely "interpretations of the Constitution. They are not Holy Writ. They do not come from Mount Olympus."[63]

But the fact is, as Connecticut's Democratic Senator Chris Dodd pointed out, Congress has been in a bind for twenty-five years, in large part because "the Supreme Court has ruled that money is speech." And though Dodd endorsed Justice Stevens' repudiation of that view in the 2000 case of *Nixon v. Shrink Missouri*, he recognized that Stevens was in the minority. "That simple conclusion, that money is speech" has meant that Congress has "been running this process out over the years where our ability to have some limitations on the amount of dollars that are spent and raised in seeking Federal office is significantly jeopardized because of the constitutionality of such provisions."[64]

Congress was building on the foundation that the Court had refashioned when ruling on earlier statutes – and the Court now took its next turn on the *Scrabble* board. "We are also mindful of the fact that in its lengthy deliberations leading to the enactment" of McCain-Feingold, the Court noted approvingly in *McConnell v. FEC*, that "Congress properly relied on the recognition of the Court's authority contained in Buckley and its progeny."[65] Few in Congress were willing to buck the Court or even confront its doctrine. As Ohio's Republican Senator Mike DeWine insisted, "The fact is, the Supreme Court has ruled that personal expenditures cannot be limited... and [we] accept that. It is the interpretation of the Supreme Court, in interpreting the First Amendment to the Constitution, which we must and do respect."[66]

"The Supreme Court's decision in *Buckley*," Wisconsin's Herb Kohl said, "has left us with the difficult task of devising a system of financing

---

62 Rep. Barney Frank (D-MA), *Congressional Record*, February 12, 2002, p 1048.
63 Sen. Arlen Specter (R-PA), *Congressional Record*, March 26, 2001, p 4522.
64 Sen. Chris Dodd (D-CT), *Congressional Record*, March 27, 2001, p 4615.
65 *McConnell v. FEC*, 540 U.S. at 137.
66 Sen. Mike Dewine (R-OH), *Congressional Record*, March 20, 2001, p 3967.

campaigns without suppressing free speech." And that is the burden he
argued Congress had to accept. The answer would be to build precisely
on the path the Court had paved in *Buckley*: acknowledge that placing
limits on campaign financing *is* a restriction of free speech and, as such,
it can only stand if it is justified by "a competing public interest." This
interest, "as articulated in *Buckley v. Valeo*, is preventing corruption of
Federal elected officials or even the appearance of corruption."[67] But
whether members of Congress found comfort and cover in the path the
Supreme Court had paved or they rejected its premise, there was broad
agreement that any new legislation had to be crafted to fit the frame the
Court had built.

Members of Congress were not the only ones who felt obliged to color
inside the lines the Court had drawn twenty-five years earlier in *Buckley*. Justice Stevens – who had struggled to break away from what he
insisted was a mistaken claim that "money is speech"[68] – was now
willing to accept the path the Court's majority laid out in 1976 and
had followed in the intervening years. Joining Justice O'Connor, Stevens
wrote the majority opinion in *McConnell v. Federal Election Commission*, upholding the BCRA's new limits on soft money and issue ads, but
never once addressed the possibility that money should be considered
property and not speech.[69] Instead, Stevens joined with his colleagues
and with Congress to focus on a test that would indeed simply rebalance
the competing interests of speech, actual corruption, and the appearance
of corruption.

This shift in the balance drew scorn from Justices Kennedy, Scalia,
and Thomas. To "make its decision work," Kennedy wrote, dissenting
in part and concurring in part, the majority "surpasses *Buckley's* limits
and expands Congress' regulatory power. In so doing, it replaces discrete
and respected First Amendment principles with new, amorphous, and
unsound rules, rules which dismantle basic protections for speech."[70]
Though Kennedy might well have dissented from any decision that upheld
the BCRA on property grounds, the difference would be the degree to
which the decisions in campaign finance might or might not spill over to
other free speech claims. This is precisely at the heart of Justice Thomas's
dissent, in which he worries that the Court had now so stretched the First
Amendment frame that it may logically lead to severe limits not only on
campaign finance but also on free speech generally and on the freedom of
the press in particular. "The chilling endpoint of the Court's reasoning,"
Thomas insisted, "is not difficult to foresee: outright regulation of the

67 Sen. Herb Kohl (D-WI), *Congressional Record*, April 2, 2001, p 5198.
68 *Nixon v. Shrink Missouri*, 528 U.S. at 398, 399.
69 *McConnell v. FEC*.
70 *McConnell v. FEC*, 540 U.S. at 287 (Kennedy, J., concurring in part, dissenting in part).

press." Although the *McConnell* ruling "does not expressly strip the press of First Amendment protection, there is no principle of law or logic that would prevent the application of the Court's reasoning in that setting." The press, Thomas concluded, "now operates at the whim of Congress."[71]

McConnell v. FEC suggested that campaign finance reform would continue to be possible, but that it would play out on an increasingly tight corner of the *Scrabble* board – one set and defined initially by the patchwork decision in *Buckley*. The Court sliced up the opinion in a myriad of pieces: Justices Stevens and O'Connor delivered the opinion of the Court upholding most of the provisions concerning soft money and issue ads, Justice Rehnquist wrote the Court's opinion on standing and jurisdictional issues, and Justice Breyer chipped in to write the Court's opinion on a portion of the act that required broadcasters to keep and make available records of all politically related broadcast advertising, ruling that this provision could survive a First Amendment challenge.[72]

McConnell continued the trend started with *Buckley* of cutting up complex legislation and leaving some parts in and some parts out, as the Court was unwilling to make a blanket ruling or fundamentally affirm or revise the underlying free speech doctrine. With the end of the Rehnquist Court, those possibilities were revisited in 2006, when the new Roberts Court struck down Vermont's very strict limits on both contributions and expenditures. Unlike *McConnell*, which seemed to have moved the balance between speech and important government interests back toward the government, the Vermont case (*Randall v. Sorrell*) was seen as an

---

71 *McConnell v. FEC*, 540 U.S. at 286 (Thomas, J., concurring in part, dissenting in part).
72 That, of course, was only the beginning: Justices Souter, Ginsburg, and Breyer joined the Stevens and O'Connor opinion; O'Connor, Scalia, Kennedy, and Souter joined the Rehnquist opinion (except with respect to §305), whereas Justice Thomas joined Rehnquist's portion of the opinion with respect to §§304, 305, 307, 316, 319, and 403(b). Justice Breyer's section of the opinion of the court was joined by Justices Stevens, O'Connor, Souter, and Ginsburg, whereas Justice Scalia filed a separate opinion concurring with the Court with respect to BCRA Titles III and IV, dissenting with respect to BCRA Titles I and V, and concurring in the judgment in part and dissenting in part with respect to BCRA Title II. Justice Thomas added a separate opinion, concurring with respect to BCRA Titles III and IV, except for §311 and §318, concurring in the result with respect to BCRA §318, concurring in the judgment in part and dissenting in part with respect to BCRA Title II, and dissenting with respect to BCRA Titles I, V, and §311. The Thomas opinion was joined by Justice Scalia – with respect to I, II-A, and II-B, whereas Justice Kennedy filed an opinion concurring in the judgment in part and dissenting in part with respect to BCRA Titles I and II – an opinion in which Chief Justice Rehnquist joined, as did Justice Scalia – except to the extent the opinion upholds new FECA §323(e) and BCRA §202. Justice Thomas joined this opinion, though only with respect to BCRA §213. For his part, Chief Justice Rehnquist filed an opinion dissenting with respect to BCRA Titles I and V, in which Justices Scalia and Kennedy joined, whereas Justice Stevens filed an opinion dissenting with respect to BCRA §305, in which Justices Ginsburg and Breyer joined.

opportunity for the new Court to revisit and overturn *Buckley*.[73] The Vermont law set strict limits on the amount of money that individuals and parties could contribute to campaigns, and perhaps more challenging to the Supreme Court's *Buckley* decision, it imposed strict limits on what individuals could spend on their own campaigns. The new Court split like the old Court – with Roberts, Alito, and Breyer joining together to rule that any restriction on what an individual could spend on his or her own campaign was absolutely forbidden by the First Amendment. They then ruled that, although it was still constitutional to impose limits on what others can give to a candidate or a political campaign, Vermont's rules set that level too low, so low that they could undercut the ability of some lesser known candidates to have a fighting chance against incumbents or those with strong party support. Three members of the Court – Anthony Kennedy, Antonin Scalia, and Clarence Thomas – voted against the Vermont rules across the board, arguing that *Buckley* itself needed to be revisited and scaled back, if not completely overturned, to square it with the First Amendment. This left three Justices – Stevens, Souter, and Ginsburg – willing to uphold the Vermont rules.

The Court clearly is not prepared to revoke *Buckley*, and the room to maneuver on the *Scrabble* board is even tighter still – and yet campaign finance reform advocates continue to insist that even that small part of the board is where they can, must, and will continue to play. Fred Wertheimer, who served as president of the public interest group, Common Cause, from 1981 to 1995 and continues to head a pro-reform lobbying effort, clearly is willing to continue to rely on what is left: The Court, Wertheimer insists, "has not disturbed the constitutional doctrine under which we've been winning cases for years."[74]

Whether Wertheimer is right or not, policy advocates have wound up in a very limited and tight corner. And the Court, for better or worse, seems unwilling to break out and jump to another precedent path. Would advocates ultimately have been better served if the Court had simply said yes – or no – to the 1974 act in *Buckley*? Although we cannot know the answer to that hypothetical question, we can learn some lessons about the risks involved in a deconstructive pattern of juridification. What happens when the Court actually does simply says yes – or no – is the subject of the next chapter.

---

73 *Randall v. Sorrell*, 438 U.S. 230 (2006). The Vermont statute imposed spending limits ranging from $2,500 for state legislative candidates to $300,000 for those running for governor – and imposed drastic limits on contributions as low as $200 for donations to parties or individual candidates for the State House and just $400 for those running for statewide offices.

74 Charles Lane, "Justices Reject Vermont's Campaign Finance Law," *Washington Post*, June 27, 2006, p 1.

7 THE SEPARATION OF POWERS

When the Court Says Yes – and No

M ANY WHO STUDY THE COURTS and the role of judges in politics and policymaking limit their examination to those areas in which judges seize control of policy choices – or have that control thrust on them. But that is only part of the story of law's allure. Juridification, as it is used here, means not only the use of courts to solve policy problems but also the ways in which legal reasoning, legal frameworks, judicial language, and legal forms have come to shape and constrain the political process itself.

Constitutional ambiguity has its virtues, but it also has its vices. "The doctrine of the separation of powers." Justice Louis Brandeis said, "was adopted by the Convention of 1787, not to promote efficiency but to preclude the exercise of arbitrary power."[1] It was not, Justice Felix Frankfurter noted, a scheme of government well designed to act with "complete, all-embracing, swiftly moving authority."[2] Ambiguity was unavoidable in such a complicated system.[3] And ambiguity was the lubrication that allowed the system to adjust, making it possible, but not easy, to act. But ambiguity can also lead to profound friction and conflict that, in turn, can prevent essential government action. It creates loopholes and gaps, which provide opportunities for exploitation and abuse.

In the wake of the urban unrest of the 1960s, the failure of the effort to end the Vietnam War, and then Watergate, there was a great demand for major reform and a growing conviction that the system simply was

---

1 *Myers v. United States*, 272 U.S. 52, 240 and 293 (1926).
2 *Youngstown Sheet & Tube Co. v. Sawyer*, 343 U.S. 579, 614 (1952).
3 Madison noted in *Federalist 37* that unlike nature "in which all the delineations are perfectly accurate, and appear to be otherwise only from the imperfection of the eye which surveys them," man-made institutions generate obscurity from "the object itself." No skill "in the science of government has yet been able to discriminate and define, with sufficient certainty, its three great provinces, the legislative, executive, and judiciary; or even the privileges and powers of the different legislative branches. Questions daily occur in the course of practice, which prove the obscurity which reins in these subjects, and which puzzle the greatest adepts in political science."

no longer capable of solving key problems through the ordinary political process of negotiation, bargaining, and elections. There was a demand for new political and institutional reforms that might provide innovative ways to work around eighteenth-century institutions that no longer seemed capable of solving critical social problems. Congress began in the early 1970s to construct legalistic solutions to these institutional and political problems. The motives for juridification here were much as they were in the policy realm: For some it was the perception that the formal allocation and reallocation of power were the only ways around profound institutional and political barriers; for others, these devices simply seemed more efficient and more effective. These new formal procedures also would allow members of Congress to avoid blame (and responsibility) for hard political choices. Law's allure seemed to promise a better, perhaps even morally superior means of governance.

The juridification of the political process often took the form of institutional or procedural innovations and rules that did not depend on the courts or did not require judicial commands or judicial blockades. Although many of these devices would be tested in court, all that was required was judicial assent or a court wiling to simply get out of the way and remain largely silent. These efforts generated three additional patterns of juridification that need to be considered: (1) those instances in which the Court says yes, allowing the political branches to formalize, legalize, and juridify the process – as they did with the establishment of the Office of Independent Counsel (special prosecutor); (2) those in which the Court says no, rejecting the effort, as it did with the effort to automate deficit reduction plans and the line-item veto provision; and (3) those in which the Court limits its role, saying relatively little, as it largely has with legislative-executive struggle over the war powers.

Each of these patterns has risks – when the Court says yes or chooses to remain silent, the changes and reallocations of power that the Court allows can erode or undermine the natural protections of Madison's eighteenth-century equilibrium of power. When the Court says no, the arguments advanced to support the failed change continue to frame the debate in future and related cases – lineal and lateral alike – not only within the courts, but also in the elected branches as well. Whether the Court says yes, no, or remains silent, these innovations reduce the ambiguity that is integral to the constitutional equilibrium: Can you eliminate ambiguity in some parts of a complicated and interdependent eighteenth-century Constitution without undercutting or destabilizing other parts? And if not, is the risk worth taking? Before we can answer the second question, we need to better understand the answer to the first. To help answer that question, this chapter examines the establishment of the Office of Independent Counsel for the investigation and prosecution of corruption and criminal activity by government officials (where the Court said yes), as well as the effort to automate deficit reduction and to hand over line-item veto authority to the president (where the Court said no). The next chapter examines the war powers and other areas in which the Court has remained relatively silent.

Ethics in Government and the Office of Independent Counsel

Watergate was the capstone of a profound shift in American society and in that society's relationship to its government that began with struggles over civil rights in the South, flared with urban violence in the North, and exploded in protests as the Vietnam War escalated. These shocks to the American system accelerated a decline in trust in government that some argue began with John F. Kennedy's assassination in Dallas in 1963. Public opinion reflected this trend – and drove it.[4] A generation whose heroes were lawyers and judges and prosecutors and journalists – Earl Warren, and Thurgood Marshall, John Sirica, Archibald Cox, Bob Woodward and Carl Bernstein – headed to law school before they went to Washington, D.C., and brought their legal training and legal instincts to government, increasingly confident that politics and political institutions were the problem and law and courts the solution. Unlike state legislatures, Congress, and the White House, the courts appeared open, transparent, and committed to justice. Public-spirited young people flocked to law schools and then into armies of reform such as those organized by Ralph Nader to press for change in policies ranging from the environment to poverty, abortion to education and civil rights. They turned to the courts in an effort to find not only a more efficient means of delivering on the promises of the American creed, but also a better, more moral, and purer way to do so.

This neo-Calvinist desire to purify politics has a long and deep history in American life. Whether it was expressed in the Jacksonian era, the abolitionist movement, the Populist-Progressive era of the 1890s and early 1900s, or the long-1960s, Samuel Huntington argues, "American society seems to evolve through periods of creedal passion and creedal passivity." There is, he writes, an "ever-present gap" between American political

---

4 And it has been a dominant feature of public opinion ever since. See John R. Hibbing and Elizabeth Theiss-Morse, *Congress as Public Enemy: Public Attitudes toward American Political Institutions*, New York: Cambridge University Press, 1995; Arthur Miller, "Political Issues and Trust in Government, 1964–1970," 68 *American Political Science Review* 3, 989–1001 (1974); Jack Citrin, "Comment: The Political Relevance of Trust in Government," 68 *American Political Science Review* 3, 973–88 (1974); Jack Citrin, Herbert McClosky, John Shanks, and Paul Sniderman, "Personal and Political Sources of Political Alienation," 5 *British Journal of Political Science* 1, 1–31 (1975).

ideals and American political institutions and practices.[5] That creedal passion hit a peak in Watergate's wake when, in 1974, national midterm elections swept a tide of reform candidates into Congress. The Democrats gained an additional forty-three seats in the House and picked up an additional three in the Senate. When Congress next met, in January 1975, there were ninety-two first-term representatives in the House – seventy-five of whom were members of the Democratic Party elected on promises of institutional reform. Reform quickly focused on the purification of politics via campaign finance laws and a depoliticized process for the investigation and prosecution of political corruption.

The corruption problem was very real and far from easy to solve. The American system leaves criminal prosecution to the executive branch, acting through the attorney general, a member of the president's cabinet and thus a political appointee. In the years leading up to Watergate, the position of attorney general increasingly went to former campaign managers or top campaign officials. J. Howard McGrath, for example, moved from chairman of the Democratic National Committee to attorney general shortly after Harry Truman's inauguration in 1949; John Kennedy appointed his brother (and former campaign manager) to head up the Justice Department in 1961; and of course, John Mitchell was serving as the chairman of the Committee to Reelect the President at the same time that he was leading the Justice Department as attorney general in 1972.

The Department of Justice, "on a per capita basis" is "the most highly politicized agency in Government," Common Cause's General Counsel Mitchell Rogovin testified in 1974. "Thirty years ago, the Collectors of Internal Revenue, the Postmasters, and the U.S. Attorneys were the backbone of the patronage system. Today, only the presidentially appointed U.S. Attorney remains."[6] Patronage has its utility, however. Having an attorney general who serves at the pleasure of the president guarantees accountability and responsiveness to popular preferences and priorities in law enforcement and criminal prosecution; it is a system that provides solid political accountability. The president is responsible for the attorney general and the choices made by the Department of Justice. If voters do not like the attorney general's priorities and prosecutorial choices, they can bring pressure on the president who, in turn, can demand changes from his agents. But what would happen if the alleged lawbreaking is being done by members of the administration itself, or even if the criminal or corrupt activities are being perpetrated by the attorney general's own

5 Samuel P. Huntington, *American Politics: The Promise of Disharmony*, Cambridge: Harvard University Press, 1981, p 4.
6 Mitchell Rogovin (General Counsel, Common Cause), testifying in "Removing Politics from the Administration of Justice," hearings on S. 2803 and S. 2978 before the Subcommittee on Separation of Power of the Committee on the Judiciary of the United States Senate, 93rd Congress, 2nd session, March 26, 1974, p 40.

superior in the White House? Suddenly, the responsive qualities of the American system appear far less advantageous.

Watergate demonstrated the problem – and, some believed, suggested the cure as well. Watergate had heroes as well as villains, and few of those stars were more luminous than Special Prosecutor Archibald Cox. When Cox refused to agree to withdraw his demand for certain Oval Office tapes, Richard Nixon decided to dismiss the special prosecutor and instructed his attorney general, Elliot Richardson, to do so. Richardson refused and then resigned. The job then fell to Richardson's deputy, William Ruckelshaus, who also refused and resigned. Finally, Robert Bork, then the solicitor general of the United States and third in command at the Justice Department, did what the others had refused to do. Cox was out. The events of that evening, October 20, 1973, would come to be known as the "Saturday Night Massacre" and generated "results precisely opposite to what the President and his lawyers had anticipated," permanently and perhaps fatally damaging the president's credibility with the public and with his own party leaders. "The news and televised images of FBI agents, following a White House directive, sealing the Special Prosecutor's office and barring access by Cox's staff, shocked and frightened the nation." Leon Jaworski, who would eventually replace Cox, "thought the FBI's actions resembled those of the Gestapo."[7]

It was widely believed that a special prosecutor slayed the dragon of Watergate, mobilizing the courts to impose accountability, and that it made sense to create a permanent and genuinely independent counsel to keep the system free of corruption – and beyond the reach of some future corrupt or dangerous administration. House and Senate hearings quickly followed the Cox dismissal, focusing on a way to remove the administration from the selection (and dismissal) of those investigating political activities and political crimes. It would take five years and several different efforts before the formal Office of Independent Counsel would be put in place by the Ethics in Government Act of 1978. But from 1973 forward, a nearly constant refrain could be heard, often led by Watergate Committee Chairman Sam Ervin of North Carolina, who in 1974 noted that "there ought to be some way to decide it other than by the political tug of war."[8] Some toyed with making the Justice Department itself an independent agency: As Texas Senator Lloyd Bentsen said during one debate on the Ethics in Government Act, "It is really time that we depoliticize the Justice Department" and end "what seems to have become the nearly standard practice of Presidents appointing as Attorney General the principal leaders of the political campaign in which they were elected.

7 Stanley I. Kutler, *The Wars of Watergate: The Last Crisis of Richard Nixon*, New York: Knopf, 1990, p 406.
8 Sen. Sam Ervin (D-NC), "Removing Politics from the Administration of Justice," p 81.

This has been done time after time and has become ingrained in the political system."[9]

In 1975, Minnesota's Democratic Senator Fritz Mondale summed up the legislative consensus that was congealing: Reactions to the abuses of the Nixon administration had produced legislative proposals ranging from "challenges to the continuation of the longest and most divisive war in our history, to the massive impoundment of funds appropriated by the Congress, to the withholding of information under the Freedom of Information Act, to the submitting of nominations for the advice and consent of the Senate." In each case, the problem was an abuse of power and congressional unwillingness or inability to do anything to respond. "The bond linking these cases," Mondale said, "was the inability to obtain redress of grievances through any means other than the courts." And the solutions for each of these problems – the War Powers Resolution of 1972,[10] the Budget Impoundment Act of 1974,[11] and the 1974 amendments to the Freedom of Information Act[12] – were each legalistic attempts to formalize and structure these political struggles. The broad lesson to be learned here, Mondale suggested, was that "illegal executive branch actions" could and had to be met by "court challenges" that would enable Congress to correct these abuses.[13]

Congressional frustration with a lack of effective tools available to deal with administration officials had reached a critical point. Representative Lee Hamilton pointed to a criminal contempt citation that the House

---

9 Sen. Lloyd Bentsen (D-TX), *Congressional Record*, June 27, 1977, p S 20974. This trend abated in the wake of Watergate. "I am pleased to see," Senator Bentsen noted, that President Carter and President Ford departed from that practice." But it has revived in more recent years, with former chief of staff to the Reagan-Bush campaign Edwin Meese serving as attorney general for Reagan, and more recently former White House Counsel Alberto Gonzales heading the Justice Department under President George W. Bush.

10 War Powers Act of 1973 (Public law 93–148). See Gordon Silverstein, *Imbalance of Powers: Constitutional Interpretation and the Making of American Foreign Policy*, New York: Oxford University Press, 1996, and Chapter 8 in this book.

11 The Congressional Budget and Impoundment Control Act of 1974 (Public Law 93–344, 2 U.S.C. § 601–688). See Louis Fisher, *Congressional Abdication on War & Spending*, College Station: Texas A&M University Press, 2000, and Louis Fisher, *Presidential Spending Power*, Princeton: Princeton University Press, 1975.

12 The original Freedom of Information Act was approved by Congress over President Lyndon Johnson's stern objections in 1966. Major revisions to the bill passed in the wake of Watergate in 1974. Though Gerald Ford was, reportedly, initially willing to sign the bill, recently released documents suggest that he was convinced to veto it by his chief of staff – Donald Rumsfeld – along with Richard Cheney, then deputy chief of staff, and Justice Department lawyer, Antonin Scalia. The House overrode the veto on November 20, 1974, by a vote of 371 to 31, whereas the Senate overturned the veto, 65–27 the next day. See Memorandum for President Ford from Ken Cole, "H.R. 12471, Amendments to the Freedom of Information Act," September 25, 1974, Gerald R. Ford Library, Document 10.

13 Sen. Walter Mondale (D-MN), "Watergate Reorganization and Reform Act of 1975," hearings on S. 495 and S. 2036 before the Committee on Government Operations, United States Senate, 94th Congress, first session (Part I), July 29, 1975, p 6.

Select Committee on Intelligence had voted out against then-Secretary of State Henry Kissinger – proposed as a way to force the production of documents concerning covert government operations – as evidence of the futility of using existing congressional tools.[14] "Even if the full House cites Kissinger for criminal contempt," Hamilton said, "he most probably will never be prosecuted because prosecutorial discretion rests with the executive branch. If a trial results, the administration's claim of executive privilege may well receive favorable consideration by a court not wanting to stigmatize the Secretary with a criminal conviction."[15]

The answer was to be more than just legislation. It would be an effort to restructure and reallocate formal powers, a legalistic solution to a political problem. Congress is engaged in "an historic mission, writing this legislation," Republican Senator Jacob Javits insisted in 1976. This sort of effort, he said, did "not follow other scandals" such as Teapot Dome. "For the first time," Javits said, "Congress is making an effort to institutionalize an instrument of self-purification."[16]

For many of the key legislators involved in this effort, however, it was important to move Congress out of the business of criminal investigation and prosecution. As "far as I see it," Connecticut's Senator Lowell Weicker noted in 1976, "the Congress' job is legislative; it is not to investigate criminal activity." Weicker made it clear that he did not want to "get Congress into the business of conducting criminal investigations."[17] The problem, some would argue, was that Congress took politics out of the criminal process by criminalizing politics itself – setting up an independent office to determine what was and was not within the bounds of the political process.

It is necessary to digress for a moment to sort out the horribly confusing set of terms used in reference to the Office of Independent Counsel. Though the terms "special prosecutor" and "independent counsel" are often confused, the 1978 statute established something quite different from the position Archibald Cox occupied before the law went into effect – and from the office Patrick Fitzgerald occupied in 2007, after the law expired. The traditional special prosecutor was someone appointed by the president or the attorney general, who could be dismissed by them, albeit at significant political cost. An independent counsel, by contrast, could be requested by the attorney general, but would be appointed by a

---

14 See Louis Fisher, "Congressional Investigations: Subpoenas and Contempt Power," Washington, DC: Congressional Research Service, April 2, 2003, p 22.
15 Sen. Lee Hamilton (D-IN), "Watergate Reorganization and Reform Act of 1975," p 126.
16 Sen. Jacob Javits (R-NY), "Provision for a Special Prosecutor," hearings on H.R. 14476, H.R. 11357, H.R. 11999, H.R. 8281, H.R. 8039, H.R. 15634, and Title I of S. 495 before the Subcommittee on Criminal Justice of the Committee on the Judiciary, United States House of Representatives, 94th Congress, Second Session, July 21, 1976, p 13.
17 Sen. Lowell Weicker (R-CT), "Provision for a Special Prosecutor," p 18.

panel of appellate court judges. The judges would then outline the parameters of the investigation, and once appointed, the counsel could only be removed for cause by those same judges.[18]

During hearings on establishing what would eventually be called the Office of Independent Counsel, New York's Representative Elizabeth Holtzman and former House Judiciary Committee Counsel John Doar neatly summed up the growing disconnect between the frustrated politicians of the Watergate era – who sought more law and less politics – and the worries expressed nearly uniformly by prominent lawyers whose government service included work in the Justice Department, House, and Senate committees, and, for some, as special prosecutors.

Doar insisted that Congress needed to take full political responsibility, not recast political corruption as a simple criminal matter. Of the 1976 legislation, Doar said, "A good part of the responsibility for preserving trust and confidence in our constitutional system of government rests with the Congress of the United States. This statute undercuts that concept." Holtzman said she was far from convinced that Congress could accomplish these goals on its own. "I must tell you in all frankness," she said, "that relying on the House of Representatives is an inadequate solution." Ultimately, she said, the House probably can come through, as it had by pressing for the impeachment of Richard Nixon, But "it took a very long time for the House of Representatives to act." Relying on political pressure and political tools to force the president to cooperate may not be acceptable, Holtzman argued.[19]

Doar's concerns were echoed again and again by lawyers who had worked in high government positions. Theodore Sorensen argued that "politics is necessarily tied up with policy," insisting that responsibility for prosecutorial choices must rest with the president: "How else can a President be held responsible for his own constitutional obligation to take care that laws be faithfully executed? He may still try to lay the blame for any failure at the door of Congress, but do not let him blame the Department of Justice as well by taking responsibility for that Department away from him."[20] Archibald Cox himself argued that it was both impossible and unwise to split public policy from prosecutorial decisions that have "vast social and economic consequences." The main reason the president

18 Between 1978 and 1999 there were twenty-one investigations conducted by those appointed to serve as independent counsels, ranging from the investigation of Jimmy Carter aide Hamilton Jordan for alleged drug use, to those of cabinet officers Mike Espy and Samuel Pierce, to the $46 million seven-year investigation of the Iran-Contra affair conducted by Lawrence Walsh, and finally, the various investigations of President and Mrs. Clinton by Ken Starr. Christopher H. Schroeder, "The Independent Counsel Statute: Reform or Repeal?", 62 *Law and Contemporary Problems* 1, 1–4 (1999).

19 John Doar and Rep. Elizabeth Holtzman (D-NY), "Provision for a Special Prosecutor," pp 173–9.

20 Theodore Sorensen, "Removing Politics from the Administration of Justice," pp 17, 19.

should be involved in these decisions, Cox testified, is that "there should be political responsibility for the decisions, and it is through the President, in the quadrennial elections and the impact upon off-term elections, that that political responsibility is made known."[21]

Lyndon Johnson's solicitor general, Erwin Griswold (who served as dean of Harvard Law School from 1946–1967), rejected the idea that law and legal process might save politics. "In my opinion," Griswold told a Senate committee, "we already have far too many questions referred to the courts. We were not established as a government by the judiciary, and we should not, I think, be taking steps to add to the tendencies which are already throwing more and more questions which arise in the administration of the government into the courts for decision."[22]

Philip Lacovara, another former solicitor general who worked for Cox on the special prosecutor's staff, said that it was "disquieting" to think that the judiciary should "routinely become the umpire in disputes of this sort" and argued that it would be "far more desirable" to "leave litigation to the private parties" whose interests are affected by executive action. The American principle of checks and balances, Lacovara testified, "provides for congressional-executive relations to be adjusted through the political process rather than through adversary litigation.[23]

Father Robert F. Drinan, a Catholic priest who represented Massachusetts in the House of Representatives and served on the Judiciary Committee during the Nixon impeachment hearings, was far from sold on relying on an independent special prosecutor to battle political corruption. Such a powerful and independent prosecutor, Drinan said, "might like his job, the publicity he gets, and then he might go from one thing to another and the Attorney General, and even the succeeding Attorney General would have such a political 'hot potato' that he would not be able to petition the court to terminate it and allow this to revert to the Department of Justice."[24] John Doar echoed this concern, adding that "this grant of power is susceptible of abuse. With the whole criminal code at his disposal, the permanent special prosecutor could embark on a self-defined crusade for all sorts of reasons including making a name for himself. The idea that any federal official, appointed not elected, should have uncontrolled power to thumb through the entire federal criminal code as a basis for investigating a targeted group of public officials is an anathema to me."[25] Despite this counsel, the Senate opted to reallocate power, building a new legal institution insulated from politics – and political accountability.

21 Archibald Cox, "Removing Politics from the Administration of Justice," p 201.
22 Erwin Griswold, "Removing Politics from the Administration of Justice," p 244.
23 Philip Lacovara, "Removing Politics from the Administration of Justice," p 279.
24 Rep. Robert Drinan (D-MA), "Provision for a Special Prosecutor," p 165.
25 Doar, "Provision for a Special Prosecutor," p 172.

The Supreme Court reviewed and allowed this innovation: It said yes to the Office of Independent Counsel. For the majority, there were two major concerns. Was there a violation of the constitutional rules allocating the appointment power to the president? And was there a violation of the broader principle of the separation of powers? On the appointment issue, the debate turned on whether or not this office would be held by what the Constitution refers to as an "Officer of the United States" or was it to be held by an "inferior Officer." This distinction matters because Officers of the United States must be appointed by the president, whereas the appointment of an inferior officer may be vested by Congress in "the Courts of Law, or in the Heads of Departments."[26] Although the majority of the Justices noted that the line between "inferior" and "principal" officers is "far from clear," they saw no need to attempt to decide exactly where the line fell "because in our view [this officer] falls on the 'inferior officer' side of that line."[27]

The more interesting problem was the broader question of the separation of powers. Here, lateral precedent played a significant role. For the majority, separation of powers had come to be defined as a barrier to one branch usurping the power of another – which was at the heart of the Court's decision two years earlier in *Bowsher v. Synar*, a 1986 case challenging the authority of Congress to vest executive power in an officer over whom Congress retained some degree of control.[28] In *Bowsher*, as in *INS v. Chadha*, which was decided in 1983, three years before *Bowsher*, the Court had made plain that, although it was very tolerant of any delegation of power by one branch to another, it would strictly prohibit any innovations that might allow the donor branch to retain any control over the powers it had delegated or assigned to another. In the case of the independent counsel, the majority's separation of powers concern focused not on what was being delegated, but rather on any strings that might be attached to that delegation, strings that would allow Congress to control this inferior officer. "Unlike both *Bowsher* and *Myers*," a 1926 case on which the Court relied in its *Bowsher* ruling,[29] "this case does not involve an attempt by Congress itself to gain a role in the removal of executive officials other than its established powers of impeachment and conviction. The Act instead puts the removal power squarely in the hands of the Executive Branch," as the independent counsel may only be removed from office "by the personal action of the Attorney General, and only for good cause."[30]

---

26 U.S. Constitution, Article II, section 2, paragraph 2.
27 *Morrison v. Olson*, 487 U.S. 654, 671 (1988) (Rehnquist, CJ, for the Majority).
28 *Bowsher v. Synar*, 478 U.S. 714 (1986) and *INS v. Chadha*, 462 U.S. 919 (1983), both of which are discussed extensively in this chapter.
29 *Myers v. United States*, 272 U.S. 52 (1926).
30 *Bowsher v. Synar*, 478 U.S. at 686.

Although the majority focused on usurpation, a loud, clear warning rang out in the form of a stinging dissent by Justice Antonin Scalia. After an extensive discussion of the separation of powers and the independent counsel provision itself, Scalia concluded his dissent with what – in hindsight – seems a rather stunningly prescient warning. Scalia said that his own experience in the Justice Department made him particularly aware of the "vast power and the immense discretion that are placed in the hands of a prosecutor with respect to the objects of his investigation." Scalia then quoted from Justice Robert Jackson, who had served as attorney general for Franklin Roosevelt. Jackson, Scalia said, had argued, "Law enforcement is not automatic. It isn't blind." A prosecutor, Jackson said, "must pick his cases, because no prosecutor can even investigate all of the cases in which he receives complaints." And if the prosecutor can choose the case, "it follows that he can choose his defendants. Therein is the most dangerous power of the prosecutor: that he will pick people that he thinks he should get, rather than cases that need to be prosecuted." Because there are no shortage of laws, Jackson continued, "a prosecutor stands a fair chance of finding at least a technical violation of some act on the part of almost anyone. In such a case, it is not a question of discovering the commission of a crime and then looking for the man who has committed it; it is a question of picking the man and then searching the law books, or putting investigators to work, to pin some offense on him."[31]

"Under our system of government," Scalia wrote in dissent, "the primary check against prosecutorial abuse is a political one. The prosecutors who exercise this awesome discretion are selected, and can be removed, by a President whom the people have trusted enough to elect. Moreover, when crimes are not investigated and prosecuted fairly, non-selectively, with a reasonable sense of proportion, the President pays the cost in political damage to his administration." If federal prosecutors abuse their power, Scalia said, "the unfairness will come home to roost in the Oval Office." This was, Scalia suggested, the positive lesson of Watergate, which he argued ultimately produced a result that was "precisely what the Founders had in mind when they provided that all executive powers would be exercised by a *single* Chief Executive." The president, Scalia wrote, is "directly dependent on the people, and, since there is only *one* President, *he* is responsible" – and the people know who is responsible. The problem with setting up an insulated and isolated Office of Independent Counsel, he continued, is that there is nowhere to turn if that prosecutor abuses this power. Turning over the selection to a panel of

---

31 *Morrison v. Olson*, 487 U.S. at 728 (Scalia, dissenting), quoting from Robert Jackson, "The Federal Prosecutor," Address delivered at the Second Annual Conference of United States Attorneys, April 1, 1940.

judges is no real protection. What happens if those judges are "politically partisan, as judges have been known to be, and select a prosecutor antagonistic to the administration, or even to the particular individual who has been selected for this special treatment? There is no remedy for that, not even a political one," Scalia insisted.

Not only would this situation be unfair to the potential target of the investigation, but perhaps more importantly, "there would be no one accountable to the public to whom the blame could be assigned." Quoting from an *amicus* brief filed in the Morrison case by three former attorneys general (Edward Levi, Griffin Bell, and William French Smith), Scalia noted that all the formal devices, all the efforts to strip out the ambiguous gray of politics, are "designed to heighten, not to check all of the occupational hazards of the dedicated prosecutor: the danger of too narrow a focus, of the loss of perspective, of preoccupation with the pursuit of one alleged suspect to the exclusion of other interests."

Scalia said he well understood the political pressure Congress must feel to approve this sort of turn to law, noting that it is "difficult to vote not to enact, and even more difficult to vote to repeal, a statute called, appropriately enough, the Ethics in Government Act. If Congress is controlled by the party other than the one to which the President belongs, it has little incentive to repeal it; if it is controlled by the same party, it dare not." Members of Congress might well feel politically unable to reject these reforms, Scalia noted, but the life-tenured Justices of the U.S. Supreme Court should not. By its "shortsighted action today," he argued, "I fear the Court has permanently encumbered the Republic with an institution that will do it great harm."[32]

Scalia's warnings dramatically gained credibility in the wake of the Reagan administration's Iran-Contra affair. After an investigation that stretched from 1986 to 1993, Lawrence Walsh spent more than $48 million (which does not include the costs of the investigation staged by a Special Select Joint Committee of Congress)[33] to produce eleven convictions (out of fourteen people charged) – of which two were reversed on appeal, two were pardoned before trial, and one was dismissed when the George H. W. Bush administration refused to submit classified information needed for the prosecution. President Bush ultimately issued executive pardons for the remaining six who were prosecuted and convicted.[34] Scalia's warnings were even more dramatically illustrated in the massive

---

32 *Morrison v. Olson*, 487 U.S. at 728–733 (Scalia, dissenting). For a more comprehensive discussion of the use of criminal prosecution in political struggles, see Benjamin Ginsberg and Martin Shefter, *Politics by Other Means: The Declining Importance of Elections*, New York: Basic Books, 1990.

33 See: Theodore Draper, *A Very Thin Line*, New York: Hill and Wang, 1991 and Lawrence E. Walsh, *Firewall: The Iran-Contra Conspiracy and Cover-Up*, New York: W.W. Norton, 1998.

34 Caspar Weinberger, Duane Clarridge, Clair George, Elliott Abrams, Alan Fiers and Robert McFarlane.

series of investigations of the Clinton White House, which reached their peak in the investigations undertaken by Independent Counsel Kenneth Starr just ten years later. These investigations cost more than $52 million (with another $6 million or so being spent on a separate special investigation of the Whitewater land deals in which the Clintons were involved),[35] ultimately generating sworn testimony by Bill Clinton that led to his impeachment in the House and trial in the Senate.[36]

Ultimately, the Clinton experience – along with several other cases in which there was wide agreement that independent counsels had run far beyond their initial mandates[37] – persuaded Congress to allow the independent counsel provisions to lapse in June 1999. The effort to formally reallocate power in the pursuit of the purification of the investigation of political corruption had run its course, albeit a very expensive course. More than $167 million was spent from 1978 to 1999, when the law expired.[38] Although some might argue that this was money well spent in the effort to assure accountability of high officials in government, few were willing to stand up and support the continuation of the office in 1999.[39] After 1999, the system essentially returned to the status quo ante, with the Justice Department appointing special counsel when political pressure or internal preferences dictate as happened in 2003 when the George W. Bush administration was pressured to appoint Patrick Fitzgerald to investigate the leak of information about undercover Central Intelligence Agency operative Valerie Plame, resulting in the resignation and then conviction of the vice president's chief of staff, I. Lewis "Scooter" Libby in 2007.[40]

---

35 GAO Financial Audits of Expenditures by Independent Counsels.
36 *Clinton v. Jones*, 520 U.S. 681 (1997). The court could have stopped this particular chain of events had there been an inclination to put Paula Jones' civil suit on hold during the Clinton presidency, rather than rejecting the president's assertion that the political risks and costs to the executive outweighed the demand for expeditious judicial resolution of the lawsuit.
37 In cases ranging from the investigation of alleged drug use by Jimmy Carter aide Hamilton Jordan in 1978, to the appointment of an independent counsel to investigate charges against Secretary of Housing Samuel Pierce in 1988, along with the investigations of Mike Espy, and Henry Cisneros among others. See Katy Harriger, *The Special Prosecutor in American Politics* (2nd ed.), Lawrence: University Press of Kansas, 2000 and Charles Johnson and Danette Brickman, *Independent Counsel: The Law and the Investigation*, Washington, DC: CQ Press, 2001.
38 David Johnston, "Attorney General Taking Control as Independent Counsel Law Dies," *New York Times*, June 30, 1999, p 1.
39 There was serious talk about making the Justice Department an independent agency after Watergate, but this ultimately was dropped. What was never seriously considered was the possibility of making the attorney general an elected official, much as is the case in many states. Such a change would require constitutional amendment, although it would have the virtue of maintaining democratic accountability, which was at the core of Scalia's concerns about severing the prosecutorial function from the executive branch.
40 Libby was later pardoned by President George W. Bush. See: Charlie Savage: *Takeover: The Return of the Imperial Presidency and the Subversion of American Democracy*, Boston: Little Brown, 2007.

The independent counsel experience was a case of juridification in which equilibrium ultimately was restored relatively easily, despite some considerable political and economic cost. It was relatively easy because the creation of the Office of Independent Counsel was not an example of an embedded, iterated pattern of juridification. In this case, the Court merely said yes; the Court *allowed* Congress to create this office and left it at that. Without layers of iterated cases and laws, the branches were not backed deep into one corner of the *Scrabble* board. The Court performed its traditional function – saying what government *may* and what it may *not* do. Then, when the political tide turned, it was relatively easy to return to and reestablish the traditional roles and the traditional equilibrium. Simply saying yes, however, left an important precedent available, a different way of thinking about the allocation and reallocation of traditional functions and powers. The status quo ante was restored, but the genie may well be out of the bottle, available again at some time down the road in a similar, lineal case – or perhaps in a rather different, lateral arena.

When the Court Says No: Automated Deficit Cuts and the Line-Item Veto

Many post-Watergate efforts to reallocate, formalize, and rigidify the separation of powers followed a similar pattern: Congress would formally acknowledge what had once been contested, allocating and delegating power explicitly to the president, and then develop innovative means to limit and control those allocations and delegations. This was the pattern in the War Powers Resolution in 1972, it would be the pattern in all sorts of policy areas like immigration control in the 1980s,[41] and it would be true as well for efforts in the 1980s and 1990s to tame uncontrolled deficits.

Proposals to reallocate and formalize the budget process were driven by various, overlapping incentives. Some saw a more rational, formal, and explicit allocation of power, along with automated procedures, as an essential way to work around profound institutional and political barriers. Others perhaps saw it as a more efficient and less politically costly alternative, a way to gain credit for securing federal funds for valued projects and avoid blame when those funds were cut – not by the vote of politically responsive elected officials, but under a predetermined formula, or at the hand of a president whose national constituency would insulate him or her from political backlash for imposing specific local budget cuts via a line-item veto. Unlike the independent counsel, however, these efforts followed a different pattern and process when they were tested in the Supreme Court: The Justices said no. Although this response

---

41 See, for example, *INS v. Chadha*, 462 U.S. 919 (1983).

might well have set off another round of efforts designed to meet the Court's constitutional objections, perhaps triggering a constructive or deconstructive pattern, this did not happen in these cases. The Court said no, and the effort ended.

But this remains an important pattern to consider because, although the policy may not have changed, the experience contributed to the broader and more subtle ways in which juridification shapes and constrains our language and our politics. Congress is no less prone to attempt to juridify in the future: The lesson that it seems to have learned is that any future effort will require more law, not less – more careful allocation, more precise and unrestricted delegation. By contrasting the reasons and arguments used by the Justices in approving the allocation of power in the independent counsel case with those used and relied on to strike down the innovations in the deficit reduction and line-item veto cases, it may be possible to better anticipate the risks as well as the rewards of law's allure when it comes to the juridification of the political process itself.

Automating the Budget Process

The Cold War, the war in Vietnam, and huge new spending induced by major domestic policy programs instituted and expanded under Lyndon Johnson and Richard Nixon, followed by the enormous rise in defense spending combined with significant tax cuts under Reagan, all layered on top of the hyperinflation of the 1970s – combined to generate explosive growth in the national debt. From a small surplus in 1969 (in standardized figures), the budget deficit rose to more than $23 billion in 1971, hit $73 billion in 1976, dropped a bit between 1977 and 1980, and then went roaring off into the stratosphere: $128 billion in 1982, $208 billion in 1983, $212 billion in 1985, and topping out at $221.2 billion in 1986 (see Figure 7.1). By the early 1980s, it was not clear what could be done about the deficit – but it was clear that few, if any, in Congress wanted responsibility for doing it, and fewer still had a clear idea of how that institution could possibly make the sorts of political choices that would be needed to significantly reduce the deficit.[42]

Inflationary pressures brought on by the costs of the Vietnam War combined with America's changing world economic role coincided with major changes in American political institutions, including structural reforms of the main political parties and revised internal rules of the House and Senate. The Democratic Party's debacle in Chicago in 1968 generated

---

42 All figures are standardized. It should be noted that the deficit, as a percentage of gross domestic product (GDP), fluctuated from just under 3 percent of GDP in 1968, reaching 5 percent of GDP in 1986. Although this is not nearly as dramatic a figure, it was the gross figures in hundreds of billions of dollars that framed the political debate about deficit reduction.

billions of dollars

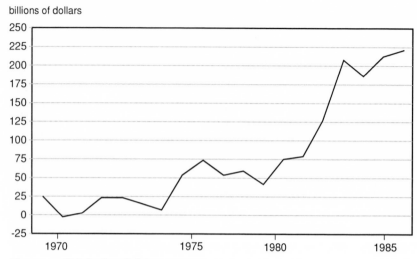

Figure 7.1. U.S. budget deficit 1969–1986.

demand for drastic reforms in the delegate selection process and the structure of the party itself.[43] The "declining influence of political parties" made it difficult for leaders "to ward off particularistic demands." Add to this the divided control of government, a rising tide of partisanship, and soaring levels of cynicism and mistrust in government and politics, and, there was every reason for all concerned to find real allure in some sort of formal, legally imposed, and strictly structured procedure that might allow members of Congress to continue to claim credit for delivering goods and services to constituents while relying on an anonymous and politically invulnerable, legally mandated, automated process to take responsibility for cutting or withdrawing those goods and services.[44]

Although a Republican-controlled Senate voted to support a balanced budget amendment to the Constitution in 1982, it was defeated in the Democratic-controlled House. By August 1983, thirty-two states had voted to call a constitutional convention to force the issue, but that effort never succeeded in garnering the votes of the thirty-four states needed. Instead, two Senate Republicans (Phil Gramm of Texas and Warren Rudman of New Hampshire), along with South Carolina Democrat Ernest

43 Nelson W. Polsby, *Consequences of Party Reform*, New York: Oxford University Press, 1983; Byron Shafer, *Quiet Revolution: The Struggle for the Democratic Party and the Shaping of Post-Reform Politics*, New York: Russell Sage Foundation, 1983, and David Truman, "Party Reform, Party Atrophy, and Constitutional Change: Some Reflections," 99 *Political Science Quarterly* 4, 637–55 (1984).
44 Darrell M. West, "Gramm-Rudman-Hollings and the Politics of Deficit Reduction," 499 *Annals of the American Academy Political and Social Science* (September 1988), p 92. See as well Polsby, *Consequences of Party Reform*, and Leroy Rieselbach, *Congressional Reform*, Washington, DC: CQ Press, 1986.

Hollings, proposed a complex, legalistic, formal set of rules that would do what the politicians would not or could not do.[45]

As the 99th Congress began to struggle with the budget in 1985, its members faced what was (for the time) historically unprecedented debt, with projected deficits for fiscal 1986 of more than $180 billion. All the choices were bad choices, and so the Gramm-Rudman-Hollings bill (often shortened to "Gramm-Rudman" much to Ernest Hollings' ultimate delight after abandoning the legislation that bore his name) began to gain traction. The bill established maximum deficit levels that, if exceeded, would legally require the president to impose a uniform reduction on all spending, except in a very few exempt categories. Some hoped the bill would force fiscal discipline – others were relieved to think it might provide political cover: Among the more appealing aspects of Gramm-Rudman was its ability to deflect blame. "If Congress [failed to] achieve its budget targets, responsibility for the painful choices would shift to the President to implement cuts specified" by the law.[46]

There were all sorts of formal mechanisms needed to construct a legal system for the automatic implementation of a balanced budget. Creating these devices took attention away from the fundamental political and economic debate, putting the focus instead on the legal formalities themselves, including their constitutionality. Among other issues, the law had to define what would constitute a deficit, who would decide if deficit thresholds had been crossed, and if so, how cuts would be implemented. Congress surely was not willing to assign this task to the White House, but could not execute these functions on its own because the power to execute the laws belongs to the executive and not the legislative branch. The solution was to assign authority to the Office of the Comptroller General, who heads the statutorily independent General Accounting Office (GAO).

Although the comptroller general actually is nominated by the president, the selection is made from a list of candidates selected by the House Speaker and the President pro tempore. Furthermore, after Senate confirmation, the comptroller general may be removed not only by impeachment (a process Congress alone controls), but also by a joint resolution of Congress in the event of a very strict and narrow set of conditions (permanent disability, inefficiency, neglect of duty, malfeasance, or conviction of a felony or for "conduct involving moral turpitude"). A joint resolution of Congress is subject to executive veto, but that veto can be overridden, leaving somewhat unclear the degree to which the comptroller general is an executive officer, a servant of Congress, or genuinely independent – and

---

45 "Effort to Amend Constitution Lags," *New York Times*, August 21, 1983, p 31.
46 Carl E. Van Horn, "Fear and Loathing on Capitol Hill: The 99th Congress and Economic Policy," 19 *PS* 1 (1986), p 25.

these legal questions would ultimately have to be decided by the Supreme Court.

Despite some debate and press coverage, this extraordinary bit of juridification was pushed through as an amendment to the regular legislation needed to raise the national debt ceiling. On October 9, 1985, without "committee hearing, economic or other analyses, and limited floor debate," Senate sponsors were able to attach the law to the debt-ceiling legislation on a 75 to 24 vote, and, a day later, the Senate approved the full debt-ceiling bill, along with Gramm-Rudman, on a vote of 51 to 37.[47]

Was this, in fact, an instance of the failure of an eighteenth-century Constitution in a twentieth-century world, or was it simply a case of political incentives driving members to focus more on their personal and political priorities than on the longer term incentives of preserving their institutional authority and power? Eric Schickler's model of "disjointed pluralism" is quite helpful in thinking about this question. The incentives that drive institutional and procedural reform are complex. Much like with precedent, there is a game of *Scrabble* here, in which choices made in earlier periods profoundly shape and constrain choices in later periods; in this instance, institutional changes designed to solve one set of problems reshape priorities and incentives in other areas.[48] This suggests that, although the Framers built institutions that were designed to create incentives for members of Congress to see their own personal power and ambition as dependent on the power and autonomy of their institution, over time these incentives had weakened and been replaced by other more powerful driving forces.[49] Was this an institutional problem or simply the lack of political will?

The rigid, formal process put in place by Gramm-Rudman was a way "to evade the hard choices that deficit reduction demands," said Maryland Republican Senator Charles Mathias, adding that it "strives for a way to reach that goal without taking responsibility."[50] Wisconsin's David Obey insisted that members were "looking for some kind of institutional magic wand," rather than having to deal with the problem at hand.[51] Even Senator Warren Rudman himself could muster little praise

47 See Jasmine Farrier, *Passing the Buck: Congress, the Budget, and Deficits*, Lexington: University Press of Kentucky, 2004, p 99.
48 See Paul Pierson, *Politics in Time: History, Institutions, and Social Analysis*, Princeton: Princeton University Press, 2004, and Chapter 3.
49 See Eric Schickler, *Disjointed Pluralism: Institutional Innovation and the Development of the U.S. Congress*, Princeton: Princeton University Press, 2001, and Kenneth A. Shepsle, "Congress Is a 'They' Not an 'It': Legislative Intent as Oxymoron," 12 *International Review of Law and Economics* 239 (1992).
50 David Broder, "The Rudman-Gramm Balanced Budget Sham," *Washington Post*, December 11, 1985, p A-23.
51 Farrier, *Passing the Buck*, pp 101–2.

for his own bill, noting that it was "a bad idea whose time has come."[52]
If nothing else, columnist Mary McGrory wrote, "it is, indisputably, an
abject and humiliating confession by Congress that it simply cannot cut
the deficit."[53] It was, McGrory noted, "a message scrawled in lipstick on
a mirror: 'Stop me before I kill again.'"[54]

Gramm-Rudman was meant to give Congress and the president political cover for hard choices on budget cutting.[55] It would allow the Republican White House to accept some cuts in military spending and give
Democrats a rationale to allow trims in domestic spending. At least, it
was supposed to do that. Instead, when it became clear that the budgetary
targets could not be met, the threat of the across-the-board reductions
created perverse incentives to develop all sorts of gimmicks and innovations to work with and through the loopholes of the law, thereby
meeting its letter without actually paying any serious political price. To
reduce the amount of cuts required, costs were shifted backward and rev-
enues moved forward: "In one particularly deft sleight of hand," Michael
Duffy reported in 1986, Congress would charge future revenue-sharing
payments from 1987 back to 1986, thus "magically wiping them off
the 1987 deficit ledger."[56] Congress also commanded the shift of federal
paydays by one day, moving them from the next fiscal year back to the
current year to move that cost out of the projected deficit that would have
triggered automatic cuts. As Comptroller General Charles Bowsher put
it, "The economic reality does not change; federal workers must still be
paid, and we've still got to borrow the money. All we've done is deceive
taxpayers by claiming a 'lower' deficit next year."[57]

The original Gramm-Rudman law was instantly challenged after President Reagan signed it on December 12, 1985. The law itself anticipated
judicial challenge and provided for an expedited appeal that would be
heard first by the district court in Washington, D.C., and then would
go directly to the U.S. Supreme Court. Congressman Mike Synar led the
challenge to the law, arguing against it in two fundamental ways: First,

52 Lois Romano, "Three Senators: Gramm, Rudman, Hollings and the Budget Revolution
They Wrought," *Washington Post*, Jan. 22, 1986, p C-1.
53 McGrory, "The Knife on Congress' Table," *Washington Post*, October 24, 1985, p A-2.
54 Mary McGrory, "The Knife on Congress' Table."
55 Initially, Hollings was delighted at the relative obscurity because the threatened cuts
were driving endless phone calls and nasty mail for his other co-sponsors: Maybe it's
just that "I got more friends in the press than Gramm and Rudman" (McCombs, "Three
Senators Gramm, Rudman, Hollings and the Budget Revolution they Wrought," p C-1.)
By 1989, Hollings publicly sought to divorce himself from the law. Ernest F. Hollings,
"Deficit Reduction, A Love Story: I Want a Divorce," *New York Times*, September 25,
1989, p A-31.
56 Michael Duffy, "Government by Gimmick," *Time*, Oct. 13, 1986.
57 Charles Bowsher, "Cooking the Books is a Bad Recipe to Cool Deficit," 169 *Journal of
Accountancy* 2 (February 1990), pp 23-5.

the law was said to delegate power beyond what the Constitution permits (*undue delegation*), and second, the law actually unconstitutionally expanded legislative power, at the expense of the executive (*usurpation*). The law, in other words, was unconstitutional because Congress both *gave away* too much power and *took* too much power, or so Synar argued.

In the end, the usurpation argument was the one that drew the Court's attention. The district court decision (notable in part because then-Circuit Court Judge Antonin Scalia was one of the judges hearing the case) ruled against the law. The three-judge panel handed down a unanimous *per curiam* decision, holding that the law was an unconstitutional attempt by Congress to hold onto powers that, once delegated, could only be exercised by someone in the executive branch. Although they made no definitive ruling on delegation, the judges sent a rather strong set of signals – built on earlier case decisions – that indicated that, although Congress could give away its power almost at will, any attempt by Congress to reclaim or control those delegations of power (short of repealing the law itself) would be strictly forbidden.[58] On the question of undue delegation, the district court noted that, though there might be something that could violate the limits of delegation, pragmatically speaking, Supreme Court rulings since the 1930s "display a much greater deference to Congress' power to delegate," motivated by concerns that an increasingly complex society made it increasingly less possible for Congress to avoid wide-ranging delegations.[59]

The Supreme Court's 1986 ruling in *Bowsher v. Synar* essentially followed the district court's reasoning, arguing that the problem was not a question of undue delegation or the abdication of its constitutional responsibilities, but rather that it was a failure to conform to a rigorous reading of the appointment power.[60] The Court focused on the selection of an officer to trigger and oversee the formulaic and automatic cuts provided for in the law. The comptroller general could be removed by Congress through impeachment (a process Congress alone controls),

---

58 A very similar doctrine is developed by the Court in *Chadha*, *Bowsher v. Synar*, and *Clinton v. City of New York*, discussed in this and the next chapter.

59 There have been two significant exceptions in which the Court did enforce a strict limit on delegation, but both came amid the Court's battle with Franklin Roosevelt. One lesson the Court seemed to learn from that experience was that a modern world probably required far more delegation than a more traditional view of the separation of powers might permit.

60 U.S. Constitution, Article 2, Section 2, Paragraph 2: "[The President] shall nominate, and by and with the Advice and Consent of the Senate, shall appoint Ambassadors, other public Ministers and Consuls, Judges of the Supreme Court, and all other Officers of the United States, whose Appointments are not herein otherwise provided for, and which shall be established by Law: but the Congress may by Law vest the Appointment of such inferior Officers, as they think proper, in the President alone, in the Courts of Law, or in the Heads of Departments."

as well as a result of a joint resolution of Congress. Joint resolutions would be subject to presidential veto. For a majority on the Supreme Court this meant that Congress held ultimate, if limited, control over the comptroller general. And this meant, the majority insisted, that Congress was unconstitutionally maintaining control of the execution of the law, in violation of the separation of powers.

Justice White, in dissent, noted that this case was the third time in the previous four years that he had "expressed the view that the Court's recent efforts to police the separation of powers have rested on untenable constitutional propositions leading to regrettable results."[61] The *Bowsher* ruling, he said, "is even more misguided." It, White argued, was a ruling based on a minor feature of a legislative plan, one that "presents no substantial threat to the basic scheme of separation of powers." But the Court's decision "to interpose its distressingly formalistic view of separation of powers as a bar to the attainment of governmental objectives through the means chosen by the Congress and the President in the legislative process," White insisted, neglects the need to protect both the constitutional diffusion of power, meant to prevent tyranny, and the constitutional recognition that appropriate cooperation between the branches is essential for a functional government.[62]

The Court focused on the question of usurpation – could Congress retain even a modicum of control over delegated powers? This ignored another fundamental problem in the separation of powers – *collusion*. Was Congress giving away powers that, constitutionally, it had no right to reallocate? Is the control over the power of the purse something Congress might constitutionally hand off to another branch or even an independent agency? But this is an aspect of the separation of powers the Court found of little interest, and, because it was possible to resolve the case without engaging the more opaque issue of the limits to delegation, the majority argued that it had "no occasion for considering appellees' other challenges to the Act, including their argument that the assignment of powers to the Comptroller General... violates the delegation doctrine."[63]

61 Justice White dissenting. The other cases were *Northern Pipeline Construction v. Marathon Pipe Line Co.*, 458 U.S. 50 (1982) and *INS v. Chadha*, 462 U.S. 919 (1983) – *Bowsher v. Synar*, 478 U.S. 714, 759 (1986),
62 *Bowsher v. Synar*, 478 U.S. at 759 (1986), Justice White dissenting. Although Justice White rejected the majority's strict, formal reading, he expressed his relief that the Court was not about to accept the solicitor general's argument that vesting any sort of executive power in an independent agency or independent officer might be constitutionally suspect. The refusal to entertain this claim, White noted, "is fully consistent with the Court's longstanding recognition that it is within the power of Congress under the 'Necessary and Proper' Clause... to vest authority that falls within the Court's definition of executive power in officers who are not subject to removal at will by the President, and are therefore not under the President's direct control." *Bowsher v. Synar*, 478 U.S. at 760–1.
63 *Bowsher v. Synar*, 478 U.S. 714, 736 (1986) (footnote 10).

Bowsher v. Synar was a case in which the Court said no. The Court explicitly rejected an invitation to turn it into a case of constructive (or deconstructive) juridification, noting that there was a constitutionally sound fallback position built into the law that would allow the Justices simply to say no and avoid any need to "perform the type of creative and imaginative statutory surgery" that had been suggested by briefs in the case. The Court's ruling did not strike down the entire statute. Congress had anticipated legal challenges and built in a fallback provision that, the majority noted, would "come into play" as a result of the Court's ruling.[64] This provision would shift the responsibilities that had been assigned to the neutral (or legislature-influenced) comptroller general back to Congress where it would be assigned to a special Joint Committee on Deficit Reduction, which would consult competing figures presented by the White House Office of Management and Budget and the Congressional Budget Office. The Committee would present a joint resolution to Congress that would then be required to follow special rules banning any amendments from the floor. It would then be sent to the president just like any ordinary legislation. In effect, Congress would simply return to its normal lawmaking process, with the exception of some streamlining internal provisions that would block amendments.

In 1986, the fallback provision worked reasonably well, but thanks, in large part, to an extraordinary set of circumstances. Because the budget cuts needed to meet the Gramm-Rudman targets already were widely known, the political damage such cuts might ordinarily be expected to generate already had been absorbed, and it was relatively easy for Congress to simply accept the reduced budget that had been previously announced.[65] The real problems would come in the next budget year. What was left of Gramm-Rudman was not much more than the ordinary budget process – run through a special Joint Committee of Congress. To benefit from the blame avoidance made possible by automated budget procedures and remain within the lines drawn by the Supreme Court, members of Congress would be forced to delegate the critical triggering decisions to a real executive officer, one exclusively accountable to the president. And that is precisely what was proposed. Instead of assigning this power to the comptroller general, Colorado Democrat Gary Hart wrote, "Gramm-Rudman II gives the President's Office of Management and Budget final power to make across the board cuts." The folks "who created the monster," Hart wrote, are writing a sequel that "promises to

---

64 *Bowsher v. Synar*, 478 U.S. at 736.
65 Ten days after the Court ruling, the House voted 339 to 72 to affirm the earlier cuts – the Senate approved the bill on a voice vote with no dissent. See Helen Dewar, "Congress Votes to Reinstate Cuts High Court Had Invalidated," *Washington Post*, July 18, 1986, p A-4.

be even more destructive than the original."[66] What could be done? One answer was to simply return to the traditional system and force Congress to accept political responsibility for budget restraint or the lack thereof. The other answer, of course, was more law.

Testifying before the Senate Governmental Affairs Committee in favor of new legislation, law professor Cass Sunstein argued that Congress should add new statutory language that would "confine executive discretion [and] ensure Executive adherence to the law." Among other things, Sunstein urged Congress to explicitly authorize lawsuits that could challenge the "economic data, assumptions and methodologies used" by the Office of Management and Budget. "The decisions of the Executive branch are usually reviewable under the standards set out in the Administrative Procedure Act, which requires courts to ensure that agency action is consistent with law and is not 'arbitrary, capricious, or an abuse of discretion,'" Sunstein testified, adding that there "is no sufficient reason to make a special exception here." The existence of review "is a useful safeguard. Perhaps the problem appeared a bit different when the calculations were to be made by the Comptroller General, an arm of Congress. But if the President or OMB is to make the decision, there should be judicial review under the ordinary standards."[67] But such an extra layer of law – and lawyers – Senator Hart noted, "not only expands the Executive branch's budgeting role but subjects the settling of the nation's accounts to litigation and endless delays."[68]

Ultimately, Congress passed a second version of Gramm-Rudman that did, in fact, rely on the Office of Management and Budget, but did not formally sanction the use of lawsuits to keep that office in line (though it did not preclude that possibility). In short, Congress simply delegated power to the executive, circumscribing the range and scope of discretion as much as possible, thereby limiting the utility and effectiveness of the automated procedure.[69] The effort to automate deficit reduction finally came to an end with the Budget Enforcement Act of 1990,[70] which shifted the focus

---

66 Gary Hart, "What Should Be Done about Gramm-Rudman? Get Rid of the Monster," *New York Times*, July 22, 1985, p A-25.
67 Cass Sunstein, in testimony before the United States Senate Committee on Governmental Affairs, "Possible Legislative Responses to *Bowsher v. Synar*," 99th Congress, second session, July 23, 1986, p 150.
68 Hart, "What Should be Done about Gramm-Rudman?"
69 The Budget and Emergency Deficit Control Reaffirmation Act of 1987 (2 U.S.C. § 900) required the director of OMB to identify and explain discrepancies between OMB and Congressional Budget Office estimates, and specified methods to be used by the Executive Office of Management and Budget in their calculations, as well as imposing procedures to be used in arriving at basic economic assumption used in calculating estimated deficit levels. These would, of course, be left to the executive branch – the Office of Management and Budget – to follow. How Congress might enforce these rules was left unstated.
70 Title XIII of the Omnibus Budget Reconciliation Act of 1990 – Public Law 101–508.

"away from deficit reduction" – the original goal of Gramm-Rudman – "and toward spending control." The problem, columnist David Broder insisted, was that this had been an effort to take "a supremely political process out of the hands of the politicians in the White House and on Capitol Hill and give it to the technicians." It was, he wrote, "bound to fail."[71] The effort to formalize and legalize the budget process, Ernest Hollings concluded, "has failed. But it is a failure not of law, but of men."[72] Indeed – but of men working with and within the constraints and frames of law. And although the Supreme Court said no, *Bowsher* built on the formalistic path of the Court's 1983 *Chadha* ruling striking down the constitutionality of legislative vetoes and the independent prosecutor decision in *Morrison v. Olson* built on *Bowsher*. The budget process may formally have returned to the status quo ante, but there were more tiles on the *Scrabble* board, and fewer options for the future. Members of Congress might have learned a lesson about the folly of juridification, but many walked away convinced that Karl Llewellyn was right when he warned new students that there is "no cure for law but more law."[73]

The Line-Item Veto

President Ulysses S. Grant is thought to have been the first president to formally articulate a rescission power when, in 1876, he sent a special message to the House informing the members that he would not spend the money they had appropriated for public works because many of the appropriations were for "works of purely private or local interest, in no sense national."[74] Since Grant, many presidents – including Hayes, Arthur, Franklin Roosevelt, Truman, Eisenhower, Nixon, Ford, Carter, Reagan, and George H.W. Bush, – endorsed something like the line-item veto,[75] often for the same reason as Grant, sometimes for partisan advantage, and sometimes in the sincere belief that a more efficient process was needed to work around the institutional impediments of the American system of "separate institutions sharing power."[76]

Of course, the appeal of the line-item veto is hardly surprising, because the power of the purse is the legislature's most significant constitutional

---

71 David Broder, "The Special Conceit of Progressivism," *Washington Post*, April 27, 1986, p C-8.
72 Hollings, "Deficit Reduction, A Love Story: I Want a Divorce."
73 Karl Llewellyn, *The Bramble Bush: On Our Law and Its Study*, Dobbs Ferry: Oceana, 1960, pp 102–8.
74 4 *Congressional Record* 5628 (1876).
75 "Legislative Line Item Veto Act of 1995 – Report of the Committee on the Budget, United States Senate on S.4," 104th Congress, first session, Report 104–109, 1995, p 5.
76 Richard Neustadt, *Presidential Power: The Politics of Leadership with Reflections on Johnson and Nixon*, New York: John Wiley, 1976, p 12.

authority and the most frustrating impediment to a president's policy agenda. What is more surprising is that members of Congress would be in the least interested in surrendering any part of this power through formal legislation or constitutional amendment. And yet, the line-item veto was one of the key pledges in the Republican "Contract with America" at the heart of Newt Gingrich's 1994 strategy for the GOP to finally regain control of Congress for the first time in forty years. The very first legislative promise in the contract was to give the president – Democrat or Republican – the power to unilaterally slice out extraneous pork in the ever-more-bloated U.S. budget. "Within the first 100 days of the 104th Congress," the contract reads, "we shall bring to the House Floor ... [a] line-item veto to restore fiscal responsibility to an out-of-control Congress, requiring them to live under the same budget constraints as families and businesses."[77]

This was not a pledge by Republican legislators to end wasteful spending nor was it a pledge to craft institutional rewards and punishments that would rein in spending. Instead, it would allow Congress to continue to bundle huge omnibus legislative packages, lacing personal members' bills into must-pass appropriations for defense and health and welfare measures, and then to authorize the president to save them from themselves. The president would cut the spending for which the local member of Congress had justly claimed credit. With a national constituency, a president can more easily absorb narrow, local blame for cuts, winning national credit for budget cutting, which suggests that perhaps this workaround really may not have been such a bad idea. But before accepting that premise, we need to consider three problems: The line-item veto undercuts the pressure on members of Congress to exercise and accept political responsibility for their choices; it may establish important lateral and lineal precedents for other assertions and delegations of power; and its ultimate success is predicated on the assumption that presidents are less likely to succumb to political pressure in making budget choices than are members of Congress.

Explicitly and formally handing veto authority to the president might have appeared to lessen the politics and replace it with formal, predictable, and transparent procedures. In fact, however, it was just as likely to only shift the locus of pork barrel politics – with the side effect of reducing the power (and responsibility) of those in Congress. Moreover, these efforts, Congressional Budget Office Director Robert Reischauer warned, were likely to "pave the way for replacing some congressional budget priorities with presidential ones." Presidents, he added, "have been known to allocate" funds toward their own "narrow constituencies." The line-item

---

77 "Republican Contract with America," http://www.house.gov/house/Contract/
CONTRACT.html.

veto, he added, "would not directly undercut that practice."[78] Furthermore, although Congress would still be the only body able to allocate
funds, the president's newly delegated ability to cut those allocations
could undermine the legislature's power, particularly in direct struggles
with the president.

Committee testimony echoed this concern. Allan Schick of the Brookings Institution noted that the legislation "would debilitate Congress's
constitutional power of the purse" permitting the president "to effectively cancel laws passed by Congress." Under the complex procedural
provisions in the proposed line-item veto bill, "Congress could override a
presidential rescission, but it would take three sets of votes for Congress to
prevail in a budgetary dispute. First, Congress would have to appropriate
the funds; second, Congress would have to pass a 'rescission disapproval
bill'; third, Congress would have to disapprove the president's disapproval of the rescission disapproval bill." And each of these steps might
require House or Senate committee hearings, separate votes, and possibly
a conference committee, meaning that more often than not "the president
would win by default."[79]

The testimony was largely ignored. A fairly common view at the time
was expressed by Peter Blute, a Republican representative from Massachusetts, who urged his colleagues "not to get sidetracked with arguments about tilting the balance of powers." The Framers of the U.S.
Constitution, Blute noted, "did not anticipate the growth of omnibus
bills.... And they certainly did not anticipate that Congress would fund
AIDS research, or disaster relief, or World Cup soccer grants, in the
Defense Department budget."[80] We have demonstrated an "institutional
inability to restrain ourselves from unnecessary pork-barrel spending,"
Republican Dan Coats said, and "perhaps the line-item veto is the
only tool we have left." Republican Majority Leader Senator Bob Dole
explained that the reason a Republican Congress "would willingly surrender so powerful a political weapon to a Democratic President" was
because of the hope that "if we cannot control ourselves, maybe the Chief
Executive can help."[81]

True to their pledge in the 1994 Contract with America, Republicans
quickly approved a line-item veto law just one month after taking control

---

78 Testimony of Robert Reischauer (Director, Congressional Budget Office), before the
Committee on Governmental Affairs and Committee on Government Reform and Over-
sight, United States Senate, on the Statutory Item Veto Proposals before the U.S. House
of Representatives, January 12, 1995.
79 Testimony of Allen Schick before the Senate Committee on Governmental Affairs,
Feb. 23, 1995.
80 Testimony of Rep. Peter Blute (R-MA) before the Senate Governmental Affairs Committee, February 23, 1995.
81 Helen Dewar, "Senate Approves Line-Item Veto Bill, 69–29," *Washington Post*, March
24, 1995, p 1.

of the House of Representatives. The next month, the Senate passed its own version of the law over the stern objection of those who, like West Virginia Democrat Robert Byrd, worried about the Senate's abject surrender of one of its most potent tools, the power of the purse. "We are not only becoming fools," Byrd said, "but lazy fools."[82] His argument did not prevail.

Although it took some time, the House and Senate arrived at a compromise in March 1996, and the law was signed by President Clinton on April 9, 1996.[83] After Clinton used the new authority to excise budget provisions that would have benefited both the City of New York and a farmer's cooperative in Snake River, Idaho, New York City brought suit, and the district court in Washington, D.C. (in an opinion by Judge Thomas F. Hogan) ruled against the statute, arguing that the law violated both the formal procedures required for legislation by the presentment clause of the U.S. Constitution and "impermissibly upsets the balance of powers so carefully prescribed by the Framers."[84]

The line "between permissible delegations of rulemaking authority and impermissible abandonments of lawmaking power is a thin one," Hogan confessed, but the line-item veto, he insisted, "impermissibly crosses the line."[85] Hogan's opinion offered two paths to the same immediate result – rejecting the law. But each path suggested very different roles for the courts and very different ground rules for future legislative innovation. One path focused on the formal questions of the specific presentment rules. The other path would require the courts to answer a far more subjective question: Just when does Congress cross the line from legitimate delegation to unconstitutional abdication? In his district court opinion, Judge Hogan offered both arguments as plausible foundations on which to build a judicial rejection of the line-item veto.

The formal question boiled down to this: If the procedure for rescission was built into the initial bill (as it was) and that was passed by both Houses and signed by the president, then would it matter that the rescissions themselves would not follow this formal process? Building on the 1983 *INS v. Chadha* case,[86] Judge Hogan argued that "while the initial passage of the Balanced Budget Act... complied with the Article I requirements, the Line Item Veto Act then authorized the President to violate those requirements by producing laws that had not adhered to" the requirements of the presentment clause. "The laws that resulted after

82 Jerry Gray, "'Lazy Fools,' Says Byrd; Champions of Cutting Spending Gladly Hand the Ax to the President," *New York Times*, March 26, 1995, section 4, p 2.
83 Public Law 104–130, 104th Congress, 110 Stat. 1200.
84 *City of New York v. Clinton*, 985 F. Supp. 168, 169 (D.D.C. 1998) (memorandum opinion by Judge Thomas Hogan).
85 *City of New York v. Clinton*, 985 F. Supp. at 181.
86 *INS v. Chadha*, discussed later in the chapter.

the President's line item veto." Hogan ruled, "were different from those consented to by both Houses of Congress." And, therefore, the resulting laws "are not valid."[87]

The other path, which would have had the Court articulate a limit to what Congress could and could not delegate, would require judges to decide whether the innovation or allocation of authority "impermissibly disrupts the balance of powers among the three branches of the government." The problem is that the line between legitimate delegation and "impermissible abandonments of lawmaking power" is thin.[88] And, at least since the great confrontation between Franklin Roosevelt and an intransigent Supreme Court in the early years of the New Deal, this is precisely the sort of line drawing the Supreme Court has assiduously avoided.

Given two foundations on which to build, Justice Stevens and the Supreme Court majority reviewing the line-item case built their ruling exclusively on formal arguments about the presentment clause. Even though the act was challenged on broader separation of powers and delegation of power issues, Stevens insisted that "the only issue we address concerns the 'finely wrought' procedure commanded by the Constitution," thereby making it "unnecessary to consider the district court's alternative holding" that the act violates the constitutionally mandated balance of powers.[89]

Stevens ruled that there was nothing in the Constitution that "gives the President the unilateral power to change the text of duly enacted statutes." A law is to be passed by Congress and sent to the president, who can either accept and sign it or veto and return it, at which point Congress can write a new law. The line-item veto essentially gave the president an independent lawmaking and not law-executing role and, therefore, failed this formal test. In dissent, Justice Breyer looked at the same formal rules and concluded that, although the line-item veto "skirts a constitutional edge," it does not cross the line. When one "measures the literal words of the Act against the Constitution's literal commands," Breyer argued, "the fact that the Act may closely resemble a different, literally unconstitutional arrangement is beside the point." Breyer insisted that "small differences matter when the question is one of literal violation of law."[90]

The more functional analysis came from Justice Kennedy, who joined the Court's result (saying no) – but for very different reasons. When the people "delegate some degree of control to a remote central authority, one branch of government ought not possess the power to shape their destiny

87 *City of New York v. Clinton*, 985 F.Supp. at 178–9.
88 *City of New York v. Clinton*, 985 F.Supp. at 181.
89 *Clinton v. City of New York*, 524 U.S. 417, 447–8 (1998).
90 *Clinton v. City of New York*, 524 U.S. at 452 (Breyer, dissenting).

without a sufficient check from the other two." Liberty, he concluded, "demands limits on the ability of any one branch to influence basic political decisions."[91] To say that the Court's role is "lessened here because the two political branches are adjusting their own powers between themselves," Justice Kennedy wrote in direct response to Justice Breyer, would be an error. "The Constitution's structure," Kennedy wrote, "requires a stability which transcends the convenience of the moment."[92] It is no answer, he added, "to say that Congress surrendered its authority by its own hand...[that] a congressional cession of power is voluntary does not make it innocuous."[93] "Abdication of responsibility is not part of the constitutional design."[94]

Justice Scalia offered a dramatically different perspective in his dissent. The line-item veto was fine, he said, not because it was a creative way to accomplish the basic goals embodied in the Constitution's separation of powers, but rather because in his view Congress was and is free to give away its power. For Scalia, the only reason to object would be if Congress tried to hold onto power it had decided to delegate away.[95]

The Court said no, as it had in the balanced budget case (*Bowsher*). But because legal decisions work differently than does the political process, and because legal decisions in one stream of cases can constrain and frame decisions in other cases – which, in turn, shape and influence the choices that legislators, litigators, and policy entrepreneurs alike work with in related political and policy arenas, we need to pay attention not simply to the decisions in these cases, but to the reasoning as well. The line-item veto was hardly the first or only time that Congress has attempted to formally reallocate power – its own or the powers of the other branches. In fact, we should look at *Clinton v. City of New York*, as the fourth in a line of cases – following the independent counsel case in 1988 (*Morrison v. Olson*), the 1986 balanced budget case (*Bowsher v. Synar*), and a critical case from 1983, *Immigration and Naturalization Service v. Chadha* that helped pave the Court's more formal path.[96] In each case, the Court confronted three choices: (1) to follow Justice White's dissents in *Chadha* and *Bowsher*, limiting its inquiry to a determination of whether or not the innovation "so alters the balance of authority among the branches of government as to pose a genuine threat to the basic division between the lawmaking power and the power to execute the law"[97]; (2) to engage – constructively or deconstructively – in shaping and revising

---

91 *Clinton v. City of New York*, 524 U.S. at 422.
92 *Clinton v. City of New York*, 524 U.S. at 449.
93 *Clinton v. City of New York*, 524 U.S. at 451–2.
94 Clinton v. City of New York, 524 U.S. at 452.
95 *Morrison* posed a different problem for Scalia – a case in which Congress took power that was appropriately assigned to the president and moved it to an independent agency – thus reallocating powers that never belonged to the legislative branch in the first place.
96 *INS v. Chadha*, 462 U.S. 919 (1983); *Morrison v. Olson*, 487 U.S. 654 (1988).
97 *Bowsher v. Synar*, 478 U.S. at 776. Justice White dissenting.

these innovations; or (3) to insist on hard limits, whether those are defined by the formal procedural process outlined in the Constitution or, more generally, as violations of the functional requirements of the separation of powers.[98]

In *INS v. Chadha*, the Supreme Court, in one blow, called into question more laws than any other Supreme Court ruling in American history.[99] The *Chadha* ruling struck down what were known as legislative vetoes – an innovation Congress and the executive had worked out over decades to provide broad delegation of administrative discretion and yet maintain a way for Congress to override those decisions in particular cases. These provisions, which had been inserted in hundreds of laws, enabled Congress to delegate broad discretion to the administration (in the *Chadha* case, discretion concerning immigration and deportation decisions) while reserving its right to overturn particular or individual decisions that concerned members of Congress.[100] Sometimes, these vetoes required a majority vote in both Houses and sometimes in just one House; in some cases, the administration's decision could be reversed by a simple majority vote in one House or Senate committee.[101]

In striking down legislative vetoes, the Court's majority relied on an extremely formal reading of the presentment clause of the U.S. Constitution – the clause that sets the precise way in which laws must be proposed, voted on by both Houses of Congress, and then "presented" to the president for signature or veto. If overruling deportation orders would require a separate law passed in both Houses and signed by the president, then Congress really would have only three choices: (1) insist on legislating each exception to the law, (2) delegate full discretion and authority to the executive, or (3) construct informal systems by which committees could continue to supervise delegations – at least to agencies and bureaus dependent on Congress for their funds and mandates.[102]

In his dissent in *Chadha*, Justice White rejected a narrow and formal test for the separation of powers, insisting that the real test ought to be a functional one: Was the legislative veto in keeping with the overarching

---

98 It is worth noting that, although the Court did permit the innovation of the independent counsel in *Morrison v. Olson*, the majority opinion focused almost exclusively on a formal reading of the appointment clause, rather than a wider structural analysis of the degree to which this innovation was, or was not, in line with broader principles and purposes of the separation of powers.

99 Barbara Hinkson Craig, *Chadha: The Story of an Epic Constitutional Struggle*, New York: Oxford University Press, 1987.

100 Louis Fisher, "The Legislative Veto: Invalidated, It Survives," 56 *Law & Contemporary Problems* 4, 293 (1993).

101 Section 244(c)(2) of the Immigration and Nationality Act.

102 Louis Fisher demonstrates that in practice, the legislative veto survived the ruling in *Chadha*, but the emphasis on the formalities of the Constitution's presentment clause, and the relative disappearance of any focus on undue delegation, is the broader framing issue that is the focus of this study. See Fisher, "The Legislative Veto," p 293.

purpose and objective of the separation of powers or perhaps did it even facilitate that structure in a modern context? If the innovation was a way to make it possible for Congress to delegate the power essential to run a modern administrative state without surrendering its vital function as a check on the exercise of that power, then the innovation should probably be tolerated. As Justice White put it, by 1983, the legislative veto had "become a central means by which Congress secures the accountability of executive and independent agencies." Without it, he added, "Congress is faced with a Hobson's choice: either to refrain from delegating the necessary authority, leaving itself with a hopeless task of writing laws with the requisite specificity to cover endless special circumstances across the entire policy landscape or, in the alternative, abdicate its lawmaking function to the executive branch and independent agencies."[103] But White's was a dissenting opinion.

Chadha and *Bowsher* were very much on the minds of the Justices two years later when they were asked to consider the establishment of the independent counsel in *Morrison v. Olson*. If Congress could not usurp executive authority by simply assigning a triggering function to the comptroller general, how then could it be acceptable for Congress to empower an independent counsel by reallocating powers (investigatory and prosecutorial authority) that ordinarily belong to the executive? Justice Scalia, who wrote a blistering dissent in the independent counsel case in 1988 (*Morrison v. Olson*), was mystified, but the majority was willing to allow it precisely because Congress made no attempt to create or preserve a role for itself in this reallocation of power. "We observe first that this case does not involve an attempt by Congress to increase its own powers at the expense of the Executive Branch," Chief Justice Rehnquist wrote in his majority opinion. This case simply does not pose a "danger of congressional usurpation of Executive branch function."[104] Although Justice Scalia agreed that there was no problem of congressional control after the fact in *Morrison*, he saw that as the wrong concern. The issue was that Congress had reallocated executive power (the prosecution of crime) from control of the executive to an independent officer, with potentially alarming risks in Scalia's view.

The problem with following the alternate path, initially suggested by Justice White in *Chadha*, was the apparent subjectivity involved in making determinations about how much delegation is too much or what sorts of powers could and could not be delegated. But to revisit the delegation doctrine also would mean revisiting one of the Court's less appealing eras, the early New Deal years in which the Court had gone to war with President Franklin Roosevelt and his supporters in Congress. "Since the

---

103 *I.N.S. v. Chadha,* 462 U.S. at 968.
104 *Morrison v. Olson,* 487 U.S. at 694.

resolution of the New Deal constitutional crisis, the non-delegation doctrine has lived a 'fugitive existence at the edge of constitutional jurisprudence.'"[105]

One of the last times the Court seriously relied on what is often
referred to as the undue delegation doctrine was in the *Schechter Poultry Corp. v. United States* – a case in which the Supreme Court struck
down FDR's National Industrial Recovery Act, which authorized industry boards appointed by the president to set and enforce wage and hour
provisions in a range of industries. In *Schechter*, the Court ruled that
"Congress is not permitted to abdicate or to transfer to others the essential legislative functions" with which it is vested.[106] The Court recognized
that Congress certainly could leave others with the responsibility for "the
making of subordinate rules within prescribed limits," but it insisted that
"the necessity and validity of such provisions, and the wide range of
administrative authority which has been developed by means of them,
cannot be allowed to obscure the limitations of the authority to delegate,
if our constitutional system is to be maintained."[107] The appropriate
question, the Court insisted in 1935, is whether or not Congress is "per-
forming its essential legislative function or . . . has attempted to transfer
that function to others."[108] It is a decision that has never been reversed,
but it is a doctrine "the Supreme Court has not seen fit to apply since that
time" either.

By 1935, it was increasingly clear that modern government would
be impossible without delegation, particularly delegation to administrative agencies. However, despite the fact that it is "impossible to imagine
a modern state in which central authorities do not delegate functions,
responsibilities, and powers to administrators,"[109] the political scholar
Theodore Lowi continued to insist that delegation must be constrained
though, as George Lovell notes, Lowi's "belief that judges can solve
the problem has waned."[110] By the 1940s, Howard Gillman writes,
"the question of whether there were constitutional limits on Congress'
authority to delegate its powers had become 'a dead issue.'"[111] That "the

---

105 George Lovell, "That Sick Chicken Won't Hunt: The Limits of a Judicially Enforced
    Non-Delegation Doctrine," 17 *Constitutional Commentary* 79 (Spring 2000), p 79,
    quoting Peter L. Aranson, Ernest Gellhorn, and Glen O. Robinson, "A Theory of
    Legislative Delegation," 68 *Cornell Law Review* 1, 17 (1982).
106 *Schechter Poultry Corp. v. United States*, 295 U.S. 495, 529 (1935).
107 *Schechter Poultry Corp. v. United States*, 295 U.S. at 530.
108 *Schechter Poultry Corp. v. United States*, 295 U.S. at 530.
109 Theodore Lowi, *The End of Liberalism*, New York: W.W. Norton, 1979, p 93.
110 George Lovell, "That Sick Chicken Won't Hunt," footnote 2, citing Theodore J. Lowi,
    "Two Roads to Serfdom: Liberalism, Conservatism, and Administrative Power," 36
    American University Law Review 295 (1987).
111 Howard Gillman, "Reconnecting the Modern Supreme Court to the Historical Evo-
    lution of American Capitalism," in Howard Gillman and Cornell Clayton (eds), *The
    Supreme Court in American Politics*, Lawrence: University Press of Kansas, 1999,

Supreme Court has shown little sustained inclination toward reviving the doctrine"[112] is important, but it has not meant that the Court is willing to ignore delegation entirely. Instead of asking the more subjective question about the nature of the power being delegated and the structure of the separation of powers, or whether Congress has provided sufficient standards to contain the abuse of the delegation, the Court has largely limited its inquiry to the formal issue of usurpation. Is one branch seizing power that belongs to another? Is one branch trying to hold onto some part of the power it has delegated away? This the Court may not allow.

This focus reframes the debate between Congress and the executive from one about the utility, risks, and extent of delegation of core functions to one about the precise legal formalities of the appointments clause or the presentment clause. This focus limits the kinds of mechanisms Congress can invent to oversee the exercise of delegated power or to control spending in a world vastly different from the one the Framers knew. But far from forcing Congress back to the aggressive defense of its prerogatives and active use of its critical tools, such as the power of the purse, law's allure may be too strong in an era in which the interests of individuals in government are less "connected with the constitutional rights of the place."[113] Instead of forcing members of Congress to revert to the tools they have, the Court's increasingly formalistic view of the separation of powers, which seems ready to allow Congress to delegate power at will, but to have no way of checking that delegation, may simply drive Congress to delegate more and more power (and responsibility) to the executive.[114]

---

p 245, quoting Peter Woll, *American Bureaucracy*, New York: W.W. Norton, 1977, p 156.

112 George Lovell, "That Sick Chicken Won't Hunt," at 80.

113 James Madison, *The Federalist* #51.

114 The Court may have said no to the line-item veto, but it has hardly removed it from the general debate. Members of Congress and presidents alike continue to float new proposals for line-item vetoes, as they did in June 2006, when Senate Majority Leader Bill Frist pledged that he would try to push a line-item veto proposal through Congress before the 2006 midterm elections. (Jim Rutenberg, "President to Press for Line Item Veto Power," *New York Times*, June 28, 2006, p A19.) The line-item veto emerged as an important feature in the early skirmishes between Rudy Giuliani and Mitt Romney in their campaign debates leading up to the 2008 presidential election. "Mayor Giuliani, in order to get more money for New York City, went to court to stop the line-item veto, and unfortunately he was successful," Romney said. "I will fight very hard to get the line-item veto back in the president's hand." (Scott Sonner, "Romney Says He Represents GOP Values," *Washington Post*, October 12, 2007.) "The main action in the Republican race is currently the squabbling between Mitt Romney and Rudy Giuliani. At the debate, Romney tried to brand Giuliani as an enemy of the line-item veto. This is, of course, fatal in a party in which everybody quails in fear of the powerful right-to-veto lobby. It's been a long time since we've had a good line-item veto fight. Not as exciting as the moment when John McCain laced into the Smoot-Hawley tariff, but quite the dust-up." (Gail Collins, "Calvin Coolidge Redux," *New York Times*, October 11, 2007, p A31.)

Allowing innovations – or rejecting them – is only part of what the Supreme Court has done in the separation of powers. The next chapter examines one more option – a pattern of juridification in which the Court remains relatively silent. Although each of these options (yes, no, and silence) may sidestep the deeply layered and far more difficult-to-reverse phenomena of constructive or deconstructive juridification, they fortified existing paths, making some choices more, and others less, likely in the future.

8   WAR POWERS AND PRECEDENT

When the Court Is Reluctant to Intervene

IT HAS LONG BEEN ASSUMED that the Supreme Court plays a far more limited role in foreign policy in general and war and emergency powers in particular than it does in other areas of public policy. Although it is true that the Court has made far fewer dramatic interventions in this area, juridification in war and emergency powers is still significant. The Court may send relatively few signals, but those that are sent powerfully shape and constrain the choices made by the elected branches. This chapter explores one important example of the juridification of war and foreign policy where the Court has remained relatively silent (the effort to formalize, rigidify, and automate the allocation and exercise of the war powers starting in 1972). The chapter then turns to focus on the expansion and acceleration of claims for prerogative powers made by modern presidents, particularly those made by the George W. Bush administration since September 11, 2001. These efforts were designed to win support – or at least acquiescence – from the Supreme Court. But these signals were misread in cases involving detainees in Guantanamo Bay, Cuba, and the chapter concludes with a close look at the 2008 case of *Boumediene et al v. Bush*, which suggests that a relatively silent Court is not a weak or insignificant Court. In foreign policy and war powers, it might be more useful to think of the Court as a fully charged capacitor, a repository of enormous power and energy, that can be triggered by those who misread its signals. This is a chapter, then, about the power of judicial signals when the Court appears reluctant to intervene.

War Powers: A Congressional Attempt at Juridification

The American commitment to the war in Vietnam was well into its second decade when the U.S. Congress began to embrace the idea that a fundamental flaw in the constitutional system had to be fixed. The problem, of course, was that it had become nearly impossible for members of Congress to vote to terminate a war. The constitutional tool given to

Congress to end a war is the power of the purse, but this is a very blunt instrument. Congress has the authority or *formal power* to cut off funds, but this is not the same thing as the *institutional capacity* or the *political ability* to do so.[1] It takes no more than 50 percent plus one of the members of Congress to authorize the deployment of troops, raise funds to support them, or institute a military draft. However, reversing these decisions likely would require a super-majority of 66 percent, because a formal, statutory reversal would only be needed when the president was opposed to it and would, therefore, surely veto any such legislative effort. Beyond the institutional problem, there is also a profound political barrier – cutting funds from ongoing military operations opens legislators to the charge that they are denying soldiers the ability to defend themselves. These institutional and political barriers became obvious in the final years of the Vietnam War.

Barely two months after taking the oath of office, Richard Nixon ordered the U.S. Air Force to begin a series of bombing raids in Cambodia on March 17, 1969. Only two members of Congress were told about this decision.[2] A year later, Nixon independently decided to widen the war, sending American ground forces into Cambodia. It was this decision – announced to Congress and the nation on April 30, 1970 – that set off major protests around the country, including the march at Kent State University during which four students were killed by National Guard troops. On Capitol Hill, the Cambodia decisions finally generated the political will to repeal the Tonkin Gulf Resolution, the only explicit legislative authorization for the use of force in the Vietnam War.[3] Nixon signed the law repealing the resolution, but repeated his long-held and frequently stated view that both the Tonkin Gulf Resolution and its repeal were "without binding force or effect," because, according to his reading

---

1 This is well explained by Richard Neustadt, who has long distinguished between formal authority and power. As he put it in the 1990 revision and expansion of his 1960 classic on presidential power, we should "keep in mind the distinction between two senses in which the word *power* is employed." One sense is when it is used "to refer to formal constitutional, statutory or customary authority," and the other is in the "sense of effective influence on the conduct of others." Neustadt suggests that the word *authority* might be substituted for power in the formal sense, whereas *influence* might be substituted for power in the more informal sense. Richard Neustadt, *Presidential Power and the Modern Presidents*, New York: Free Press, 1990, p 321.

2 Mississippi Democrat John Stennis and Georgia's Richard Russell, both members of the Senate Armed Services Committee. Richard Nixon, *The Memoirs of Richard Nixon*, New York: Grosset & Dunlap, 1978, p 382.

3 After less than three days of discussion and debate, the House passed the Tonkin Gulf Resolution without any opposition, and, in the Senate, only two negative votes were cast. The legislative branch resolved that the United States was "prepared, as the President determines, to take all necessary steps, including the use of armed force, to assist" Southeast Asian nations in defending their freedom.

of the Constitution, the exercise of the war powers was well within the president's exclusive constitutional prerogative.[4]

That left Congress with only one way to force Nixon to end the war – cutting off funds. However, despite the expansion of the war to Cambodia, the secret bombing runs, and the growing domestic opposition to the war, Congress remained unable to muster majorities to cut off funds for all military operations. Efforts were made – and failed – in 1970 and again in 1971. Finally, in May 1973, a bill to cut off all funds for military action in Indochina passed with sufficient support to override Nixon's veto. As dramatic as passage of this bill might have been, however, it came four months after Nixon had signed the Paris peace accords to end the war in Vietnam. The vote to cut off the money was not necessarily meaningless, because significant bombing operations continued in Cambodia, but even on this point Nixon was able to negotiate a six-week extension of funds.[5]

The Vietnam saga generated broad support for an effort to restructure the war powers that had been floating around Congress for many years. Two Senators – New York Republican Jacob Javits and Missouri Democrat Thomas Eagleton – pressed for a law that would preemptively reverse the political and institutional burdens by formalizing the delegation and revocation of the war powers.[6] Instead of requiring Congress to act to remove troops, the idea was to create a preemptive way to reverse the

---

4 In calling on Congress to approve the Tonkin Gulf Resolution, President Johnson asked "Congress, on its part to join in *affirming* the national determination" and recommended "a Resolution expressing the *support* of the Congress for all necessary action" (Special Message to Congress on U.S. Policy in Southeast Asia, August 5, 1964: Printed in Lyndon B. Johnson, Public Papers of the Presidents, 1963–1964, p 91, emphasis added.) In the eyes of the president, the resolution would affirm his decision and support it: It would not *authorize* it, nor would it legitimate it, because such authorization was not necessary. As Johnson noted in 1967, "We did not think the resolution was necessary to do what we did and what we are doing. But we thought it was desirable." (News Conference, August 18, 1967: Printed in Public Papers of the Presidents, Lyndon Johnson, 1967, p 794.) Indeed, it was, because with the resolution the administration was persuasively able to argue that it had defeated all possible objections: If the administration did, in fact, need congressional authorization then, even though the word was not used, any reading of the resolution clearly suggested that Congress had in fact provided that authorization. As Nicholas Katzenbach (then Under Secretary of State) argued, "If the President needed authority, I think he got that authority." If, on the other hand, one rejected the notion that he needed authority, then one could see on the resolution only what its words actually said – that Congress offered support and affirmation for the president's policy: If the president "did not need that authority," Katzenbach continued, "then I think he got the support and sense of Congress on this." When pressed as to his own interpretation, however, Katzenbach reflected the Johnson administration position that in fact the president "does have that authority" without the resolution. (Senate Report on U.S. Commitments to Foreign Powers, p 141).

5 Richard Madden, "Nixon Agrees to Stop Bombing in Cambodia by Aug. 15 with New Raids Up to Congress," *New York Times*, June 30, 1970, p 1.

6 Jacob K. Javits, *Who Makes War: The President versus Congress*, New York: Morrow, 1973.

burden, writing a law that would order troops withdrawn *unless* Congress acted affirmatively to continue the mission. In other words, where once congressional silence constituted congressional approval, the law was designed to turn the tables, transforming congressional silence into formal, legal, explicit *disapproval*. By not voting, a member of Congress would be forcing the president to end the war – and a war could *only* continue if Congress voted explicitly and affirmatively to support the policy.

The War Powers Resolution of 1973 is fairly short. It starts with a statement that the law is designed to "fulfill the intent of the framers of the Constitution," and to ensure that the president's use of American armed forces would be allowed only "pursuant to (1) a declaration of war, (2) specific statutory authorization, or (3) a national emergency created by attack upon the United States, its territories or possessions, or its armed forces." The President was instructed to consult with Congress before introducing American forces "into hostilities or into situations where imminent involvement in hostilities is clearly indicated by the circumstances." In addition to consultation, and in the absence of a declaration of war, the president was required to submit a formal report to Congress no more than forty-eight hours after U.S. armed forces were introduced into hostilities or situations where hostilities were "clearly indicated by circumstances," as well as when the president sent American troops into foreign territories "while equipped for combat." In these circumstances, the president's report to Congress would trigger a clock, and sixty days after the report, the president was required to "terminate any use of United States Armed Forces" that had been identified in the president's report "unless the Congress declared war, had provided specific statutory authorization or had extended the clock by adding an additional sixty-day period. In addition, the president could get an additional thirty days if he "certifies to the Congress in writing that unavoidable military necessity" requires such an extension.

In essence, the bill formally authorized the president to use military force without a declaration of war, but traded that authorization for what many supporters hoped would be a reversal of the traditional political burden: Ending a war before had required Congressional action (a statute that would likely be vetoed, and then an override of that veto). Now, ending a war would require nothing – once the clock was formally triggered, the war would have to end after sixty days *unless* Congress affirmatively acted to formally authorize the president's use of force. But there were at least three major problems with this approach: (1) despite explicitly denying that it was doing so, the law formally authorized the president to use force, something the Constitution left ambiguous and unclear; (2) it was entirely predicated on the assumption that the President would trigger the clock by reporting the use of force – absent that, Congress itself could trigger the clock, or order the removal of forces by passing a concurrent resolution, but of course that would put everyone right back where they had been in Vietnam, with Congress politically constrained to pass a law that might appear to undercut support for troops in the field, and (3) the use of a legislative veto provision that would ostensibly require the president to remove forces at any time should Congress care to pass a concurrent resolution requiring the president to do so. (Unlike ordinary legislation, a concurrent resolution is not presented to the president for signature or veto.)

Although this sort of statute might be politically advantageous for Congress – particularly if a court could ever be persuaded to entertain a legal action designed to force the president to comply with it – it would cede some measure of formal power to the president to use force at his or her discretion. It would formally delegate to the president the power to use the military not only to repeal an imminent attack or invasion, but largely as the chief executive saw fit. The original Senate bill attempted to narrowly categorize and contain the instances in which this authority was to be delegated, but provided concrete authorization nevertheless – an authority presidents had long asserted, but one that was ambiguous, always contested, and constitutionally unclear. Testifying before a House committee considering the resolution in 1970, former Attorney General Nicholas Katzenbach argued that the bill would pose a "real danger that the President's authority would be expanded rather than ordered." The fact that the president has to "assert this authority without formal congressional sanction... has a moderating effect on his actions," Katzenbach said. Formalizing this authority would eliminate that ambiguity, shifting the presidential use of the war power from shaky to firm ground. The president would have "an additional power in his hands. He can cite it to justify his acts over a fairly broad spectrum of factual situations."[7] The president, he added, will "use those provisions [in the law] which support his own interpretation and reject those which he believes are incorrect. Thus he will make political use of those provisions he likes and treat the others as inoperative."[8]

In exchange for this formal delegation, Congress innovatively attempted to reverse the political burden that had made it so hard to end the Vietnam War. The president's preemptive authorization would be limited: in some versions to just thirty days, in others to as much as ninety days. At the end of that time, the authorization would expire and the president would be statutorily required to return the troops and end

---

7 Testimony of Nicholas Katzenbach in hearings before the Subcommittee on National Security Policy and Scientific Development of the Committee on Foreign Affairs, "Congress, the President, and the War Powers," U.S. House of Representatives, 91st Congress, second session, July 28, 1970, p 303.
8 Katzenbach, "Congress, the President, and the War Powers," p 303.

the engagement. The only way the use of force could continue at that point would be if Congress formally met and affirmatively authorized an extension. If this plan worked as intended, ending a war would require no action and no political courage, because congressional silence alone would terminate the war.

A conference committee was assigned to blend the bills passed by each house of Congress in July 1973. Senator Eagleton, one of the bill's original sponsors, insisted that what emerged was far worse than no bill at all. The conference committee, Eagleton insisted, had produced a law stating "that the President can send us to war wherever and whenever he wants to."[9] Eagleton's claim was echoed at the other end of the political spectrum by Barry Goldwater, one of the Senate's leading conservative opponents of the entire effort by Congress to juridify the war powers. The conference report, Goldwater announced, "puts into the law language that is not contained in the Constitution, but only assumed to be there because of the delegation of Commander-in-Chief powers to the President."[10]

Despite the political reality that the law might actually favor and not degrade executive power, President Nixon vetoed it, arguing that it was an unconstitutional invasion of executive power. Nixon was opposed, conservatives and war hawks in both parties were opposed, and a number of stalwart doves like Eagleton were opposed as well – and yet, Congress was able to muster the two-thirds necessary in each house to override the president's veto. Why? The explanation has relatively little to do with a debate about constitutional law. In part, it passed because the vote came just days after Nixon dismissed Archibald Cox – the Watergate Special Prosecutor – as well as the attorney general and deputy attorney general who refused to carry out Nixon's orders in what came to be known as the "Saturday Night Massacre,"[11] and a frustrated Congress was eager to send a clear message of direct opposition to the president. New York Representative Bella Abzug, for example, spoke for many of her liberal colleagues when she announced that the veto override was about Nixon far more than it was about the allocation of the war powers. The bill itself gave presidents too much power, Abzug said, although she hoped it might ultimately "prove to be, in fact, limiting." But this vote, she indicated, was about Nixon. Until this vote, she said, "Congress has not been able to override any Presidential veto in this session." But this vote, coming "at a time of revulsion of the people against the crimes and corruption in this administration.... This could be a turning point in the struggle to control an administration that has run amuck. It could accelerate the demand for the impeachment of the President. On that basis, I will vote

9 Sen. Thomas Eagleton, *Congressional Record*, November 7, 1973, p 36177.
10 Quoted in Thomas F. Eagleton, *War and Presidential Power: A Chronicle of Congressional Surrender*, New York: Liveright, 1974, p 207.
11 Stanley Kutler, *The Wars of Watergate: The Last Crisis of Richard Nixon*, New York: Knopf, 1990.

to override the veto." Congressman Ron Dellums, a liberal Democrat from Oakland, California, urged his colleagues to resist falling for "symbolic politics." Remember, he told his colleagues, "Richard Nixon is not going to be President forever," and a vote against Nixon – at the cost of strengthening the executive's claim to unilateral war powers – was not a very good deal at all.[12] But in the end this override was a chance to defeat Nixon, and that was an opportunity that could not be resisted. One unnamed senator, Eagleton later said, agreed with him that this law would actually undermine the constitutional balance of power. "Tom," this senator reportedly told Eagleton, "I love the Constitution, but I hate Nixon more."[13] And so the War Powers Resolution became law in 1973.

Since then, the United States has been involved in military operations and combat around the world – including the use of force to retake the *S.S. Mayaguez* (1975); the aborted effort to rescue American hostages in Iran (1980); and fighting in Grenada (1983); the Persian Gulf (1987–1988); Panama (1989–1990); the Persian Gulf, Kuwait, and Iraq (1991); Somalia (1992–1995); Haiti (1993); Bosnia (1995); Serbia and Kosovo (1999); Afghanistan (2002); and Iraq (2003). Yet, the War Powers Resolution has been formally invoked by Congress just once, and has never been subjected to any formal judicial review.[14]

In the past three decades, Congress has toyed with revisions and even the outright repeal of the War Powers Resolution. In 1988, four leading Senators (Byrd, Nunn, Warner, and Mitchell) proposed Senate Joint Resolution 323 in the 100th Congress. Their concern, as Senator Warner noted on the Senate floor, was that the

War Powers Resolution does not assist the Congress in making constructive contributions to policies involving the use of U.S. Armed Forces, and at times, the War Powers Resolution can actually prevent the Congress from exercising its authority over and accepting its responsibility for the use of the Armed Forces. Quite bluntly, the War Powers Resolution has not worked in the past, is not working now, and will not work in the future.[15]

---

12 Abzug, *Congressional Record*, November 7, 1973, p 36221 and Dellums, p 36220.
13 See Eagleton's testimony in Senate hearings, "The War Powers after 200 Years," U.S. Senate, July 13, 1988, p 16.
14 A part of the Multinational Force in Lebanon Resolution in 1983 "determined that the requirements of section 4(a) of the War Powers Resolution had been triggered on August 29, 1983, and that Congress authorized the continued participation of the U.S. Marines" in the conflict for eighteen months. But long before that clock would run out, a Marine barracks in Lebanon was destroyed by a truck bomb on October 23, 1983; President Reagan announced that the Marines would be withdrawn a few months later, and on March 30, 1984 – just six months after the eighteen-month clock had started – President Reagan announced that U.S. forces were no longer being deployed as part of the Multinational Force in Lebanon. Richard Grimmett, "Congressional Use of Funding Cutoffs since 1970 involving U.S. Military Forces and Overseas Deployments," Congressional Research Service Report for Congress, January 16, 2007.
15 *Congressional Record*, January 25, 1989, p 466.

Among the reasons Warner cited to explain why the law had not been used was the fact that the Supreme Court had cast a constitutional shadow over the legislative veto provision, which was the critical mechanism to automatically reverse the political burdens, making it easier to end wars and harder to continue them.[16]

This shadow was cast by the *Immigration and Naturalization Service v. Chadha* case, in which a divided Court ruled that all legislative action – both delegations of power as well as actions to revoke delegations of power – had to follow the formal procedure for lawmaking laid out in Article I of the U.S. Constitution. As discussed in the last chapter, *Chadha* insisted on a formal reading of the presentment clause, with each legislative act formally presented to the president for his signature or veto. That the president had signed the original legislation – which included the legislative veto provision – was ruled irrelevant. This meant that, although Congress was free to delegate, it would be tightly constrained should it choose to terminate that delegation. The only way a termination would meet the Court's formal requirement would be if it were part of a new law, presented to the president for a signature or veto. Because the president might be expected to veto any effort to limit executive power, the normal ratchet (50% plus one to delegate, 67% to revoke it) would apply. In fact, it might be even more one-sided because the Court seemed unwilling to block delegation, but more than willing to reject restraints on those delegations. Should the War Powers Resolution ever find its way to Court, in other words, *Chadha* suggests that the delegation might survive, but that the limit to that delegation might not. This would be a rather dramatic illustration of the risks of deconstructive juridification.

This left Congress with three options: (1) recognize the risk posed by the Court's ruling in *Chadha* and its likely application to the War Powers Resolution and write a new law that might somehow still succeed in reversing the political burden; (2) repeal the flawed War Powers Resolution of 1973 and return to the status quo ante – putting war powers back into the political gray zone and forcing presidents to struggle for power, authority, and legitimacy when it comes to the deployment of U.S. forces; or (3) leave the flawed law on the books, ignoring it or hiding behind it.

In their 1988 proposal, Senators Byrd, Nunn, Mitchell, and Warner pursued the first option, proposing to repeal the 1973 law. Far from returning the question to the political realm, however, their new proposal actually enhanced juridification. To guarantee that the president would cooperate with Congress, this new proposal added a very different legal

---

16 This is something Mark Tushnet refers to as "judicial overhang," which, he argues, distorts legislation and legislative debate and promotes irresponsibility. Mark Tushnet, *Taking the Constitution Away from the Courts*, Princeton: Princeton University Press, 1999, pp 57–65.

mechanism, formally giving members of Congress judicial standing to bring suit in U.S. courts "for declaratory judgment and injunctive relief" when the president and the U.S. Armed Forces "have not complied with any provision" of the law. This solution was, for Thomas Eagleton, a "cure worse than the known disease,"[17] and it failed, as did a similar law introduced by Indiana Democrat Lee Hamilton in the House the next year. That left the other two options – work around or ignore the existing law despite its explicit and formal delegation of what had never before been formally delegated in advance of a conflict, or repeal the law and return to political ambiguity.

The full repeal option actually came close to fruition. When the Republican Party took control of both houses of Congress for the first time in forty years in 1994, among their first priorities was passing what Senate Majority Leader Robert Dole labeled the Peace Powers Act of 1995, a law that would repeal the War Powers Resolution and, in Dole's words, "untie the President's hands in using American forces to defend American interests."[18] A similar bill in the House proposed by Republican Henry Hyde of Illinois won the impassioned support of Newt Gingrich, the first Republican Speaker of the House in forty years. Gingrich told the House that he was rising "for what some Members might find an unusual moment, an appeal to the House to, at least on paper, increase the power of President Clinton."[19] Despite that unusual plea, Hyde's amendment failed, but it was a close vote (201–217).[20] In part, it failed because many who thought the law already delegated too much power to the president agreed with Eagleton's 1988 argument that, although reverting to "the basic words of the Constitution" would be ideal in the abstract, any explicit repeal of the law might be seen by politicians and judges alike as an affirmative endorsement by Congress of "the President's unilateral right to wage war however and whenever he liked."[21] The War Powers Resolution remained law, but Congress sought to work around it instead of invoking its risky mechanisms.

---

17 Eagleton's testimony in Senate hearings, "The War Powers after 200 Years," p 366.
18 *The Washington Post*, Jan. 5, 1995, p A 10. This proposal echoed an earlier debate in Congress over the Bricker Amendment, a 1953 effort to regulate executive agreements with international organizations and, at the same time, to limit the treaty power, mandating that no law passed in pursuance of a treaty would be held constitutional if that law would not have passed constitutional scrutiny in the absence of the treaty. This episode is considered in Chapter 3 and is carefully analyzed in Duane Tananbaum, *The Bricker Amendment Controversy: A Test of Eisenhower's Political Leadership*, Ithaca: Cornell University Press, 1988.
19 The proposed amendment was attached to H.R. 1561, Fiscal 1996–1997 Foreign Aid and State Department Authorization.
20 Dellums was one of the few liberal Democrats who voted against the original War Powers Resolution and supported Nixon's veto on the ground that the resolution as written actually ceded to the president powers delegated to Congress by the Constitution.
21 Eagleton's testimony in Senate hearings, "The War Powers after 200 Years," p 366.

In August 1990, President George H. W. Bush began to order the deployment of U.S. military forces to the Persian Gulf after Iraq had invaded and occupied Kuwait. The deployment rapidly escalated, as Bush ordered "a heavy U.S. Army Corps and a Marine expeditionary force" along with "three aircraft carriers, a battleship, [and other] appropriate escort ships" into the Gulf on November 8, 1990.[22] Congress, however, would not extensively debate the military buildup until January 1991 – by which time more than 500,000 troops were positioned and combat ready in the Middle East. Any claim that the troops in the Gulf region did not face imminent hostilities – the criterion that is supposed to automatically start the War Powers Resolution's clock – in the five months between August 1990 and January 1991, when Congress finally passed an authorization for the use of force, is simply untenable.[23]

Something rather similar happened in the wake of the attacks on the United States in 2001, which generated instant and nearly unanimous support for another authorization for the use of force. The 2001 authorization was explicitly limited to the use of force against those whom the president determined had "planned, authorized, committed, or aided the terrorist attacks that occurred on September 11, 2001, or harbored such organizations or persons, in order to prevent any future acts of international terrorism against the United States by such nations, organizations or persons."[24] A year later, however, Congress handed the president a third and even more open-ended formal delegation of power to use force, this time directed at Iraq. In the 2002 version of the authorization, Congress formally stated that the president was legally "authorized to use the Armed Forces of the United States as he determines to be necessary and appropriate in order to (1) defend the national security of the United States

22 George H. W. Bush, letter to Thomas Foley, Speaker of the House of Representatives, November 16, 1990. Printed in the *Congressional Record*, January 12, 1991, p 1091.
23 Section 4 (a) of the War Powers Resolution of 1973 states, "In the absence of a declaration of war, in any case in which United States Armed Forces are introduced (1) into hostilities or into situations where imminent involvement in hostilities is clearly indicated by the circumstances... the President shall submit within 48 hours to the Speaker of the House of Representatives and to the President pro tempore of the Senate a report, in writing." Section 5 (b) continues: "Within sixty calendar days after a report is submitted or is required to be submitted... the President shall terminate any use of United States Armed Forces with respect to which such report was submitted (or required to be submitted), unless the Congress (1) has declared war or has enacted a specific authorization for such use of United States Armed Forces, (2) has extended by law such sixty-day period, or (3) is physically unable to meet as a result of an armed attack upon the United States. Such sixty-day period shall be extended for not more than an additional thirty days if the President determines and certifies to the Congress in writing that unavoidable military necessity respecting the safety of United States Armed Forces requires the continued use of such armed forces in the course of bringing about a prompt removal of such forces."
24 Senate Joint Resolution 23, signed into law by President George W. Bush on September 18, 2001, as Public Law 107-40, 115 Stat. 224 (2001).

against the continuing threat posed by Iraq; and (2) enforce all relevant United Nations Security Council Resolutions regarding Iraq."[25]

Maine Democrat Thomas Allen argued that the 2002 resolution went far beyond the 2001 authorization, giving the president nearly unlimited discretion to use force "as he determines to be necessary and appropriate." The Gulf War resolution of 1991, Allen said, "did not delegate decisions on 'force as he determines.' The post-September 11 use-of-force resolution did not use the words 'as he determines.' Not even the Gulf of Tonkin resolution," Allen noted, "used the words 'as he determines.'" This resolution, Allen insisted, "represents an abdication of Congress' constitutional role."[26]

One might argue that the War Powers Resolution was simply ineffective. But although it failed to increase the congressional role in the deployment of force, it still left intact the formal, statutory authority for the president to use force – authority that had been constitutionally ambiguous before 1973. While Congress continued to delegate and authorize executive power, every president from Nixon through George W. Bush consistently, regularly, loudly, and clearly insisted that the provisions of the War Powers Resolution designed to check or limit these delegations and other exercises of war powers were unconstitutional.[27] When the first President Bush secured a formal authorization for the use of force in Kuwait and Iraq in January 1991, he made clear in a signing statement that in his view the administration's "request for congressional support did not, and my signing this resolution does not, constitute any change in the long-standing positions of the Executive branch on either the President's constitutional authority to use the Armed Forces to defend vital U.S. interests or the constitutionality of the War Powers Resolution."

A very similar pattern unfolded when the second President Bush was handed authorizations for the use of force from Congress in 2001 (for Afghanistan) and in 2002 (for Iraq). Like his father before him, George W. Bush noted in 2001 that, "in signing this resolution, I maintain the longstanding position of the executive branch regarding the President's constitutional authority to use force, including the Armed Forces of the United States and regarding the constitutionality of the War Powers Resolution."[28] The second President Bush went a bit further in his signing statement attached to the 2002 authorization for the use of force in Iraq. He insisted that, although he appreciated the congressional support, he

---

25 House Joint Resolution 114, passed by the House on October 10, 2002.
26 *Congressional Record*, October 8, 2002, p H 7245–6.
27 Gordon Silverstein, *Imbalance of Powers: Constitutional Interpretation and the Making of American Foreign Policy*. New York: Oxford University Press 1996.
28 President George W. Bush, "Statement on Signing the Authorization for Use of Military Force," *Weekly Compilation of Presidential Documents*, September 21, 2001, pp 1319–55.

had no constitutional or statutory need for it. "While I appreciate receiving that support," Bush wrote, "my request for it did not, and my signing this resolution does not, constitute any change in the long-standing positions of the executive branch on either the President's constitutional authority to use force to deter, prevent, or respond to aggression or other threats to U.S. interests or on the constitutionality of the War Powers Resolution."[29]

Was this language merely a matter of semantics? When seen exclusively through a political lens, perhaps. But each administration – from Nixon through Clinton and Bush – seemed to have understood the value, the importance of precedent that might govern any future court struggle over executive power. By providing specific statutory authority for the use of force for sixty to ninety days, Congress had removed any claim that the president lacked constitutional authority to use force without prior congressional authorization. Presidents agreed that they had this authority – and more. They argued that they had this authority without restriction or limit. In essence, by formalizing the ambiguous authority to use force, Congress had undercut its own constitutional position without gaining anything in terms of practical control on the use of force.

One risk this poses is what might happen in the event Congress was interested in challenging a president on the use of force. This is precisely what the presidents were focusing on in their statements – an effort to shape future judicial rulings, an effort to shape or even redefine the default assumptions courts might use to decide if a president had overstepped his or her constitutional limits. Default assumptions signal which path would meet greater and which would meet less resistance. A default that favors Congress would raise the costs for a president's assertion of prerogative power, whereas a default that favors the executive likely would encourage those assertions. Because default assumptions, triggers, and conditions are not static, shifting them can profoundly reframe the political and policy debate.[30] Shaping these default assumptions was very much a part of what these presidents were attempting to do. And to do it, they needed a good grasp of just what the Court's default assumptions were and what was likely to trigger even a reluctant Court to intervene.

Law is Different: Precedent and the Power of Default Assumptions

The Supreme Court has never accepted the idea that foreign policy is free of all constitutional constraint. It has intervened in foreign policy cases

---

29 President George W. Bush, "Statement on signing the authorization for use of military force against Iraq resolution of 2002," *Weekly Compilation of Presidential Documents*, Oct 21, 2002.

30 Another example of the power of what Mark Tushnet refers to as "judicial overhang." See Mark Tushnet, *Taking the Constitution Away from the Courts*, Princeton: Princeton University Press, 1999. pp 57–65.

a number of times, even when the government insisted that these rulings might imperil national security.[31] Despite regular pendulum swings in power between Congress and the executive branch, certain fundamental assumptions about the Constitution and foreign policy developed early and were steadily maintained by all three branches, at least until World War I. This traditional interpretation can be summed up in three broad principles: (1) The national government (Congress *and* the president, together) has broad, but *not* unlimited power in foreign affairs; (2) specific limits or restrictions in the Constitution apply to foreign and domestic policy alike – including provisions assigning powers to the judicial branch itself – and these will be enforced by the Supreme Court even in war and emergencies; and (3) Congress has constitutional authority (should it choose to exercise that authority) in foreign and domestic affairs alike.[32]

Although aggressive presidents from Thomas Jefferson to Abraham Lincoln and Theodore Roosevelt all pushed the limits and boundaries of the traditional interpretation, none rejected it; none asserted that there were separate or unlimited prerogative powers in the executive branch. This began to change in the aftermath of two world wars, and particularly in the midst of the Cold War, as presidents increasingly came to argue that the Constitution should be read to provide and support inherent and unassailable prerogative powers in the executive branch. This argument became more explicit and more dramatic in the Johnson and Nixon administrations, rising to a zenith in the George W. Bush administration.

While presidents were increasingly pressing their more aggressive prerogative claims in speeches, public documents, legislative proposals, and court briefs, the Supreme Court never abandoned these three basic principles. What has changed is the threshold the Court sets for determining

---

31 See the full discussion of this doctrine in Silverstein, *Imbalance of Powers*. An example of this sort of case would be *New York Times v. United States*.

32 Supreme Court Justice George Sutherland, who had served as a very conservative senator from the state of Utah before joining the Supreme Court, attempted to articulate a complicated theory by which foreign and domestic powers could be constitutionally separated. Sutherland spelled this out in a book he wrote while still in the Senate – George Sutherland, *The Constitution and World Affairs*, New York: Columbia University Press, 1919. But Sutherland's concerns were about the vertical separation of powers – the question of the allocation of power between the national government and the state governments. He wanted to find a way to make sure the national government would exercise strong and centralized power in foreign affairs and yet protect the states against a strong national government in domestic policy. When he joined the Supreme Court, he had an opportunity to put this theory into law in *U.S. v. Curtiss-Wright Export Corporation*, 299 U.S. 304 (1936). But this is a badly misunderstood and misquoted case. The question in this case was one of delegation – could the Congress delegate foreign policy power to the executive? Sutherland insisted it could – but was at pains to argue that, although such a delegation was constitutional in foreign policy (where power belonged exclusively to the *national government* – president *and* Congress), it was not in domestic policy, where power was located in the states, and the national government allowed only limited and specific authority. For a full discussion, see Gordon Silverstein, *Imbalance of Powers: Constitutional Interpretation and the Making of American Foreign Policy*, New York: Oxford University Press, 1997, pp. 37–41.

just when and what Congress must do assert its authority in foreign affairs and to bring the Court in on its side in a struggle with the executive. Because war and emergency powers inherently involve unanticipated challenges and problems, there are great ambiguities about these powers written into the Constitution: The power to declare war is exclusively assigned to Congress, as are the powers to raise and support armies and navies and to tax and spend. The president, however, is assigned the duty to serve as Commander in Chief of those armed forces, to negotiate treaties, and to represent the United States and speak on its behalf with other nations. Default assumptions about where the boundaries between these powers might lie and what might trigger judicial intervention to police those boundaries are vitally important.

The Supreme Court's traditional default assumptions in this arena were most cogently summarized in a formula first articulated by Justice Robert Jackson in 1952. When a strike in the steel industry in the midst of the Korean War led President Truman to order American steel mills to be seized and run by the government to support the war effort, the Supreme Court said no, rejecting the executive's constitutional claims. In a concurrence in the case, Justice Jackson argued that separation of powers disputes fall into three distinct categories – cases in which the president "takes measures incompatible with the expressed or implied will of Congress (where the president acts against the express will of Congress); cases falling in what Jackson called a "zone of twilight" in which the president and Congress have concurrent powers and, in effect, must struggle for control; and finally cases in which the president acts *together with* Congress. "When the President acts pursuant to an express or implied authorization of Congress," Jackson wrote, "his authority is at its maximum, for it includes all that he possesses in his own right plus all that Congress can delegate." In these circumstances, "and in these only," Jackson said, the president may be said "to personify the federal sovereignty."[33]

These outer boundaries were not new in 1952 – Justice Jackson was building on longstanding interpretations, evident as early as 1804 – and they have been confirmed again and again in cases since, including cases decided at the peak of the Cold War, in the midst of the Vietnam War, and during the extended conflicts that were triggered by the attacks on the United States on September 11, 2001.[34] What has changed, however, are the default assumptions about what is needed to move a case

---

33 *Youngstown Sheet & Tube v. Sawyer.*
34 *Little v. Barreme*, 6 U.S. 170 (1804); *Youngstown Sheet & Tube v. Sawyer*, 343 U.S. at 613; *Perez v. Brownell*, 356 U.S. 44 (1958); *New York Times v. United States*, 403 U.S. 713, 732–733 (1971); *Hamdi v. Rumsfeld*, 542 U.S. 507 (2004); *Rasul et al v. Bush*, 542 U.S. 466 (2004); *Hamdan v. Rumsfeld*, 548 U.S. 557 (2006); *Boumediene et al v. Bush*, 553 U.S. ___ (2008); *Munaf et al v. Geren*, 553 U.S. ___ (2008). See also

from one category to another. Just what is sufficient to indicate legislative approval – or disapproval? Is the burden on the legislature or on the executive? Does legislative silence mean tacit approval – or does silence mean a lack of explicit approval? Where once the Court largely assumed that only clear and explicit authorization could place a case in the most permissive, president *together with* Congress category, whereas congressional silence would be read as implicit disapproval (pushing a case into the most restrictive president *versus* Congress category), by the 1980s, those defaults were shifting: Congressional silence was increasingly read as tacit approval, and anything short of explicit legislative disapproval was read as tacit authorization.[35]

If the standards that define the boundaries of each category have changed, there will, of course, be dramatic changes in what officials in each branch of the government assume is required of them – and what they are allowed to do. Changing these boundaries alters incentives and risks. In the steel seizure case, the Court adhered to a default assumption that congressional silence constituted at best a lack of approval and, more likely, tacit disapproval. That assumption continued to hold for nearly thirty years after the steel case, until the Supreme Court dramatically blurred Jackson's rigid category/boundaries in the wake of the Iran hostage crisis of 1979–1980.

President Jimmy Carter's response to the seizure of American hostages in Iran in 1979 included freezing Iranian assets and convincing the international community to do the same. These frozen assets became Carter's primary leverage in negotiations for the hostages' release. Although the impact of the freeze fell mostly on Iran and Iranians, it also pinched those who sold goods and provided services to Iran, including many U.S. firms such as the American International Group (AIG) and Dames & Moore International (an engineering firm that had built nuclear power facilities in Iran, but had not yet been paid for its work when Iran's assets were frozen).[36] In an Executive Agreement formalizing negotiations with Iran, Carter assigned the frozen assets to an international tribunal that, in turn, was empowered to resolve all claims against Iran.

In *American International Group v. Islamic Republic of Iran*, a case taking up the question of the asset freeze, the U.S. Court of Appeals for the District of Columbia ruled that, although Carter had clear authority to freeze foreign assets under the International Emergency Economic Powers Act (IEEPA), he had no express or implied grant of power from Congress in that law to suspend the claims of American nationals against Iran.

Gordon Silverstein, *Imbalance of Powers: Constitutional Interpretation and the Making of American Foreign Policy*, New York: Oxford University Press, 1997.
35 *Dames & Moore v. Regan*, 453 U.S. 654 (1980), discussed at length later in the chapter.
36 *Dames & Moore v. Regan*.

Nevertheless, the court found that "there is a long-standing practice of settling private American claims against foreign governments through executive agreements."[37] Here the appeals court found support for an executive initiative in foreign policy not in the Constitution itself, nor in a particular act of Congress. It was the *lack of action* by Congress and the precedent of a pattern of silence that were said to matter. In this decision, the court pointed to a pattern of previous behavior, ruling that absent an explicit effort to foreclose the option selected by the president, the court would defer to the executive branch. The court was quick to note that it "would be confronted with a very different case if Congress had enacted legislation, or even passed a resolution, indicating its displeasure with the Iranian agreements."[38]

The Supreme Court grappled with these issues in a related case, *Dames & Moore v. Regan*. Then-Associate Justice William Rehnquist's opinion for the Court in *Dames & Moore* held that the president's actions had been constitutional. Even though the presidential freeze was not explicitly authorized by an act of Congress, the IEEPA and the Hostage Act of 1868, he wrote, were clear indications of congressional acceptance of broad executive discretion in similar circumstances to those presented by the case. Rehnquist argued that the courts cannot expect Congress to "anticipate and legislate with regard to every possible action the President may find it necessary to take or every possible situation in which he might."[39] Taken together with the evidence of other related delegations of power in the IEEPA and the Hostage Act, Rehnquist concluded, "Congress has *implicitly* approved the practice of claim settlement by Executive agreement."[40]

But there was a problem with this argument. Far from being a law designed to delegate power to the executive, the IEEPA was a post-Vietnam, post-Watergate effort explicitly designed to *limit* and *reduce* executive power and executive discretion. Rehnquist was able to find delegation in a bill designed to *limit* delegation in part because the final

---

37 See *American International Group, Inc. v. Islamic Republic of Iran*, 657 F.2d 430, 444 (1981), noting that "the President has entered into binding settlements with foreign nations compromising the claims of U.S. nationals at least 10 times since 1952 without seeking the advice and consent of the Senate."

38 *American International v. Iran*, 657 F.2d at 445.

39 *Dames & Moore v. Regan*, 453 U.S. at 678.

40 *Dames & Moore v. Regan*, 453 U.S. at 680 (emphasis added). Although Rehnquist argued for broad executive discretion, he explicitly rejected the notion that there was an executive prerogative: "We do not decide," Rehnquist wrote, "that the President possesses plenary power to settle claims, even as against foreign governmental entities." 453 U.S. at 688. Similarly, the appeals court in *American International* held that "to the extent that denominating the President as the 'sole organ' of the United States in international affairs constitutes a blanket endorsement of plenary Presidential power over any matter extending beyond the borders of this country, we reject that characterization." *American International v. Iran*, 657 F.2d at 438, n.6.

bill that emerged was a shadow of its original self, having been watered down considerably to secure support in both houses of Congress, much as had happened with the War Powers Resolution. Both started out as clear efforts to limit executive power, but by the time they emerged from the legislative process, both had lost much of their bite. The final version of the IEEPA failed to define what constituted an emergency and dropped any penalties for presidents who failed to consult with Congress.

Rehnquist's strained transformation of a law designed to limit executive power into one that would actually fortify executive claims drew a stinging rebuke from Justices Blackmun, Brennan, Marshall, and Powell in a dissent in a later case, *Regan v. Wald*, which challenged a Treasury Department regulation prohibiting property transactions with Cuba or Cuban citizens. Writing for the majority in *Regan v. Wald*, Justice Rehnquist insisted that the legislative history of the IEEPA was unclear, that its language was broad, and that the president's action was a logical construction of that language. The dissent would have none of it, arguing that the whole intent of IEEPA was to *restrict* the burgeoning discretion being exercised by the chief executive. In a separate statement, Justice Powell added that "the judgment of the Court [in this case] may well be in the best interest of the United States," but that the Court's proper role should be limited to "ascertaining and sustaining the intent of Congress."[41] For Powell, as for Blackmun, Brennan, and Marshall, the legislative intent of this statute was clear: Congress wanted to *limit* executive discretion.

But the majority found some ambiguity in the legislative record and chose to read the words of the IEEPA rather literally, insisting that because Congress had not clearly foreclosed this option, it was within the president's discretionary authority. The default assumption appeared to have flipped – where Justice Jackson's steel case concurrence limited the executive's independent constitutional authority, insisting on explicit delegation of power, now the Court would interpret ambiguity and silence as tacit delegation. This meant, of course, that for Congress to win the support of the Court, legislators would have to invoke and explicitly insist on their prerogatives – the Court seemed to be signaling that it would no longer be as willing to ride in and protect Congress from its own tendency to avoid politically costly debates. Congressional silence or ambiguity would now be more likely to be read as a *lack of approval*. Clear, explicit, formal, and unambiguous legislative *dis*-approval now would be required. Anything less, the Court signaled, might now be interpreted as tacit approval.

The *Dames & Moore* suit argued that the president lacked authority to strip the firm of its right to judicial process in American courts. In his majority opinion, then-Associate Justice William Rehnquist ruled that the

41 *Regan v. Wald*, 468 U.S. 222, 262 (1983).

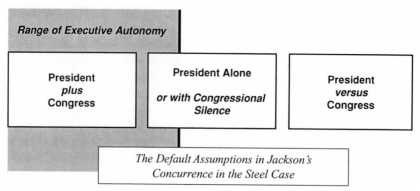

Figure 8.1.

Court would adhere to Jackson's basic categories, but would take a far less rigid view of the lines separating the three. In foreign affairs, Justice Rehnquist noted, in his opinion in *Dames & Moore v. Regan*, cases are likely to fall "not neatly in one of three pigeonholes, but rather at some point along a spectrum running from explicit congressional authorization to explicit congressional prohibition."[42] Softening the barriers between these categories allows the default assumptions about what is required to move from one category to another to soften as well. Where Congress explicitly opposes the president, the Court continues to defend legislative prerogatives, as it insisted it would in the 1952 steel case. But short of meeting this far higher standard of formal opposition, the Court since *Dames & Moore* has been increasingly willing to find implicit delegation of power to the president, even where the legislative language is far from clear.

Under Jackson's categories, as interpreted and applied in the 1950s and 1960s, the president's range of executive autonomy looked something like that shown in Figure 8.1. In *Dames & Moore*, the Rehnquist Court shifted that line significantly, suggesting that silence likely would be interpreted as tacit consent (see Figure 8.2).

Just as legislative precedent builds on judicial precedent and shapes executive precedent, so too has foreign policy precedent been reinforced by and (and influenced) lateral cases concerning the default assumption when it came to executive discretion in domestic policy. In a case having nothing whatever to do with war and foreign policy, the Supreme Court made clear what Rehnquist had only hinted at in the *Dames & Moore* case – that default assumptions about executive power and its limits might now be reversing. When Congress is explicit and clear and actively states its preferences, the Court ruled, in *Chevron v. Natural*

---

42 *Dames & Moore v. Regan*, 453 U.S. at 669. Justice Rehnquist noted, however, that "we have in the past found and do today find Justice Jackson's classification of executive actions into three general categories analytically useful."

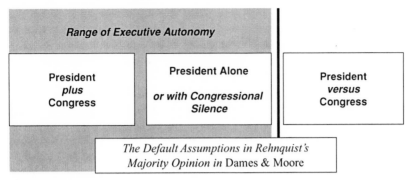

Figure 8.2.

Resource Defense Council in 1984, that preference will be honored. When Congress is ambiguous or silent, the administration's interpretation of a statute will be accepted. In a law review article, Justice Scalia made clear his view that this is an appropriate rule of thumb. *Chevron* he insisted, puts Congress on notice that ambiguity, or gaps, or silences will be read as tacit delegations. Congress, he wrote, "now knows that the ambiguities it creates, whether intentionally or unintentionally, will be resolved, within the bounds of permissible interpretation, not by the courts," but by administration officials.[43] If Congress disapproves of the administration's interpretation, legislators are free to pass an explicit statute that makes clear their preferences. This is perfectly simple in theory – but extraordinarily difficult in practice given the institutional barrier of overcoming a filibuster in the Senate or a presidential veto.

Chevron created what Mark Richards, Herbert Kritzer, and Joseph Smith refer to as a jurisprudential regime – a case in which the Court's ruling powerfully shapes and constrains the frames in which future cases will be considered and decided.[44] That these critical regime-defining cases also spill over laterally should hardly be surprising. Adding *Chevron* to the rulings in *Regan v. Wald* and *Dames & Moore*, it becomes increasingly clear that, although Jackson's steel seizure categories may still be operative, the default thresholds that determine the category – and therefore the constitutional barrier – triggered in each category can move significantly. When Congress actually, formally fortifies these assumptions by passing

43 *Chevron v. Natural Resources Defense Council*, 467 U.S. 837 (1984); Antonin Scalia, "Judicial Deference to Administrative Interpretations of Law," 1989 *Duke Law Journal* 511, 517 (1989). For a more complete examination of the implications of this shift, see Gordon Silverstein, "Statutory Interpretation and the Balance of Institutional Power," 56 *Review of Politics* 3, 475–503 (1994).
44 Mark Richards and Herbert Kritzer, "Jurisprudential Regimes in Supreme Court Decision Making," 96 *American Political Science Review* 2, 305–320 (2002); Mark Richards, Herbert Kritzer and Joseph Smith, "Does *Chevron* Matter?" 28 *Law & Policy* 4, 444–469 (2006).

legislation that explicitly delegates, there is every reason to consider the impact of this legislative precedent if and when the Court ever comes to consider the question. Even if the Court does not, it continues to offer support and fortification for presidential actions and ever-more aggressive assertions of prerogative power.

These cycles are not cast in stone – courts change as do precedents both lateral and lineal. A 2001 case, *U.S. v. Mead*, significantly softened *Chevron's* default preference for administrative discretion.[45] As discussed in Chapter 5, Justice Scalia himself was appalled by the *Mead* decision precisely because he saw it as fundamentally reversing the default assumption back toward Congress. Whereas *Chevron* left discretion as largely a zero-sum, winner-take-all proposition, the majority in *Mead* insisted that they were not replacing *Chevron* so much as refining it. The wide range of "statutory variation has led the Court to recognize more than one variety of judicial deference, just as the Court has recognized a variety of indicators that Congress would expect *Chevron* deference," the majority ruled. *Mead* in no way overturned or reversed *Chevron*, but even if *Mead* significantly waters down *Chevron's* default assumption, it will not automatically water down or revise or rewrite the myriad decisions that have been shaped by this ruling and those it generated over the years, at least not in the short run.[46]

Default Assumptions and the Prerogative Claims of the Bush Administration

From the steel case in 1952 through Vietnam and on to the Iran hostage crisis, Kosovo, and even the first Gulf War in 1991, the struggle over war and foreign policy has largely been a struggle over ambiguity: Just what would constitute congressional delegation or the denial of that delegation? But since 9/11, the Bush administration has worked hard to revise the constitutional boundaries of the separation of powers in war and foreign policy – not only in terms of executive power independent of Congress, but even executive power versus the power of the judicial branch. The Bush administration had a clear focus on legal and constitutional argument – its objective was not simply to explain the utility or even the necessity of actions taken, but to assert, secure, and fortify

45 *United States v. Mead Corp.*, 533 U.S. 218 (2001).
46 Note well that the Court is free to reverse precedent and to reverse earlier decisions. Here, there were eight Justices who agreed that the *Chevron* deference principle should not apply as a simple either-or proposition. But they were in no way prepared to reverse or strike it down. The Justices will typically go well out of their way to preserve what they can of earlier decisions – often in the process damping or trimming, skewing or framing their newer doctrine to allow them to avoid the direct reversal. This is another important consequence of the reality that judicial decision making is different from the process that governs in the elected branches.

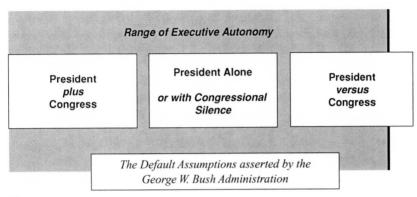

Figure 8.3.

explicit, legal and constitutional arguments for the formal expansion of the traditional (and ambiguous) boundaries of executive power. Its focus and objective was to break down Jackson's barriers and expand the president's independent authority even in what had been Jackson's third category (see Figure 8.3).

The attack of September 11, 2001, was without parallel or precedent. Nothing in our eighteenth-century Constitution directly addressed a situation in which an organized group – under no national command, wearing no uniforms, and not being signatories to any treaties or legal obligations – would execute an act of war of this magnitude on American soil, against American civilians. It is unsurprising that those charged with responding to these attacks might feel the need to exercise extraordinary, even extra-constitutional powers. But unlike Jefferson, Lincoln, and even Theodore Roosevelt, they insisted not only that they had done what was needed to be done but that they also had the right and the formal legal authority to do so. To reach this conclusion required a dramatic reinterpretation of the U.S. Constitution. But thanks to the steady juridification of American politics in the years since World War II and especially to what Assistant Attorney General Jack Goldsmith refers to as the "post-Watergate hyper-legalization of warfare, and the attendant proliferation of criminal investigators," the Bush administration did not even consider the need to make a political case for their actions. "The President had to do what he had to do to protect the country," Goldsmith writes. "And the lawyers had to find some way to make what he did legal."[47]

A set of very creative and smart young lawyers – including Goldsmith, Jay Bybee, John Yoo, Patrick Philbin, and Robert Delahunty, among others – led by Vice President Cheney's chief of staff, David Addington,

47 Jack Goldsmith, *The Terror Presidency: Law and Judgment Inside the Bush Adminis-tration*. New York: W.W. Norton, 2007, p 81.

developed creative and aggressive legal theories that they believed would reset the constitutional debate, fortifying the president's claims to exclusive, constitutional, executive power. The foundation for their arguments was laid in the midst of the Cold War that followed World War II and gained strength during the Johnson and Nixon administrations, flowering in the Reagan administration's efforts to fund the Contras fighting in Nicaragua, despite explicit statutory provisions that appeared to ban such assistance. The Iran-Contra affair was one of the earliest examples of an extensive and very legalistic effort to work around Congress. In the aftermath of 9/11 the Bush administration took the next logical step, not only using legal argument to work around Congress, but affirmatively using legal argument to assert and defend a bold prerogative interpretation that held that in foreign affairs the president alone had final authority, and when the national security is imperilled (a judgment left to the executive), the president was legitimately entitled to override constitutional constraints to preserve and protect that security.[48]

This position was clearly articulated by Attorney General Michael Mukasey in his confirmation hearings in October 2007. He was asked whether the president could authorize a subordinate to act in violation of an explicit statute. He could, Mukaskey told the Senate Judiciary Committee, if he was acting "within the authority of the President to defend the country." In that case, "the President is not putting somebody above the law; the President is putting somebody within the law."[49] This statement seemed to echo a famous pair of answers Richard Nixon gave David Frost, a British journalist, about the so-called Huston plan for spying on domestic dissidents.[50]

FROST: *So what in a sense, you're saying is that there are certain situations . . . where the president can decide that it's in the best interests of the nation or something, and do something illegal.*

NIXON: Well, when the president does it, that means that it is not illegal.

FROST: *By definition?*

NIXON: Exactly. Exactly. If the president, for example, approves something because of the national security, or in this case because of a threat to internal peace and order of significant magnitude,

---

48 This argument is most clearly articulated in John Yoo, *The Powers of War and Peace: The Constitution and Foreign Affairs after 9/11*, Chicago: University of Chicago Press, 2006.

49 Attorney General Designate Michael Mukasey testifying before the Senate Judiciary Committee, October 18, 2007. Cited in Philip Shenon, "Senators Clash with Nominee over Torture and Limits of Law," *New York Times*, October 19, 2007, p 1.

50 A plan attributed to then Deputy White House Counsel Thomas Huston for surveillance on domestic dissidents.

then the president's decision in that instance is one that enables those who carry it out, to carry it out without violating a law. Otherwise they're in an impossible position.

Later, in the interview, Frost returned to the earlier statement about the Huston Plan and the president's authority to override constitutional or statutory provisions:

FROST: *Is there anything in the Constitution or the Bill of Rights that suggests the president is that far of a sovereign, that far above the law?*

NIXON: No, there isn't. There's nothing specific that the Constitution contemplates in that respect. I haven't read every word, every jot and every tittle, but I do know this. . . . As far as a president is concerned, that in wartime, a president does have certain extraordinary powers which would make acts that would otherwise be unlawful, lawful if undertaken for the purpose of preserving the nation and the Constitution, which is essential for the rights we're all talking about.[51]

In their effort to build a new constitutional understanding and legal commitment to executive power, the Bush administration and its lawyers explicitly rejected the traditional interpretation, arguing that the executive alone has constitutional authority under Article II not only to use American military force as he sees necessary, but also to eavesdrop on American citizens and to unilaterally interpret or even terminate treaties such as the Geneva Convention Accords on the Treatment of Prisoners and the U.N. Convention Against Torture. Not only did the Bush administration assert independent and unfettered constitutional power, but it also consistently and formally insisted that these powers cannot constitutionally be interfered with by Congress or even by the federal courts. In signing a defense appropriations bill in 2005 that contained a provision banning torture, President George W. Bush wrote, "The executive branch shall construe Title X in Division A of the Act, relating to detainees, in a manner consistent with the constitutional authority of the President to supervise the unitary Executive branch and as Commander in Chief and *consistent with the constitutional limitations on the judicial power*, which will assist in achieving the shared objective of the Congress and the President, evidenced in Title X, of protecting the American people from further terrorist attacks."[52]

---

51 "Excerpts from Interview with Nixon about Domestic Effects of Indochina War." *New York Times*, May 20, 1977, p A16.

52 President's Statement on Signing of H.R. 2863, the Department of Defense, Emergency Supplemental Appropriations Bill, December 30, 2005. See http://www.whitehouse.gov/news/releases/2005/12/print/20051230-8.html (emphasis added).

Signing statements were an important tool for the Bush administration in its efforts to develop and embed a fundamental shift in the allocation of constitutional power and authority. Used for various purposes over the years, signing statements developed prominence during the Reagan administration as part of an announced policy by Attorney General Edwin Meese to articulate and advance executive precedent and interpretations that might be available to the courts when controversial laws were tested and applied. The purpose, Meese said, was "to make sure that the president's own understanding of what's in a bill... is given consideration at the time of statutory construction later on by a court." In short, signing statements are designed to influence, to frame and constrain the Court's decision, to shape the "jurisprudential regime" in which the Court situates its rulings.[53] To ensure that signing statements would indeed have this impact, Meese announced that he had "arranged with the West Publishing Company that the presidential statement on the signing of a bill will accompany the legislative history from Congress so that all can be available to the court for future construction of what that statute really means."[54] (The West Publishing Company was one of two dominant firms publishing formal reports of federal and state judicial decisions and related legal materials, so this inclusion likely would have real influence over lawyers, judges, and legal academics trained to consider all relevant formal materials and, whether they agree or not, to cite them and consider their arguments.)

Default Assumptions, Precedent, and Guantanamo Bay

All of these efforts – court cases, legal memos, speeches, and signing statements – suggested an administration keenly aware of the importance of default assumptions and judicial precedent. Two streams of cases litigated by the Bush administration, however, well illustrate the risks of juridification, particularly in an arena in which the Court has remained relatively silent. A long series of cases involving Jose Padilla, an American citizen seized at Chicago's O'Hare airport in 2002 as a suspect in

53 Richards and Kritzer, "Jurisprudential Regimes."
54 Address by Attorney General Edwin Meese III, National Press Club, Washington, DC, Feb. 25, 1986, quoted in Marc N. Garber and Kurt A. Wimmer, "Presidential Signing Statements as Interpretations of Legislative Intent: An Executive Aggrandizement of Power," 24 *Harvard Journal on Legislation* 363, 366 (1987). In a 1993 memo, Clinton Assistant Attorney General Walter Dellinger noted that signing statements that purport to "create legislative history for the use of the courts was uncommon – if indeed it existed at all – before the Reagan and Bush Presidencies," though earlier administrations had used signing statements "to raise and address the legal or constitutional questions they believed were presented by the legislation they were signing," with examples of that sort dating back at least to the Jackson and Tyler administrations. Memorandum for Bernard N. Nussbaum, Counsel to the President, from Walter Dellinger, Assistant Attorney General, November 3, 1993, available at http://www.usdoj.gov/olc/signing.htm.

a plot to detonate a "dirty bomb" inside the United States, well illustrate the workings of an administration that understood the importance of judicial signals and how an adverse legal ruling (and the precedent it would establish) might undercut their broader constitutional objectives. A series of cases concerning detainees being held at Guantanamo Bay, Cuba, however, illustrate that this same administration was equally capable of ignoring or resisting clear judicial signals that, had they been heeded, might have prevented just the sort of ruling (and precedent) it had worked so hard to avoid in the Padilla case.

Jose Padilla was seized on May 8, 2002, classified by the executive branch as an "enemy combatant," and transferred to the custody of the U.S. Defense Department. For several years he was held in U.S. military prisons without any formal charges being filed and was denied access to any legal counsel. Padilla sued, seeking a writ of habeas corpus to force the government to present evidence showing why he should not be released and giving him an opportunity to challenge that evidence. The initial suit was dismissed by the Supreme Court for a technical flaw, but in 2005 a corrected suit was heard by a three-judge panel of the Fourth Circuit Court of Appeals in Richmond, Virginia. In his opinion, Judge J. Michael Luttig (who was then widely believed to be on George Bush's short list for Supreme Court nominees)[55] ruled that the administration was allowed to hold Padilla, but not because of any inherent executive prerogative power, but rather because the Authorization for the Use of Military Force (AUMF) passed by Congress provided statutory support for the Bush administration to detain and hold Padilla as an enemy combatant.[56]

Padilla appealed this ruling to the U.S. Supreme Court, but suddenly, on December 21, 2005, the administration filed papers to shift Padilla out of the military system, instead filing specific civilian charges against him. Oddly, this is what Padilla had long been demanding and what Luttig had said the administration did *not* have to do. And yet, it did take that action – but that was not all. The administration then petitioned the appeals court to *withdraw* its judgment and opinion in the Padilla case, arguing that giving Padilla what he wanted made the case moot. In short,

55 Todd Purdum, "Strong Ties Bind Players in Battle for Seat on Court," *New York Times*, July 18, 2005, p 1.
56 This ruling explicitly relied on the Supreme Court's decision in *Hamdi v. Rumsfeld*, 542 U.S. at 517, which similarly held that an American citizen could be detained as an enemy combatant, but, again, as Luttig ruled, this authority was built on the AUMF – a Supreme Court plurality explicitly noted, "We do not reach the question whether Article II provides such authority," because "Congress has in fact authorized Hamdi's detention, through the AUMF." *Hamdi v. Rumsfeld*, 542 U.S. at 517. The U.S. Code, O'Connor wrote for the plurality, states that "no citizen shall be imprisoned or otherwise detained by the United States except pursuant to an Act of Congress" (18 U.S.C.S. 4001(a)), and in this case, O'Connor ruled, the AUMF constituted a sufficient legislative act, despite the fact that it said nothing at all about how or when or if American citizens might be detained.

it seemed as if the administration wanted to make sure the Supreme Court would *not* have an opportunity to issue a ruling – one way or the other – in this case. Or at least that was how Judge Luttig saw it.

Not only did Luttig refuse to do as he was asked, but he issued an extraordinarily stinging rebuke to the government in a written opinion rejecting the request. The government's transfer of Padilla and the withdrawal of the appeals court's decision would, Luttig wrote, "compound what is, in the absence of explanation, at least an appearance that the government may be attempting to avoid consideration of our decision by the Supreme Court"; because of that, he held, the appeals court would "deny both the motion and suggestion."[57] This, he wrote, is a decision that could and should be made only by the U.S. Supreme Court.

The Supreme Court accepted the government's decision to give Padilla what he sought and foreclose further review – although Justices Kennedy and Stevens, joined by recently appointed Chief Justice John Roberts, issued a rather unusual warning to the president: Although the Court would grant the government's petition, in light of the previous changes in Padilla's custody status "and the fact that nearly four years have passed since he first was detained, Padilla, it must be acknowledged, has a continuing concern that his status might be altered again." To make sure that would not happen, the Supreme Court instructed the lower courts that would now hear the civilian case that "were the Government to seek to change the status or conditions of Padilla's custody" the district court "should act promptly to ensure that the office and purposes of the writ of *habeas corpus* are not compromised," adding that "Padilla, moreover, retains the option of seeking a writ of *habeas corpus* in this Court."[58]

The government's actions, Judge Luttig asserted in his rejection of the request to withdraw the circuit court opinion, have left impressions that

we would have thought the government [could] ill afford to leave extant. And these impressions have been left, we fear, at what may ultimately prove to be substantial cost to the government's credibility before the courts, to whom it will one day need to argue again in support of a principle of assertedly like importance and necessity to the one that it seems to abandon today. While there could be an objective that could command such a price as all of this, it is difficult to imagine what that objective would be.[59]

Why the sudden change? Why the extraordinary request for Luttig to withdraw his opinion? It is far too soon for us to know for sure, but one plausible reason (one of the few, frankly) turns on the power of precedent.

57 *Padilla v. Hanft*, 432 F.3d 582 (Order of the U.S. Circuit Court of Appeals for the Fourth Circuit, filed December 21, 2005).
58 *Padilla v. Hanft*, 547 U.S. 1062 (2006).
59 *Padilla v. Hanft*, 547 U.S. 1062 (2006).

In the Supreme Court case on which Luttig relied – *Hamdi v. Rumsfeld* – Justice O'Connor ruled that the AUMF provided sufficient authority for the government to provide an extremely truncated procedure for determining whether or not Hamdi could be held as an illegal combatant in a military prison; it thereby obviated any need for the Court to address the more extensive constitutional argument advanced by the government that the executive had the exclusive power to seize and detain enemy combatants with *or without* congressional authorization.[60] In other words, because the case *could* be resolved under Jackson's third category – in which Congress could be understood to have explicitly or implicitly delegated power to the president – the Court would not decide the broader constitutional question about exclusive executive power.

Yaser Hamdi, an American citizen, was seized by the U.S. military in Afghanistan in 2001. Accused of fighting against the Americans, he was declared an "enemy combatant" and held in a military prison in Virginia. A district court ruled that the government could not hold him; the Fourth Circuit Court of Appeals reversed the lower court, arguing for judicial deference. Hamdi appealed to the Supreme Court, which held that the AUMF provided the president with the authority to hold American citizens as enemy combatants, but that Hamdi nevertheless had a right to formal judicial process that could determine if he was, in fact, an enemy combatant.

By avoiding a Supreme Court ruling on the broader executive prerogative question in the *Padilla* case, the administration dodged the risk that the Court might take the *Hamdi* decision one step further, explicitly rejecting the executive's prerogative claims under Article II. The Court avoided this in the *Hamdi* case because there, Justice O'Connor had argued, the administration had congressional authority to act under the AUMF – which meant the Court did not have to rule on the president's broader prerogative claim.

A plausible case can be made that the administration very much preferred no precedent to a bad one. In the wake of the *Hamdi* decision in 2004, in fact, the *Los Angeles Times* reported, "authorities have moved repeatedly to avoid judicial review by changing the status of prisoners, shipping them overseas or making adjustments in conditions of their confinement – sometimes days before suspects were to appear in court."[61]

In the Fourth Circuit's initial ruling in September 2005, Judge Luttig's opinion relied almost entirely on the implied delegation of the congressional AUMF. There was no mention in the opinion of any inherent

---

60 *Hamdi v. Rumsfeld*, 542 U.S. 507 (2004).
61 Richard B. Schmitt, "Sidestepping Courts in the War on Terrorism: U.S. Seeks Leverage by Moving Detainees or Changing Their Status Before Scheduled Hearings. Critics Call It Legal Dodge Ball," *Los Angeles Times*, November 30, 2005, p 18.

executive authority, no support at all for any claims that the power to seize and detain enemy combatants in any way could be built on the president's powers as Commander in Chief or on his role as the nation's chief executive. Even if the government prevailed, then, at best this would be a precedent that would further support the importance of congressional authorization. And, as easy as that might be to secure, it would not advance the broader constitutional claim for exclusive power. That the Court might also take the opportunity to address the prerogative claims that Justice O'Connor so explicitly avoided in *Hamdi* was a risk the government may not have been willing to take.

Establishing strong precedents for executive power and avoiding those that might undercut these claims seem to have been the administration's top priorities: Good precedents were better than no precedents, but no precedent was vastly to be preferred to a bad judicial precedent. The administration seemed to have understood the risks and potential rewards of reluctant and even silent courts. Far from struggling with Congress over politics and policy, the Bush administration – more than any before – articulated and exercised an extraordinarily focused legal strategy.[62] It seemed to have understood that law is different and that a long-term strategy may sometimes dictate short-term strategic sacrifices. The saga of the administration's legal effort to assert exclusive and plenary executive power over the detention and interrogation of non-American citizens held at Guantanamo Bay, Cuba, however, illustrates a very different pattern from the one suggested by the Padilla case.

Separation of Powers, Prerogative Claims, and the Third Branch of Government

In the *Hamdi* case, the Court went out of its way to avoid making any sort of definitive constitutional ruling, instead signaling that Congress had provided sufficient statutory authority for the president to seize and detain American citizens as enemy combatants. The Court also ruled that Hamdi, and others like him, were entitled to a more thorough hearing process, a signal to Congress that formal legislation would be needed and that the president could not seize citizens as enemy combatants without at least some legislative support. The Court sent a similar set of signals in two cases involving non-Americans who had been seized and were being held as enemy combatants at the U.S. Naval Station at Guantanamo Bay.

Much hinges on the unusual status of Guantanamo Bay. The Bush administration made a very deliberate and considered decision to use

---

62 Jane Mayer, "The Hidden Power: The Legal Mind behind the White House's War on Terror," *New Yorker*, July 3, 2006, p 44.

Guantanamo as a prison facility – in large part on the legal advice of Deputy Assistant Attorneys General Patrick Philbin and John Yoo.[63] Guantanamo is a unique territory – although it technically remains a part of the sovereign nation of Cuba, the United States has had full military and legal control of this territory since signing a treaty with Cuba in 1903.[64] This status suggested to Bush administration lawyers Patrick Philbin and John Yoo that the United States might be able to house prisoners in a secure location over which the United States had total military and legal control (thanks to the treaty), and yet, because it was still technically the territory of a foreign, sovereign nation, the U.S. prison at Guantanamo would neither be subject to the control and supervision of the U.S. federal courts nor governed by the standards and limits of the U.S. Constitution.[65] For an administration that craved a free hand, unconstrained by the legislative or judicial branch, Guantanamo seemed ideal.

On the same day it decided *Hamdi v. Rumsfeld*, the Court also handed down a 6–3 decision in a case called *Rasul et al v. Bush*,[66] in which twelve Kuwaitis and two Australian nationals being held in Guantanamo filed petitions for habeas corpus with the district court in Washington, D.C. The district court refused to hear the cases, arguing that the federal courts had no jurisdiction over aliens held outside the United States. The U.S. Supreme Court reversed this holding, however, ruling that, although Guantanamo Bay was not a part of the United States, it was under the sovereign control of the United States and therefore subject to congressional statutes laying out the rules for habeas corpus review (28 U.S. Code 2241). The signal seemed clear – if the problem was a flawed statute, the easy answer was a new statute.

Although the administration was loathe to accept any constraints on its legal discretion, the Detainee Treatment Act of 2005 was rushed through Congress. The new law explicitly stated that "no court, justice or judge shall have jurisdiction to consider . . . an application for . . . habeas corpus filed by or on behalf of an alien detained . . . at Guantanamo,"[67] effectively endorsing the administration's commitment "to push its legal discretion

---

63 Patrick Philbin and John Yoo, "Memorandum for William J. Haynes, General Counsel, Department of Defense: RE: Possible Habeas Jurisdiction over Aliens Held in Guantanamo Bay, Cuba. December 28, 2001.

64 Lease to the United States by the Government of Cuba of Certain Areas for Naval or Coaling Stations in Guantanamo and Bahia Honda, July 2, 1903. http://www.yale.edu/lawweb/avalon/diplomacy/cuba/cuba003.htm.

65 John Yoo and Robert J. Delahunty, "Memorandum for William J. Haynes, General Counsel, Department of Defense: Application of Treaties and Laws to al Qaeda and Taliban Detainees." January 9, 2002. http://www1.umn.edu/humanrts/OathBetrayed/Yoo-Delahunty%201-9-02.pdf.

66 *Rasul et al v. Bush*, 542 U.S. 466 (2004).

67 Detainee Treatment Act of 2005.

to its limit" and its rejection of "any binding legal constraints on detainee treatment under the laws of war."[68]

In both *Hamdi* and *Rasul*, the Court had signaled its discomfort with the procedures the president had unilaterally established to conduct military commissions to try enemy combatants. The next year, it considered the case of Salim Ahmed Hamdan, a driver for Osama bin Laden, who was captured in Afghanistan and held at Guantanamo Bay. Salim Hamdan raised a different challenge to the detentions and denial of judicial process, arguing that these commissions could not be allowed because their use in these circumstances was a violation of the rules set out in the Geneva Accords, an international treaty to which the United States was a signatory. Common Article 3 of the Third Geneva Convention precludes the use of evidence to convict a prisoner unless the prisoner has had a chance to see or hear that evidence and to present a defense – but were enemy combatants being held in Guantanamo entitled to the protections of the Geneva Accords?[69]

In a December 2001 memo to William Haynes, the general counsel for the Department of Defense, Deputy Assistant Attorneys General Yoo and Philbin argued that *Johnson v. Eisentrager*, a post-World War II case involving German prisoners being held in camps in occupied Germany, was the only relevant precedent.[70] And in that case, the Court ruled that alien enemies who had served in governments at war with the United States had no right to habeas petitions nor the right to claim immunity from military trials and punishment.[71]

These propositions were initially tested in 2006 in *Hamdan v. Rumsfeld*. In a 5–3 decision, the Supreme Court rejected these claims, ruling that the Geneva Accords were law – enforceable in the federal courts – and that military commissions, as the administration had deployed them in this case, had violated the Uniform Code of Military Justice as well as the Geneva Accords. Reaction was swift. John Yoo commented to *The New York Times* that the Court "is attempting to suppress creative thinking."[72] Across the street on Capitol Hill, members of Congress read this new signal as yet another invitation to provide the president with

---

68 Jack Goldsmith, *The Terror Presidency: Law and Judgment inside the Bush Administration*, pp 119–20.

69 *Hamdan v. Rumsfeld*, 548 U.S. 557 (2006).

70 *Johnson v. Eisentrager*, 339 U.S. 763 (1950). John Yoo also strenuously insisted that – as a matter of American statutory and constitutional law, as well as a matter of international law – the Geneva Accords would not apply to enemy combatants who fought for no country and wore no uniform.

71 John Yoo and Robert J. Delahunty, "Memorandum for William J. Haynes, General Counsel, Department of Defense: Application of Treaties and Laws to al Qaeda and Taliban Detainees." January 9, 2002. http://www1.umn.edu/humanrts/OathBetrayed/Yoo-Delahunty%201-9-02.pdf.

72 Adam Liptak, "The Court Enters the War, Loudly," *New York Times*, July 2, 2006, Section 4, p 2.

statutory cover, which they promptly did in the Military Commissions Act of 2006.

In response to the ruling, Republican Senators Lindsey Graham and Jon Kyl issued a joint statement, saying that "working together, Congress and the administration can draft a fair, suitable, and constitutionally permissible tribunal statute."[73] Senate Judiciary Chairman Arlen Specter "introduced a bill immediately," providing blanket statutory authority for the new procedures and eliminating the remaining avenues for habeas petitions. Specter ushered the bill through the Senate, despite the fact that he told reporters the law was "patently unconstitutional on its face." Nevertheless, the chair of the Senate Judiciary Committee said that he had decided to support the bill because he thought it had a number of good items and was convinced that "the Court will clean it up" by striking down the unconstitutional provisions dealing with habeas corpus.[74]

The opportunity to "clean it up" came in 2008. Having closed all the statutory loopholes with these laws, the only question left was whether or not these statutes were constitutional. And that is the question the Supreme Court – which had been so carefully avoiding it since the war began in 2001 – finally would address in the 2008 case of *Boumediene et al v. Bush*. The Court's answer came in a stinging 5–4 ruling written by Justice Anthony Kennedy. The only case that seemed to offer a precedent supporting the administration was *Johnson v. Eisentrager*, in which the Supreme Court rejected the claims of two German nationals who argued that they should not be subjected to U.S. military tribunals.[75] In *Boumediene*, the Supreme Court ruled that *Eisentrager* may be good law, but it did not apply to Guantanamo. The right to petition for a writ of habeas corpus is so central to the American constitutional system, the majority ruled, that there is but one way to suspend its application – by following the formal and explicit procedure required by Article I, section 9, clause 2 of the Constitution.[76] Although the Detainee Treatment Act of 2005 and the Military Commissions Act of 2006 had explicitly stripped the courts of jurisdiction to hear habeas pleas coming out of Guantanamo, Congress had explicitly *not* "suspended" the "privilege of the writ of habeas corpus."

And what of Guantanamo and its unique status? Here the Court ruling implied that the Bush administration may have been a bit too clever. Unlike the prisoner camp in Germany at issue in *Eisentrager*, the Court

---

73 Linda Greenhouse, "Supreme Court Blocks Guantanamo Tribunals," *New York Times*, June 29, 2006, p 1.

74 Charles Babington and Jonathan Weisman, "Senate Approves Detainee Bill Backed by Bush," *Washington Post*, September 28, 2006. p A01.

75 *Johnson v. Eisentrager* 339 U.S. 763 (1950).

76 "The privilege of the Writ of *Habeas Corpus* shall not be suspended, unless when in Cases of Rebellion or Invasion the public Safety may require it."

ruled, Guantanamo has been and remains under the total and exclusive control of the United States and is likely to remain so for the near and distant future. The German camp was clearly temporary and clearly an integral part of the sovereign state of Germany. The administration insisted that Guantanamo was neither domestic nor foreign and thus excluded from constitutional and statutory rules – and that this status was established by a treaty-contract the U.S. had signed with Cuba in 1903. But the Court rejected this contention, arguing that the reality of control was and is dispositive. If Guantanamo is under the control of the United States, the Court held, then American forces on Guantanamo were subject to constitutional limits and statutory rules, including treaties such as the Geneva Accords that were incorporated into American law.

In *Boumediene*, the majority argued that it is constitutionally impermissible to assert that the executive could simply execute a lease agreement with a foreign government that would "contract away" constitutional provisions such as the rules about the suspension of the writ of habeas corpus. "The Constitution," Justice Kennedy wrote, "grants Congress and the President the power to acquire, dispose of, and govern territory, not the power to decide when and where its terms apply." The government's view, Kennedy said, is that "by surrendering formal sovereignty over any unincorporated territory to a third party, while at the same time entering into a lease that grants total control over the territory back to the United States, it would be possible for the political branches to govern without legal constraint."[77]

Although there may be times when the Court must abstain from certain questions concerning the boundaries of sovereignty, Kennedy insisted, "to hold that the political branches have the power to switch the Constitution on or off at will" is quite another thing altogether. Such a position "would permit a striking anomaly in our tripartite system of government, leading to a regime in which Congress and the President, not this Court, say 'what the law is.'"[78]

The Third Branch of Government and the Power of Precedent

And this brings us to one aspect of the separation of powers that has been relatively missing in the discussion of patterns of juridification: The Court is not only a referee, but can be an interested party as well. In *Boumediene*, the Court saw not simply an aggressive executive claiming independent power or pressing Congress to delegate power to the administration – it saw the elected branches employing creative devices such as the lease

---

77 *Boumediene et al v. Bush*, 533 U.S. ____ (2008).
78 *Boumediene et al v. Bush*, 533 U.S. ____ (2008).

with Cuba to usurp what the majority saw as the independent power of the judicial branch itself.[79]

Recall that there are two broad conditions under which the Court traditionally has been willing to intervene in foreign policy: (1) cases in which the government violates the explicit, constitutionally guaranteed rights of American citizens and (2) cases in which the president alone, against, or together with Congress violates explicit constitutional limits on the exercise of powers that are not assigned to the executive branch or that are assigned to others. Typically, when we think about the usurpation of power, we are thinking about the struggle between the president and Congress. but there is a third branch to consider, and the Court has been and continues to be extremely sensitive to any usurpation of judicial power, whether its power is usurped by the president alone or together with Congress.

The Bush administration's creative effort to find a way around existing law and judicial interpretation may have backfired a bit. Then again, *Boumediene* was a 5–4 decision that drew two very strongly worded dissents (from Chief Justice John Roberts and Justice Antonin Scalia). It was a case that the administration likely could have avoided had it been more sensitive to signals in the earlier cases (*Rasul, Hamdi,* and *Hamdan*) and established more than a perfunctory judicial process to handle those being held in Guantanamo. Ironically, part of the rebuke to the Bush administration also could have been avoided if it had not decided to hold these prisoners in Guantanamo. It might also have been avoided if the administration had read the earlier signals about the application of the Geneva Accords and accepted the reality that the third branch of government is, and has long been, a vigilant guardian of its own constitutional and institutional powers.

It is too soon to be able to fully sort out why the Bush administration reacted so differently in the *Padilla* case – why it removed the case and sought to terminate any chance of an adverse precedent – and in contrast, why in *Hamdi, Hamdan, Rasul,* and *Boumediene,* it pressed its claim, ignored signal after signal, and eventually helped drive a five-Justice majority to insist on defending judicial prerogatives against the assertive claims it was making. *Boumediene* itself could be a short-lived precedent; default patterns can change. But Congress ought to carefully consider the open-ended delegation that would be left behind should its effort to juridify the war powers ever wind up in court. Presidents might pay close attention to the Bush administration's clear and uncompromising

---

79 By contrast, Justice Scalia saw this as the core of the problem with this decision. "What drives today's decision," Scalia wrote in dissent, "is neither the meaning of the Suspension [of *habeas corpus*] Clause, nor the principles of our precedents, but rather an inflated notion of judicial supremacy." *Boumediene et al v. Bush,* 533 U.S. ____ (2008).

insistence not only on juridifying but also on constitutionalizing its claims to power. As the Court made clear in this series of cases, there is great latitude for the president *together with* Congress. And as the Court suggested in *Dames & Moore* along with *Chevron*, it can take precious little to move a case into that category. And yet the Bush administration insisted on pressing its constitutional case until, eventually, it got decisions (and precedents) diametrically at odds with its objectives. A reluctant Court can still shape and constrain policy choices, particularly when one or more of the elected branches are eager to embrace juridification.

Part III
Law's Allure: Costs and Consequences

9 TOBACCO

How Law Saves – and Kills Politics

E FFORTS TO PROTECT PRIVACY and save the environment, reduce poverty, end segregation, assure integration; and demands for fiscal responsibility, an end to political corruption, better and more equitable representation, the reform of the criminal justice system, and the allocation of the war powers – all these and more are problems that are being increasingly structured, framed, shaped, and constrained by judicial rules and automated legal procedures. Legal language dominates our political debates and has for a long time. Law's allure is deeply embedded in a American political system in which an intentionally fragmented government interacts with a political culture deeply suspicious of politics and imbued with a language of rights and rules, liberty and equity.

This is not an argument against the use of law, legal language, or judicial process – these are woven into the fabric of the American political system. Instead, this book is an effort to encourage politicians, policy advocates, and scholars alike to understand when and how these tools can be used most effectively and when their use, when a reliance on law, and legal language, and judicial decisions poses the greatest risks for the goals of those who choose to turn to the law and the courts. The question is not *whether* law and judicial process is to be employed or not, but rather when and under what conditions.

At their best, litigation and judicial orders can break through profound political and institutional barriers that can be broken in no other way short of violent or massive systemic, institutional, or constitutional change. Properly used, law can and should be the battering ram that opens the way for genuine and lasting political change. Medieval armies understood that the battering ram was a necessary, but not sufficient, part of their battle strategy. The battering ram clears the way for a full assault, but it is the assault and not the battering ram that will achieve the objective. In the decades-long struggle to regulate, restrict, and even eliminate the manufacture and marketing of tobacco, litigation was a battering ram that finally broke through, clearing the way for the political changes that would enable real change. But law's allure proved too strong, turning tobacco from being an object lesson that might help us better understand how law can save politics into one that might explain how law can kill politics.

Tobacco: The Icarus Tale of Law's Allure

What once was touted as an elixir for good health is now universally condemned as an agent of death, with those who choose to smoke cigarettes exiled to street corners to indulge their habit come rain or snow or blazing heat. But tobacco survives. In fact, it thrives. A November 2007 report from the Centers for Disease Control estimates that nearly 21 percent of the American population – more than 45 million Americans – smoke regularly. Among young adults, the rate is even higher, reaching nearly 24 percent of the population between the ages of 18 and 24.[1] These numbers are down dramatically from 1965, when more than half of all adult men in America were smokers, and down even from 1995 when smokers represented 25 percent of the American population.[2] But although the percentages have declined, 45 million smokers still translate into big profits on Wall Street, where "tobacco has been not only accepted but also preferred. Stock prices for tobacco companies in the Standard & Poor's 500-stock index rose 8.6 percent" in the first half of 2005, a time when that index rose overall by less than 1 percent.[3] And for the five years between May 2002 and May 2007, tobacco outperformed the Dow Jones Industrial Average by more than 2 to 1, with the Dow Jones average rising about 30 percent, but tobacco stocks rising 70 percent. During that time, the stock prices of leading tobacco makers soared: British American Tobacco, for example, posted 184 percent gains in that five-year period and R. J. Reynolds' U.S. division rose 82 percent.[4]

Who would have imagined this picture in the mid-1990s, when tobacco executives were imploring Congress to impose strict regulation on their industry, offering stunning amounts of money in voluntary penalties, and pledging to voluntarily eliminate advertising in exchange for liability protection? Tobacco might have been the quintessential case of the

---

1 Figures are from the Centers for Disease Control, December, 2007. See http://www.cdc.gov/tobacco/data_statistics/factsheets/adult_cig_smoking.htm.
2 Robert Kagan and William Nelson, "The Politics of Tobacco Regulation in the United States," in Robert Radin and Stephen Sugarman, eds, *Regulating Tobacco*, New York: Oxford University Press, 2001, p 11.
3 "Wall Street Loves Tobacco. Well, for Now," *New York Times*, March 6, 2005, "Sunday Money" section, p 8.
4 http://www.marketwatch.com. In the five years from May 2002 to May 2007, R. J. Reynolds' American unit reported earnings up 82 percent, British American Tobacco rose 184 percent, Imperial Tobacco 183 percent, and Altria rose 65 percent. In the year ending March 31, 2008, British American Tobacco's stock price rose nearly 18 percent, whereas the Dow Jones Industrial average declined by nearly 8 percent.

effective use of courts *together with* legislation and administrative regulation. It might have been a powerful case study of how to deploy the judicial sword to force legislative action and compromise. It should have been the story of how law saves politics; it should have been a demonstration of how law can serve as a weapon, cutting through the institutional and political barriers of a deliberately fragmented eighteenth-century system, one in which policy change is far easier to stop than to initiate. Instead, this is a case study of the perils of a reliance on law and judicial process as an alternative to politics and a way to achieve policy goals without the need for sordid compromise.

Litigation forced the tobacco companies to come to the negotiating table and actually agree to provisions and limits they had fought for decades. They agreed to submit to federal regulation that could mandate additional or larger warnings on cigarette packages, to control and even eliminate tobacco advertising and marketing programs, and to regulate and restrict the levels of different chemicals in cigarettes. They also agreed to pay defined penalties if youth smoking failed to be reduced by specific amounts. Under the agreement, the tobacco companies would pay the states and the national government $368.5 billion over twenty-five years, with specific percentages of that money explicitly allocated to support programs to help people quit smoking and to fund antismoking advertising.[5] They agreed to do all this in exchange for explicit limits on future legal liability, an end to the state litigation, and the setting of strict caps on the level of damages that could be sought by individuals and class action litigants.

Was it a good deal? Greek mythology tells of Icarus and his father, Daedalus, who were imprisoned on the island of Crete. To escape the island, Daedalus used wax and string and feathers to fashion wings for himself and Icarus, warning his son that he must not fly too high because the hot sun would melt the wax. The wings worked, but as Icarus flew through the air, he ignored his father's warning, soaring higher and higher – until the wax in his wings melted and Icarus crashed and died in the sea. Like Icarus, litigation allowed policy advocates who sought to eradicate tobacco to fly far, to batter down profound political and institutional barriers. But instead of using law *together with* politics, they decided they did not need to compromise, that they could fly higher still. Although they did not crash into the sea, the case of the antitobacco advocates does provide an illustration of how law can save politics – and how law can kill politics as well.

For policy advocates who had unsuccessfully fought Big Tobacco for so long, seeing that state lawsuits, class action litigation, and a barrage

---

5 Joe Nocera, "If It's Good for Philip Morris, Can it Also Be Good for Public Health?", *New York Times Magazine*, June 18, 2006, p 46.

of individual liability suits had forced their seemingly unconquerable foe to come hat in hand, asking to be regulated by the Federal Drug Administration, suggested that compromise was unnecessary: If litigation brought them this far, why not rely on litigation to bring them the whole way? They insisted that litigation could do the job – the whole job – without any need for compromise. They seem to have made a fundamental miscalculation. Tobacco use is way down in the United States, though it is still a phenomenally profitable business. Robert Kagan and William Nelson may well be correct in asserting that the policy we have quite accurately reflects popular preferences.[6] But from the perspective of those who fought tobacco all these years, who came so close to their goal, the tobacco story might be thought of as the Icarus tale of juridification.

Tobacco has a long and storied history in America; the popularity of smoking and cigarettes grew steadily across the decades from the days of the earliest colonies into the twentieth century, spiking dramatically first in World War I and later in World War II when tobacco farmers actually were excused from the military draft "because their crop was judged essential to the war effort."[7] Soon after World War II, however, several studies began to show increasingly convincing evidence of a link between tobacco and cancer, ultimately leading the Surgeon General of the United States to issue a report in 1964 concluding that cigarette smoking "is a health hazard of sufficient importance in the United States to warrant appropriate remedial action."[8] This report, Martha Derthick writes, galvanized antismoking efforts into a more cohesive political movement that "consisted of a struggle to define and pursue the 'appropriate remedial action'" called for in the Surgeon General's report.[9] There were three broad avenues available for this movement, one focusing on litigation, one focusing on regulation and legislation, and a third relying on public education about the risks and dangers of smoking for smokers, for taxpayers, and for those who endure second-hand smoke.[10]

On the legislative front, the Surgeon General's report translated into a labeling law for cigarettes in 1965, requiring the now-famous warning:

6 Robert A. Kagan and William Nelson, "The Politics of Tobacco Regulation in the United States."

7 Martha A. Derthick, *Up in Smoke: From Legislation to Litigation in Tobacco Politics* (2nd ed.), Washington, DC: CQ Press, 2005, p 8.

8 Public Health Service, "Smoking and Health: Report of the Advisory Committee to the Surgeon General of the Public Health Service," Washington, DC: U.S. Government Printing Office, 1964, p 33.

9 Derthick, *Up in Smoke*, p 11.

10 Kagan and Nelson, "The Politics of Tobacco Regulation in the United States." Kagan and Nelson argue that tobacco policy reflects neither the preferences of the tobacco manufacturers nor those of the antitobacco lobbyists, but rather fairly closely reflects public opinion and was achieved through a mix of public education, litigation, and regulation.

"Caution: Cigarette Smoking May Be Hazardous to Your Health."[11] This labelling law proved to be a two-edged sword. Although it marked an important policy change and government statement, it also served "as a powerful shield for the industry," one that tobacco firms would use both retrospectively and prospectively in the courtroom to fight off waves of liability litigation.[12]

The Surgeon General's report and the labeling law made it clear that manufacturers would henceforth know they were producing a dangerous product, but it also allowed them to argue that, before this date, manufacturers might well have been able to believe their product was safe. They could tell juries that they had only recently "learned of the potential health dangers associated with cigarettes" and therefore they "could not be held liable for harming smokers."[13] This argument only compounded the difficulty of winning a suit in the 1960s, when product liability standards focused on helping consumers get the product for which they paid, rather than helping make sure the product they purchased was safe. The legal standard in product liability suits in that period required that a product be shown to be "dangerous to an extent beyond that which would be contemplated by the ordinary consumer who purchases it," meaning that if you bought tobacco, and got tobacco, and that tobacco was unadulterated, then you were not going to win.[14] And even if the product, cumulatively, was dangerous, that did not constitute liability on the manufacturer's part. As the American Law Institute's restatement of the law of torts put it in 1965,

Good whiskey is not unreasonably dangerous merely because it will make some people drunk, and is especially dangerous to alcoholics; but bad whiskey, containing a dangerous amount of fuel oil, is unreasonably dangerous. Good tobacco is not unreasonably dangerous merely because the effects of smoking may be harmful; but tobacco containing something like marijuana may be unreasonably dangerous. Good butter is not unreasonably dangerous merely because, if such

11 This was a much watered-down version of the warning initially proposed by the Federal Trade Commission that would have said, "Cigarette smoking is dangerous to health and may cause death from cancer and other diseases." Graham Kelder and Richard Daynard, "The Role of Litigation in the Effective Control of the Sale and Use of Tobacco," 8 *Stanford Law & Policy Review* 63, 67 (1997), quoting 29 Fed. Reg. 8325 (1964).

12 Lynn Mather, "Theorizing about Trial Courts: Lawyers, Policymaking and Tobacco Litigation," 23 *Law & Social Inquiry* 4, 904 (1998). Mather also quotes Lee Fritschler and James Hoefler who argue that the 1965 bill was "more of a victory for cigarettes than it was for health." Lee Fritschler and James Hoefler, *Smoking and Politics* (5th ed.), Englewood Cliffs: Prentice Hall, 1996, p 89.

13 Maria Bianchini, "The Tobacco Agreement That Went Up in Smoke: Defining the Limits of Congressional Intervention into Ongoing Mass Tort Litigation," 87 *California Law Review* 703, 710 (1999).

14 American Law Institute, Restatement (Second) of Torts, 1965. Quoted in Derthick, *Up in Smoke*, p 29.

be the case, it deposits cholesterol in the arteries and leads to heart attacks; but bad butter, contaminated with poisonous fish oil, is unreasonably dangerous.[15]

Add the warning, which made it clear that a consumer was assuming health risks in using this product, and it is hardly surprising that early litigation efforts failed.

In lawsuits filed in the 1980s, the tobacco industry turned the label in their favor, successfully arguing "that smokers knew the risks of smoking and chose to smoke anyway. The plaintiffs were thus to blame for their own illnesses. The fact that the Surgeon General's warning was stamped on every package of cigarettes after 1965 served to reinforce the assumption of risk argument."[16] Indeed, for more than twenty years after the Surgeon General's warnings were added to cigarette packages, no tobacco company lost a jury trial. And even when one finally did lose in June 1988, in the New Jersey case of *Cipollone v. Liggett*, the damage award was overturned on appeal.[17] Not until 1996 did a jury again decide in favor of a smoker, and this verdict, like the Cipollone case, was overturned.[18] The labels helped an industry that needed little help. Big Tobacco had deep pockets and a clear, unified understanding that to lose one case would mean to lose them all – meaning they could and would litigate each case and concede nothing. Their resources were legendary: "To paraphrase General Patton, the way we won these cases," one R. J. Reynolds' attorney wrote, "was not by spending all of Reynolds' money, but by making that other son-of-a-bitch spend all of his money."[19]

A major barrier to any effort to regulate tobacco was legislation that explicitly prohibits the Food and Drug Administration (FDA) from allowing the sale of any product it deems unsafe. The Food, Drug and Cosmetic Act (FDCA) charges the agency with the responsibility "to ensure that any product regulated by the FDA is 'safe' and 'effective' for its intended

---

15 ALI, Restatement (Second) of Torts, section 402A, comment i, 1965, cited in Robert Rubin, "A Sociolegal History of the Tobacco Tort Litigation," 44 *Stanford Law Review* 853, 863 (1992).

16 Mather, "Theorizing about Trial Courts," p 904.

17 On June 13, 1988, a Newark, New Jersey, jury awarded damages to the husband of Rose Cipollone, a lifelong smoker. But the decision was reversed on appeal, *Cipollone v. Liggett*, 893 F.2d 541 (1990). The case eventually made it to the U.S. Supreme Court, where in a complicated ruling, the Justices concluded that the 1965 labeling law did not automatically preempt any actions brought under state law for damages. However, a 1969 law did preempt some of the Cipollone family's claims that the tobacco company's failure to warn and fraudulent misrepresentations claims, though it did leave room for the possibility of claims based on express warranty or conspiracy to defraud. *Cipollone v. Liggett*, 505 U.S. 504, 505 and 520–30 (1992) – see below.

18 *Grady Carter v. Brown & Williamson Tobacco Corp.*, No. 95–934-CA CV-B (Fla. Duval Cir. Ct. Dec. 5, 1996) resulted in a jury award of $750,000. This, too, was overturned on appeal.

19 *Haines v. Liggett Group, Inc.*, 814 F. Supp. 414, 421 (D.N.J. 1993) (quoting an April 29, 1988, internal memorandum by R. J. Reynolds' attorney J. Michael Jordan).

use."[20] But because tobacco is, according to the FDA itself, not only unsafe but also cannot be made to be safe, it would seem to preclude any regulation of this product. The only option would be an outright ban, which was not only politically impossible, but legally impossible as well, as the Supreme Court would later conclude in a case against the Brown & Williamson tobacco company in 2000. Congress, the Court would rule, "has foreclosed the removal of tobacco products from the market," and Congress has "directly addressed the problem of tobacco and health through legislation on six occasions since 1965,"[21] stopping "well short of ordering a ban," thereby making clear "its intent that tobacco products remain on the market."[22]

By the early 1990s, it appeared that tobacco makers were immune to federal regulation, litigation, and legislation, though they were facing more and more state-level restrictions including workplace limits, bans on smoking in public places, and ever-higher taxes.[23] The tobacco lobby had a strong hand in politics not only in Washington, D.C., where tobacco-state legislators controlled key committees in both Houses of Congress, but also in many states where a wide range of powerful interests – ranging from farmers to factory workers, delivery people, and retailers – relied on tobacco for their livelihood. In short, any attack on tobacco would face profound political and institutional barriers – it would take a mighty sword to slice through this Gordian knot.

In 1992, the U.S. Supreme Court revived a case brought by Rose Cipollone's family against three major tobacco firms in 1983, claiming that their advertising had misrepresented the risks of smoking. A smoker for forty-two years, Mrs. Cipollone died at the age of fifty-eight, a year after filing the suit. A jury awarded her family $400,000 in 1988, but that award was reversed by the Third Circuit Court of Appeals that ruled that Cipollone's case could not proceed because state law damage suits were preempted by national law. The Supreme Court reversed that decision in part, suggesting that, although some state actions might be preempted by federal law, others could proceed. In its ruling, the Court made it clear that "federal law does not preempt claims based on warranty, fraud

---

20 *FDA v. Brown & Williamson Tobacco Corp.*, 529 U.S. 120, 134 (2000).
21 See Federal Cigarette Labeling and Advertising Act (FCLAA), Pub. L. 89–92, 79 Stat. 282; Public Health Cigarette Smoking Act of 1969, Pub. L. 91–222, 84 Stat. 87; Alcohol and Drug Abuse Amendments of 1983, Pub. L. 98–24, 97 Stat. 175; Comprehensive Smoking Education Act, Pub. L. 98–474, 98 Stat. 2200; Comprehensive Smokeless Tobacco Health Education Act of 1986, Pub. L. 99–252, 100 Stat. 30; Alcohol, Drug Abuse, and Mental Health Administration Reorganization Act, Pub. L. 102–321, §202, 106 Stat. 394, cited in *FDA v. Brown & Williamson Tobacco Corp.*
22 *FDA v. Brown & Williamson Tobacco Corp.* 529 U.S. at 137.
23 See Kagan and Nelson, "The Politics of Tobacco Regulation in the United States." See as well the comments of FDA Commissioner Charles Edwards during hearings before the Consumer Subcommittee of the Committee on Commerce, on S. 1454, "Public Health Cigarette Amendments of 1971," 92d Cong., second session, p 239 (1972).

and misrepresentation or conspiracy."[24] Although the Cipollone family ultimately decided to drop its case, this ruling did provide an opportunity for others.[25] The litigation sword might have some potential after all.

To slice through the knot, however, a plaintiff still had to overcome three significant barriers. First there was a financial barrier – how could individual plaintiffs possibly challenge the legal resources of these phenomenally profitable, multinational corporations? Second, there was a procedural barrier – tort actions are decided by juries, and juries seemed steadfast in their refusal to find against the tobacco firms. Public opinion polls in the 1990s made clear that the public was convinced smoking caused cancer, but nevertheless felt strongly that this was a risk smokers had brought on themselves.[26] Even with sympathetic plaintiffs, the tobacco companies' track record with juries was daunting. Finally, plaintiffs faced a legal barrier – negligence and liability suits might be *possible* now, but they would not be easy, particularly when the plaintiffs were individuals who were (at least since 1965) explicitly warned about the dangers of the product they were using. By the late 1980s, however, it seemed all three of these problems could be solved.

The financial challenge would be met by speculative plaintiffs' attorneys who would fund this litigation in the expectation of a tremendous collective payday, drawing resources in part from their extremely lucrative success with Agent Orange and the Dalkon shield, among others.[27] Some of these attorneys pursued large, private class action suits – including *Castano v. American Tobacco Co.* in Louisiana[28] and *Engle et al v. Liggett Group* in Florida.[29] The more potent threat to Big Tobacco,

---

24 Mather, "Theorizing about Trial Courts," p 909, and see Linda Greenhouse, "The Supreme Court: Court Opens Way for Damage Suits over Cigarettes," *New York Times*, June 25, 1992, p 1.

25 Charles Strum, "Major Lawsuit on Smoking Is Dropped," *New York Times*, November 6, 1992, p B1.

26 Kagan and Nelson, "The Politics of Tobacco Regulation in the United States;" W. Kip Viscusi, *Smoking: Making the Risky Decision*, New York: Oxford University Press, 1992; and Lydia Saad, "The Survey Data Reviewed: Smoking and American Values," 9 *Public Perspective* 1 (1998).

27 Robert Kagan, "The Tort Law System," Chapter 7 of *Adversarial Legalism: The American Way of Law*, Cambridge: Harvard University Press, 2001. Also, see Ronald Bacigal, *The Limits of Litigation: The Dalkon Shield Controversy*, Durham: Carolina Academic Press, 1990; Peter Schuck, *Agent Orange on Trial: Mass Toxic Disasters in the Courts*, Cambridge: Belknap, 1986, cited in Rubin, "A Sociolegal History of the Tobacco Tort Litigation," p 864.

28 *Castano v. American Tobacco Co.*, 160 F.R.D. 544 (E.D. La. 1995), reversed by 84 F.3d 734 (5th Circuit) 1996.

29 In 1994, a Florida court certified a nationwide class action, in which the class initially was defined as "All United States citizens and residents, and their survivors, who have suffered, presently suffer or have died from diseases and medical conditions caused by their addiction to cigarettes that contain nicotine." In 1996, however, the class was slashed back to include only Florida residents and citizens. *R. J. Reynolds Tobacco Co. v. Engle*, 672 So.2d 39, 42 (Fla.App. 1996). After trial, a jury awarded the named plaintiffs

however, appeared to be the suits that were filed by the combined forces of private attorneys, such as Mississippi's Dickie Scruggs, and state attorneys general, such as Mississippi's Mike Moore.[30] With private attorneys shouldering the financial risk, the state attorneys general could engage in a no-cost war, bringing legal weapons to the fight that private attorneys could only dream about. The incentives for the state attorneys general were clear – not only would a victory provide great political advantages to these elected officials, but even a loss could produce political credit for a valiant fight on behalf of their constituents without incurring significant legal bills.

The second barrier was a procedural one. Tobacco had a nearly perfect track record in jury trials. Even if there was a growing willingness on the part of juries to find corporations guilty for producing dangerous products and failing to warn people about those dangers in other products, verdicts in tobacco cases remained a stubborn exception. The 1988 *Cipollone* case was the first time that a tobacco maker lost a jury verdict, but even that victory was pretty thin.[31] Not only was the fairly modest $400,000 damage award reversed on appeal, but it was also later reported that the *Cipollone* jury was badly divided over its verdict. Some jurors "told reporters at the time that they were worried that they had done the wrong thing. Some cried about having given in to more dominant jurors."[32] As sad as the plaintiffs' cases might be, juries were easily persuaded that these plaintiffs had made a choice – albeit a tragic one – to smoke. And that decision carried with it risks.

So, to beat the tobacco companies in court meant either coming up with new arguments for those juries or finding a way to sue the companies without a jury. State Attorney General Mike Moore was able to do both. The state of Mississippi had a split court system, and it would be possible to bring this suit in what was called Chancery Court – a court developed out of the equity tradition of Anglo-American law, in which verdicts were reached by judges, not by juries. In addition, Moore would make a very

---

$12.7 million dollars in compensatory damages, and the entire class $145 billion in punitive damages. But, on July 6, 2006, the Florida Supreme Court reversed the bulk of the decision, decertifying the class action and rejecting the $145 billion punitive damage award as excessive. *Engle v. Liggett Group*, 945 So.2d 1246 (Fla. 2006).

30 In March 2008, Scruggs pled guilty to a federal charge that he conspired to bribe a judge. Richard Fausset, Jenny Jarvie and Henry Weinstein, "Legal Legend Dickie Scruggs Pleads Guilty in Bribery," *Los Angeles Times*, March 15, 2008, p 1.

31 On June 13, 1988, a Newark, New Jersey, jury awarded damages to the husband of Rose Cipollone, a lifelong smoker. But the decision was reversed on appeal, *Cipollone v. Liggett*, 893 F.2d 541 (1990).

32 Joan Biskupic, "Activist Jurors Help Carve out New Law," *Washington Post*, Aug. 30, 1999, p 1. The other case, *Grady Carter v. Brown & Williamson Tobacco Corp.*, No. 95–934-CA CV-B (Fla. Duval Cir. Ct. Dec. 5, 1996) resulted in a jury award of $750,000. This, too, was overturned on appeal.

different claim than had been made in the past, which brings us to the third challenge that had to be met – the legal argument itself.

Smokers might well have known the risks they took when they indulged their habit, Moore acknowledged, but, as he put it, "The State of Mississippi never smoked a cigarette. Yet it has paid the medical expenses of thousands of indigent smokers who did."[33] He would sue to recover the money the state had been forced to spend to care for those who had been made ill by this product – and would make this argument to a judge and not a jury. "Rather than depending on tort law, the [Mississippi] suit would rely on equitable theories of recovery. Mississippi would claim that the tobacco companies had been 'unjustly enriched' because they had not borne the costs of the by-products of their enterprise. The state would ask to be indemnified as an innocent third party for its medical expenditures on behalf of smokers."[34] The state asserted that it had been forced to spend millions in the treatment of disease that might easily have been avoided had there been no cigarettes on the market and, more important, had the companies not engaged in deceptive marketing of a product that they knew would cause disease. A remedy for this violation was something a Chancery Court was well equipped to provide – and once the precedent was established there, it would be far easier to seek a remedy in ordinary courts in other states.[35]

Ultimately, this litigation might not succeed (few of the lawyers involved were genuinely optimistic about being able to survive the appeals process), but one thing these new suits could do was to raise costs – and risks – for the tobacco companies. And risk is anathema to the tobacco multinationals. Losing one suit is insignificant, but forty other states followed the examples set by Mississippi and Florida, as did a host of individuals and lawyers filing class action claims. All these suits started to add up to significant risk and unpredictability. To reduce risk, the tobacco firms might very well be willing to negotiate and compromise, even accept a consent decree that could accomplish what regulation (thanks to the rules hemming in the FDA) and even ordinary litigation alone

---

33 Mike Moore, "The States Are Just Trying to Take Care of Sick Citizens and Protect Children." 83 *ABA Journal* 53 (1997), quoted in Mather, "Theorizing about Trial Courts," p 911.
34 Derthick, *Up in Smoke*, p 75.
35 See Edward Correia and Patricia Davidson, "The State Attorney Generals' Tobacco Suits: Equitable Remedies," 7 *Cornell Journal of Law & Public Policy* 843 (1998). As discussed in Chapter 2, federal courts in America are constitutionally bound to consider cases in *both* law *and* equity, but this is not the case in every state. Some states continue the English tradition of maintaining separate trial courts for these two functions. Mississippi is one of those states. As Martha Derthick explains, in Mississippi cases in equity are handled by what is called *Chancery* Court (borrowing from the English tradition), where decisions were rendered by a *chancellor* – a judge, not a jury.

could not. Litigation might just force them to seek and accept a political compromise – law just might save politics.

Political Compromise?

Lawsuits and uncertainty brought Big Tobacco to the bargaining table, but only politics could seal the deal, because the one thing the tobacco companies demanded was the elimination of the uncertainty about their level of legal risk.[36] To meet this demand, Congress would have to place a cap on future liability, limiting suits against tobacco makers.[37] The courts and legal decisions alone could not do that – it would require a statute, an act of Congress. If the story ended here, it might have been a stunning tale of how law saves politics, a demonstration of the great success and efficacy of litigation *together with* politics, of judicial swords slashing through political and institutional barriers that had so long blocked any reform in this area, forcing negotiation and compromise and a political solution. Of course, unfortunately, that is not where the story ends.

On April 16, 1997, the *Wall Street Journal* reported that representatives of the state attorneys general and the tobacco companies were putting the

36 "The complex agreement, negotiated by a group of state attorneys general, plaintiffs' lawyers, and industry representatives, would require cigarette companies to pay $368.5 billion over the next twenty-five years to compensate states for the costs of treating smoking-related illness, to finance nationwide antismoking programs, and to underwrite health care for millions of uninsured children. Under the terms of the settlement, the tobacco industry would admit for the first time in prominent new warning labels on every package of cigarettes that smoking by an estimated 45 million Americans is lethal and addictive. The plan imposes strict new limits on tobacco marketing and advertising, including a ban on vending machines and outdoor billboards. And it gives the Food and Drug Administration new powers to regulate nicotine as a drug and cigarettes as drug delivery devices.... In exchange for their concessions, the tobacco companies won the promise of relief from dozens of potentially ruinous lawsuits filed by states and diseased smokers ... [and] cigarette makers would be allowed to continue to sell their products without the threat of concerted legal action against them. Cigarette company stocks rose this week in anticipation of a deal capping the industry's liability." John Broder, "Cigarette Makers in a $368 Billion Accord to Curb Lawsuits and Curtain Marketing," *New York Times*, June 21, 1997, p 1.

37 According to the *New York Times*, the agreement stipulated that present actions by state attorneys general "are legislatively settled. No future prosecution of such actions." It also mandated that as to civil liability for past conduct, "i.e., suits by persons claiming injury or damage caused by conduct taking place prior to the effective date of the act" all punitive damages claims are "resolved as part of overall settlement. No punitive damages [will be allowed] in individual tort actions." All trials would henceforth be individual trials only, "no class actions, joinder, aggregations, consolidations, extrapolations or other devices to resolve cases other than on the basis of individual trials, without defendant's consent." Furthermore, there would be an "annual aggregate cap for judgments/settlements: 33 percent of annual industry base payment (including any reductions for volume decline). If aggregate judgments/settlements for a year exceed annual aggregate cap, excess does not have to be paid that year and rolls over." "Excerpts from Agreement between States and Tobacco Industry," *New York Times*, June 25, 1997.

finishing touches on their secret negotiations for a definitive settlement.[38] Who was at the table was stunning: executives from the top tobacco firms, state attorneys general, the key plaintiffs attorneys, and one lone representative of the many interest groups that had been battling against tobacco for decades – Matt Myers of the Campaign for Tobacco-Free Kids.[39] But if who *was* there was stunning, who was *not there* was shocking. There were no regulators – no one from the Federal Trade Commission or the FDA – and there were no doctors – no one from the Centers for Disease Control or the National Institutes of Health. There was no one from the White House or from anywhere near the White House, and, with the sole exception of some informal contact with Mississippi Republican Senator Trent Lott (who was the brother-in-law of the key plaintiffs' attorney in this case, Dickie Scruggs of Pascagoula, Mississippi), there was no one from either House of Congress.

As Martha Derthick put it in rather understated language, "That no member of Congress had brokered the big tobacco deal – that it had been wholly imported from outside the institution – was a major handicap."[40] This absence of congressional involvement was all the more important because, as drafted, the agreement would actually fall within the jurisdiction of "no fewer than seven Senate committees" – Agriculture, Commerce, Environment and Public Works, Finance, Indian Affairs, Judiciary, and Labor and Human Resources.[41]

Politics is about adjustment, negotiation, tradeoffs. A deal such as the global tobacco settlement would typically be seen as a starting point for political maneuvering – not a fait accompli, all or nothing, take it or leave it. Seeing a deal that included astronomical sums of money, commitments to reduce teen smoking that had real teeth, and voluntary restrictions on advertising practices suggested to many how much more might be possible. However, for the lawyers and their clients who had approved this deal, it was not a starting point. It was a finished package, a contract, a settlement, a legal deal with little room for maneuver. The problem is that room for maneuver is what makes politics work.

Battlelines were immediately drawn, with many in the antitobacco community steadfast in their conclusion that, if the tobacco companies would agree to this deal voluntarily, it meant that the agreement either was a Trojan horse or that the manufacturers were on the run: If the judicial sword could get them to agree to this deal, it could get them

---

38 Alix Freedman and Suein Hwang, "Peace Pipe: Philip Morris, RJR and Tobacco Plaintiffs Discuss a Settlement," *Wall Street Journal*, April 16, 1997, p 1.

39 See Michael Pertschuk, *Smoke in Their Eyes: Lessons in Movement Leadership from the Tobacco Wars*, Nashville: Vanderbilt University Press, 2001, for a full and detailed account of the negotiations.

40 Derthick, *Up in Smoke*, p 144.

41 Derthick, *Up in Smoke*, p 122.

to agree to a whole lot more. Failing that, the judicial sword could and should and would simply vanquish them. Los Angeles Representative Henry Waxman, probably the most strident advocate for strict tobacco regulation in the House at the time, summed up this sentiment in an op-ed shortly after the agreement was reached: "In some ways, the tobacco industry's position reminds me of Paul Newman and Robert Redford's final moments in *Butch Cassidy and the Sundance Kid*, when the duo are trapped in a market square by the Bolivian army. They have no place to go, no place to hide."[42]

On June 5, 1997, the former head of the Food and Drug Administration, David Kessler, and former Surgeon General C. Everett Koop assembled an advisory committee to consider the proposal. The panel's response was not favorable. Dudley Hafner of the American Heart Association called parts of the plan "absolutely unacceptable," whereas Kessler summed up the group's initial thoughts by saying that it would be "absolutely unacceptable for the terms of the settlement to go forward."[43]

The Senate assigned the bill – which was needed to implement many provisions in the act, and above all to impose the liability caps that were the key as far as Big Tobacco was concerned – to the Commerce Committee, chaired by Arizona Republican John McCain. But as the McCain bill worked its way through the process, it was quickly ratcheted up from the levels and terms of the master legal agreement, as senators demanded higher payments and higher liability caps (eventually eliminating the liability cap entirely). Even House Speaker Newt Gingrich realized this was a train he could not afford to miss, telling tobacco lobbyists on their own private plane, "I will not let Bill Clinton get to the left of me on this." The bottom line for Gingrich was clear: "We're not going to support anything the industry is for."[44]

Finally, the tobacco companies balked. This industry, R. J. Reynolds CEO Steven Goldstone said, is not "like a Brinks truck overturned in the middle of a highway."[45] The original agreement had called for payments of $368.5 billion to state and federal governments (over twenty-five years) to cover medical expenses, as well as to fund health programs, education,

---

42 Henry A. Waxman (D-CA), "A Look at the Tobacco Settlement: Don't Sign it; On Balance, a Bad Deal for Public Health," *Washington Post*, June 29, 1997, p C3. Waxman forgot how the movie actually ended – Butch and Sundance run out of the saloon doors and into a hail of gunfire – but then the picture freezes and the audience never learns for sure whether they lived or died. In fact, historians are still divided over whether or not Robert Leroy Parker and Harry Longabaugh escaped from Boliva and returned to the United States or not.

43 John Schwartz, "Advisory Panelists Strongly Critical of Tobacco Deal," *Washington Post*, June 26, 1997, p A3.

44 Ceci Connolly and John Mintz, "For Cigarette Industry, a Future without GOP Support," *Washington Post*, March 29, 1998, p 1.

45 John Schwartz. "Tobacco Firms Say They'd Rather Fight," *Washington Post*, April 9, 1998, p 1.

and antismoking campaigns. The McCain bill, as it was shaping up, was at that point coming in at about $516 billion over twenty-five years. The initial agreement called for a liability cap of $5 billion a year, with a ban on all future class action lawsuits; the McCain bill bumped the cap up to $6.5 billion a year, but, more significantly, eliminated the lawsuit immunity entirely.[46]

For many Democrats and key health and antitobacco organizations, even these provisions were not enough. Any negotiation, anything short of total vindication and the eradication of the industry was unacceptable: The fact that the industry was working the Halls of Congress seeking a deal was mistakenly taken as a sign that total victory was within reach. One advocacy group insisted that negotiating with the tobacco industry for immunity of any kind was "immoral and threatens to undermine decades of work by committed public health activists to curb the ravages of the tobacco corporations." Their message was clear: "We say: No immunity. No deal. Let the prosecutions commence."[47] Politics was unacceptable – law was the way to go. If the incentive to juridify had initially been to break through profound political and institutional barriers, for many at this stage, the incentives had shifted, and there was a sense that a legal victory was normatively and morally superior to a negotiated political compromise.

For those deeply invested in judicial strategies to advance policy goals, there was another issue to consider: precedent. A deal that would provide liability limits for tobacco would set a precedent that other powerful business interests might emulate.[48] For some, like Ralph Nader, the weapon itself, the judicial sword, was too important to compromise or negotiate away:

Nader was prepared to face the possibility that the refusal to provide any liability relief might jeopardize the fate of the public health provisions. He no longer held any faith that a future FDA, subject to control by a corporate-funded and -indentured White House, would take bold regulatory steps, no matter how theoretically broad its authority. He believed that maintaining the integrity of the tort liability system ultimately held greater promise for corporate accountability than did shaky regulatory schemes.[49]

---

46 David Rosenbaum, "Cigarette Makers Quit Negotiations on Tobacco Bill," *New York Times*, April 9, 1998, p 1.
47 Pertschuk, *Smoke in Their Eyes*, p 107.
48 Congress had provided liability limits in other cases – most notably for nuclear power and for airlines in the aftermath of 9/11. But these were both instances where there was a profound public need that these industries were supplying. Liability caps for tobacco would set a rather important and very different sort of precedent. For a discussion of the struggle over liability limits in the case of asbestos, see Kagan, *Adversarial Legalism*, Chapter 7.
49 Pertschuk, *Smoke in Their Eyes*, p 134.

The tobacco industry, Martha Derthick reports, spent millions of dollars for lobbying and advertising, but "the industry was rebuffed" when a bill finally emerged from McCain's committee that provided absolutely no liability protection. At that point, the tobacco industry reversed course, going back on defense, "back to its accustomed task of opposition."[50] The Commerce Committee approved the McCain bill 19–1, but the bill failed on the floor after the Senate voted 61–37 to adopt an amendment eliminating not only all lawsuit immunity but also even the $6.5 billion/year liability cap. With no legislation left to fight, Big Tobacco abandoned Capitol Hill and turned instead to cut deals with the states, providing payments of $40 billion to the initial four states that had brought suit and then $206 billion "to the remaining 46 states to settle lawsuits over the health care costs attributed to smoking."[51] These payments are far from trivial, but they are also far short of what might have been accomplished by law *together with* politics at the national level.

This was not the end for those who opposed this legislation – merely the end of the first act. On January 19, 1999, the curtain rose on the second act when President Bill Clinton stunned his aides and the health community alike during the State of the Union address with a pledge to support a massive federal suit that would, much as had the state suits, seek huge payments from tobacco for costs incurred by the federal Medicaid and Medicare programs. "Smoking has cost taxpayers hundreds of billions of dollars under Medicare and other programs," Clinton told the Joint Session of Congress. "You know, the states have been right about this. Taxpayers shouldn't pay for the cost of lung cancer, emphysema, and other smoking-related illnesses, the tobacco companies should. So tonight I announce that the Justice Department is preparing a litigation plan to take the tobacco companies to court and with the funds we recover to strengthen Medicare."[52]

What's Good for the States Is Good for the Federal Government?

If it could work for the states, why not for the federal government? For many, the real lesson of the failed tobacco legislative effort was that regulation by legislation was simply no longer possible and that the judicial sword not only was a better way to go, but perhaps was the only effective strategy. Following Clinton's pledge, the Justice Department filed suit on September 22, 1999, seeking $280 billion in damages for conspiracy to defraud and mislead the public and for reimbursement of the federal

50 Derthick, *Up in Smoke*, p 142.
51 Mather, "Theorizing about Trial Courts," p 898.
52 Bill Clinton, State of the Union Address, January 19, 1999, reproduced in the *Washington Post*, January 20, 1999, p A-12.

government's expenditures to treat disease brought on by tobacco. Robert Reich, former Secretary of Labor for Clinton, embraced regulation-by-lawsuit just a few weeks after the State of the Union address. Years ago, Reich wrote, "courts championed the cause of civil rights. That's because legislatures, which decide things by majority rule, couldn't be counted on to protect the rights of minorities." Now, he said, courts are taking over the regulatory responsibility once exercised by Congress. "Maybe that's because politicians – more dependent than ever on industry for campaign contributions – can't be trusted to protect the rest of us from big business." This might mean, Reich concluded, that the "era of big government may be over, but the era of regulation through litigation has just begun."[53]

While one part of the administration pursued a federal judicial remedy, another part – the Food and Drug Administration – built its own novel claim. The FDA had long since concluded that tobacco was a dangerous product and nicotine an addictive substance. Under normal circumstances, the FDA could and would have acted to regulate and even ban such a dangerous product, but tobacco was different. Not only was tobacco explicitly excluded from the FDA's jurisdiction but also "the FDA consistently stated before 1995 that it lacked jurisdiction over tobacco, and Congress has enacted several tobacco-specific statutes fully cognizant of the FDA's position."[54] The FDA had, indeed, recognized that the government faced a real dilemma with tobacco. The FDA operates under statutory authority originally granted in the Food, Drug, and Cosmetic Act (FDCA). The FDA's charge under this act is "to ensure that any product regulated by the FDA is 'safe' and 'effective' for its intended use."[55] But there's the rub. Tobacco was, according to the FDA, not only unsafe but also could not be made to be safe. In short, under the ordinary interpretation of the FDCA, if the government regulated tobacco, the FDA would have to ban it. "In fact, based on these provisions," the Supreme Court noted, "the FDA itself has previously taken the position that if tobacco products were within its jurisdiction, 'they would have to be removed from the market because it would be impossible to prove they were safe for their intended us[e].'"[56]

FDA Commissioner David Kessler came up with a new approach in 1995. Although the FDA continued to insist that tobacco was unsafe, Kessler argued that, in determining safety, it must consider "not only the

---

53 Robert Reich, "Regulation Is Out, Litigation Is In," *USA Today*, February 11, 1999, p A15.
54 *FDA v. Brown & Williamson Tobacco Corp.*, 529 U.S. at 131.
55 *FDA v. Brown & Williamson Tobacco Corp.*, 529 U.S. at 134.
56 *FDA v. Brown & Williamson Tobacco Corp.*, 529 U.S. at 136–7, quoting statement of FDA Commissioner Charles Edwards, "Public Health Cigarette Amendments of 1971," p 239.

risks presented by a product but also any of the countervailing effects of use of that product, including the consequences of not permitting the product to be marketed."[57] In other words, tobacco is unsafe, but banning it outright would create an even more dangerous situation for smokers who were addicted to nicotine. Not only would they turn to a black market for unregulated products but they would also suffer through withdrawal symptoms. Therefore, the FDA reasoned, regulating tobacco would be possible under this more sophisticated reading of the statute.

What might possibly have led David Kessler to conclude that this statutory move would work? Precedent, U.S. Supreme Court precedent. In a famous ruling in 1984, the Supreme Court appeared to shift its traditional default assumption about legislative intent and statutory interpretation. The burden, the Court ruled in *Chevron USA v. Natural Resources Defense Council*, would be on Congress, not the administration.[58] When Congress fails to speak directly to a regulatory issue, the Court would give the administrative agency broad latitude. If a statute "is silent or ambiguous with respect to the specific issue," the Court held in 1984, the question for the Court is "whether the agency's answer is based on a permissible construction of the statute."[59] In the 2000 *Brown & Williamson* case, Justice Breyer (in dissent) argued that this was an easy question: The FDA's interpretation should prevail. Not so for the majority, which found that the complications created by conflicting provisions in law that supported the tobacco industry were enough to suggest that Congress had "directly spoken to the precise question at issue." Citing *Chevron*, the majority in *Brown & Williamson* said that when the "intent of Congress is clear, that is the end of the matter; for the Court, as well as the agency, must give effect to the unambiguously expressed intent of Congress."[60] Congress, the majority concluded, has "clearly precluded the FDA from asserting jurisdiction to regulate tobacco products." In light of "this clear intent," they ruled, "the FDA's assertion of jurisdiction is impermissible."[61]

---

57 61 Fed. Reg. 44413 (1996).
58 Here, much as with the war powers and legislative vetoes, the shifting default presumption favoring federal agencies moved widely and laterally in something like what Mark Richards and Bert Kritzer describe as a jurisprudential regime. See Mark Richards and Herbert Kritzer, "Jurisprudential Regimes in Supreme Court Decision Making," 96 *American Political Science Review* 2, 305–320 (2002) and Mark Richards, Herbert Kritzer and Joseph Smith, "Does *Chevron* Matter?" 28 *Law & Policy* 4, 444–69 (2006).
59 *Chevron USA v. Natural Resources Defense Council*, 467 U.S. 837, 843 (1984).
60 *Chevron v. NRDC*, 467 U.S. at 842–3.
61 *FDA v. Brown & Williamson Tobacco Corp.*, 529 U.S. at 125–126. Here we can also think about the spillover effects of precedent. *FDA v. Brown & Williamson* was decided in 2000 – the next year, in *United States v. Mead Corp.*, 533 U.S. 218 (2001), the Supreme Court significantly limited the scope of its deference to agency interpretation – or at least this is how Justice Scalia interpreted the decision in a scathing dissent in which he wrote, "Today's opinion makes an abusive change in judicial review of federal administrative action.... What was previously a general presumption of authority in

In 2000, therefore, the Supreme Court took David Kessler's end run around a recalcitrant Congress off the table. It also put a serious crimp in the Clinton administration's plan to emulate the states and achieve in litigation far more than they had been offered in political negotiation over legislation, because the March 2000 ruling in *Brown & Williamson* would serve as the key precedent cited by the U.S. District Court for the District of Columbia when it dismissed two of the foundational claims on which the Clinton administration had built its case against the tobacco companies on September 28, 2000.

One of those foundational claims was built on assertions that the tobacco companies could be held liable for the money spent by the government under Medicare (under the Medical Care Recovery Act [MRCA] of 1962) and the Federal Employees Health Benefits Act.[62] But in her ruling for the district court, Judge Gladys Kessler (no relation to the FDA's David Kessler) ruled that the MCRA was designed to aid in the recovery of costs in individual cases, but was not meant by Congress to apply in such sweeping class action procedures. Further, she noted, Medicare did not exist when the MCRA became law. "Applying the principles" from the *Brown & Williamson* case that had been handed down by the U.S. Supreme Court just six months earlier,[63] Kessler wrote that "this court concludes that Congress did not intend that MCRA be used as a mechanism to recover" Medicare costs. Judge Kessler also threw out a second foundational claim under Medicare's secondary payer provisions, which would have served as an alternative vehicle for tort actions. Congress, Kessler ruled, "did not intend" these statutes to serve as such broad vehicles for tort actions, which, she added, "is precisely how the Government attempts to use" them in this case.[64]

That left the government with one judicial club – a novel action under the Racketeer Influenced and Corrupt Organizations Act (RICO) that Judge Kessler allowed to move forward.[65] Eventually, however, the RICO club itself would be whittled down to almost nothing by a federal appeals court in 2005.[66] The government had sought $289 billion in damages under the RICO theory – but in a ruling by Judge David Sentelle of the D.C. Circuit Court of Appeals, the government was precluded from

---

agencies to resolve ambiguity in the statutes they have been authorized to enforce has been changed to a presumption of no such authority, which must be overcome by affirmative legislative intent to the contrary."

62 The Medical Care Recovery Act of 1962 (42 U.S.C. 2651–3) and the Federal Employees Health Benefits Act of 1959 (5 U.S.C. 8901–13).

63 *FDA v. Brown & Williamson Tobacco Corp.*, 529 U.S. 120 (2000).

64 *U.S. v. Philip Morris Inc.*, 116 F. Supp. 2d 131 (D.D.C. 2000). Memorandum Opinion by Judge Gladys Kessler, September 28, 2000.

65 18 U.S.C. 1961–1968.

66 *U.S. v. Philip Morris Inc.*, 396 F.3d 1190 (DC Cir. 2005). Now under appeal to the U.S. Supreme Court.

seeking damages determined by past profits. At best, the appeals court ruled, the government could ask for penalties designed to prevent and restrain *future* bad acts. The language in the RICO Act, Judge Sentelle ruled, "indicates that the jurisdiction is limited to forward-looking remedies that are aimed at future violations" and not designed to recover ill-gotten gains from earlier practices.[67]

Although Judge Kessler issued a 1,742-page ringing denunciation of the tobacco companies and ruled that they had, in fact, engaged in RICO violations, the final remedies she could order in 2006, were dramatically limited, not only by the appeals court ruling, but even more so by the Bush administration that had taken over the case and had slashed the penalties it sought from the $130 billion that had been left as a possibility after the appeals court ruling to just $10 billion. Even that was more than Judge Kessler felt she could impose under the appeals court ruling. The best she could do, the *New York Times* editorialized, was to impose a detailed "public shaming" on Big Tobacco. "There are plenty of shameful acts depicted" in the voluminous court ruling, the *Times* wrote, but "there is apparently nothing that can be done to force them to disgorge their ill-gotten profits or punish them for past mendacities." Judge Kessler clearly wanted to impose harsh penalties, but felt she could not impose even the very modest penalties sought by the Bush administration. "All the judge felt she could do was to order the companies to mount an advertising campaign to correct years of misrepresentations and to stop using such misleading terms as 'light' or 'low tar' or 'mild' to imply health benefits." The prospects for reining in "this rogue industry," the *Times* concluded, "seem limited unless Congress finds the gumption to crack down" or the tobacco companies themselves decide to terminate a very profitable enterprise.[68] Needless to say, even Kessler's mild ruling was promptly appealed by the tobacco companies.

Tobacco Lives – and Thrives

In 2001, the Philip Morris company announced a plan to change its name to the Altria Group. This conglomerate not only manufactured and marketed Marlboro cigarettes but also owned Kraft Foods. The name change was part of a longer term plan to split the company's tobacco interests from its food products. Oddly, the goal was not to get rid of the tobacco business – the goal was to get rid of Kraft Foods, which was putting a tremendous drag on the high-flying tobacco business. On January 31, 2007, the Altria Group formally announced its plan to sell off all of its remaining interest in Kraft Foods, and this sale was completed on

67 *U.S. v. Philip Morris Inc.*, 396 F.3d 1190, 1198 (2005).
68 "Tobacco Racketeers Get Off Easy," *New York Times* (editorial), August 20, 2006.

March 30, 2007. Altria's stock price at that point hit $65.90 a share. A year later, in March 2008, Altria's stock had zipped up to $73.83 a share. Meanwhile, what happened to Kraft Foods? In January 2007, Kraft was selling for $34.92 a share. In March 2007, its stock price had actually fallen to $29.26, rising just a bit in March 2008 to $30.82. Tobacco lives and thrives. Altria, one mutual fund portfolio manager told the *New York Times*, is "just a cash cow. The free cash flow on this business is just tremendous." Although much of this growth is attributable to sales in developing countries and not in the United States, where "the number of American smokers usually drops about one or two percent a year," even in the United States "Altria continues to generate sizable profits by raising prices." As a Morgan Stanley analyst told Andrew Martin of the *New York Times* in January 2007, at times "it seems like an unending stream of bad news" for tobacco. "And then lo and behold, manufacturers release their results... and they are good." This same analyst noted that U.S. tobacco company stocks "have beaten the Standard & Poor's 500-stock index in each of the last six years."[69]

For Ralph Nader and other tobacco foes, lawsuits were essential – and litigation combined with state regulation would do what Congress could not. When the tobacco lobbyists succeeded in killing the far more restrictive final version of the McCain bill that eliminated all liability caps and litigation restrictions, Ralph Nader's press release insisted that it was

a Pyrrhic victory for Big Tobacco. Their desire to end uncertainty has boomeranged. Moreover, even if no bill is passed, the drug-dealing tobacco industry will remain on the defensive, as state and private litigation continues and registers increasing success, researchers cull through internal industry documents to further demonstrate the industry's calculated strategy to addict the young, deceive and prevaricate, and states and localities enact tough tobacco control regulations.[70]

Nader was wrong. Federal litigation seems to have hit a dead end. Even if a new administration were to revive a judicial effort, the statutes on the books, as well as the rulings on RICO and Medicare, leave few avenues available. The states have gotten a financial windfall from their tobacco litigation. Some have spent it well, others have squandered it, but one thing the settlement most certainly did not do was put tobacco out of business. Taxes and restrictions on where and when people may smoke are important. But because of the First Amendment and of long-developed rules about federal preemption when it comes to commercial activity, any limits on marketing techniques, product ingredients, and promotion – all of which were part of the voluntary agreement tobacco offered to Congress in 1997 – are beyond the states' reach. Unlike a politically

69 Andrew Martin, "Wall Street Finds a Lot to Like about Tobacco," *New York Times*, January 31, 2007, p 1.
70 Pertschuk, *Smoke in Their Eyes*, p 238.

negotiated settlement under which the tobacco companies would simply agree to cease advertising, a law banning advertising would be subject to litigation. Could a state enforce these sorts of regulations, or was it preempted by existing national regulation? And could a state ban advertising, or would doing so run afoul of the First Amendment? In 2001, the U.S. Supreme Court answered both questions.[71] In *Lorillard Tobacco v. Reilly*, the Supreme Court struck down a series of Massachusetts regulations governing the advertising and sale of tobacco products, in part, because they were preempted by federal law (the Federal Cigarette Labeling and Advertising Act) and, in part, because some of the state regulations violated the First Amendment's free speech clause.

The only way that these limits could be achieved was through national legislation and a national, negotiated political agreement or settlement. There was a moment when that achievement seemed possible, but that moment is gone. Law's allure was too strong. Like Icarus soaring above the waves, many of those battling the manufacture and sale of tobacco believed that the legal weapons that brought them so close to their goal surely could do anything. And so they soared too high, and the moment passed. Law could have saved politics – meaning that litigation was able to break through profound political and institutional barriers, making a long and enduring political solution possible. Instead, one could argue, law killed politics. A great deal was accomplished to be sure – but was it as much as could have been accomplished by law *together with* politics? Was the promise worth the peril?

---

71 *Lorillard Tobacco v. Reilly, Attorney General of Massachusetts*, 533 U.S. 525 (2001).

CONCLUSION

The Promise and Peril of Law's Allure

THE AMERICAN SYSTEM is fragmented and divided – intentionally. The constitutional system drawn up in a stuffy, hot, crowded Philadelphia meeting hall in the summer of 1787 was designed to make change possible, but very difficult.[1] The great challenge was to find a way to make the government efficient, to make it strong enough "to control the governed," and yet make sure that it could not become tyrannical. To accomplish both of these goals, power in America was divided and then divided and divided again. "In the compound republic of America," James Madison wrote in the *Federalist Papers*, "power surrendered by the people is first divided between two distinct governments" – the national government and the state government – "and then the portion allotted to each subdivided among distinct and separate departments." This would provide a "double security" Madison wrote: "The different governments will control each other, at the same time that each will be controlled by itself."[2]

This is not a prescription for efficiency. As Justice Brandeis noted in 1926, the purpose of the separation of powers "was, not to avoid friction, but, by means of the inevitable friction incident to the distribution of the governmental powers among three departments, to save the people from autocracy."[3] The American government is not designed to respond nimbly to crisis and change. It is a government that is *capable* of that response, but not easily. To work within the political system is slow and often frustrating – and sometimes futile. No surprise then that there would be great appeal in an alternative path to policy goals, one that could bypass these inefficiencies. Part of law's allure is precisely the apparent promise of relatively quick, relatively cheap, and relatively decisive action in place of the bargaining, tradeoffs, negotiations, and persuasion that

---

1 The Philadelphia Convention opened on May 25, 1787 and the final draft was signed on September 17, 1787.
2 James Madison, *Federalist 51*.
3 *Myers v. United States*, 272 U.S. 52, 240 (1926) (Brandeis, J., dissenting).

might, in the end, be blocked or sidetracked by all sorts of political and institutional roadblocks.

Efficiency is not the only appeal underlying law's allure. In a nation of immigrants, one in which deep religious, social, and economic differences flourished, law emerged as something approaching a common civil religion. Thomas Grey notes that, although the Constitution itself states that "no religious test shall ever be required as a qualification to any office or public trust under the United States," that very same sentence in the Constitution *requires* that all public officials in the United States – every Senator and Representative, "the members of the several state legislatures, and all executive and judicial officers, both of the United States and of the several states – shall be bound by oath or affirmation to support this Constitution." Although Americans foreclosed the possibility of a national church with the First Amendment, "the worship of the Constitution would serve the unifying function of a national civil religion."[4]

The Constitution and legal language, legal forms, legal ideas, and legal arguments are deeply cherished aspects of American political culture.[5] The American creed, so deeply legalistic, is inherently suspicious of government and power. The various elements of the American creed "unite in imposing limits on power and on the institutions of government," Samuel Huntington writes. "The essence of constitutionalism [in America] is the restraint of governmental power through fundamental law." One problem this restraint breeds, Huntington argues, is that the "more intensely Americans commit themselves to their national political beliefs, the more hostile or cynical they become about their political institutions."[6]

Legal frames, legal modes of analysis, and legal argument are more than ideas and the foundation for a civic religion – they shape and constrain our language and our practice of politics and have done so from the start, a fact Alexis de Tocqueville famously noted in the 1830s. Many quote Tocqueville's line about how "scarcely any political question arises in the United States that is not resolved, sooner or later, into a judicial question." But few continue to the next sentence: "Hence," he adds, "all parties are obliged to borrow, in their daily controversies, the ideas, and even the language, peculiar to judicial proceedings." Not only that, but because "most public men are or have been legal practitioners, they introduce the customs and technicalities of their profession into the management of

---

4 Thomas Grey, "The Constitution as Scripture," 37 *Stanford Law Review* 1, 18 (1984). Sanford Levinson's *Constitutional Faith* (Princeton: Princeton University Press, 1988) provides a comprehensive treatment of the loyalty oaths, the Constitution, and the "faith community" it generates in the United States.

5 See, among others, Michael Kammen, *A Machine That Would Go of Itself: The Constitution in American Culture*, New York: Knopf, 1986.

6 Samuel Huntington, *American Politics: The Promise of Disharmony*, Cambridge: Harvard University Press, 1981, pp 33, 41.

public affairs." The language of the law spreads broadly into the society; "the spirit of the law, which is produced in the schools and courts of justice, gradually penetrates beyond their walls into the bosom of society, where it descends to the lowest classes, so that at last the whole people contract the habits and the tastes of the judicial magistrate."[7]

The Best Use of Law's Allure

Law's allure offers both promise and peril. The question we need to ask is not whether law and legal process and legal language and argument ought to be a part of our political process, but rather when and under what conditions. Relying on legal process and legal arguments, using legal language, and substituting or replacing ordinary politics with judicial decisions and legal formality can shape and constrain the political and policy horizon. But when is that risk worth taking? When it is essential, and when it does it unnecessarily jeopardize the goals of those who chose to juridify in the first place?

For those pursuing policy objectives that face profound political and institutional barriers, turning to the courts, employing juridification, makes good sense – provided that they take advantage of these break-throughs juridification may offer, and then return to secure their gains through the ordinary political process of negotiation, bargaining, elections, and persuasion. As the paradigmatic case studies here illustrate, turning to the courts is a powerful tool, but relying on them exclusively is a strategy fraught with risk. The most effective use of judicial rulings is as something of a battering ram, breaking through those political and institutional barriers. But failing to follow through with the political arts of persuasion puts these gains at risk if – and almost inevitably when – the judiciary changes, new judges take over, and new judicial modes of interpretation and new judicial preferences begin to emerge. At that point, if the initial gains have not been cemented into the political culture through the political arts, those gains face real jeopardy.

It is useful to recall that the Legal Defense Fund (LDF), which organized and managed a great deal of the litigation efforts to end segregation and pursue active integration, worked in tandem with its sister institution, the National Association for the Advancement of Colored Peoples (NAACP) which focused on the traditional political process. By contrast, those who sought not only to liberalize abortion laws in America, but also sought the total repeal of all restrictions on a woman's right to choose abortion were far less effective at cementing their judicial gains through political means. For some – those who sought liberalization – the rulings in *Roe v. Wade* were sufficient, or nearly so, and some wind went out of their political

---

7 Alexis de Tocqueville, *Democracy in America*, book I, chapter 16.

sails. For others, political energy dissipated in the wake of the failure of the Equal Rights Amendment to secure the thirty-eight states needed to ratify a constitutional revision.[8] That an increasingly conservative Court chipped away at *Roe* without reversing it for more than thirty years only made it easier to continue to rely on courts rather than shifting attention to the political process.

Michael McCann is quite right to say that court cases can serve a constitutive function – both court decisions that support one's policy goals and, perhaps more powerfully, those court decisions that undercut or block those goals.[9] Court decisions from *Dred Scott v. Sandford* to *Lochner v. New York*, from the busing rulings such as *Swann v. Charlotte-Mecklenburg School District* to those forbidding school prayer, and from affirmative action cases to capital punishment and many more have galvanized not only supporters, but more often opponents. No case has served a more powerful constitutive function than has *Roe v. Wade*, which may have taken a bit of the urgency out of the right to choose movement. More important perhaps, it galvanized and inspired a major political movement that, in turn, elected Ronald Reagan, George H. W. Bush, and his son, George W. Bush – who, in turn, not only put Antonin Scalia, Clarence Thomas, John Roberts, and Samuel Alito on the U.S. Supreme Court, but have also fundamentally recast the face and direction of the lower federal courts as well.[10]

Law can save politics by breaking through the barriers that are a part of the American system; law can kill politics when deference to judicial authority, precedent cycles, and deconstructive patterns take the wind out of the political sails and, as happened with tobacco, when law's allure becomes so powerful that the means become the ends. Then, at the very moment when legal weapons should be laid aside and political methods relied on, the allure of law is too strong and the ends may be put at risk because of a false assumption that if law can break through an enemy's defenses, then surely law can vanquish the enemy entirely.

Relying on law and courts and juridification to lock in and hold policy gains is a risky choice – not only because of the ways in which legal decision making can shape and constrain those policy goals, but also

8 Jane Mansbridge, *Why We Lost the ERA*, Chicago: University of Chicago Press, 1986.
9 Michael W. McCann (ed), *Law and Social Movements*, Burlington: Ashgate, 2006; Michael W. McCann, *Rights at Work: Pay Equity Reform and the Politics of Legal Mobilization*, Chicago: University of Chicago Press, 1994; Michael W. McCann, "Causal versus Constitutive Explanations (or, On the Difficulty of Being So Positive...)," 21 *Law & Social Inquiry* 2, 457–82 (1996).
10 Frank Cross, *Decision Making in the U.S. Courts of Appeals*, Palo Alto: Stanford University Press, 2007; Sheldon Goldman, *Picking Federal Judges: Lower Court Selection from Roosevelt through Reagan*, New Haven: Yale University Press, 1999; Lee Epstein and Jeffrey Segal, *Advise and Consent: The Politics of Judicial Appointments*. New York: Oxford University Press, 2007; Michael J. Gerhardt, *The Federal Appointments Process: A Constitutional and Historical Analysis*, Durham: Duke University Press, 2003.

because, ultimately, although the courts are insulated and do respond to different incentives, speak a different language, and see things in a different time horizon, courts change and judges and Justices quit, retire, and die. And when they are replaced, there is no reason to assume that these new judges will necessarily continue to serve as a bulwark, protecting and guaranteeing these same political goals. The only way to protect those policy gains is to change minds. Legal rulings can help, to be sure, but only if they are followed up by the traditional political arts of negotiating, bargaining, and persuading.

The Risks and Rewards of Juridification

The juridification of policy and politics alike – the reliance on judicial rulings; the desire to formalize, proceduralize, rigidify, and legalize; the substitution of legal rules and rulings for the political arts of negotiation, bargaining, elections, and persuasion – has been a part of the American political system and American political culture from the start. But juridification began to accelerate and expand in the late 1950s and early 1960s. The Supreme Court was not alone responsible for this, but the Court opened its doors as detailed in Chapter 2, indicating that the Justices would now entertain cases that asked not only for the Court to say what government could and could not do, but also those that would ask the Court to say what the government *must* do as well. The Court's doors were open, and legislators, litigators, and lobbyists alike marched through, coming to rely increasingly on judicial rulings. These same policy advocates and practitioners moved away from the gray ambiguity of political negotiation and persuasion, seeking to formalize and codify political practices and the allocation of power within the government itself, increasingly framing their debates and conversations in legal terms, constitutionalizing and juridifying political debates. These efforts at juridification were neither uniformly successful nor uniformly failures. To evaluate the wisdom or folly of juridification, we need to step back and create a road map of the motives or incentives that drove policy advocates to choose to juridify, and the patterns and process of juridification that followed.

Motives and incentives matter, because they suggest the degree of risk a policy advocate might reasonably be willing to tolerate. The American system is designed to make change difficult, and there are profound institutional and political barriers that stand in the way, that make it virtually impossible to achieve deeply coveted policy goals. The Senate filibuster rule is one such barrier. Federalism is another. Both are examples of the ways in which the intentional fragmentation of power in America creates space for judicial authority and a demand for it as well. Even with majority support, some policy changes simply cannot hope to break through these barriers. For those seeking to end segregation, the fact that national majorities were coming to support their position simply was not enough to make a difference. At the national level, a determined and politically skilled set of southern Senators could block legislation – not only because they and their supporters understood the power of seniority and they, in turn, controlled key committees but also because they understood and were willing to rely on the filibuster to defeat proposals they opposed. Federalism – which limited the reach and scope of national authority – only made it more difficult for a national majority to impose its will.

These profound institutional and political barriers certainly suggested that courts and legal rulings might be the only way around – or through – these impediments. That juridification might be risky obviously is of less concern to those who see no other viable path to their goals. By contrast, those for whom the ordinary political process appears viable – even if difficult – might be well advised to avoid the risks of juridification. Abortion offers one illustration. Those fighting for change in abortion laws in the United States in the 1960s and 1970s could be broadly grouped into two camps. For those who wanted to reform and liberalize these laws, the political path appeared viable – with some states making independent strides toward reform and with national opinion moving in their direction. For those who sought to end all restrictions on a woman's right to choose abortion, however, the political barriers were formidable. For both groups, there were – and are – real perils in a reliance on judicial rulings to secure their policy goals. Unlike a political strategy in which it would have been necessary to change public opinion before embedding these protections in law, a judicial strategy allowed policy change without necessarily changing minds. This would be fine as long as the courts were staffed by sympathetic jurists. But changes in judicial appointments could (and have) put these policy accomplishments at great risk. Reform advocates – who seemed to have a viable alternative path – should not have been as willing as they were to take on this risk. Those seeking total repeal, with no viable political path to follow, probably were right to have accepted the higher long-term risk of a judicial strategy.

Motives and incentives tell us a great deal about the level of risk tolerance a politician or policy advocate might have for juridification. But motives do not tell us very much about the risks themselves – about the perils of juridification. To better understand those variable risks, we need to consider the various patterns that juridification tends to follow. The case studies in this book were selected as paradigmatic examples of these different motives and patterns, useful in helping construct a road map of juridification. This map is meant to be the start and not the end of this inquiry. It is meant to help us break through our tendency to examine the branches in isolation from each other, and in so doing, miss a great deal of the important ways in which judicial decision making and legal frames and language shape and constrain out policy options and our political choices. An interbranch approach, one in which ideas and arguments as well as institutional incentives and practice, will help to fill in the details of the basic map outlined in this book and help us understand more precisely when and why law shapes, constrains, saves and kills politics.[11]

Patterns of Juridification

There are a number of patterns juridification can follow. In some instances the Court has quickly (or not so quickly) terminated these efforts, as happened with the attempt to automate budget reform. In other cases, the Court has allowed or approved these efforts, as happened with the special prosecutor. Of course, the Court has performed these classic functions from the beginning – saying what the government *may* and what it may *not* do. When the Court says no or when the Court is relatively silent, as it largely has been with the allocation of the war powers, judicialization is left to the political branches, for better or worse. Frederick Schauer argues persuasively that a great many important political issues do not end up in the Supreme Court. But juridification is not merely a matter of judicial rulings – it is a matter of how issues are framed, understood, and implemented. Juridification also takes place when Congress attempts to formalize, even automate the political process; and when Congress attempts to eliminate ambiguity and discretion, emulating, even imitating the language and practices of courts and judicial decision making.[12]

When judges command the government to act or open their courthouse doors to an iterated process in which one layer of court rulings is constructed on top of the initial legislation, triggering more legislation, which triggers a new court ruling, and the pattern repeats, we can see the emergence of *constructive* or *deconstructive* patterns of juridification. Why do some of these iterated, layered patterns follow a constructive pattern, whereas others end up following a deconstructive pattern, in which courts undo or revise legislative efforts in directions quite at odds with what those advocates had in mind? This book cannot definitively answer that question. But if the map here is compelling, this book can help set us on a road to the answer. Part of that answer likely lies in the degree of alignment or basic ideological agreement between and among Congress, the president, and the federal courts.[13] When the federal judiciary is in

11 Jeb Barnes, "Bringing the Courts Back In: Interbranch Perspectives on the Role of Courts in American Politics and Policy Making," 10 *Annual Review of Political Science*, pp 25–43 (2007); Mark C. Miller and Jeb Barnes (eds), *Making Policy, Making Law: An Interbranch Perspective*, Washington, D.C.: Georgetown University Press, 2004.

12 See Frederick Schauer, "The Supreme Court 2005 Term, Foreword: The Court's Agenda – and the Nation's," 120 *Harvard Law Review* (2006).

13 Institutional alignment fits well with what some refer to as the "regime theory" of judicial decision making. See Cornell Clayton and J. Mitchell Pickerill, *The Supreme Court in the Political Regime: How Politics Structures the Exercise of Judicial Review*,

general ideological and/or partisan agreement with the dominant political coalition in the elected branches (or at least with Congress), there is at least a better chance of a constructive pattern. By contrast, the reform-minded Democratic Congress that swept into office in the wake of the Watergate scandal was not exactly in line with a federal judiciary that had begun a wrenching turn away from the Warren Court, on its way eventually to becoming the far more assertively conservative Rehnquist and then the Roberts Court. That important reform legislation might generate deconstructive patterns should not be terribly surprising. We might also expect that as Congress itself becomes more bitterly divided and less capable of unified action, not only in regard to the Executive branch, but within its own body, and even within its own Party caucuses, the Court is more likely to become a staunch ally for some, and a clear enemy for others, making constructive patterns less and less likely.[14] Divided government, and fractured political coalitions also appear likely to encourage ever more space in which an aggressive Court might be able to set, or re-set agendas. As Keith Whittington argues, if political coalitions "are fragmented or insecure or if coalition partners disagree [about] myriad issues" courts can become increasingly useful. And, as he notes, "when the signals about constitutional priorities" coming from the leaders of fractious political coalitions become increasingly weak, even more space opens for the courts to become increasingly independent agents.[15]

Party cohesion and institutional alignment tell an important part of the story. Unfortunately, another, equally important part of the story is the one far less easily observed, measured and counted. The other part of the explanation for why some issues end up in a constructive pattern, and others in a deconstructive pattern hinges on understanding that although Court and Congress may be speaking about the same issues they are responding to different incentives, have different institutional interests, work in different timeframes, and speak in slightly different languages. Even in eras of unified government, the way judges articulate, explain and rationalize their choices, and the way earlier decisions influence, shape and constrain later judicial decisions are distinctly different from

Chicago: University of Chicago Press, forthcoming. See, as well, Jack Balkin and Sanford Levinson, "The Processes of Constitutional Change: From Partisan Entrenchment to the National Surveillance State," 75 *Fordham Law Review* 489 (2006).

14 See Polsby, *How Congress Evolves: Social Bases of Institutional Change*, New York: Oxford University Press, 2003; Sarah Binder, *Minority Rights, Majority Rule: Partisanship and the Development of Congress*, New York: Cambridge University Press, 1997; Jon R. Bond and Richard Fleisher, *Polarized Politics: Congress and the President in a Partisan Era*, Washington, D.C.: CQ Press, 2000; Barbara Sinclair, *Party Wars: Polarization and the Politics of National Policy Making*, Norman: Oklahoma University Press, 2006; David Mayhew, *Divided We Govern: Party Control, Lawmaking and Investigations, 1946–2002* (2d ed.), New Haven: Yale University Press, 2005.

15 Whittington, *Political Foundations*, p 274.

the patterns, practices, rhetoric, internal rules, and driving incentives that operate in the elected branches and among bureaucrats. Legalistic policy may produce similar results in the short-term, but it can limit, direct, shape, and constrain those policies in the longer-run in ways quite different from what might have been expected by those who chose a legalistic route in the first place.

Unstitching Complex Legislative Quilts

Institutional alignment helps explain when and why we might see a constructive pattern – but does not fully explain the deconstructive pattern. For that we need to consider judicial practices and judicial canons of construction and interpretation, including how easy Congress makes it for the Supreme Court to unstitch the increasingly complex quilts of legislation that are put together on Capitol Hill.

One issue to consider here is severability. Deconstructive patterns seem more likely to emerge out of policy governed by complex statutes or regulations, of which Justices are likely to find some parts more constitutionally compatible than others. Faced with this sort of legislation, the Court has two choices: The Justices can reject the full package of laws and regulations, or they can pick and choose, severing what they believe to be unconstitutional parts from those parts they believe survive scrutiny. This choice is made easier for the Justices when Congress – as is common practice now – inserts what is known as a severability or separability clause. These clauses generally state that if any provision of the law is held to be invalid, "the validity of the remainder of the Act and the application of such provision to other persons and circumstances shall not be affected thereby."[16] This makes great sense from an efficiency perspective, ensuring that hard-fought legislative gains are not repealed because a clause or subclause is found to be invalid.

Yet, severability clauses invite deconstructive patterns of juridification. The initial framing case in the deconstructive pattern of juridification in campaign finance reform provides a clear example. Chief Justice Warren Burger argued that the complex campaign finance regulations of 1974 had to stand or fall as a package – and should not be severed and deconstructed. By dissecting the act and casting off vital parts, Burger insisted, the Court "fails to recognize that the whole of this Act is greater than the sum of its parts."[17] Burger noted that a severability clause allows the Court to dissect the law, but does not require it to do so. When the remaining parts of the law leave a "comprehensive, integrated statutory

16 2 U.S.C. 454 (1970 ed., Supp. IV).
17 *Buckley v. Valeo*, 424 U.S. 1, 235–6 (1976) (Burger, C.J., concurring in part and dissenting in part).

scheme" unworkable, the Court should refuse to do so.[18] Burger was
in dissent however; the clause was there, and the majority in *Buckley v.
Valeo* used it to salvage the pieces of the complex and interdependent law
they felt could be allowed under the Constitution.

One way to perhaps fend off deconstructive patterns would be for
Congress to stop inserting severability clauses as a routine matter. It is
true that the Court has long maintained that, even without a formal severability clause, the "unconstitutionality of a part of an Act does not
necessarily defeat or affect the validity of its remaining provisions." The
Court insists that it has the duty to decide if the legislature would not
have enacted the remaining, constitutional part of the law "independently of that which is not" constitutional. If so, "the invalid part may
be dropped if what is left is fully operative as a law."[19] This means that
Congress cannot necessarily stop the Court from severing constitutional
from unconstitutional parts of a law. But Congress certainly does not need
to make it quite so easy. The Court may insist that it can and will sever
unconstitutional provisions, but in fact, even in the case where it asserted
this independent authority, the Court has rarely needed to decide if it is
really willing to carry out this threat. The case quoted above – *Champlin
Refining Co. v. Corporation Commission of Oklahoma* – involved a law
where Congress had, in fact, provided a severability clause. "Section 10"
of the law under review the Court states in its opinion, "declares that
the invalidity of any part of the Act shall not in any manner affect the
remaining portions." That, the Court concluded, "discloses an intention
[by Congress] to make the Act divisible and creates a presumption that,
eliminating invalid parts, the legislature would have been satisfied with
what remained and that the scheme of regulation derivable from the
other provisions would have been enacted," regardless of the Court's
decision.[20] In other words, the Court asserts the independent authority
to sever, but does so in cases in which the legislation has already provided
a formal clause calling on the courts to do just that.

Although Congress might not be able to prevent the Supreme Court
from attempting to deconstruct legislation, severing some parts from

---

18 *Buckley v. Valeo*, 424 U.S. at 255.
19 *Champlin Refining Co. v. Corporation Commission of Oklahoma*, 286 U.S. 210, 234
   (1932), cited and quoted in *Buckley v. Valeo*, 424 U.S. at 109.
20 *Champlin Refining*, 286 U.S. at 234. It is worth noting the layered, *together with*
   quality of this ruling. In *Champlin*, the Court asserts the general interpretive principle
   of severability and then lists a series of supporting cases (*Connolly v. Union Sewer Pipe
   Co.*, 184 U.S. 540; *Pollock v. Farmers' Loan & Trust Co.*, 158 U.S. 601; *Regan v.
   Farmers' Loan*, 154 U.S. 362; *Field v. Clark*, 143 U.S. 649), suggesting that this is a
   deeply embedded judicial canon of interpretation. But immediately after this, the Court
   notes that in the case before it, Congress had, in fact, put in place the equivalent of a
   severability clause. The Court thus fortifies the broader and more controversial claim to
   have the authority to sever with or without legislative authorization in a case where, in
   effect, there is legislative authorization.

the rest, legislators certainly do not have to make it that much easier by inserting these clauses. And even if a Court does insist on severing parts of a complex bill, there is nothing that requires the Congress to accept the patchwork legislation that is returned to them: The power to repeal the law is still in congressional hands, subject to executive veto. But Congress tends to defer to the Court's interpretation of the Constitution, and more so in recent years, as Keith Whittington catalogues in his recent book. This is only compounded by the degree to which presidents have also been complicit in the empowering of the courts.[21]

Severability is only one of the important judicial canons of construction influencing the emergence of deconstructive patterns of juridification. Another has to do with shifting default assumptions. Congress legislates in general terms, and the courts apply those laws in specific cases. In writing laws for the future, members of Congress look back retrospectively, seeking guidelines and signals that might suggest how their work is likely to be read and interpreted in the future. When the Court shifts its default assumptions, laws passed under one set of assumptions might later come to be interpreted or applied in ways quite contrary to the expectations of legislators who supported those laws initially.

The Power of Default Assumptions

In foreign policy and war powers, Justice Robert Jackson articulated the Court's dominant default assumption about the scope of executive prerogative in foreign policy in the steel seizure case of *Youngstown Sheet & Tube v. Sawyer* in 1952. He argued that, to exercise any more than the powers explicitly assigned to the executive, a president would need clear, affirmative support from Congress. Congressional silence, or any indication of congressional opposition, would be enough for the Court to side with Congress and against the president.

By 1981, however, that default assumption had shifted rather dramatically. In his opinion for the Court in the Iran hostage case of *Dames & Moore v. Regan*, Justice Rehnquist argued that the Court would need evidence, not of congressional intent to expand executive discretion, but rather of congressional intent to *narrow* executive discretion. Absent clear limits and explicit restrictions, statutes would be read far more generously than had been the case under Jackson's interpretation of the default assumption. This could, of course, dramatically shift the balance of power, particularly when the Court is interpreting statutes that were

21 Whittington, *Political Foundations* (2007).

written when a very different default assumption was in place. Where did the president get the authority to suspend all claims against the government of Iran, and shift their resolution out of American courts and instead vest them in an international tribunal in Algeria (Chapter 8)?[22] Rehnquist based his ruling on an act of Congress – the International Economic Emergency Powers Act (IEEPA) – that had been passed specifically and explicitly to trim back on delegations of power to the president that had accumulated over the course of two world wars, the Cold War, and the conflicts in Korea and Vietnam. Rehnquist argued that this was a statute that actually delegated power. And indeed it did, but the idea was that this new, more modest delegation would replace the earlier, far broader delegations. But because it was a *delegation* of power, it did not explicitly limit or forbid the president from doing what he had done in 1980. Rehnquist argued that the president was well within his constitutional mandate. Would Congress have phrased the IEEPA in quite the same way if the default assumption in 1977 (when the law was written) had been understood as Rehnquist would apply it in 1981, rather than as Jackson had articulated it in 1952?

Another profoundly important default shift came about in 1984, in the *Chevron v. Natural Resources Defense Council* case – which shifted again, and quite dramatically, in 2001 in the case of *U.S. v. Mead.*[23] In 1981, the new Reagan administration issued regulations concerning air pollution that seemed contrary to the language of the Clean Air Act of 1977 and its subsequent amendments. The Supreme Court, however, disagreed, instituting a rather dramatic new default assumption that would give agencies tremendous discretion unless Congress in relevant statutes explicitly and clearly precluded or forbade the choices the agency had made. Much like the shift from Jackson to Rehnquist, this shift profoundly altered the default assumptions about how congressional silence might be read. Where before one might have expected the burden to fall on agencies to show where in the statute they found explicit authority to do as they had done, now the burden would run the other way, forcing those opposed to agency interpretation to show where in the statute what the agency had done was forbidden. Absent rewriting statute after statute, this shift in the default assumption could potentially lead to significant opportunities for deconstructive juridification based on laws that had been written when different default assumptions were operative. The *Chevron* default assumption itself was significantly recast twenty years later in a case called *United States v. Mead* – the consequences of which

22 *Youngstown Sheet & Tube v. Sawyer,* 343 U.S. 579 (1952); *Dames & Moore v. Regan,* 453 U.S. 654 (1981).
23 *United States v. Mead Corp.,* 533 U.S. 218 (2001).

for statutes written in the period between the two shifts are only just beginning to become apparent.[24]

Steel seizure and *Dames & Moore*, *Chevron* and the *Mead* case – these default assumptions, and more importantly the shifts they represent, are aspects of the ways in which judicial canons, judicial practices, judicial language, judicial incentives, and judicial time horizons shape and constrain policy and politics that have been juridified. There are two more that bear some attention and they are related to each other.

War and emergency powers provide a powerful reminder that ours is a constitutional system and not a civil code. To contain the "accurate detail of all the subdivisions of which its great powers will admit, and of all the means by which they may be carried into execution," Chief Justice John Marshall wrote in 1819, our Constitution would have to "partake of the prolixity of a legal code, and could scarcely be embraced by the human mind. It would probably never be understood by the public." Instead, we have a document whose very nature "requires that only its great outlines should be marked, its important objects designated, and the minor ingredients which compose those objects be deduced from the nature of the objects themselves."[25]

Most read this as a gloss on the Court's responsibilities (and power) when it comes to constitutional interpretation. But there is another lesson here. Each of the separate institutions, and those who occupy them, needs to understand the risks of insisting on hard lines and explicit definitions in a system that relies on ambiguity, signals, and flexibility. Constitutional ambiguity is a lynchpin of Madison's mechanical separation of powers.[26] "Some play must be allowed for the joints of the machine," Justice Oliver Wendell Holmes said.[27] Stripping out that ambiguity, insisting on hard, clear answers, is particularly dangerous in a system in which ambiguity is the lubricant that makes it possible for an eighteenth-century machine to continue to run hundreds of years after its designers left this Earth. President George W. Bush refused to read the clear signals sent by the Supreme Court in 2004 (in *Hamdi v. Rumsfeld* and *Rasul v. Bush*) and again in 2006 (in *Hamdan v. Rumsfeld*), signals that he could quite easily have followed and that would have enabled him to accomplish his policy objectives by adjustment, compromise, and negotiation. Instead,

---

24 Cass Sunstein, "Administrative Law Goes to War," 118 *Harvard Law Review* 2663 (2005); Ronald M. Levin, "*Mead* and the Prospective Exercise of Discretion," 54 *Administrative Law Review* 771 (2002).

25 *McCulloch v. Maryland*, 17 U.S. 316, 407 (1819)

26 As President Woodrow Wilson once remarked, if you pick up a copy of Madison's *Federalist Papers* "some parts of it read like a treatise on astronomy instead of a treatise on government. They speak of the centrifugal and the centripetal forces. . . . The whole thing is a calculation of power and an adjustment of parts." (Woodrow Wilson, Address to the Woman Suffrage Convention, Atlantic City, September 8, 1916).

27 *Missouri, Kansas & Texas Railway v. Clay May* 194 U.S. 267, 270 (1904).

he insisted on explicit, clear, and unequivocal allocation of formal, legal and constitutional power. Their signals ignored, a narrow Court majority finally made a clear ruling, rejecting the president's claims and assertions – even in the midst of war.[28]

Judicial Motives, Incentives, and Constraints Are Different – and They Matter

The United States of America, a continent-spanning superpower with global economic, military, and diplomatic interests and responsibilities, functions under a set of rules that were drawn up more than 200 years ago. The U.S. Constitution has been formally amended just twenty-seven times – and one of those (the Twenty-First) was put in place to repeal an earlier amendment (the Nineteenth) concerning the prohibition of the sale or use of alcohol. That ours is an old and largely unrevised constitution has led to any number of efforts to innovate, to adapt, and to work with and around the mechanics of a system designed in an era the dominant paradigm was set by Sir Isaac Newton's work in physics and mechanics, shaping and influencing everything from literature to the design of government institutions.[29] Some of the innovations and adaptations that have been devised and deployed since then are compatible with this eighteenth-century system – but some undermine, weaken, and destroy its delicate balancing act.

At the turn of the twentieth century, the Supreme Court focused its attention on the vertical separation of powers, concerned primarily with the allocation and distribution of power between the national and state governments. The Court's attention turned to the horizontal distribution of power (executive, legislative, and judicial power on the national level) in the Great Depression years and was at the core of its battle with Franklin Roosevelt. In this struggle, the Court aggressively resisted efforts both by one branch to usurp the powers of the others, and efforts by the executive and legislative branches to collude with each other, ruling legislation unconstitutional that would delegate broad and often undefined powers to the executive. The Supreme Court's decisions triggered FDR's effort to pack the Court with his own appointees in his failed court reorganization plan of 1937.[30] Ultimately, of course, FDR outlasted his opponents on the Court, placing eight of his own nominees

---

28 *Boumediene et al v. Bush* (2008).
29 Michael Foley, *Laws, Men and Machines: Modern American Government and the Appeal of Newtonian Mechanics*, London: Routledge, 1990. For a full discussion of the power and importance of scientific paradigms and shifts in those paradigms, see Thomas S. Kuhn, *The Structure of Scientific Revolutions*, Chicago: University of Chicago Press, 1996.
30 See *A.L.A. Schechter Poultry Corporation v. United States*, 295 U.S. 495 (1935), and, among others, Franklin Roosevelt, "Fireside Chat," March 9, 1937. See as well Joseph

on the High Court – in addition to choosing to elevate the one remaining Justice he had not named (Harlan Fiske Stone) to serve as Chief Justice. If there was one lesson these nine, and those who followed them, learned rather dramatically from this period, it was to be far less concerned about the delegation of power.

This is not to say that the Supreme Court forswore the supervision of the separation of powers – but rather that in recent years the concern has been largely in only one direction, with the Court aggressively patrolling to make sure that one branch (typically the Congress) cannot and will not usurp the powers of another (typically the executive).[31] Chapter 7 details a number of instances in which the Court made clear that it would allow Congress to give away its power, but would aggressively enforce a highly formalistic reading of the Constitution's presentment clause, among other provisions, to reject any innovation that appeared to delegate with one hand, but limit, constrain, or contain that delegation with another. Giving away power, the Court seemed to say in the 1980s and 1990s, was fine – trying to hold onto any part of the power that had been delegated was not.

This canon of judicial construction has created hydraulic pressures that risk seriously distorting the separation and balance of powers. Because our eighteenth-century Constitution unquestionably requires a good deal of delegation from the legislative to the administrative branch, the Court's rulings suggest that Congress has no choice but to erode its own power to assure some measure of efficiency and effectiveness in the American political process. Put the Court's reluctance to enforce undue delegation (protect against collusion) together with the Court's willingness to sever constitutionally questionable innovations (such as legislative vetoes) from otherwise constitutionally tolerable delegations of power, and one has a prescription for a mighty deconstructive pattern. Consider what might happen should the War Powers Resolution of 1973 ever find its way to court.

The War Powers Resolution was an explicit effort to trade off the formal delegation of war powers (which had until that time been contested and constitutionally ambiguous at best) for an innovation that was meant to reverse the political and institutional barriers that prevented Congress from slowing, redirecting, or ending conflicts once they have begun. Should the 1973 law ever make it to Court, however, one can well imagine the Court ruling that the delegation of power is quite acceptable, but the innovative restraint is not. What was meant to be an important tool rebalancing the separation of powers would turn into

McKenna, *Franklin Roosevelt and the Great Constitutional War: The Court-Packing Crisis of 1937*, New York: Fordham University Press, 2001.
31 Note, though, the Supreme Court's aggressive response in *City of Boerne v. Flores*, 521 U.S. 507 (1997), to congressional efforts to limit the scope and reach of judicial power in the Religious Freedom Restoration Act of 1993.

an extraordinary and unprecedented delegation of power, a power that appears to be a core function for a legislature in a representative democracy. Should the Court hesitate to unstitch this particular legislative quilt, the Justices can simply turn to Section 9 of the War Powers Resolution – the "separability clause":

SEC. 9. If any provision of this joint resolution or the application thereof to any person or circumstance is held invalid, the remainder of the joint resolution and the application of such provision to any other person or circumstance shall not be affected thereby.[32]

The only real protection against the possibility that a law explicitly designed to limit the president might actually provide the chief executive with nearly unfettered authority to exercise powers explicitly assigned by the Constitution to Congress would be to rewrite or to repeal the law. Neither is likely to happen.[33]

The Power of Precedent

There is one last aspect of the importance of judicial rules of interpretation to consider here – the Court's reluctance to overturn its own precedents and its preference to simply extend, expand, or redefine existing pathways instead. This book offers a number of cautionary tales about the judicial preference to avoid retracing its steps, thereby opening constitutional pathways that long have been sealed, and instead being far more willing to expand and extend pathways that have already been developed. Consider the fact (explored in Chapter 3) that America's civil rights law has been built on the commerce clause of the U.S. Constitution. This was not because the commerce clause was the only constitutional foundation that might make sense. In fact, there were at least two other options (the privileges and immunities and the equal protection clauses of the Fourteenth Amendment). But each of these had been largely foreclosed by Supreme Court cases that were handed down shortly after that Amendment was ratified – the privileges and immunities clause by the *Slaughterhouse Cases* of 1877 and the equal protection clause by the *Civil Rights Cases* of 1883.[34] To build this law on those clauses would require the Court to reverse these venerable and deeply embedded decisions. This is certainly something the Court *could* do – but not something a majority of the Justices wanted to do, particularly if there was a way to avoid doing so.

32 *War Powers Resolution*, Public Law 93–148, 93rd Congress, H. J. Res. 542, November 7, 1973.
33 See Gordon Silverstein, *Imbalance of Powers: Constitutional Interpretation and the Making of American Foreign Policy*, New York: Oxford University Press, 1997.
34 *The Slaughterhouse Cases*, 83 U.S. 36 (1873); *The Civil Rights Cases*, 109 U.S. 3 (1883).

In their conference after oral argument in 1964, Justice Black made clear his preference for the Fourteenth Amendment, but noted that "Congress limited the act to the Commerce Clause." Otherwise, Black added, "I would be for overruling the *Civil Rights Cases*." But Justice Harlan suggested that Solicitor General Cox, the administration, and Congress had probably been correct in a pragmatic sense. "I would stand by the *Civil Rights Cases*," Harlan said, "and hold this act unconstitutional" if it were before the Court as a Fourteenth Amendment case. But, he added, "I have no problem under the Commerce Clause." Justice Stewart made clear that "resting on the Commerce Clause" he would uphold the law – a position Justice White said that he would join.[35]

That civil rights was built on the commerce clause was a choice Congress made *together with* the Court. That this framework has or perhaps might yet skew, shape, or frame how we think about civil rights, how to articulate a case for rights, how and where to extend rights, and where and when the Constitution might impede that extension is an open question – though cases from 1995 and 2000 suggested that, for a majority of the Court, the extension of commerce as a rationale for the constitutionality of national legislation does, indeed, have real limits.[36]

None of this is to say that Congress could not build on a different path or that the Court never can or will return and revisit a path it abandoned years ago. But, much like Robert Frost, "knowing how way leads on to way," it is doubtful that we "should ever come back."[37] Paths are not destiny, but because of judicial canons of construction, they do exercise great influence over how we think and frame and argue about constitutional questions, public policy, politics, and the political process itself. The choice of a path and legal language and constitutional arguments about that language needs to be determined by more than just an evaluation of the short-term and single-case probability of success or failure. Politics is capable of highly specific decisions that can be reversed with the next election – and often are. Judges are equally able to reverse decisions – but, are far more reluctant to do so. There are powerful institutional and professional norms that pressure Justices to avoid, as Justice Owen Roberts argued in 1944, making decisions that are like "a restricted railroad ticket, good for this day and train only."[38] This may not preclude

35 Supreme Court Conference of October 5, 1964, quoted in Del Dickson (ed), *The Supreme Court in Conference: 1940–1985*, New York: Oxford University Press, 2001, p 726.
36 *United States v. Lopez*, 514 U.S. 549 (1995); *United States v. Morrison*, 529 U.S. 598 (2000).
37 Robert Frost, "The Road Less Traveled."
38 *Smith v. Allwright*, 321 U.S. 649, 665 (1944) (Roberts, J., dissenting). Owen Roberts was dissenting, it should be noted, because he felt that the majority had too cavalierly overturned a Supreme Court ruling that had been made on a similar case just nine years earlier.

a policy entrepreneur from achieving his or her short term goal in Court – but it may shape and constrain that advocate's options in the future.

Courts, Congress, and the Executive – Together with Each Other

Juridification and the patterns it follows are never a matter of a single choice, a single case, a single statute – nor are they the responsibility of any single institution or actor. This is not a story about a grasping imperial court filled with power-hungry judges. Nor is it a story of simple abdication by politicians unwilling to fight for anything more than the spotlight and a generous contribution from their favorite lobbyist. This is a story about an eighteenth-century system trying to adapt to twenty-first-century demands – and the costs of the adaptations we have made.

The interaction of government, law, and politics profoundly shapes and constrains policy and practice in every facet of public and private life, from elections to education, from torture to trade and finance, from marriage to war, from adoption to abortion. We cannot hope to understand American politics without paying close attention to the separate institutions that comprise the government. But it is equally true that we cannot hope to understand the American system without understanding how these institutions interact, overlap, frame, and constrain each other. Those who study the courts seem trapped in a cyclical and almost endless struggle between those who see the Court as "radicals in robes" or "justice in robes"; between arguments about "the least dangerous branch" versus "the most democratic branch"; between those who lament that the court is "overruling democracy" and those who gently urge a policy of "taking the Constitution away from the courts."[39] These are debates that cannot be won because the courts never have and never can act on their own.

One problem is the focus on courts as independent agents, making individual choices. Law and politics in America are fully integrated and yet very different. But we tend to think about, write about, and read about the judicial branch as a distinct and disconnected institution. The artificial divide that has grown up between those who study law and those who study government and politics is largely an accident of history, but one that is now making it increasingly hard to solve some of the nation's most pressing problems.

39 Cass Sunstein, *Radicals in Robes: Why Extreme Right Wing Courts Are Wrong for America*, New York: Basic Books, 2005; Ronald Dworkin, *Justice in Robes*, Cambridge: Harvard University Press, 2006; Alexander Bickel, *The Least Dangerous Branch: The Supreme Court at the Bar of Politics*, Indianapolis: Bobbs-Merrill, 1962; Jeffrey Rosen, *The Most Democratic Branch: How the Courts Serve America*, New York: Oxford University Press, 2006; Jamin Raskin, *Overruling Democracy: The Supreme Court vs. the American People*, New York: Routledge, 2003; Mark Tushnet, *Taking the Constitution Away from the Courts*, Princeton: Princeton University Press, 1999.

Detached from the classic liberal arts, American legal scholarship developed its own traditions and emerged as a separate discipline, centered in postgraduate schools of law that traditionally emphasized professional training, but have since the early twentieth century becoming increasingly concerned with scholarly research. That there were separate (and excellent) schools of law created disincentives for traditional social science disciplines such as economics and political science to explore and study law and legal institutions. Conversely, law faculties saw little reason to duplicate the efforts of traditional social science disciplines and tended to deemphasize the study of political institutions and government structures.

The growth of the American national government, the end of the Cold War, and the emergence of new states and their hunger for constitutional systems and solutions, along with the growing interest in concepts such as the rule of law and its application to an increasingly global economic and political system, have led both the social sciences and the legal academy to pay attention once again to these long neglected questions – lawyers are now thinking about the lessons social science can teach; sociologists, economists, and those who study political science are now paying closer attention to law and legal institutions. But they are doing so largely within their separate worlds, creating in some cases unnecessary duplication and in others wasting efforts on theories and claims that have been well treated, fully developed, and long ago discarded by the other disciplines.

We need to understand how these institutions, how law and politics interact, shape, and frame each other if we ever hope to be able to understand the pathology and promise of American politics and the capacity of the American political system. We need that understanding to be able to decide if we have reached a point at which an eighteenth-century Constitution requires fundamental restructuring or, alternatively, if that machine is still not only functional but, on balance, is able to maintain a social and political equilibrium unlikely to be improved on by major reform.

What is clear is that tinkering with this machine has consequences. Law and judicial decision making seem to offer efficiency, clarity, transparency, and the elimination of ambiguity. Ambiguity, however, is the grease in the creaking, clanking, eighteenth-century Madisonian machine that continues to govern this continent-spanning nation more than 200 years later. Cleaning this out, and replacing it with legal clarity, legal formality, and strict allocations of power, is a very risky process indeed – it is building a new and very different building on an old foundation. Doing so does not strike someone who has spent a few years living next to one of the world's most dangerous earthquake fault lines as a particularly good idea. If a new building is wanted, a new foundation is needed. Conversely, if the foundation is still considered sound and desirable, new construction must be designed to fit it well. The expansion and acceleration of juridification in the years since the early 1960s have not been the product of that sort of careful calculation. This book is an effort to help politicians and policy entrepreneurs, lawyers, judges, and those who study them begin to think about the perils and promise of law's allure in a more systematic way: It is not meant to be the last word on the subject, but rather a goad for others to develop these themes and arguments, to build and test more systematic studies of juridification that will help us make sense of this incredibly complex and incredibly important interactive set of problems.

Law's allure is built into American political culture, something that was recognized well before there was a United States. Urging his readers to take arms against the British monarch, Tom Paine insisted that if America must have a king, then that king ought to be the law. "But where says some is the King of America? I'll tell you Friend," Paine wrote, "he reigns above, and doth not make havoc of mankind like the Royal Brute of Britain." But Paine recognized that Americans still craved formality and pomp and circumstance:

That we may not appear defective even in earthly honors, let a day be solemnly set apart for proclaiming the Charter; let it be brought forth placed on the divine law, the word of God; let a CROWN be placed thereon, by which the world may know, that so far as we approve of monarchy, that in American, THE LAW IS KING.

Paine, however, recognized that there is real danger in the unquestioning obedience to rules and documents; there is real peril in complacency and deference and the worship of formal rules. He knew that crowning the charter might be risky, and quickly added, "But lest any ill use should afterwards arise, let the CROWN at the conclusion of the ceremony be demolished, and scattered among the people whose RIGHT it is."[40]

---

40 Thomas Paine, *Common Sense*, 1776.

BIBLIOGRAPHY

Ackerman, Bruce. 1991. *We the People: Foundations*. Cambridge, MA: Harvard University Belknap Press.

Adler, Jonathan. 2002. "Fables of the Cuyahoga: Reconstructing a History of Environmental Protection." 14 *Fordham Environmental Law Journal* 89.

Anderson, Frederick R. and Robert H. Daniels. 1973. *NEPA in the Courts: A Legal Analysis of the National Environmental Policy Act*. Baltimore: Johns Hopkins University Press.

Anechiarico, Frank and James Jacob. 1996. *The Pursuit of Absolute Integrity: How Corruption Control Makes Government Ineffective*. Chicago: University of Chicago Press.

Apple, Jr., R.W. 1989. "Justice and the Public." *New York Times*, April 10, p B6.

Arthur, W. Brian. 1989. "Competing Technologies, Increasing Returns, and Lock-In by Historical Events." 99 *Economic Journal* (March).

Bacigal, Ronald. 1990. *The Limits of Litigation: The Dalkon Shield Controversy*. Durham: Carolina Academic Press.

Baker, Peter. 2005. "Parties Gear Up for High Court Battle." *Washington Post*, June 27, p A2.

Balkin, Jack, ed. 2002. *What* Brown v. Board of Education *Should Have Said*. New York: New York University Press.

Balkin, Jack, ed. 2005. *What* Roe v. Wade *Should Have Said*. New York: New York University Press.

Balkin, Jack and Sanford Levinson. 2006. "The Processes of Constitutional Change: From Partisan Entrenchment to the National Surveillance State." 75 *Fordham Law Review* 489.

Banks, Christopher P. and John C. Green. 2001. *Superintending Democracy: The Courts and the Political Process*. Akron: University of Akron Press.

Barnes, Jeb. 2004. *Overruled? Legislative Overrides, Pluralism and Contemporary Court-Congress Relations*. Stanford: Stanford University Press.

Barnes, Jeb. 2007. "Bringing the Courts Back In: Interbranch Perspectives on the Role of Courts in American Politics and Policy Making." 10 *Annual Review of Political Science*, pp 25–43.

Barnes, Robert. 2007. "Justices Continue Trend of Hearing Fewer Cases." *Washington Post*, Jan. 7, p 4.

Barone, Michael. 1985. "The Deficit Panic: If We Won't Pay Now, Why Will We Later?" *Washington Post*, Oct. 27, p B1.

Baum, Lawrence. 2006. *Judges and Their Audiences: A Perspective on Judicial Behavior.* Princeton: Princeton University Press.

Bell, Derrick. 2004. *Silent Covenants:* Brown v. Board of Education *and the Unfulfilled Hopes for Racial Reform.* New York: Oxford University Press.

Berry, Jeffrey M. 1977. *Lobbying for the People: The Political Behavior of Public Interest Groups.* Princeton: Princeton University Press.

Bestor, Arthur. 1964. "The American Civil War as a Constitutional Crisis." 69 *American Historical Review* 2, p 327.

Bianchini, Maria. 1999. "The Tobacco Agreement That Went Up in Smoke: Defining the Limits of Congressional Intervention into Ongoing Mass Tort Litigation." 87 *California Law Review* 703.

Bickel, Alexander. 1961. "Forward: The Passive Virtues." 75 *Harvard Law Review* 40.

Bickel, Alexander. 1962. *The Least Dangerous Branch: The Supreme Court at the Bar of Politics.* Indianapolis: Bobbs-Merrill.

Bickel, Alexander. 1967. "Skelly Wright's Sweeping Decision." *New Republic*, July 8, p 11.

Binder, Sarah. 1997. *Minority Rights, Majority Rule: Partisanship and the Development of Congress.* New York: Cambridge University Press.

Biskupic, Joan. 1999. "Activist Jurors Help Carve Out New Law." *Washington Post*, Aug. 30, p 1.

Black, H. C., et al. 1992. *Black's Law Dictionary* (7th ed.). St. Paul: West Publishing.

Black, Charles. 1997. *A New Birth of Freedom: Human Rights Named and Unnamed.* New Haven: Yale University Press.

Blackstone, William. 1979 [1765]. *Commentaries on the Laws of England.* Chicago: University of Chicago Press.

Blichner, Lars Chr. and Anders Molander. 2005. "What is Juridification?" University of Oslo, Centre for European Studies, Working Paper, no. 14, March.

Bond, Jon R. and Richard Fleisher. 2000. *Polarized Politics: Congress and the President in a Partisan Era.* Washington, DC: Congressional Quarterly Press.

Bowman, Frank. 2001. "Falling Out of Love with America: The Clinton Impeachment and the Madisonian Constitution." 60 *Maryland Law Review* 5.

Bowsher, Charles. 1990. "Cooking the Books is a Bad Recipe to Cool Deficit." 169 *Journal of Accountancy* 2, 23–5.

Brandwein, Pamela. 2006. "The Civil Rights Cases and the Lost Language of State Neglect," in Ronald Kahn and Ken Kersch (eds.), *The Supreme Court and American Political Development*, Lawrence: University Press of Kansas.

Brandwein, Pamela. 2007. "A Judicial Abandonment of Blacks? Rethinking the 'State Action' Cases of the Waite Court," 41 *Law & Society Review* 4, 997.

Brennan, William J. 1986. "Constitutional Adjudication and the Death Penalty: A View from the Court." 100 *Harvard Law Review* 313.

Brenner, Saul and Harold Spaeth. 1995. *Stare Indecisis; The Alteration of Precedent on the Supreme Court, 1946–1992.* New York: Cambridge University Press.

Brenner, Saul and Charlotte Mare Stier. 1996. "Retesting Segal and Spaeth's Stare Decisis Model," 40 *American Journal of Political Science*, 4, 1036–48.

Brigham, John. 1987. *The Cult of the Court.* Philadelphia: Temple University Press.

Brisbin, Richard. 1996. "Slaying the Dragon: Segal, Spaeth and the Function of Law in Supreme Court Decision-Making." 4 *American Journal of Political Science*, pp 1004–1017.

Broder, David. 1985. "The Rudman-Gramm Balanced Budget Sham." *Washington Post*, Dec. 11, p A-23.

Broder, David. 1986. "The Special Conceit of Progressivism." *Washington Post*, April 27, p C-8.

Broder, John. 1997. "Cigarette Makers in a $368 Billion Accord to Curb Lawsuits and Curtail Marketing." *New York Times*, June 21, p 1.

Bryce, James. 1893. *The American Commonwealth*. New York: MacMillan.

Burke, Thomas. 2002. *Lawyers, Lawsuits and Legal Rights: The Battle over Litigation in American Society*. Berkeley: University of California Press.

Bussiere, Elizabeth. 1994. "The Failure of Constitutional Welfare Rights in the Warren Court," 109 *Political Science Quarterly* 1, 105–31.

Bussiere, Elizabeth. 1997. *(Dis)Entitling the Poor: The Warren Court, Welfare Rights, and the American Political Tradition*. University Park: Pennsylvania State University Press.

Bussiere, Elizabeth. 2004. "The 'New Property' Theory of Welfare Rights; Promises and Pitfalls." 2 *The Good Society*, pp 1–9.

Cahn, Edgar and Jean Cahn. 1964. "The War on Poverty: A Civilian Perspective." 73 *Yale Law Journal* 1317.

Cahn, Edgar and Jean Cahn. 1970. "Power to the People or the Profession? The Public Interest in Public Interest Law." 79 *Yale Law Journal* 1005.

Cain, Bruce. 1985. "Assessing the Partisan Effects of Redistricting." 79 *American Political Science Review* 2, 320–33.

Campbell, Colton and John Stack. 2001. *Congress Confronts the Court: The Struggle for Legitimacy and Authority in Lawmaking*. Lanham, MD: Rowman & Littlefield.

Canon, David. 1999. *Race, Redistricting and Representation: The Unintended Consequences of Black Majority Districts*. Chicago: University of Chicago Press.

Cardozo, Benjamin. 1924. *The Growth of the Law*. New Haven: Yale University Press.

Carter, Stephen. 1987. "From Sick Chicken to Synar: The Evolution and Subsequent De-Evolution of the Separation of Powers." *Brigham Young University Law Review* 719.

Century Foundation. 2000. *Uncertain Justice: Politics and America's Courts – The Reports of the Task Forces of Citizens for Independent Courts*. New York: Century Foundation Press.

Chayes, Abraham. 1976. "The Role of the Judge in Public Law Litigation." 89 *Harvard Law Review* 1281.

Citrin, Jack. 1974. "Comment: The Political Relevance of Trust in Government." 69 *American Political Science Review* 3, 973–88.

Claude, Richard. 1970. *The Supreme Court and the Electoral Process*. Baltimore: Johns Hopkins University Press.

Clayton, Cornell and Howard Gillman, eds. 1999. *Supreme Court Decision-Making: New Institutionalist Approaches*. Chicago: University of Chicago Press.

Clayton, Cornell and J. Mitchell Pickerill. Forthcoming. *The Supreme Court in the Political Regime: How Politics Structures the Exercise of Judicial Review*. Chicago: University of Chicago Press.

Coleman, Christopher, Lawrence Nee and Leonard Rubinowitz. 2005. "Social Movements and Social-Change Litigation: Synergy in the Montgomery Bus Protest," 30 *Law & Soc. Inquiry* 4, 663–701.

Collins, Gail. 2007. "Calvin Coolidge Redux." *New York Times*, Oct. 11, p A31.

Connolly, Ceci and John Mintz. 1998. "For Cigarette Industry, a Future without GOP Support." *Washington Post*, March 29, p 1.

Cooper, Charles. 1988. "Stare Decisis: Precedent and Principle in Constitutional Adjudication." 401 *Cornell Law Review* 73.

Cooper, Samuel. 1994. "Considering 'Power' in Separation of Powers." 46 *Stanford Law Review* 2, p 361.

Corrado, Anthony, Thomas Mann and Trevor Potter, eds. 2003. *Inside the Campaign Finance Battle*. Washington DC: Brookings Institution Press.

Correia, Edward and Patricia Davidson. 1998. "The State Attorney Generals' Tobacco Suits: Equitable Remedies." 7 *Cornell Journal of Law & Public Policy* 843.

Cortner, Richard. 2001. *Civil Rights and Public Accommodations: The Heart of Atlanta Motel and McClung Cases*. Lawrence: University Press of Kansas.

Council for Public Interest Law. 1976. *Balancing the Scales of Justice: Financing Public Interest Law in America*. Washington, DC: Council for Public Interest Law.

Cox, Archibald. 1966. "The Supreme Court – 1965 Term." 80 *Harvard Law Review* 91.

Craig, Barbara Hinkson. 1987. *Chadha: The Story of an Epic Constitutional Struggle*. New York: Oxford University Press.

Crenson, Matthew and Benjamin Ginsberg. 2002. *Downsizing Democracy: How America Sidelined its Citizens and Privatized its Public*. Baltimore: Johns Hopkins University Press.

Cross, Frank and Emerson Tiller. 1998. "Judicial Partisanship and Obedience to Legal Doctrine: Whistleblowing on the Federal Courts of Appeals." 107 *Yale Law Journal* 2155.

Curry, Rebecca. 2008. "Legislatures, Lawsuits and Loopholes: The Politics of Judicial Review in U.S. Campaign Finance Policy." PhD dissertation in the Jurisprudence and Social Policy Program at the University of California, Berkeley.

Cushman, Barry. 1998. *Rethinking the New Deal Court: The Structure of a Constitutional Revolution*. New York: Oxford University Press.

David, Paul. 1985. "CLIO and the Economics of QWERTY." 75 *American Economic Review*.

Davis, Martha. 1995. *Brutal Need: Lawyers and the Welfare Rights Movement, 1960–1973*. New Haven: Yale University Press.

Department of Justice. 1963. "The Constitutionality of the Public Accommodations Provisions of Title II." In *Hearings Before the Committee on Commerce, United States Senate, 88th Congress, 1st Session on S. 1732*, part 2. Washington, DC: U.S. Government Printing Office.

Derthick, Martha A. 2005. *Up in Smoke: From Legislation to Litigation in Tobacco Politics* (2nd ed.). Washington, DC: Congressional Quarterly Press.

Dewar, Helen. 1986. "Congress Votes to Reinstate Cuts High Court Had Invalidated." *Washington Post*, July 18, p A-4.

Dewar, Helen. 1995. "Senate Approves Line-Item Veto Bill, 69–29." *Washington Post*, March 24, p A-1.

De Witt, Karen. 1992. "Huge Crowd Backs Right to Abortion in Capital March." *New York Times*, April 6, p A1.

Dickson, Del (ed.). 2001. *The Supreme Court in Conference: 1940–1985*. New York: Oxford University Press.

Doyle, Vincent. 1963. "The Power of Congress to Prohibit Racial Discrimination in Privately Owned Places of Public Accommodation." In *Hearings Before the Committee on Commerce, United States Senate, 88th Congress, 1st Session on S. 1732*, part 2. Washington, DC: U.S. Government Printing Office.

Dudziak, Mary L. 2002. *Cold War Civil Rights Race and the Image of American Democracy*. Princeton: Princeton University Press.

Duffy, Michael. 1986. "Government by Gimmick." *Time*, Oct. 13.

Dworkin, Ronald. 1986. *Law's Empire*. Cambridge: Harvard University Press.

Dworkin, Ronald. 2006. *Justice in Robes*. Cambridge: Harvard University Press.

Eagleton, Thomas F. 1974. *War and Presidential Power: A Chronicle of Congressional Surrender*. New York: Liveright.

Easterbrook, Gregg. 1995. *A Moment on The Earth: The Coming Age of Environmental Optimism*. New York: Viking.

Ehrenreich, Barbara. 1989. "Mothers Unite." *New Republic*, July 10, p 30.

Ellis, Richard. 1971. *The Jeffersonian Crisis: Courts and Politics in the Young Republic*. New York: W.W. Norton.

Ely, James. 2002. *Railroads and American Law*. Lawrence: University Press of Kansas.

Ely, John Hart. 1973. "The Wages of Crying Wolf: A Comment on *Roe v. Wade*." 82 *Yale Law Journal* 920.

Ely, John Hart. 1993. *War and Responsibility: Constitutional Lessons of Vietnam and its Aftermath*. Princeton: Princeton University Press.

Epstein, Lee. 1985. *Conservatives in Court*. Knoxville: University of Tennessee Press.

Epstein, Lee and Jack Knight. 1997. *Choices Justices Make*. Washington, DC: Congressional Quarterly Press.

Epstein, Lee and Joseph Kobylka. 1992. *The Supreme Court and Legal Change: Abortion and the Death Penalty*. Chapel Hill: University of North Carolina Press.

Epstein, Lee and Jeffrey Segal. 2007. *Advise and Consent: The Politics of Judicial Appointments*. New York: Oxford University Press.

Farber, Daniel. 2007. *Retained by the People: The 'Silent' Ninth Amendment and the Constitutional Rights Americans Didn't Know They Had*. New York: Perseus Books.

Farrell, William E. 1970. "Opponents of the Abortion Law Gather Strength in the Legislature But Many Lawmakers Would Prefer to Let the Courts Settle Controversy." *New York Times*, Jan. 26, p 19.

Farrier, Jasmine. 2004. *Passing the Buck: Congress, the Budget, and Deficits*. Lexington: University Press of Kentucky.

Fausset, Richard, Jenny Jarvie, and Henry Weinstein. 2008. "Legal Legend Dickie Scruggs Pleads Guilty in Bribery." *Los Angeles Times*, March 15, p 1.

Federal Election Commission. 1981. *Legislative History of the Federal Election Campaign Act of 1971*. Washington, DC: U.S. Government Printing Office.

Feeley, Malcolm M. 2007. "The Black Basis of Constitutional Development," in Harry N. Schieber (ed.)., *Earl Warren and the Warren Court; The Legacy in American and Foreign Law*. Lanham, MD: Lexington Books.

Feeley, Malcolm M. and Edward Rubin. 1998. *Judicial Policy Making and the Modern State: How the Courts Reformed America's Prisons*. New York: Cambridge University Press.

Fehrenbacher, Don. 1961. "Lincoln, Douglas and the 'Freeport Question.'" 3 *American Historical Review* 66, 599–617.

Fehrenbacher, Don. 1978. *The Dred Scott Case: Its Significance in American Law and Politics*. New York. Oxford University Press.

Fenno, Richard. 1973. *Congressmen in Committees*. Boston: Little, Brown & Co.

Fenno, Richard. 1978. *Home Style: House Members in Their Districts*. Boston: Little, Brown & Co.

Ferejohn, John and Barry Weingast. 1992. "A Positive Theory of Statutory Interpretation," 12 *International Review of Law and Economics*, pp 263–79.

Ferejohn, John. 2002. "Judicializing Politics, Politicizing Law," 65 *Law and Contemporary Problems* 3, 41.

Fisher, Louis. 1975. *Presidential Spending Power*. Princeton: Princeton University Press.

Fisher, Louis. 1988. *Constitutional Dialogues*. Princeton: Princeton University Press.

Fisher, Louis. 1993. "The Legislative Veto: Invalidated, It Survives." 4 *Law & Contemporary Problems* 56, 293.

Fisher, Louis. 1999. *American Constitutional Law* (3rd ed.). Durham: Carolina Academic Press.

Fisher, Louis and David Gray Adler. 2007. *American Constitutional Law* (7th ed.). Durham: Carolina Academic Press.

Fisher, Louis. 2000. *Congressional Abdication on War & Spending*. College Station: Texas A&M University Press.

Fisher, Louis. 2003. *Congressional Investigations: Subpoenas and Contempt Power*. Washington, DC: Congressional Research Service, April 2.

Fisher, Louis. 2005. *Military Tribunals and Presidential Power: American Revolution to the War on Terrorism*. Lawrence: University Press of Kansas.

Fisher, William, Morton Horowitz, and Thomas Reed, eds. 1993. *American Legal Realism*. New York: Oxford University Press.

Fleishman, Joel L. and Carol Greenwald. 1976. "Public Interest Litigation and Political Finance Reform." 1 *Annals of the American Academy of Political and Social Science* 425, 114–23.

Foley, Michael. 1990. *Laws, Men and Machines: Modern American Government and the Appeal of Newtonian Mechanics*. London: Routledge.

Forbath, William E. 1991. *Law and the Shaping of the American Labor Movement*. Cambridge: Harvard University Press.

Ford Foundation. 1973. *The Public Interest Law Firm: New Voices for New Constituencies*. New York: Ford Foundation.

Ford Foundation and the American Bar Association. 1976. *Public Interest Law: Five Years Later*. New York: Ford Foundation.

Freedman, Alix and Suein Hwang. 1997. "Peace Pipe: Philip Morris, RJR and Tobacco Plaintiffs Discuss a Settlement." *Wall Street Journal*, April 16, p 1.

Freund, Paul. 1963. "Constitutional Bases for the Public Accommodations Bill – A Brief on the Constitutional Issues." In *Hearings Before the Committee on Commerce, United States Senate, 88th Congress, 1st Session on S. 1732*, part 2. Washington, DC: U.S. Government Printing Office.

Friedman, Lawrence. 1995. *Total Justice*. New York: Russell Sage Foundation.

Frymer, Paul. 2003. "Acting When Elected Officials Won't: Federal Courts and Civil Rights Enforcement in U.S. Labor Unions, 1935–85." 3 *American Political Science Review* 97, 483–499.

Frymer, Paul. 2008. *Black and Blue: African Americans, the Labor Movement and the Decline of the Democratic Party*, Princeton: Princeton University Press.

Galanter, Marc. 1983. "The Radiating Effects of Courts," in Keith Boyum and Lynn Mather (eds.), *Empirical Theories of Courts*. New York: Longman Press.

Garber, Marc N. and Kurt A. Wimmer. 1987. "Presidential Signing Statements as Interpretations of Legislative Intent: An Executive Aggrandizement of Power." 24 *Harvard Journal on Legislation* 363.

Garrow, David J. 1998. *Liberty and Sexuality: The Right to Privacy and the Making of* Roe v. Wade. Berkeley: University of California Press.

Gerhardt, Michael J. 1991. "The Role of Precedent in Constitutional Decisionmaking and Theory." 60 *George Washington Law Review* 68.

Gerstmann, Evan. 2003. *Same Sex Marriage and the Constitution.* New York: Cambridge University Press.

Gerstmann, Evan. 2005. "Litigating Same-Sex Marriage: Might the Courts Actually Be Bastions of Rationality?" 38 *PS: Political Science and Politics* 2, 217–20.

Gillman, Howard. 1993. *The Constitution Besieged: The Rise and Decline of Lochner Era Police Powers Jurisprudence.* Durham: Duke University Press.

Gillman, Howard. 1999. "Reconnecting the Modern Supreme Court to the Historical Evolution of American Capitalism," in Howard Gillman and Cornell Clayton (eds.), *The Supreme Court in American Politics.* Lawrence: University Press of Kansas.

Gillman, Howard. 2001. "What's Law Got to Do with It? Judicial Behavioralists Test the 'Legal Model' of Judicial Decision Making." 26 *Law & Social Inquiry* 465.

Gillman, Howard. 2002. "How Political Parties Can Use the Courts to Advance Their Agendas: Federal Courts in the United States, 1875–1891." 96 *American Political Science Review* 3, 511–524.

Gillman, Howard and Cornell Clayton, eds. 1999. *The Supreme Court in American Politics: New Institutionalist Interpretations.* Lawrence: University Press of Kansas.

Ginsberg, Benjamin and Martin Shefter. 1990. *Politics by Other Means: The Declining Importance of Elections.* New York: Basic Books.

Ginsburg, Ruth Bader. 1985. "Some Thoughts on Autonomy and Equality in Relation to *Roe v. Wade.*" 63 *North Carolina Law Review* 375.

Ginsburg, Ruth Bader. 1992a. "Speaking in a Judicial Voice." 67 *NYU Law Review* 1185.

Ginsburg, Ruth Bader. 1992b. "A Moderate View on Roe." *Constitution* (Spring-Summer 1992), p 17.

Glendon, Mary Ann. 1989. *Abortion and Divorce in Western Law.* Cambridge: Harvard University Press.

Goffman, Erving. 1974. *Frame Analysis: An Essay on the Organization of Experience.* New York: Harpers.

Goldman, Sheldon. 1999. *Picking Federal Judges: Lower Court Selection from Roosevelt through Reagan.* New Haven: Yale University Press.

Goldsmith, Jack. 2007. *The Terror Presidency: Law and Judgment inside the Bush Administration.* New York: W.W. Norton.

Goldstein, Amy and Charles Babington. 2005. "Miers Once Vowed to Support Ban On Abortion; But Conservatives Still Question Nominee's Views." *Washington Post,* Oct. 19, p 1.

Graber, Mark. 1999. *Rethinking Abortion: Equal Choice, the Constitution and Reproductive Politics,* Princeton: Princeton University Press.

Graber, Mark. 1993. "The Non-Majoritarian Difficulty: Legislative Deference to the Judiciary." 7 *Studies in American Political Development,* pp 35–73.

Graber, Mark. 2006. *Dred Scott and the Problem of Constitutional Evil.* New York: Cambridge University Press.

Graglia, Lino. 1976. *Disaster by Decree: The Supreme Court Decisions on Race and the Schools.* Ithaca: Cornell University Press.

Graham, Fred. 1968. "'68 Ending With No Executions, First Such Year in U.S. Records." *New York Times,* Dec. 31, p 17.

Graham, Fred. 1969. "Court Fight for Legal Abortions Spurred by Washington Ruling." *New York Times,* Nov. 12, p 30.

Graham, Fred. 1972. "Court Spares 600." *New York Times,* June 30, p 1.

Gray, Jerry. 1995. "'Lazy Fools,' Says Byrd; Champions of Cutting Spending Gladly Hand the Ax to the President." *New York Times,* March 26, p 2.

Gray, John Chipman. 1963. *The Nature and Sources of the Law*. Boston: Beacon Press.

Green, David. 1987. *Shaping Political Consciousness: The Language of Politics in America from McKinley to Reagan*. Ithaca: Cornell University Press.

Greenberg, Jack. 1994. *Crusaders in the Court*. New York: Basic Books.

Greenhouse, Linda. 1970. "Constitutional Question: Is There a Right to Abortion?" *New York Times Magazine*, Jan. 25, p 20.

Greenhouse, Linda. 1992. "The Supreme Court: Court Opens Way for Damage Suits Over Cigarettes." *New York Times*, June 25, p 1.

Greenhouse, Linda. 2005. *Becoming Justice Blackmun*. New York: Times Books.

Greenhouse, Linda. 2006. "Supreme Court Blocks Guantanamo Tribunals." *New York Times*, June 29, p 1.

Greenhouse, Linda. 2007. "In Steps Big and Small, the Supreme Court Moved Right." *New York Times*, July 1, p 1.

Greider, William. 1992. *Who Will Tell the People: The Betrayal of American Democracy*. New York: Simon & Schuster.

Grey, Thomas. 1984. "The Constitution as Scripture." 37 *Stanford Law Review* 1.

Grimmett, Richard. 2007. "*Congressional Use of Funding Cutoffs Since 1970 Involving U.S. Military Forces and Overseas Deployments*." Report for Congress. Washington, DC: Congressional Research Service, January 16.

Guinier, Lani. 1995. *The Tyranny of the Majority: Fundamental Fairness in Representative Democracy*. New York: Free Press.

Gunningham, Neil, Robert A. Kagan, and Dorothy Thornton. 2003. *Shades of Green: Business, Regulation and Environment*. Stanford: Stanford University Press.

Hacker, Jacob and Paul Pierson. 2005. *Off Center: The Republican Revolution and the Erosion of American Democracy*. New Haven: Yale University Press.

Habermas, Jurgen. 1986. "Law as Medium and Law as Institution," in Gunther Teubner (ed.), *Dilemmas of Law in the Welfare State*. New York: Walter de Gruyter.

Haltom, William and Michael McCann. 2004. *Distorting the Law: Politics, Media and the Litigation Crisis*. Chicago: University of Chicago Press.

Harriger, Katy. 2000. *The Special Prosecutor in American Politics* (2nd ed.). Lawrence: University Press of Kansas.

Hart, Gary. 1985. "What Should be Done about Gramm-Rudman? Get Rid of the Monster." *New York Times*, July 22, p A25.

Hasen, Richard L. 2003. *The Supreme Court and Election Law: Judging Equality from Baker v. Carr to Bush v. Gore*. New York: New York University Press.

Hazard, Geoffrey. 1969. "Social Justice through Civil Justice." 36 *University of Chicago Law Review* 699.

Heale, M. J. 2005. "The Sixties as History: A Review of the Political Historiography." 33 *Reviews in American History*, pp 133–52.

Hibbing, John and Elizabeth Theiss-Morse. 1995. *Congress as Public Enemy: Public Attitudes toward American Political Institutions*. New York: Cambridge University Press.

Hill, Gladwin. 1969. "Environment May Eclipse Vietnam as College Issue." *New York Times*, Nov. 30, p 1.

Hirschl, Ran. 2000. "The Political Origins of Judicial Empowerment through Constitutionalization: Lessons from Four Constitutional Revolutions." 25 *Law and Social Inquiry*, pp 91–148.

Hobson, Charles. 1996. *The Great Chief Justice: John Marshall and the Rule of Law*. Lawrence: University Press of Kansas.

Hollings, Ernest F. 1989. "Deficit Reduction, A Love Story: I Want a Divorce." *New York Times*, Sept. 25, p A-31.

Hunter, Marjorie. 1964. "Packed Senate Galleries Tense; 10 Minute Vote Makes History." *New York Times*, June 11, 1964, p 21.

Huntington, Samuel P. 1981. *American Politics: The Promise of Disharmony*. Cambridge: Harvard University Press.

Hyman, Harold. 1975. *A More Perfect Union: The Impact of the Civil War and Reconstruction of the Constitution*. New York: Knopf.

Issacharoff, Samuel. 1993. "Judging Politics: The Elusive Quest for Judicial Review of Political Fairness." 71 *Texas Law Review* 1643.

Issacharoff, Samuel. 2002. "Gerrymandering and Political Cartels." 116 *Harvard Law Review* 593.

Jacobson, Peter D. and Kenneth E. Warner. 1999. "Litigation and Public Health Policy Making: The Case of Tobacco Control," 24 *Journal of Health Politics, Policy and Law* 4, 769–804.

Javits, Jacob K. 1973. *Who Makes War: The President versus Congress*. New York: Morrow.

Jay, Stewart. 1997. *Most Humble Servants: The Advisory Role of Early Judges*. New Haven: Yale University Press.

Johnson, Earl. 1974. *Justice and Reform: The Formative Years of the OEO Legal Services Program*. New York: Russell Sage Foundation.

Johnson, Charles and Danette Brickman. 2001. *Independent Counsel: The Law and the Investigation*. Washington, DC: CQ Press.

Johnston, David. 1999. "Attorney General Taking Control as Independent Counsel Law Dies." *New York Times*, June 30, p 1.

Kagan, Robert A. 2001. *Adversarial Legalism: The American Way of Law*. Cambridge, MA: Harvard University Press.

Kagan, Robert. 2004. "American Courts and the Policy Dialogue: The Role of Adversarial Legalism," in Mark Miller and Jeb Barnes (eds), *Making Policy, Making Law: An Interbranch Perspective*. Washington, DC: Georgetown University Press, 2004.

Kagan, Robert A. and William P. Nelson. 2001. "The Politics of Tobacco Regulation in the United States," in Robert L. Rabin and Stephen D. Sugarman (eds.), *Regulating Tobacco*, New York: Oxford University Press.

Kahn, James B., Judith Bourne, and Carl W. Tyler, Jr. 1971. "The Impact of Recent Changes in Therapeutic Abortion Laws." 14 *Clinical Obstetrics and Gynecology* 1130.

Karlan, Pamela. 2003. "Disarming the Private Attorney General." *University of Illinois Law Review* 183.

Kammen, Michael. 1986. *A Machine That Would Go of Itself: The Constitution in American Culture*. New York: Knopf.

Karst, Kenneth. 1977. "The Supreme Court 1976 Term – Foreword: Equal Citizenship under the Fourteenth Amendment." 91 *Harvard Law Review* 1.

Katzmann, Robert A. *Courts and Congress*. 1997. Washington: Brookings Institution Press.

Kelder, Graham and Richard Daynard. 1997. "The Role of Litigation in the Effective Control of the Sale and Use of Tobacco." 8 *Stanford Law & Policy Review* 63.

Kinsley, Michael. 2001. "Readme: Flagging Interest." *Slate* on-line magazine, July 19, 2001. http://slate.msn.com/Readme/01-07-19/Readme.asp.

Klarman, Michael. 2006. *From Jim Crow to Civil Rights: The Supreme Court and the Struggle for Racial Equality*. New York: Oxford University Press.

Knight, Jack and Lee Epstein. 1996. "The Norm of Stare Decisis." 40 *American Journal of Political Science*, pp 1018–1035.

Koh, Harold Hongju. 1990. *The National Security Constitution: Sharing Power after the Iran-Contra Affair.* New Haven: Yale University Press.

Kovach, Bill. 1970. "Abortion Reform is Voted by the Assembly, 76 to 73." *New York Times*, April 10, p 1.

Kramer, Larry D. 2004. *The People Themselves: Popular Constitutionalism and Judicial Review.* New York: Oxford University Press.

Kritzer, Herbert M. and Mark J. Richards. 2003. "Jurisprudential Regimes and Supreme Court Decision Making: The Lemon Regime and Establishment Clause Cases." 37 *Law & Society Review* 4, 827–840.

Kritzer, Herbert M. and Mark J. Richards. 2005. "The Influence of Law in the Supreme Court's Search-and-Seizure Jurisprudence." 33 *American Politics Research* 1, 33–55.

Kuhn, Thomas S. 1996. *The Structure of Scientific Revolutions.* Chicago: University of Chicago Press.

Kurland, Philip B. 1974. "The Judicial Road to Social Welfare." 48 *Social Service Review*, pp 481–493.

Kurland, Philip B. 1978. *Watergate and the Constitution.* Chicago: University of Chicago Press.

Kutler, Stanley I. 1990. *The Wars of Watergate: The Last Crisis of Richard Nixon.* New York: Knopf.

Lakoff, George. 2002. *Moral Politics: How Liberals and Conservatives Think* (2nd ed.). Chicago: University of Chicago Press.

Lamm, Richard D. 1971. "Therapeutic Abortion: The Role of State Government." 14 *Clinical Obstetrics and Gynecology* 4, 1204–1207.

Lane, Charles. 2006. "Justices Reject Vermont's Campaign Finance Law." *Washington Post*, June 27, p 1.

Layton, Azza Salama. 2000. *International Politics and Civil Rights Policies in the United States 1941–1960.* New York: Cambridge University Press.

Lazarus, Richard. 2004. *The Making of Environmental Law.* Chicago: University of Chicago Press.

Leupp, Frances. 1912. "Roosevelt the Politician." *Atlantic*, June 1912.

Levi, Margaret. 1997. "A Model, a Method, and a Map: Rational Choice in Comparative and Historical Analysis," in Mark Lichbach and Alan Zuckerman (eds.), *Comparative Politics: Rationality, Choice and Structure.* Cambridge: Cambridge University Press.

Levin, Ronald M. 2002. "*Mead* and the Prospective Exercise of Discretion." 54 *Administrative Law Review* 771.

Levinson, Sanford. 1990. *Constitutional Faith.* Princeton: Princeton University Press.

Lipset, Seymour Martin. 1996. *American Exceptionalism: A Two-Edged Sword.* New York: W.W. Norton.

Liptak, Adam. 2006. "The Court Enters the War, Loudly." *New York Times*, July 2, p 2.

Liroff, Richard A. 1976. *A National Policy for the Environment: NEPA and Its Aftermath.* Bloomington: Indiana University Press.

Llewellyn, Karl. 1960. *The Bramble Bush: On Our Law and its Study.* Dobbs Ferry, NY: Oceana.

Llewellyn, Karl. 1989. *The Case Law System in America.* Chicago: University of Chicago Press.

Loevy, Robert. 1997. *The Civil Rights Act of 1964: The Passage of the Law that Ended Racial Segregation.* Albany: SUNY Press.

Lovell, George. 2003. *Legislative Deferrals: Statutory Ambiguity, Judicial Power and American Democracy.* Cambridge: Cambridge University Press.

Lowi, Theodore. 1979. *The End of Liberalism.* New York: W.W. Norton.

Lublin, David. 1999. *The Paradox of Representation: Racial Gerrymandering and Minority Interests in Congress.* Princeton: Princeton University Press.

Luks, Samantha and Mike Salamone. 2008. "Abortion," in Nathaniel Persily, Jack Citrin and Patrick Egan (eds.), *Public Opinion and Constitutional Controversy.* New York: Oxford University Press.

Madden, Richard. 1970. "Nixon Agrees to Stop Bombing in Cambodia by Aug. 15 with New Raids up to Congress." *New York Times*, June 30, p 1.

Maltz, Earl. 1988. "The Nature of Precedent." 66 *North Carolina Law Review* 367.

Maltz, Earl. 1990. *Civil Rights, the Constitution and Congress, 1863–1869.* Lawrence: University Press of Kansas.

Maltzman, Forrest, James Spriggs, and Paul Wahlbeck. 1999. "Strategy and Judicial Choice: New Institutionalist Approaches to Supreme Court Decision-Making." in Cornell W. Clayton and Howard Gillman (eds), *Supreme Court Decision-Making: New Institutionalist Approaches.* Chicago: University of Chicago Press.

Maltzman, Forrest, James Spriggs, and Paul Wahlbeck. 2000. *Crafting Law on the Supreme Court: The Collegial Game.* Cambridge: Cambridge University Press.

Mansbridge, Jane. 1986. *Why We Lost the ERA.* Chicago: University of Chicago Press.

Martin, Andrew. 2007. "Wall Street Finds a Lot to Like about Tobacco." *New York Times*, Jan. 31, p 1.

Mather, Lynn. 1998. "Theorizing about Trial Courts: Lawyers, Policymaking and Tobacco Litigation." 23 *Law & Social Inquiry* 897–940.

Mayer, Jane. 2006. "The Hidden Power: The Legal Mind behind the White House's War on Terror." *New Yorker*, July 3, p 44.

Mayhew, David. 1974. *Congress: The Electoral Connection.* New Haven: Yale University Press.

Mayhew, David. 2005. *Divided We Govern: Party Control, Lawmaking and Investigations, 1946–2002* (2nd ed.). New Haven: Yale University Press.

McCann, Michael W. 1986. *Taking Reform Seriously: Perspectives on Public Interest Liberalism.* Ithaca: Cornell University Press.

McCann, Michael W. 1994. *Rights at Work: Pay Equity Reform and the Politics of Legal Mobilization.* Chicago: University of Chicago Press.

McCann, Michael W. 1996. "Causal versus Constitutive Explanations (or, On the Difficulty of Being So Positive . . .)." 21 *Law & Social Inquiry* 457–82.

McCann, Michael W. 2006a. *Law and Social Movements.* Burlington: Ashgate.

McCann, Michael W. 2006b. "Legal Mobilization and Social Reform Movements: Notes on Theory and its Application," in Michael W. McCann (ed.), *Law and Social Movements.* Burlington: Ashgate.

McConnell, Michael. 2000. "The Redistricting Cases: Original Mistakes and Current Consequences." 24 *Harvard Journal of Law and Public Policy* 103.

McDowell, Gary. 1982. *Equity and the Constitution: The Supreme Court, Equitable Relief and Public Policy.* Chicago: University of Chicago Press.

McGrory, Mary. 1985. "The Knife on Congress' Table." *Washington Post*, Oct. 24, p A-2.

McKenna, Joseph. 2001. *Franklin Roosevelt and the Great Constitutional War: The Court-Packing Crisis of 1937.* New York: Fordham University Press.

Melnick, R. Shep. 1983. *Regulation and the Courts: The Case of the Clean Air Act.* Washington, DC: Brookings Institution Press.

Melnick, R. Shep. 1991. *The Politics of the New Property: Welfare Rights in Congress and the Courts.* Washington, DC: Brookings Institution Press.

Melnick, R. Shep. 1994. *Between the Lines: Interpreting Welfare Rights.* Washington, DC: Brookings Institution Press.

Melnick, R. Shep. 1996. "Federalism and the New Rights." 14 *Yale Law & Policy Review* 325.

Meltsner, Michael. 1973. *Cruel and Unusual: The Supreme Court and Capital Punishment.* New York: Random House.

Meyer, David S. and Steven A. Boutcher. 2007. "Signals and Spillover: *Brown v. Board of Education* and other Social Movements." 5 *Perspectives on Politics,* 81–93.

Mikva, Abner J. 1995. "Justice Brennan and the Political Process: Assessing the Legacy of *Baker v. Carr.*" *University of Illinois Law Review* 683.

Miller, Arthur. 1974. "Political Issues and Trust in Government, 1964–1970." 68 *American Political Science Review* 951–972.

Miller, Mark C. 2004. "The View of the Courts from the Hill," in Mark C. Miller and Jeb Barnes (eds), *Making Policy, Making Law: An Interbranch Perspective.* Washington, DC: Georgetown University Press.

Miller, Mark C. and Jeb Barnes. 2004. *Making Policy, Making Law: An Interbranch Perspective.* Washington, DC: Georgetown University Press.

Mills, Kay. 2004. *Changing Channels: The Civil Rights Case That Transformed Television.* Jackson: University Press of Mississippi.

Moore, Mike. 1997. "The States Are Just Trying to Take Care of Sick Citizens and Protect Children." 83 *ABA Journal* 53.

Morris, John. 1972. "Memos Show New Plans to Narrow U.S. Legal Aid." *New York Times,* Feb. 19, 1972, p 16.

Moulton, Beatrice A. 1968. "*Hobson v. Hansen*: The De Facto Limits on Judicial Power." 20 *Stanford Law Review* 1249.

Murphy, Walter. 1964. *The Elements of Judicial Strategy.* Chicago: University of Chicago Press.

Mutch, Robert E. *Campaigns, Congress and Courts: The Making of Federal Campaign Finance Law.* New York: Praeger.

Nelson, William. 1974. "The Impact of the Antislavery Movement upon Styles of Judicial Reasoning in Nineteenth Century America." 87 *Harvard Law Review* 513.

Nelson, William. 1988. *The Fourteenth Amendment: From Political Principle to Judicial Doctrine.* Cambridge, MA: Harvard University Press.

Neustadt, Richard E. 1990. *Presidential Power and the Modern Presidents: The Politics of Leadership from Roosevelt to Reagan.* New York: Free Press.

Newmyer, R. Kent. 1986. *The Supreme Court under Marshall and Taney.* Wheeling, IL: Harlan Davidson.

Newton, Merlin. 1995. *Armed with the Constitution: Jehovah's Witnesses in Alabama and the U.S. Supreme Court.* Tuscaloosa: University of Alabama Press.

Nixon, Richard. 1978. *The Memoirs of Richard Nixon.* New York: Grosset & Dunlap.

Nocera, Joe. 2006. "If It's Good for Philip Morris, Can it Also Be Good for Public Health?" *New York Times Magazine,* June 18, p 46.

North, Douglass. 1990. *Institutions, Institutional Change and Economic Performance.* New York: Cambridge University Press.

North, Oliver. 1987. *Taking the Stand: The Testimony of Lieutenant Colonel Oliver L. North*. New York: Pocket Books.

Nossiff, Rosemary. 1994. "Why Justice Ginsburg Is Wrong about States Expanding Abortion Rights." 27 *PS: Political Science and Politics* 227–31.

Nossiff, Rosemary. 2001. "Abortion Policy before *Roe*: Grassroots and Interest Group Mobilization." 13 *Journal of Policy History* 463–78.

O'Connor, Karen and Lee Epstein. 1983. "The Rise of Conservative Interest Group Litigation." 45 *Journal of Politics* 479.

O'Connor, Karen and Lee Epstein. 1984. "Rebalancing the Scales of Justice: Assessment of Public Interest Law." 7 *Harvard Journal of Law & Public Policy* 483.

Oelsner, Lesley. 1975. "High Court's Queries Hint Doubt on Parts of New Election Law." *New York Times*, Nov. 11, p 1.

Ogletree, Charles. 2004. *All Deliberate Speed: Reflections on the First Half-Century of* Brown v. Board of Education. New York: W.W. Norton.

Orfield, Gary. 1996. *Dismantling Desegregation: The Quiet Reversal of* Brown v. Board of Education. New York: The New Press.

Orfield, Gary and Chungmei Lee. 2004. "Brown at 50: King's Dream or Plessy's Nightmare?" Cambridge, MA: Civil Rights Project, Harvard University.

Orren, Karen. 1976. "Standing to Sue: Group Conflict in the Federal Courts." 70 *American Political Science Review* 723.

Osborn, John Jay. 1971. *The Paper Chase*. New York: Houghton-Mifflin.

Packwood, Bob. 1971. "The Role of the Federal Government." 14 *Clinical Obstetrics and Gynecology* 1213.

Paine, Thomas. 2004 [1776]. *Common Sense*. New York: Penguin Books.

Parsons, William Chase. 1989. *A Secular Faith: The Supreme Court and the Free Exercise Doctrine*. Unpublished Senior Honors Thesis, Harvard College, 1989. (Available from Harvard University Libraries, Harvard Archives).

Paulsen, Michael Stokes. 2000. "Abrogating Stare Decisis by Statute: May Congress Remove the Precedential Effect of Roe and Casey?" 109 *Yale Law Journal* 1535.

Paulsen, Michael Stokes. 2003. "The Worst Constitutional Decision of All Time." 78 *Notre Dame Law Review* 995.

Perine, Keith. 2003. "Both Parties Find Political Benefit from Battle over Judicial Nominees." *Congressional Quarterly Weekly Report*, Oct. 4, p 2431.

Perry, Barbara. 1999. *The Priestly Tribe: The Supreme Court's Image in the American Mind*. Westport, CT: Praeger.

Perry, H.W. 1991. *Deciding to Decide: Agenda Setting in the United States Supreme Court*. Cambridge, MA: Harvard University Press.

Persily, Nathaniel. 2002. "Reply: In Defense of Foxes Guarding Henhouses: the Case for Judicial Acquiescence to Incumbent-Protecting Gerrymanders." 116 *Harvard Law Review* 649.

Persily, Nathaniel, Jack Citrin, and Patrick Egan, eds. 2008. *Public Opinion and Constitutional Controversy*. New York: Oxford University Press.

Pertschuk, Michael. 2001. *Smoke in Their Eyes: Lessons in Movement Leadership from the Tobacco Wars*. Nashville: Vanderbilt University Press.

Peters, Shawn Francis. 2002. *Judging Jehovah's Witnesses: Religious Persecution and the Dawn of the Rights Revolution*. Lawrence: University Press of Kansas.

Pfeffer, Leo. 1973. "The Supremacy of Free Exercise." 61 *Georgetown Law Journal* 1115.

Pierson, Paul. 2000. "Increasing Returns, Path Dependence, and the Study of Politics." 94 *American Political Science Review* 251–67.

Pierson, Paul. 2004. *Politics in Time: History, Institutions, and Social Analysis.* Princeton: Princeton University Press.

Pollak, Louis H. 1962. "Judicial Power and 'the Politics of the People.'" 72 *Yale Law Journal* 81.

Polsby, Nelson W. 1983. *Consequences of Party Reform.* New York: Oxford University Press.

Polsby, Nelson W. 2004. *How Congress Evolves: Social Bases of Institutional Change.* New York: Oxford University Press.

Powe, Jr., Lucas. 2000. *The Warren Court and American Politics.* Cambridge, MA: Harvard University Press.

Powell, H. Jefferson and Jeb Rubenfeld. 1998. "Laying it on the Line: A Dialogue on Line Item vetoes and Separation of Powers." 47 *Duke Law Journal* 1171.

Purdum, Todd. 2005a. "Strong Ties Bind Players in Battle for Seat on Court." *New York Times,* July 18, p 1.

Purdum, Todd. 2005b. "Potentially, the First Shot in All-Out Ideological War." *New York Times,* Nov. 1, p 22.

Rabin, Robert L. and Stephen D. Sugarman (eds.). 2001. *Regulating Tobacco.* New York. Oxford University Press.

Rabkin, Jeremy. 1989. *Judicial Compulsions: How Public Law Distorts Public Policy.* New York: Basic Books.

Rabkin, Jeremy. 1998. "The Secret Life of the Private Attorney General." 61 *Law & Contemporary Problems* 179.

Raskin, Jamin. 2003. *Overruling Democracy: The Supreme Court vs. the American People.* New York: Routledge.

Reed, Douglas S. 2001. *On Equal Terms: The Constitutional Politics of Equal Opportunity.* Princeton: Princeton University Press.

Reich, Charles A. 1964. "The New Property." 73 *Yale Law Journal* 733.

Reich, Charles A. 1965. "Individual Rights and Social Welfare: The Emerging Legal Issues." 74 *Yale Law Journal* 1245.

Reich, Robert. 1999. "Regulation Is Out, Litigation Is In." *USA Today,* Feb. 11, p A15.

Richards, Mark and Herbert Kritzer. 2002. "Jurisprudential Regimes in Supreme Court Decision Making." 96 *American Political Science Review* 2, 305–320.

Richards, Mark, Herbert Kritzer, and Joseph Smith. 2006. "Does Chevron Matter?" 28 *Law & Policy* 444–69.

Rieselbach, Leroy. 1986. *Congressional Reform.* Washington, DC: Congressional Quarterly Press.

Rohde, David and Harold Spaeth. 1976. *Supreme Court Decision Making.* San Francisco: W.H. Freeman.

Rosen, Jeffrey. 2006. *The Most Democratic Branch: How the Courts Serve America.* New York: Oxford University Press.

Rosenbaum, David. 1998. "Cigarette Makers Quit Negotiations on Tobacco Bill." *New York Times,* April 9, p 1.

Rosenberg, Gerald. 1991. *The Hollow Hope: Can Courts Bring about Social Change?* Chicago: University of Chicago Press.

Rosenkranz, E. Joshua (ed.). 1999. *If Buckley Fell: A First Amendment Blueprint for Regulating Money in Politics.* New York: Century Foundation Press.

Rosenthal, Jack. 1971a. "Nixon Proposes New Legal Aid Unit." *New York Times,* May 16, p 1.

Rosenthal, Jack. 1971b. "President Vetoes Child Care Plan as Irresponsible." *New York Times*, Dec. 10, p 1.

Rubenstein, William B. 2004. "On What a 'Private Attorney General' Is – And Why It Matters." 57 *Vanderbilt Law Review* 2129.

Rubin, Robert. 1992. "A Sociolegal History of the Tobacco Tort Litigation." 44 *Stanford Law Review* 853.

Rutenberg, Jim. 2006. "President to Press for Line Item Veto Power." *New York Times*, June 28, p A19.

Ryden, David K (ed.). 2000. *The U.S. Supreme Court and the Electoral Process.* Washington, DC: Georgetown University Press.

Saad, Lydia. 1998. "The Survey Data Reviewed: Smoking and American Values." 9 *Public Perspective* 1.

Saletan, William. 2003. *Bearing Right: How Conservatives Won the Abortion War.* Berkeley: University of California Press.

Sandler, Ross and David Schoenbrod. 2004. *Democracy by Decree: What Happens When the Courts Run Government.* Yale University Press.

Sarat, Austin and Stuart Scheingold (eds.). 2006. *Cause Lawyers and Social Movements.* Stanford: Stanford University Press.

Sarat, Austin, Bryant Garth and Robert A. Kagan (eds.). 2002. *Looking Back at Law's Century.* Ithaca: Cornell University Press.

Sax, Joseph L. 1971. *Defending the Environment: A Strategy for Citizen Action.* New York: Knopf.

Scalia, Antonin. 1989. "Judicial Deference to Administrative Interpretations of Law." *Duke Law Journal* 511.

Scalia, Antonin. 1997. *A Matter of Interpretation: Federal Courts and the Law.* Princeton: Princeton University Press.

Schauer, Frederick. 2006. "The Supreme Court 2005 Term, Foreword: The Court's Agenda – and the Nation's." 120 *Harvard Law Review* 4.

Scheingold, Stuart and Austin Sarat (eds). 2004. *Something to Believe in: Politics, Professionalism and Cause Lawyering.* Stanford: Stanford University Press.

Schickler, Eric. 2001. *Disjointed Pluralism: Institutional Innovation and the Development of the U.S. Congress.* Princeton: Princeton University Press.

Schmitt, Richard B. 2005. "Sidestepping Courts in the War on Terrorism: U.S. Seeks Leverage by Moving Detainees or Changing Their Status before Scheduled Hearings. Critics Call It Legal Dodge Ball." *Los Angeles Times*, Nov. 30, p 18.

Schoenbrod, David. 1995. *Power without Responsibility: How Congress Abuses the People through Delegation.* New Haven: Yale University Press.

Schoenbrod, David. 2005. *Saving Our Environment from Washington: How Congress Grabs Power, Shirks Responsibility and Shortchanges the People.* New Haven: Yale University Press.

Schotland, Roy A. 2002. "Commentary: The Limits of Being 'Present at the Creation.'" 80 *North Carolina Law Review* 1505.

Schroeder, Christopher H. 1999. "The Independent Counsel Statute: Reform or Repeal?" 62 *Law & Contemporary Problems* 1–4.

Schubert, Glendon. 1965. *The Judicial Mind.* Evanston, IL: Northwestern University Press.

Schuck, Peter H. 1986. *Agent Orange on Trial: Mass Toxic Disasters in the Courts.* Cambridge, MA: Belknap Press.

Schuck, Peter H. 2000. *The Limits of Law: Essays on Democratic Governance*. Boulder, CO: Westview Press.

Schuck, Peter H. and E. Donald Elliott. 1990. "To the Chevron Station: An Empirical Study of Federal Administrative Law." *Duke Law Journal* 984.

Schwartz, Bernard (ed.). 1970. *Statutory History of the United States: Civil Rights, Part II*. New York: Chelsea House.

Schwartz, Bernard (ed.). 1985. *The Unpublished Opinions of the Warren Court*. New York: Oxford University Press.

Schwartz, John. 1997. "Advisory Panelists Strongly Critical of Tobacco Deal." *Washington Post*, June 26, p A3.

Schwartz, John. 1998. "Tobacco Firms Say They'd Rather Fight." *Washington Post*, April 9, p 1.

Segal, Jeffrey A. and Harold Spaeth. 1993. *The Supreme Court and the Attitudinal Model*. Cambridge: Cambridge University Press.

Segal, Jeffrey A. and Harold Spaeth. 2002. *The Supreme Court and the Attitudinal Model Revisited*. Cambridge: Cambridge University Press.

Shafer, Byron. 1983. *Quiet Revolution: The Struggle for the Democratic Party and the Shaping of Post-Reform Politics*. New York: Russell Sage Foundation.

Shapiro, Martin. 1964. *Law and Politics in the Supreme Court: New Approaches to Political Jurisprudence*. New York: Free Press.

Shapiro, Martin. 1968. *The Supreme Court and Administrative Agencies*. New York: Free Press.

Shapiro, Martin. 1981. *Courts: A Comparative and Political Analysis*. Chicago: University of Chicago Press.

Shapiro, Martin. 1988. *Who Guards the Guardians? Judicial Control of Administration*. Athens: University of Georgia Press.

Shapiro, Martin. 2002. "The Giving Reasons Requirement," in Martin Shapiro and Alec Stone Sweet (eds.), *On Law, Politics and Judicialization*. New York: Oxford University Press.

Shapiro, Martin and Alec Stone Sweet. 2002. *On Law, Politics and Judicialization*. New York: Oxford University Press.

Shenon, Philip. 2007. "Senators Clash with Nominee Over Torture and Limits of Law." *New York Times*, Oct. 19, p 1.

Shepsle, Kenneth A. 1992. "Congress Is a 'They' Not an 'It': Legislative Intent as Oxymoron." 12 *International Review of Law and Economics* 239.

Shklar, Judith. 1964. *Legalism: Law, Morals, and Political Trials*. Cambridge, MA: Harvard University Press.

Sinclair, Barbara. 2006. *Party Wars: Polarization and the Politics of National Policy Making*. Norman: Oklahoma University Press.

Silverstein, Gordon. 1994. "Statutory Interpretation and the Balance of Institutional Power." 56 *Review of Politics* 475–503.

Silverstein, Gordon. 1997. *Imbalance of Powers: Constitutional Interpretation and the Making of American Foreign Policy*. New York: Oxford University Press.

Skocpol, Theda. 1999. "Advocates without Members: The Recent Transformation of Civic Life," in Theda Skocpol and Morris Fiorina (eds), *Civic Engagement in American Democracy*, Washington, DC: Brookings Institution Press.

Skocpol, Theda. 2003. *Diminished Democracy: From Membership to Management in American Civic Life*. Norman: University of Oklahoma Press.

Slabach, Frederick G. 1998. *The Constitution and Campaign Finance Reform*. Durham: Carolina Academic Press.

Smith, Rogers. 1988. "Political Jurisprudence, the 'New Institutionalism,' and the Future of Public Law." 82 *American Political Science Review*, pp 89–108.

Smith, Rogers. 1992. "If Politics Matters: Implications for a 'New Institutionalism.'" 6 *Studies in American Political Development*, pp 1–36.

Smith, Rogers. 1995. "Ideas, Institutions, and Strategic Choices." 28 *Polity*, pp 135–40.

Songer, Donald and Stefanie Lindquist. 1996. "Not the Whole Story: The Impact of Justices' Values on Supreme Court Decision Making." 40 *American Journal of Political Science* 4, 1049–63.

Sonner, Scott. 2007. "Romney Says He Represents GOP Values." *Washington Post*, Oct. 12.

Spaeth, Harold and Jeffrey Segal. 1999. *Majority Rule or Minority Will: Adherence to Precedent on the U.S. Supreme Court.* Cambridge, UK: Cambridge University Press.

Spitzer, Robert. 1997. "The Constitutionality of the Presidential Line-Item Veto." 112 *Political Science Quarterly* 261.

Stefancic, Jean and Richard Delgado. 1996. *No Mercy: How Conservative Think Tanks and Foundations Changed America's Social Agenda.* Philadelphia: Temple University Press.

Stewart, Richard B. 1977. "The Development of Administrative and Quasi-Constitutional Law in Judicial Review of Environmental Decisionmaking: Lessons from the Clean Air Act." 62 *Iowa Law Review* 713.

Stone Sweet, Alex. 2000. *Governing with Judges: Constitutional Politics in Europe.* London: Oxford University Press.

Stone Sweet, Alex. 2002. "Judicialization and the Construction of Governance," in Martin Shapiro and Alec Stone Sweet (eds.), *On Law, Politics and Judicialization.* New York: Oxford University Press.

Story, Joseph. 1836. *Commentaries on Equity Jurisprudence as Administered in England and America.* Boston: Hilliard, Gray & Co.

Story, Joseph. 1838. *Commentaries on Equity Pleadings and the Incidents Thereto according to the Practice of the Courts of Equity of England and America.* Boston: C.C. Little and J. Brown.

Strum, Charles. 1992. "Major Lawsuit on Smoking Is Dropped." *New York Times*, Nov. 6, p B1.

Sullivan, Kathleen. 1992. "The Supreme Court 1991 Term, Foreword: The Justices of Rules and Standards," 106 *Harvard Law Review* 22.

Sunstein, Cass. 1992. "What's Standing after *Lujan?* Of Citizen Suits, 'Injuries' and Article III." 91 *Michigan Law Review* 163.

Sunstein, Cass. 1999. *One Case at a Time: Judicial Minimalism on the Supreme Court.* Cambridge, MA: Harvard University Press.

Sunstein, Cass. 2005a. "Administrative Law Goes to War." 118 *Harvard Law Review* 2663.

Sunstein, Cass. 2005b. *Radicals in Robes: Why Extreme Right Wing Courts Are Wrong for America.* New York: Basic Books.

Sutherland, George. 1919. *The Constitution and World Affairs*, New York: Columbia University Press.

Tamanaha, Brian Z. 2006. *Law as a Means to an End: Threat to the Rule of Law.* New York: Cambridge University Press.

Tocqueville, Alexis de. 2003 [1835]. *Democracy in America.* New York: Penguin.

Tragardh, Lars and Michael X. Delli Carpini. 2004. "The Juridification of Politics in the United States and Europe: Historical Roots, Contemporary Debates and Future

Prospects," in Lars Tragardh (ed.), *After National Democracy: Rights, Law and Power in America and the New Europe*. Portland: Hart Publishing.

Trubeck, David. 1978. "Environmental Defense I: Introduction to Interest Group Advocacy in Complex Disputes." In Burton Weisbrod, Joel Handler and Neil Komesar (eds.), *Public Interest Law: An Economic and Institutional Analysis*. Berkeley: University of California Press.

Truman, David. 1984. "Party Reform, Party Atrophy, and Constitutional Change: Some Reflections." 99 *Political Science Quarterly* 637–55.

Tsai, Robert. 2008. "Reconsidering Gobitis: An Exercise in Presidential Leadership." 86 *Washington University Law Review* 2.

Tushnet, Mark. 1995. "Themes in Warren Court Biographies." 70 *New York University Law Review* 748.

Tushnet, Mark. 1999. *Taking the Constitution Away from the Courts*. Princeton: Princeton University Press.

Tversky, Amos and Daniel Kahneman. 1981. "The Framing of Decisions and the Psychology of Choice." 211 *Science* 453.

Ulmer, S. Sydney. 1971. "Earl Warren and the Brown Decision," 33 *Journal of Politics* 3.

Urofsky, Melvin I. 2005. *Money and Free Speech: Campaign Finance Reform and the Courts*. Lawrence: University Press of Kansas.

Van Horn, Carl E. 1986. "Fear and Loathing on Capitol Hill: The 99th Congress and Economic Policy," 19 *PS* 1, pp 23–9.

Viscusi, W. Kip. 1992. *Smoking: Making the Risky Decision*. New York: Oxford University Press.

Viscusi, W. Kip (ed.). 2002. *Regulation through Litigation*. Washington: Brookings Institution Press.

Vose, Clement. 1967a. *Caucasians Only: The Supreme Court, the NAACP and the Restrictive Covenant Cases*. Berkeley: University of California Press.

Vose, Clement. 1967b. "School Desegregation: A Political Scientist's View." 2 *Law & Society Review*, pp 141–50.

Waldron, Jeremy. 2006. "The Core of the Case against Judicial Review." 115 *Yale Law Journal* 1346.

Wardle, Lynn and Mary Anne Wood. 1982. *A Lawyer Looks at Abortion*. Provo: Brigham Young University Press.

Warren, Charles. 1928. *The Supreme Court in United States History*. Boston: Little Brown & Co.

Warren, Charles. 1994. *Congress, the Constitution and the Supreme Court*. Buffalo, NY: William S. Hein & Co.

Warren, Earl. 1977. *The Memoirs of Earl Warren*. Garden City: Doubleday.

Waxman, Henry A. 1997. "A Look at the Tobacco Settlement: Don't Sign it; On Balance, a Bad Deal for Public Health." *Washington Post*, June 29, p C3.

Weaver, R. Kent. 1986. "The Politics of Blame Avoidance." 6 *Journal of Public Policy* 371.

Weaver, R. Kent. 1987. *The Politics of Blame Avoidance*. Washington, DC: Brookings Institution Press.

Weaver, Warren. 1969. "Pollution: The Oil Threat to the Beaches." *New York Times*, Feb. 9, p E2.

Weaver, Warren. 1971. "Campaigning Bill Passed by House." *New York Times*, Dec. 1, p 1.

Wehr, Elizabeth. 1985. "Support Grows for Balancing Federal Budget." *Congressional Quarterly Weekly Report*, Oct. 5, pp 1975–8.

West, Darrell. 1988. "Gramm-Rudman-Hollings and the Politics of Deficit Reduction" 499 *Annals of the American Academy of Political and Social Science*, pp 90–100.

White, G. Edward. 2000. *The Constitution and the New Deal*. Cambridge: Harvard University Press.

Whittington, Keith. 2001. "The Road Not Taken: Dred Scott, Judicial Authority and Political Questions." 63 *Journal of Politics* 365.

Whittington, Keith. 2007. *Political Foundations of Judicial Supremacy: The Presidency, the Supreme Court and Constitutional Leadership in U.S. History*. Princeton: Princeton University Press.

Wicker, Tom. 2002. "Remembering the Johnson Treatment." *New York Times*, May 9, p 39.

Wiecek, William. 1977. *The Sources of Antislavery Constitutionalism in America, 1760–1848*. Ithaca: Cornell University Press.

Wiecek, William. 1998. *The Lost World of Classical Legal Thought: Law and Ideology in America, 1886–1937*. New York: Oxford University Press.

Will, George. 2001. "Second Thoughts about Soft Money." *Washington Post*, March 8, p. A21.

Woodward, Bob and Scott Armstrong. 1979. *The Brethren: Inside the Supreme Court*. New York: Simon & Schuster.

Yoo, John. 2006. *The Powers of War and Peace: The Constitution and Foreign Affairs ater 9/11*. Chicago: University of Chicago Press.

Yoon, Albert. 2003. "Love's Labor Lost: Judicial Tenure among Federal Court Judges: 1945–2000." 91 *California Law Review* 1029.

INDEX

LaVergne, TN USA
25 October 2010
202120LV00002B/41/P